Foundations of PyGTK Development

GUI Creation with Python

Second Edition

W. David Ashley

Andrew Krause

apress®

Foundations of PyGTK Development: GUI Creation with Python

W. David Ashley
AUSTIN, TX, USA

Andrew Krause
Leesburg, VA, USA

ISBN-13 (pbk): 978-1-4842-4178-3
https://doi.org/10.1007/978-1-4842-4179-0

ISBN-13 (electronic): 978-1-4842-4179-0

Library of Congress Control Number: 2018966864

Managing Director, Apress Media LLC: Welmoed Spahr
Acquisitions Editor: Celestin Suresh John
Development Editor: James Markham
Coordinating Editor: Divya Modi

Cover designed by eStudioCalamar

Cover image designed by Freepik (www.freepik.com)

Distributed to the book trade worldwide by Springer Science+Business Media New York, 233 Spring Street, 6th Floor, New York, NY 10013. Phone 1-800-SPRINGER, fax (201) 348-4505, e-mail orders-ny@springer-sbm.com, or visit www.springeronline.com. Apress Media, LLC is a California LLC and the sole member (owner) is Springer Science + Business Media Finance Inc (SSBM Finance Inc). SSBM Finance Inc is a **Delaware** corporation.

For information on translations, please e-mail rights@apress.com, or visit http://www.apress.com/rights-permissions.

Apress titles may be purchased in bulk for academic, corporate, or promotional use. eBook versions and licenses are also available for most titles. For more information, reference our Print and eBook Bulk Sales web page at http://www.apress.com/bulk-sales.

Any source code or other supplementary material referenced by the author in this book is available to readers on GitHub via the book's product page, located at www.apress.com/978-1-4842-4178-3. For more detailed information, please visit http://www.apress.com/source-code.

Printed on acid-free paper

I dedicate this book to my wife.
Without you, all of this would not be possible.
—W. David Ashley

Table of Contents

About the Author

W. David Ashley is a technical writer for SkillSoft, where he specializes in open source, particularly Linux. As a member of the Linux Fedora documentation team, he recently led the Libvert project documentation and wrote the Python programs included with it. He has developed in 20 different programming languages during his 30 years as a software developer and IT consultant. This includes more than 18 years at IBM and 12 years with American Airlines.

About the Technical Reviewers

 **Jonathan Giszczak** is a professional software developer with extensive experience writing software for the military and financial services industries, as well as the game industry. He graduated from the University of Michigan with a degree in computer engineering. He has been writing C, C++, and Python applications since the 1990s, including applications in Motif and PyGTK.

 **Peter Gill** loves spending time with his family in Newfoundland, Canada. He is currently a software developer at TownSuite, where he specializes in release deployment and leading a full stack web development team. Peter loves learning programming language and has used Python, Ruby, Rust, Io, Prolog, Java, C, C++, C#, VB, JavaScript, Typescript, Bash, PowerShell and is currently focused on C# with ASP .NET Core and Typescript. He is a huge advocate open source software. He loves to use Git, Jenkins, Docker, and other tools related to automated deployments.

Acknowledgments

I would like to express my gratitude to the many people who have made this book possible. Many thanks go to Daniel Berrange of Red Hat, whose assistance has certainly decreased the number of errors in the book. I would also like to thank Peter Gill and Jonathan Giszczak for their fine technical reviewing skills. You were very tough on every paragraph I wrote and every example I coded, but this book is better today because of the hard work you put into the project.

I would like to extend a special thanks to Andrew Krause for his encouragement and help. Without him, this update to his original book would not have been possible.

In addition, I would like to thank the people at Apress who put so many hours of hard work into the book. I could not imagine writing for any other publisher. It is a great organization that makes the writing process enjoyable.

Finally, I need to acknowledge my wife, who has supported me in every step of the process. Without you, I would not be who I am today and for that I am forever grateful.

—W. David Ashley

Introduction

One of the most important aspects of an application is the interface that is provided to interact with the user. With the unprecedented popularity of computers in society today, people have come to expect those user interfaces to be graphical, and the question of which graphical toolkit to use quickly arises for any developer. For many, the cross-platform, feature-rich GTK+ library is the obvious choice.

Learning GTK+ can be a daunting task, because many features lack documentation and others are difficult to understand even with the API documentation. *Foundations of PyGTK Development* aims to decrease the learning curve and set you on your way to creating cross-platform graphical user interfaces for your applications.

Each chapter in this book contains multiple examples that help you further your understanding. In addition to these examples, the final chapter of this book provides five complete applications that incorporate topics from the previous chapters. These applications show you how to bring together what you have learned to accomplish in various projects.

Each chapter starts with an overview, so that you are able to skip around if you want. Most chapters also contain exercises to test your understanding of the material. I recommend that you complete all the exercises before continuing, because the best way to learn GTK+ is to use it.

At the end of this book, there are multiple appendixes that serve as references for various aspects of GTK+. These appendixes include tables listing signals, styles, and properties for every widget in GTK+. These appendixes will remain a useful reference after you have finished reading the book and begin creating your own applications. In addition, Appendix D explains the solutions to all the exercises in the book.

Who Should Read This Book

Because this book begins with the basics and works up to more difficult concepts, you do not need any previous knowledge of GTK+ development to use this book. This book does assume that you have a decent grasp of the Python programming language. You should also be comfortable with running commands and terminating applications (Ctrl+C) in a Linux terminal.

In addition to a grasp of the Python programming language, some parts of this book may be difficult to understand without some further knowledge about programming for Linux in general. You will get more out of this book if you already comprehend basic object-oriented concepts. It is also helpful to know how Linux handles processes.

You can still use this book if you do not already know how to implement object orientation or manage processes in Linux, but you may need to supplement this book with one or more online resources. A list of helpful links and tutorials can be found on the book's web site, which is located at www.gtkbook.com. You can also find more information about the book at www.apress.com.

How This Book Is Organized

Foundations of PyGTK Development is composed of 14 chapters. Each chapter gives you a broad understanding of its topic. For example, Chapter 4 covers container widgets and introduces many of the most important widgets derived from the Gtk.Container class.

Because of this structure, some chapters are somewhat lengthy. Do not feel as though you have to complete a whole chapter in one sitting, because it can be difficult to remember all the information presented. Also, because many examples span multiple pages, consider focusing on just a few examples at a time; try to understand their syntax and intent.

Each chapter provides important information and unique perspectives that help you to become a proficient PyGTK developer.

Chapter 1 teaches you how to install the GTK+ libraries and their dependencies on your Linux system. It also gives an overview of each of the GTK+ libraries, including GObject, GDK, GdkPixbuf, Pango, and ATK.

Chapter 2 introduces the Gtk.Application and Gtk.ApplicationWindow classes. These classes are fundamental classes that wrap the program logic and provide some useful features for your application. While a GTK+ program can be written without utilizing these classes, you will find the creation process much easier and more object-oriented if you utilize these classes.

Chapter 3 steps through two Hello World applications. The first shows you the basic essentials that are required by every GTK+ application. The second expands on the first while also covering signals, callback functions, events, and child widgets. You then learn about widget properties and the Gtk.Button and Gtk.Label widgets.

Chapter 4 begins by introducing the `Gtk.Container` class. Next, it teaches you about horizontal and vertical boxes, grids, fixed containers, horizontal and vertical panes, notebooks, and event boxes.

Chapter 5 covers basic widgets that provide a way for you to interact with users. These include toggle buttons, specialized buttons, text entries, and spin buttons.

Chapter 6 introduces you to the vast array of built-in dialogs. It also teaches you how to create your own custom dialogs.

Chapter 7 is a general overview of the most useful features of Python. It covers many Python features that are directly useful to the GTK+ programmer but not necessarily covered in depth in many Python introductory texts.

Chapter 8 introduces you to scrolled windows. It also gives in-depth instructions on using the text view widget. Other topics include the clipboard and the Gtk.SourceView library.

Chapter 9 covers two types of widgets that use the `Gtk.TreeModel` object. It gives an in-depth overview of the tree view widget and shows you how to use combo boxes with tree models or strings.

Chapter 10 provides two methods of menu creation: manual and dynamic. It covers menus, toolbars, pop-up menus, keyboard accelerators, and the status bar widget.

Chapter 11 is a short chapter about how to design user interfaces with the Glade user interface builder. It also shows you how to dynamically load your user interfaces using `Gtk.Builder`.

Chapter 12 teaches you how to create your own custom GTK+ widgets by deriving them from other widgets.

Chapter 13 covers many of the remaining widgets that do not quite fit into other chapters. This includes several widgets that were introduced in GTK+ 2.10, including recent files and tray icon support.

Chapter 14 gives you a few longer, real-world examples. They take the concepts you have learned throughout the book and show you how they can be used together.

The appendixes act as references to widget properties, signals, styles, stock items, and descriptions of exercise solutions.

Official Web Site

You can find additional resources on the book's official web site, found at `www.gtkbook.com`. This web site includes up-to-date documentation, links to useful resources, and articles that supplement what you learn in this book. There is also find a link to the downloadable source code for every example in this book. The Apress web site (`www.apress.com`,) is another great place to find more information about this book.

When you unzip the source code from the web site, you will find a folder that contains the examples in each chapter and an additional folder that holds exercise solutions. You can run all the files within the current folder.

CHAPTER 1

Getting Started

Welcome to *Foundations of PyGTK Development*. In this book, you acquire a thorough knowledge of the GIMP Toolkit (GTK+), which allows you to create comprehensive graphical programs. Before continuing, you should be aware that this book is aimed at Python programmers, so we assume that you already have a good understanding of the Python language, and you can jump right into using GTK+. Time is not spent on bringing you up to speed on Python.

To get the most out of this book, you should follow each chapter sequentially and study all the examples in each chapter. Getting started with GTK+ on Linux is very easy because most distributions are bundled with everything you need to create and run Python/GTK+ programs. We cover Windows and macOS installation procedures later in this chapter.

There are a few tools that should be installed to get you started without running into trouble. First, Python 3.x should be installed. It is required to run GTK+ 3.x Python programs. Second, the GTK+ 3.x runtime libraries should be installed. These libraries come with many dependencies installed, including GObject, Pango, GLib, GDK, GdkPixbuf, and ATK. Be sure to install all the dependent libraries.

You do *not* need to install the GNU Compiler Collection. You are not compiling any C/C++ programs in the examples provided in this book. You only need Python 3.x and the GTK+ 3.x runtime libraries to be installed to run the example programs.

Differences Between GTK+ 2.x and 3.x

If you are proficient in GTK+ 2.x, you may be surprised by the changes in version 3.x. There are both small and large changes to the GTK+ API and the Python classes that wrap those libraries. While the basics for most widgets are unchanged, there are a lot of small "gotchas" that can cause you grief until you understand why and where the changes have been made.

© W. David Ashley and Andrew Krause 2019
W. D. Ashley and A. Krause, *Foundations of PyGTK Development*,
https://doi.org/10.1007/978-1-4842-4179-0_1

1

The reason for most of these changes is due to a change in the GTK+ philosophy. The GTK+ 2.x libraries were designed around consistency between all GTK+ programs, with the use of GTK+ themes as the basis for that consistency. This philosophy completely changed with the GTK+ libraries. While themes are still available, it is now easier to create GTK+ programs that have their own look and feel separate from the current GTK theme. While this gives the developer greater control, it also requires some extra programming steps to achieve the look and feel. It also removes some APIs that make a widget easy to create and control.

The following is a partial list of the differences between GTK+ 2.x and 3.x. Some of these items have simple workarounds, but others require a little more work on the programmer's part because they are different enough to cause source code porting problems.

- Many standard stock icons have been removed, mostly the ones used on push buttons and menu items. If you need these icons, you must provide your own set.

- All the 2.x constants are now grouped in a 3.x Python class as attributes. If you are porting source code, this is a major area that needs to be addressed.

- Some containers have been eliminated. For instance, the `Gtk.Hbox` and `Gtk.Vbox` widgets have been removed and you now must specify the orientation of a `Gtk.Box` via a parameter when creating a new `Gtk.Box` instance. Note that the `Gtk.Box` class is now a real class in GTK+ 3.x, not an abstract class.

- Default packing for containers has been removed; all packing parameters must be supplied to the API.

- Some standard dialogs have been removed. You must create your own dialogs to replace them.

- There are two new major classes that are very useful for the overall control of large and small applications: the `Gtk.Application` class and the `Gtk.ApplicationWindow` class. While these classes are not strictly needed for simple applications, you still find them useful for even the simplest of applications. For that reason, we base all the examples in this book on these two classes to wrap our widget examples.

Creating menus is much easier using the `Gtk.Application` and `Gtk.ApplicationWindow` classes. This required complex programming in the GTK+ 2.x environment and is reduced to creating an XML file to represent the menu you want to create in the 3.x environment.

Installing GTK+ 3.x

Before you can create programs, you must install Python, GTK+, and all the dependent libraries. This section covers installing GTK+ on Linux and other Unix-like operating systems. It does not cover how to install GTK+ on macOS or Windows. You need to research the correct way to install GTK+ and Python in those OS environments.

Most modern Linux distributions include Python and GTK+ as part of their respective repositories. You simply need to select Python 3 (this is sometimes installed by default) and GTK+ 3.x (use the latest version available, as shown in Figure 1-1) from the package install program in your Linux distribution and then install those packages along with all the dependent packages.

To test your installation, run the following command.

```
/usr/bin/gtk3-demo
```

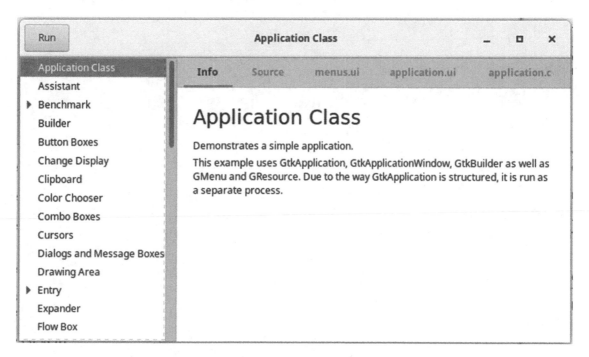

Figure 1-1. *GTK+ 3 demo program*

If the program exists and the widget documentation window appears, then the GTK+ installation was successful.

Summary

This chapter introduced GTK+ Version 3.x and Python 3 along with some installation prerequisites. It presented some post-installation tests to ensure that GTK+ was successfully installed. And it discussed some differences between GTK+ 2.x and 3.x.

After successfully installing GTK+ 3.x and Python 3, your environment should be ready to build your first Python/GTK+ program.

Chapter 2 further discusses Gtk.Application and the Gtk.ApplicationWindow, the base classes that you should use for all Python 3 GTK+ 3.x programs.

CHAPTER 2

The Application and ApplicationWindow Classes

A new set of classes were introduced in GTK+ 3.x: `Gtk.Application` and `Gtk.ApplicationWindow`. These classes are designed to be the base instances for your GUI application. They wrap the application and the main window behavior of your application. They have many built-in features and provide containers for the functions in your application. The `Gtk.Application` and `Gtk.ApplicationWindow` classes are described in detail in this chapter because they are the basis for all the example programs in this book.

The Gtk.Application Class

`Gtk.Application` is the base class of a GTK application. Its primary purpose is to separate your program from Python `__main__` function, which is a Python implementation detail. The philosophy of `Gtk.Application` is that applications are interested in being told what needs to happen and when it needs to happen in response to actions from the user. The exact mechanism by which Python starts applications is uninteresting.

`Gtk.Application` exposes a set of signals (or virtual methods) that an application should respond to.

- `startup`: Sets up the application when it first starts. The virtual method name for this signal is do_startup.

- `shutdown`: Performs shutdown tasks. The virtual method name for this signal is do_shutdown.

© W. David Ashley and Andrew Krause 2019
W. D. Ashley and A. Krause, *Foundations of PyGTK Development*,
https://doi.org/10.1007/978-1-4842-4179-0_2

- activate: Shows the default first window of the application (like a new document). The virtual method name for this signal is do_activate.

- open: Opens files and shows them in a new window. This corresponds to someone trying to open a document (or documents) using the application from the file browser, or similar. The virtual method name for this signal is do_open.

When your application starts, the startup signal is fired. This gives you a chance to perform initialization tasks that are not directly related to showing a new window. After this, depending on how the application is started, either activate or open signal is called next.

The signal name and the receiving method name should not be the same. The receiving method name should have an on_ prefix. For instance, a signal named paste should have a connect call that looks something like the following.

```
action = Gio.SimpleAction.new("paste", None)
action.connect("activate", self.on_paste)
self.add_action(action)
```

Note that you have to specify the new signal name and the corresponding method name. By convention in GTK+ 3.x, signals that are built into an existing class have a do_ prefix for their corresponding method names. Callbacks should have method names with an on_ prefix. Adding a prefix to the method name prevents inadvertently overriding method names that are not a part of the signal mechanism.

Gtk.Application defaults to applications being single-instance. If the user attempts to start a second instance of a single-instance application, then Gtk.Application signals the first instance, and you receive additional activate or open signals. In this case, the second instance exits immediately without calling startup or shutdown signals.

For this reason, you should do essentially no work at all from Python's __main__ function. All startup initialization should be done in Gtk.Application do_startup. This avoids wasting work in the second-instance case where the program exits immediately.

The application continues to run as long as it needs to. This is usually as long as there are any open windows. You can also force the application to stay alive by using the hold method.

On shutdown, you receive a shutdown signal where you can do any necessary cleanup tasks (such as saving files to disk).

Gtk.Application does not implement __main__ for you; you must do so yourself. Your __main__ function should be as small as possible and do almost nothing except create your Gtk.Application and run it. The "real work" should always be done in response to the signals fired by Gtk.Application.

Primary vs. Local Instance

The *primary instance* of an application is the first instance that is run. A *remote instance* is an instance that has started but is not the primary instance. The term *local instance* is refers to the current process, which may or may not be the primary instance.

Gtk.Application only emits signals in the primary instance. Calls to the Gtk.Application API can be made in primary or remote instances (and are made from the vantage of being the local instance). When the local instance is the primary instance, method calls on Gtk.Application result in signals being emitted locally. When the local instance is a remote instance, method calls result in messages being sent to the primary instance and the signals are emitted there.

For example, calling the do_activate method on the primary instance emits the activate signal. Calling it on a remote instance results in a message being sent to the primary instance, and it emits the activate signal.

You rarely need to know if the local instance is primary or remote. In almost all cases, you should call the Gtk.Application method that you are interested in and have it forwarded or handled locally, as appropriate.

Actions

An application can register a set of actions that it supports in addition to the default activate and open actions. Actions are added to the application with the GActionMap interface, and invoked or queried with the GActionGroup interface.

As with the activate and open signals, calling activate_action on the primary instance activates the named action in the current process. Calling activate_action on a remote instance sends a message to the primary instance, causing the action to be activated there.

Dealing with the Command Line

Normally, Gtk.Application assumes that arguments passed on the command line are files to be opened. If no arguments are passed, then it assumes that an application is being launched to show its main window or an empty document. When files are given, you receive these files (in the form of GFile) from the open signal; otherwise, you receive an activate signal. It is recommended that new applications make use of this default handling of command-line arguments.

If you want to deal with command-line arguments in more advanced ways, there are several (complementary) mechanisms by which you can do this.

First, the handle-local-options signal is emitted, and the signal handler gets a dictionary with the parsed options. To make use of this, you need to register your options with the add_main_option_entries method. The signal handler can return a non-negative value to end the process with this exit code, or a negative value to continue with the regular handling of command-line options. A popular use of this signal is to implement a --version argument that works without communicating with a remote instance.

If handle-local-options is not flexible enough for your needs, you can override the local_command_line virtual function to entirely take over the handling of command-line arguments in the local instance. If you do so, you are responsible for registering the application and for handling a --help argument (the default local_command_line function does this for you).

It is also possible to invoke actions from handle-local-options or local_command_line in response to command-line arguments. For example, a mail client may choose to map the --compose command-line argument to an invocation of its compose action. This is done by calling activate_action from the local_command_line implementation. If the command line being processed is in the primary instance, then the compose action is invoked locally. If it is a remote instance, the action invocation is forwarded to the primary instance.

Note in particular that it is possible to use action activations instead of activate or open. It is perfectly reasonable that an application could start without an activate signal ever being emitted. activate is only supposed to be the default "started with no options" signal. Actions are meant to be used for anything else.

Some applications may wish to perform even more advanced handling of command lines, including controlling the life cycle of the remote instance and its exit status once it quits, as well as forwarding the entire contents of the command-line arguments, the environment, and forwarding stdin/stdout/ stderr. This can be accomplished using the HANDLES_COMMAND_LINE option and the command-line signal.

Example

Listing 2-1 provides a very simple example of an instance derived from the Gtk.Application class.

Listing 2-1. An Example of the Gtk.Application Class

```python
class Application(Gtk.Application):

    def __init__(self, *args, **kwargs):
        super().__init__(*args, application_id="org.example.myapp",
                         flags=Gio.ApplicationFlags.HANDLES_COMMAND_LINE,
                         **kwargs)
        self.window = None
        self.add_main_option("test", ord("t"), GLib.OptionFlags.NONE, GLib.
        OptionArg.NONE, "Command line test", None)

    def do_startup(self):
        Gtk.Application.do_startup(self)
        action = Gio.SimpleAction.new("quit", None)
        action.connect("activate", self.on_quit)
        self.add_action(action)

    def do_activate(self):
        # We only allow a single window and raise any existing ones
        if not self.window:
            # Windows are associated with the application
            # when the last one is closed the application shuts down
            self.window = AppWindow(application=self, title="Main Window")
        self.window.present()

    def do_command_line(self, command_line):
        options = command_line.get_options_dict()
        if options.contains("test"):
            # This is printed on the main instance
            print("Test argument received")
        self.activate()
        return 0
```

This example is a very simple instance of the Gtk.Application class. This example will be enhanced throughout this book as you gain knowledge of GTK+ 3.x.

Line 23 of the example shows how to create an instance of the Gtk.ApplicationWindow class.

The next section outlines the Gtk.ApplicationWindow class.

The Gtk.ApplicationWindow Class

The Gtk.ApplicationWindow class is the main visible window for your application. Under default conditions, this is the one and only main window visible to the user, unless the application has been set to "multi-instance" (the default is "single-instance").

Gtk.ApplicationWindow is a Gtk.Window subclass that offers extra functionality for better integration with Gtk.Application features. Notably, it can handle both the application menu as well as the menu bar (see Gtk.Application.set_app_menu() and Gtk.Application.set_menubar()).

When the Gtk.ApplicationWindow is used in coordination with the Gtk. Application class, there is a close relationship between the two classes. Both classes create new actions (signals) that may be acted upon by either class. But the Gtk. ApplicationWindow class is responsible for the full functionality of the widgets contained in the window. It should be noted that the Gtk.ApplicationWindow class also creates a connection for the delete-event that activates the do_quit method of the associated Gtk.Application class.

Actions

The Gtk.ApplicationWindow class implements the Gio.ActionGroup and Gio. ActionMap interfaces to let you add window-specific actions exported by the associated Gtk.Application with its application-wide actions. Window-specific actions are prefixed with win. Prefix and application-wide actions are prefixed with the app. prefix. Actions must be addressed with the prefixed name when referring to them from a Gio. MenuModel.

Note that widgets placed inside the Gtk.ApplicationWindow class can also activate these actions if they implement the Gtk.Actionable interface.

Locking

As with `Gtk.Application`, the GDK lock is acquired when processing actions arrive from other processes, and should therefore be held when activating actions locally (if GDK threads are enabled).

Example

Listing 2-2 is a very simple version of the integration between the `Gtk.Application` class and the `Gtk.ApplicationWindow` class. This example becomes the building block for all subsequent examples in this book.

Listing 2-2. An Example of the Gtk.Application and the Gtk.ApplicationWindow Classes

```python
#!/usr/bin/python3

import sys
import gi
gi.require_version('Gtk', '3.0')
from gi.repository import GLib, Gio, Gtk

# This would typically be its own
file MENU_XML="""
<?xml version="1.0" encoding="UTF-8"?> <interface>
    <menu id="app-menu">
        <section>
            <attribute name="label" translatable="yes">Change label
            </attribute> <item>
                <attribute name="action">win.change_label</attribute>
                <attribute name="target">String 1</attribute>
                <attribute name="label" translatable="yes">String 1
                </attribute> </item>
            <item>
                <attribute name="action">win.change_label</attribute>
                <attribute name="target">String 2</attribute>
                <attribute name="label" translatable="yes">String 2
                </attribute> </item>
```

```
            <item>
                <attribute name="action">win.change_label</attribute>
                <attribute name="target">String 3</attribute>
                <attribute name="label" translatable="yes">String 3
                </attribute> </item>
            </section>
            <section>
                <item>
                    <attribute name="action">win.maximize</attribute>
                    <attribute name="label" translatable="yes">Maximize
                    </attribute> </item>
            </section>
        <section>

        <item>
            <attribute name="action">app.about</attribute>
            <attribute name="label" translatable="yes">_About</attribute>
        </item>
        <item>
            <attribute name="action">app.quit</attribute>
            <attribute name="label" translatable="yes">_Quit</attribute>
            <attribute name="accel"><Primary>q</attribute>
        </item>
        </section>
    </menu>
</interface>
"""

class AppWindow(Gtk.ApplicationWindow):

    def __init__(self, *args, **kwargs):

        super().__init__(*args, **kwargs)

        # This will be in the windows group and have the "win" prefix
        max_action = Gio.SimpleAction.new_stateful("maximize", None,
                                        GLib.Variant.new_boolean(False))
```

```python
        max_action.connect("change-state", self.on_maximize_toggle)
        self.add_action(max_action)
        # Keep it in sync with the actual state
        self.connect("notify::is-maximized",
                    lambda obj, pspec: max_action.set_state(
                    GLib.Variant.new_boolean(obj.props.is_maximized)))
        lbl_variant = GLib.Variant.new_string("String 1")
        lbl_action = Gio.SimpleAction.new_stateful("change_label",
                                        lbl_variant.get_type(),
                                        lbl_variant)
        lbl_action.connect("change-state", self.on_change_label_state)
        self.add_action(lbl_action)
        self.label = Gtk.Label(label=lbl_variant.get_string(),
                                margin=30)
        self.add(self.label)
    def on_change_label_state(self, action, value):
        action.set_state(value)
        self.label.set_text(value.get_string())

    def on_maximize_toggle(self, action, value):
        action.set_state(value)
        if value.get_boolean():
            self.maximize()
        else:
            self.unmaximize()

class Application(Gtk.Application):

    def __init__(self, *args, **kwargs):
        super().__init__(*args, application_id="org.example.myapp",
                    flags=Gio.ApplicationFlags.HANDLES_COMMAND_LINE,
                    **kwargs)
        self.window = None
        self.add_main_option("test", ord("t"),
                        GLib.OptionFlags.NONE, GLib.OptionArg.NONE,
                        "Command line test", None)
```

```python
    def do_startup(self):
        Gtk.Application.do_startup(self)
        action = Gio.SimpleAction.new("about", None)
        action.connect("activate", self.on_about)
        self.add_action(action)
        action = Gio.SimpleAction.new("quit", None)
        action.connect("activate", self.on_quit)
        self.add_action(action)
        builder = Gtk.Builder.new_from_string(MENU_XML, -1)
        self.set_app_menu(builder.get_object("app-menu"))

    def do_activate(self):
        # We only allow a single window and raise any existing ones
        if not self.window:
            # Windows are associated with the application
            # When the last one is closed the application shuts down
            self.window = AppWindow(application=self, title="Main Window")
        self.window.present()

    def do_command_line(self, command_line):
        options = command_line.get_options_dict()
        if options.contains("test"):
            # This is printed on the main instance
            print("Test argument received")
        self.activate()
        return 0

    def on_about(self, action, param):
        about_dialog = Gtk.AboutDialog(transient_for=self.window, modal=True)
        about_dialog.present()

    def on_quit(self, action, param):
        self.quit()

if __name__ == "__main__":
    app = Application()
    app.run(sys.argv)
```

This example is a full-blown program that should be run from the command line. It modifies the command-line window and adds a menu to it for controlling the application. Most of the menu options are non-functional examples but prove useful for explaining how menu actions act and which class performs the actions specified by the menu XML file.

The top three lines specify the environment for the Python program. Line 5 establishes the Python environment as version 3.x. This is required for all Python programs running GTK 3.x. The next lines establish the Python and GTK imports. It specifically imports the GTK 3.x import libraries. Make sure that you import the modules using the gi interface so that you have the latest modules, because there may be more than one set of modules installed on your system.

The next lines describe the menu XML interface. Each menu item is described by one of three XML attributes. The first is the action attribute. It names an action and the name prefix specifies which class receives the action signal. An app prefix means that Gtk.Application processes the action signal. A win prefix means that Gtk.ApplicationWindow processes the signal. The second attribute is target, which specifies the string that displays in the menu item. The third attribute is label, which specifies whether or not the target attribute string should be translated.

Normally, this XML information is stored in its own file and read at runtime, but to simplify the example, we have included it inline.

The next lines describe the Gtk.ApplicationWindow subclass AppWindow, which encapsulates the main window behavior and all the main window widgets. In this example, there are no widgets contained in the main window. It only intercepts action signals from the menu and acts on those signals.

The main thing to note about the menu signal methods is that they have the same name as specified in the menu XML but with an on_ prefix. The next lines turn two of the four window actions into automatic toggles. The next lines catch the other two signals as method calls.

The Gtk.Application subclass Application encapsulates the application behavior. It provides the application startup and command-line processing, and processes two menu XML signals. As with the methods processed by Gtk.ApplicationWindow, the Gtk.Application method names have an on_ prefix.

First, the initialization for the Gtk.Application subclass calls the superclass to initialize it and then sets up a new command-line option.

The next lines perform the activation activities for the class, and create the `Gtk.ApplicationWindow` subclass.

Next, two signal methods are defined in the menu XML that are destined for the `Gtk.Application` subclass.

At the bottom is the actual start of the Python program. The only work that should be done here is to create the class or subclass of `Gtk.Application`.

Summary

This chapter covered the `Gtk.Application` and the `Gtk.ApplicationWindow` classes and the integration of the two classes. We covered how these classes can improve your application and make it more object oriented. The classes can also improve the readability and maintenance of your application.

In subsequent chapters, we cover most of the other GTK+ widgets while using the classes covered in this chapter as the basis for integrating the widgets into sample programs.

## CHAPTER 3

Some Simple GTK+ Applications

This chapter introduces some simple GTK+ applications and a few GTK+ widgets. We cover topics that are utilized in the upcoming chapters and example applications.

The following concepts are covered in this chapter.

- The basic function and method calls used by all GTK+ Python applications
- The object-oriented nature of the GTK+ widget system
- The role that signals, callbacks, and events play in your application
- How to alter textual styles with the Pango Text Markup Language
- Some useful functions and methods for widgets
- How to make a clickable label
- How to get and set properties (attributes) using the widget methods

It is important that you grasp the concepts presented so that you have a proper foundation.

Hello World

Practically every programming language book in the world starts with a Hello World example. While this book is no different, the example it uses is more complicated than most other language examples. This is because we base our example around the `Gtk.Application` and `Gtk.ApplicationWindow` classes. This makes the example program somewhat longer, and, at first glance, overblown for such a simple GTK+ window. But it also allows good explanations for how GTK+ works and how the Python bindings wrap the APIs into a very good object-oriented system.

Listing 3-1 is one of the simplest applications in this book, but it provides the basis for explaining how a GTK+ application should be organized and how the GTK+ hierarchy of widgets work. This is the basic code that every GTK+ application you create in Python should have!

Listing 3-1. HelloWorld.py

```
#!/usr/bin/python3

import sys
import gi
gi.require_version('Gtk', '3.0')
from gi.repository import Gtk

class AppWindow(Gtk.ApplicationWindow):

    def __init__(self, *args, **kwargs):
        super().__init__(*args, **kwargs)

class Application(Gtk.Application):

    def __init__(self, *args, **kwargs):
        super().__init__(*args, application_id="org.example.myapp",
                         **kwargs)
        self.window = None

    def do_activate(self):
        if not self.window:
            self.window = AppWindow(application=self, title="Main Window")
        self.window.present()

if __name__ == "__main__":
    app = Application()
    app.run(sys.argv)
```

Figure 3-1 contains everything you need for a complete GTK+ 3.x Python program.

Figure 3-1. *HelloWorld.py*

If you have previous experience with GTK+, you may notice some GTK+ 2.x common elements are missing. We explicitly make this a Python 3 program at line 1. This is necessary because the GTK+ 3.x modules are only available in Python version 3.x. This declaration allows lines 4–6 to properly establish the GTK+ 3.x environment.

Lines 8–11 support the visible GTK+ window. The only activity we need to support for this application is calling the super class to initialize it. But there seems to be some missing activities! All of those missing elements are either contained in the Gtk.ApplicationWindow superclass or they are supported in the Gtk.Application class. One of the default supporting actions connects the delete-event to a default method to quit the application.

Lines 13–23 support the application logic. One of the four default methods for the Gtk.Application class are defined in our subclass. The do_activate method performs the activation activities needed.

do_activate is called when the application is activated (after startup). In this case, two functions are needed. First, we check to see if this is the initial call to the method, and if it is, we create the Application GTK+ window instance. Second, we activate and show (present) the main application window.

Lines 25–27 are the only Python statements needed to start our application. No other statements are necessary, and in fact, none should be added. All the application work should take place in the `Gtk.Application` class or the `Gtk.ApplicationWindow` class or their subclasses. This prevents any unnecessary work taking place for a "single instance" application that has attempted to start up another application instance.

GTK+ Widget Hierarchy

The GTK+ application programming interface is actually a C language API. However, it is organized in such a way that an object-oriented language like Python can wrap the C API so that the entire set of APIs are turned into a set of classes organized in a hierarchy.

The transition from GTK+ 2.x to 3.x made changes that have helped other languages create object-oriented bindings that are easier to maintain and easier to implement. For instance, while Python 2.x supported abstract classes, they were buried in the collection classes and were hard to implement in your own code. Python 3.3 supplies the `collections.abc` module, which makes it easy for you to subclass classes in the module to create your own abstract classes. Also, the GTK+ 3.x API drastically reduces the number of abstract classes. In the future, all of them will probably be eliminated.

The GTK+ 3.x object hierarchy is documented by the PyGObject API Reference (`http://lazka.github.io/ pgi-docs/#Gtk-3.0`) document. This is the Python GTK+ 3.x reference document. It covers everything you need to know about the Python object bindings to GTK+, including the object hierarchy, supported classes, interfaces, functions, methods, and properties. While the document is mostly comprehensive, it lacks information concerning some new classes. We hope that this book provides that information, as well excellent examples on how to use all the widgets and classes.

While it is important to have an understanding of the GTK+ hierarchy, it is still possible to create good GUI applications with only a superficial understanding. But the more you understand the hierarchy, the better control you have over your application.

Extending HelloWorld.py

Even though Listing 3-1 is a complete application, obviously it is not very useful. So let's add useful features and method calls to provide visible information and visual appeal to our application (see Listing 3-2).

Listing 3-2. HelloWorld with Label

```python
#!/usr/bin/python3

import sys
import gi
gi.require_version('Gtk', '3.0')
from gi.repository import Gtk

class AppWindow(Gtk.ApplicationWindow):

    def __init__(self, *args, **kwargs):
        super().__init__(*args, **kwargs)
        label = Gtk.Label.new("Hello World!")
        label.set_selectable(True)
        self.add(label)
        self.set_size_request(200, 100)

class Application(Gtk.Application):

    def __init__(self, *args, **kwargs):
        super().__init__(*args, application_id="org.example.myapp",
                         **kwargs)
        self.window = None

    def do_activate(self):
        if not self.window:
            self.window = AppWindow(application=self, title="Hello World!")
        self.window.show_all()
        self.window.present()

if __name__ == "__main__":
    app = Application()
    app.run(sys.argv)
```

Figure 3-2 is the result of running Listing 3-2. Note that the label is already highlighted.

Figure 3-2. *HelloWorld with label*

We now have an application that displays data, and thus is a little more useful. Let's take a look at the changes we made to the program to achieve this result.

Lines 12–15 are where most of the changes have been made. On line 12, we create Gtk.Label with text "Hello World!" contained within it. On line 13, we make that text selectable. This allows the user to select the text and copy it to the clipboard. On line 14, we add the label to the Gtk.ApplicationWindow default container. All main windows in GTK+ derive from Gtk.Container, so it is possible to add widgets to that container. Line 15 resizes Gtk.ApplicationWindow.

Line 27 shows all the widgets contained by Gtk.ApplicationWindow. We need this method call because the present method does not perform that function. It only shows the main window.

These are the only changes made to Listing 3-1. As you can see, it does not take a lot of effort to add new functionality to a Python GTK+ application.

The GTK.Label Widget

A GTK.Label widget was created in Listing 3-2. This was accomplished with the following invocation.

```
label = Gtk.Label.new("Hello World!")
```

This call creates a new label with the specified text included. The text may include Python escape sequences (such as "\n"), which GTK+ uses to format your text on the screen.

There are lots of useful methods that GTK.Label supports. The following is list of some of the more useful ones.

- set_selectable: This method turns on/off the text's selectability. The default is off. This is very useful for things like error messages, where the user may wish to copy the text to the clipboard.

- set_text: This method replaces the current label text with the specified new text.

- set_text_with_mnemonic: This method replaces the current label text with the specified new text. The new text may or may not have a mnemonic contained within it. If characters in the text are preceded by an underscore, they are underlined, which indicates that they represent a keyboard accelerator called a *mnemonic*. The mnemonic key can be used to activate another widget, chosen automatically, or explicitly using Gtk.Label.set_mnemonic_widget.

- get_text: This method retrieves the current label text.

Layout Containers

The Gtk.ApplicationWindow and Gtk.Window classes both indirectly derive from the Gtk.Container widget. This means that all the methods in the Gtk.Container are available to the derived windows.

By using the add method, widgets or other container types can be added to a main window. That is how GTK.Label is added to the main window. It follows when you add a widget to a container that a parent/child relationship is formed; the container becomes the parent and the label becomes a child of the container.

The parent/child relationship between widgets is very important in GTK+ for many reasons. For example, when a parent widget is destroyed, GTK+ recursively destroys all the child widgets, no matter how deeply nested they are.

Containers also have a default sizing algorithm. This can be both good and bad news. In many cases, the default sizing is just what you want; but in many cases, it is not. You can override the default sizing by resizing the main window.

Another sizing helper for the container is the set_border_width method. It allows you to create a border around the text so that when the user shrinks the window manually, the window has a minimum size determined by the size of text and the border width.

There is more information on containers and layouts in Chapter 4.

Signals and Callbacks

GTK+ is a system that relies on signals and callback methods. A signal is a notification to your application that the user has performed some action. You can tell GTK+ to run a method or function when the signal is emitted. These are called *callback methods/functions*.

Caution   GTK+ signals are not the same as POSIX signals! Signals in GTK+ are propagated by events from the X Window System. Each provides separate methods. These two signal types should not be used interchangeably.

After you initialize your user interface, control is given to the gtk_main() function through the Gtk.Application class instance, which sleeps until a signal is emitted. At this point, control is passed to other methods/functions.

As the programmer, you connect signals to their methods/callback functions. The callback method/function is called when the action has occurred and the signal is emitted, or when you have explicitly emitted the signal. You also have the capability of stopping signals from being emitted at all.

Note   It is possible to connect signals at any point within your applications. For example, new signals can be connected within callback methods/functions. However, you should try to initialize mission-critical callbacks before calling gtk_main() or the present() method in the Gtk.Application instance.

There are many types of signals, and just like functions, they are inherited from parent structures. Many signals are generic to all widgets, such as "hide" and "grab-focus" or specific to the widget such as the Gtk.RadioButton signal "group-changed". In any case, widgets derived from a class can use all the signals available to all of its ancestors.

Connecting the Signal

Our first example of connecting to a signal intercepts the "destroy" signal from a main window so that we can choose how to handle that signal. One of the main reasons for handling this signal ourselves is to perform an action prior to having the window automatically destroyed by the GTK+ system.

```
widget.connect("destroy", self.on_window_destroy, extra_param)
```

GTK+ emits the "destroy" signal when widget.destroy() is called on the widget or when False is returned from a delete_event() callback method/function. If you reference the API documentation, you see that the destroy signal belongs to the Gtk.Object class. This means that every class in GTK+ inherits the signal. You can be notified of the destruction of any GTK+ structure/instance.

There are two required parameters to every connect() call. The first is the name of the signal you want to track. Each widget has many possible signals, all of which are found in the API documentation. Remember that widgets are free to use the signals of their ancestors, since each widget is actually an implementation of each of its ancestors. You can use the "Object Hierarchy" section of the API to reference parent classes.

```
widget.connect("signal_name", function_name, extra_param)
```

When typing the signal name, the underscore and dash characters are interchangeable. They are parsed as the same character, so it does not make any difference which one you choose. I use the underscore character in all the examples in this book.

The second parameter in the connect() method is the callback method/function which is called when the signal is emitted. The format of the callback method/function depends on the function prototype requirements of each specific signal. An example callback method is shown in the next section.

The last parameter in the connect() method allows you to send extra parameters to the callback method/function. Unlike the C version of the g_signal_connect() function, the Python version of the connect() method call allows you to pass as many extra parameters as you need for the callback method/function. This is very useful because it prevents the artificial creation of a single variable container that wraps a number of variables/classes that you wish to pass to a callback/method.

In this instance of connect(), a single label is passed to the callback method.

```
widget.connect("destroy", self.on_window_destroy, label)
```

The return value for connect() is the handler identifier of the signal. You can use this with GObject.signal_handler_block(), GObject.signal_handler_unblock(), and GObject.signal_handler_disconnect(). These functions stop a callback method/function from being called, re-enable the callback function, and remove the signal handler from a widget's handler list, respectively. More information is in the API documentation.

Callback Methods/Functions

Callback methods/functions specified in `connect()` are called when the signal is emitted on the widget to which it was connected. For all signals, with the exception of events, callback methods/functions are in the following form.

```
# a callback function
def on_window_destroy(widget, extra_arg)
```

```
# a callback method
def on_window_destroy(self, widget, extra_arg)
```

You can find an example format of a callback method/function for each signal in the API documentation, but this is the generic format. The `widget` parameter is the object that performed the `connect()` call.

There are other possible required arguments that may appear in the middle as well, although this is not always the case. For these parameters, you need to reference the documentation of the signal you are utilizing.

The last parameter of your callback method/function corresponds to the last parameter of `connect()`. Remember that there can be as many of these optional arguments as you need, but the number of extra parameters from the `connect()` call and the number of extra arguments in the callback method/ function definition must be the same.

You should also note that the first argument to the method version of the callback is the `self` argument required by Python in method definitions; otherwise, the function and method definitions are the same.

Events

Events are special types of signals that are emitted by the X Window System. They are initially emitted by the X Window System and then sent from the window manager to your application to be interpreted by the signal system provided by GLib. For example, the `"destroy"` signal is emitted on the widget, but the `"delete-event"` event is first recognized by the underlying `Gdk.Window` of the widget, and then emitted as a signal of the widget.

The first instance of an event you encountered was the "delete-event". The "delete-event" signal is emitted when the user tries to close the window. The window can be exited by clicking the Close button on the title bar, using the Close pop-up menu item in the taskbar, or by any other means provided by the window manager.

Connecting events to a callback function is done in the same manner with connect() as with other GTK + signals. However, your callback function is set up slightly differently.

```
# an event callback function
def on_window_destroy(widget, event, extra_arg)
```

```
# an event callback method
def on_window_destroy(self, widget, event, extra_arg)
```

The first difference in the callback method/function is the boolean return value. If True is returned from an event callback, GTK+ assumes the event has already been handled and it does not continue. By returning False, you are telling GTK+ to continue handling the event. False is the default return value for the function, so you do not need to use the "delete-event" signal in most cases. This is only useful if you want to override the default signal handler.

For example, in many applications, you may want to confirm the exit of the program. By using the following code, you can prevent the application from exiting if the user does not want to quit.

```
# an event callback method
def on_delete_event(self, widget, event, extra_arg):
    answer = # Ask the user if exiting is desired.
    if answer:
        return False
    else:
        return True
```

By returning False from the "delete-event" callback function, widget.destroy() is automatically called on the widget. This signal automatically continues with the action, so there is no need to connect to it unless you want to override the default.

In addition, the callback function includes the Gdk.Event parameter. Gdk.Event is a union of the Gdk.EventType enumeration and all the available event structures. Let's first look at the Gdk.EventType enumeration.

Event Types

The Gdk.EventType enumeration provides a list of available event types. These can be used to determine the type of event that has occurred, since you may not always know what has happened.

For example, if you connect the "button-press-event" signal to a widget, there are three different types of events that can cause the signal's callback function to be run: Gdk.EventType.BUTTON_PRESS, Gdk.EventType.2BUTTON_PRESS, and Gdk. EventType.3BUTTON_PRESS. Double-clicks and triple-clicks emit the Gdk.EventType. BUTTON_PRESS as a second event as well, so being able to distinguish between different types of events is necessary.

Appendix B provides see a complete list of the events available to you. It shows the signal name that is passed to connect(), the Gdk.EventType enumeration value, and a description of the event.

Let's look at the "delete-event" callback function. We already know that "delete-event" is of the type Gdk.EventType.DELETE, but let's assume for a moment that we did not know that. We can easily test this by using the following conditional statement.

```
def delete_event(self, window, event, data):
    if event.type == Gdk.EventType.DELETE:
        return False
    return True
```

In this example, if the event type is Gdk.EventType.DELETE, False is returned, and widget.destroy() is called on the widget; otherwise, True is returned, and no further action is taken.

Using Specific Event Structures

Sometimes, you may already know which type of event has been emitted. In the following example, we know that a "key-press-event" is always emitted.

```
widget.connect("key-press-event", on_key_press)
```

In this case, it is safe to assume that the type of event is always Gdk.EventType.KEY_ PRESS, and the callback function can be declared as such.

```
def on_key_press(widget, event):
```

Since we know that the type of event is a Gdk.EventType.KEY_PRESS, we do not need access to all of the structures in Gdk.Event. We only have use for Gdk.EventKey, which we can use instead of Gdk.Event in the callback method/function. Since the event is already cast as Gdk.EventKey, we have direct access to only the elements in that structure.

```
Gdk.EventKey.type                # GDK_KEY_PRESS or GDK_KEY_RELEASE
Gdk.EventKey.window              # The window that received the event
Gdk.EventKey.send_event          # TRUE if the event used XSendEvent
Gdk.EventKey.time                # The length of the event in milliseconds
Gdk.EventKey.state               # The state of Control, Shift, and Alt
Gdk.EventKey.keyval              # The key that was pressed
Gdk.EventKey.length              # The length of string
Gdk.EventKey.string              # A string approximating the entered text
Gdk.EventKey.hardware_keycode    # Raw code of the key that was pressed or
                                   released
Gdk.EventKey.group               # The keyboard group
Gdk.EventKey.is_modifier         # Whether hardware_keycode was mapped
```

There are many useful properties in the Gdk.EventKey structure that we use throughout the book. At some point, it would be useful for you to browse some of the Gdk.Event structures in the API documentation. We cover a few of the most important structures in this book, including Gdk.EventKey and Gdk.EventButton.

The only variable that is available in all the event structures is the event type, which defines the type of event that has occurred. It is a good idea to always check the event type to avoid handling it in the wrong way.

Further GTK+ Methods

Before continuing on to further examples, I would like to draw your attention to a few functions that will come in handy in later chapters and when you create your own GTK+ applications.

Gtk.Widget Methods

The Gtk.Widget structure contains many useful functions that you can use with any widget. This section outlines a few that you need in a lot of your applications.

It is possible to destroy a widget by explicitly calling widget.destroy() on the object. When invoked, widget.destroy() drops the reference count on the widget and all of its children recursively. The widget, along with its children, are then destroyed and all memory is freed.

widget.destroy()

Generally, this is only called on top-level widgets. It is usually only used to destroy dialog windows and to implement menu items that quit the application. It is used in the next example to quit the application when a button is clicked.

You can use widget.set_size_request() to set the minimum size of a widget. It forces the widget to be smaller or larger than it would normally be. It does not, however, resize the widget so that it is too small to be functional or able to draw itself on the screen.

widget.set_size_request(width, height)

By passing −1 to either parameter, you are telling GTK+ to use its natural size, or the size that the widget would normally be allocated to if you do not define a custom size. This is used if you want to specify only the height or only the width parameter. It also allows you to reset the widget to its original size.

There is no way to set a widget with a width or height of less than 1 pixel, but by passing 0 to either parameter, GTK+ makes the widget as small as possible. Again, it is not resized so small that it's non-functional or unable to draw itself.

Because of internationalization, there is a danger in setting the size of any widget. The text may look great on your computer, but on a computer using a German translation of your application, the widget may be too small or large for the text. Themes also present issues with widget sizing, because widgets are defaulted to different sizes, depending on the theme. Therefore, it is best to allow GTK+ to choose the size of widgets and windows in most cases.

You can use widget.grab_focus() to force a widget to grab the keyboard focus. This only work on widgets that can handle keyboard interaction. One example of a use for widget.grab_focus() is sending the cursor to a text entry when the search toolbar is shown in Firefox. It could also be used to give focus to a Gtk.Label that is selectable.

widget.grab_focus()

Often, you want to set a widget as inactive. By calling `widget.set_sensitive()`, the specified widget and all of its children are disabled or enabled. By setting a widget as inactive, the user is prevented from interacting with the widget. Most widgets are also grayed out when set as inactive.

```
widget.set_sensitive(boolean)
```

If you want to re-enable a widget and its children, you need only to call this method on the same widget. Children are affected by the sensitivity of their parents, but they only reflect the parents' settings, instead of changing their properties.

Gtk.Window Methods

You have now seen two examples using the `Gtk.Window` class. You learned how to set the title of a window and add a child widget. Now, let's explore a few more functions that allow you to further customize windows.

All windows are set as resizable by default. This is desirable in most applications, because each user has different size preferences. However, if there is a specific reason for doing so, you can use `window.set_resizable()` to prevent the user from resizing the window.

```
window.set_resizable(boolean)
```

Caution   You should note that the ability to resize is controlled by the window manager, so this setting may not be honored in all cases!

The preceding caution brings up an important point. Much of what GTK+ does interacts with the functionality provided by the window manager. Because of this, not all of your window settings may be followed on all window managers. This is because your settings are merely hints that are either used or ignored. You should keep in mind that your requests may or may not be honored when designing applications with GTK+.

The default size of `Gtk.Window` can be set with `window.set_default_size()`, but there are a few things to watch out for when using this method. If the minimum size of the window is larger than the size you specify, this method is ignored by GTK+. It is also ignored if you have previously set a larger size request.

```
window.set_default_size(width, height)
```

Unlike `widget.set_size_request()`, `window.set_default_size()` only sets the initial size of the window; it does not prevent the user from resizing it to a larger or smaller size. If you set a height or width parameter to 0 , the window's height or width is set to the minimum possible size. If you pass –1 to either parameter, the window is set to its natural size.

You can *request* that the window manager move the window to the specified location with `window.move()`; however, the window manager is free to ignore this request. This is true of all functions that require action from the window manager.

```
window.move(x, y)
```

By default, the position of the window on the screen is calculated with respect to the top-left corner of the screen, but you can use `window.set_gravity()` to change this assumption.

```
window.set_gravity(gravity)
```

This function defines the gravity of the widget, which is the point that layout calculations consider (0, 0). Possible values for the `Gdk.Gravity` enumeration include `Gdk.Gravity.NORTH_WEST`, `Gdk.Gravity.NORTH`, `Gdk.Gravity.GRAVITY_NORTH_EAST`, `Gdk.Gravity.WEST`, `Gdk.Gravity.CENTER`, `Gdk.Gravity.EAST`, `Gdk.Gravity.SOUTH_WEST`, `Gdk.Gravity.SOUTH`, `Gdk.Gravity.SOUTH_EAST`, and `Gdk.Gravity.STATIC`.

North, south, east, and west refer to the top, bottom, right, and left edges of the screen. They are used to construct multiple gravity types. `Gdk.Gravity.STATIC` refers to the top-left corner of the window itself, ignoring window decorations.

If your application has more than one window, you can set one as the parent with `window.set_transient_for()`. This allows the window manager to do things such as center the child above the parent or make sure one window is always on top of the other. We explore the idea of multiple windows and transient relationships in Chapter 6 when discussing dialogs.

```
window.set_transient_for(parent)
```

You can set the icon that appears in the taskbar and title bar of the window by calling `window.set_icon_from_file()`. The size of the icon does not matter, because it is resized when the desired size is known. This allows the scaled icon to have best quality.

```
window.set_icon_from_file(filename)
```

True is returned if the icon was successfully loaded and set.

Caution   Icons are a complex topic and have many behavioral complexities, including icon sets, scaling, and interactions with themes. See the GTK+ documentation for more information.

Process Pending Events

At times, you may want to process all pending events in an application. This is extremely useful when you are running a piece of code that takes a long time to process. This causes your application to appear frozen, because widgets are not redrawn if the CPU is taken up by another process. For example, in an integrated development environment that I created called OpenLDev, I have to update the user interface while a build command is being processed; otherwise, the window would lock up and no build output would be shown until the build was complete.

The following loop is the solution for this problem. It is the answer to a great number of questions from new GTK+ programmers.

```
while Gtk.events_pending():
    Gtk.main_iteration()
```

The loop calls Gtk.main_iteration(), which processes the first pending event for your application. This continues while Gtk.events_pending() returns True, which tells you whether there are events waiting to be processed.

Using this loop is an easy solution to the freezing problem, but a better solution is to use coding strategies that avoid the problem altogether. For example, you can use idle functions found in GLib to call a function only when there are no actions of greater importance to process.

Buttons

Gtk.Button is a special kind of container that can only contain a single child. However, that child can be a container itself, thus allowing a button to contain multiple widgets. The Gtk.Button class is a clickable entity. It can be connected to a defined method of the owning container or window.

Gtk.Button is an action widget. That is, when it is clicked, an action is expected to be taken. The programmer has full control of that action by processing the signal emitted when the button is clicked. So let's take a look at how Gtk.Button works in another simple example (see Listing 3-3).

Listing 3-3. HelloWorld with Button

```python
#!/usr/bin/python3

import sys
import gi
gi.require_version('Gtk', '3.0')
from gi.repository import Gtk

class AppWindow(Gtk.ApplicationWindow):

    def __init__(self, *args, **kwargs):
        super().__init__(*args, **kwargs)
        self.set_border_width(25)
        button = Gtk.Button.new_with_mnemonic("_Close")
        button.connect("clicked", self.on_button_clicked)
        button.set_relief(Gtk.ReliefStyle.NORMAL)
        self.add(button)
        self.set_size_request(200, 100)

    def on_button_clicked(self, button):
        self.destroy()

class Application(Gtk.Application):

    def __init__(self, *args, **kwargs):
        super().__init__(*args, application_id="org.example.myapp",
                         **kwargs)
        self.window = None

    def do_activate(self):
        if not self.window:
            self.window = AppWindow(application=self,
                                    title="Hello World!")
        self.window.show_all()
        self.window.present()
```

```
if __name__ == "__main__":
    app = Application()
    app.run(sys.argv)
```

Figure 3-3 shows the result of running Listing 3-3. Note how the button is centered by default.

Figure 3-3. *HelloWorld with button*

Those of you who are experienced GTK+ 2.x developers may wonder why we did not use a stock button instead. Stock buttons have been deprecated since GTK+ 3.1 and should not be used in new code. This may come as a huge surprise because this causes a lot of work when upgrading a 2.x application to a 3.x application. But all is not as bad as it first seems. By converting to non-stock buttons, your application becomes more portable for all supported platforms.

Let's take a detailed look at the button code. There is some interesting code.

Line 12 sets the border width around the button to be created later. Lines 13–16 create the button and connect it to a method in the Gtk.Application instance. Line 13 creates a button with the mnemonic label "_Close". The underline indicates that the letter C is the mnemonic. When the user presses Alt+C, the "clicked" signal is emitted by the button.

Line 14 connects the "clicked" signal produced by the button to the on_button_ clicked method in the Gtk.ApplicationWindow instance. It does this by obtaining the instance from the kwargs argument. The dictionary name application was assigned a value on line 28, and that value was fetched on line 14 to point to the correct Gtk. Application instance method.

You may be wondering why we did not connect the button signal to a method local to the Gtk.ApplicationWindow class. This is because the signal to quit the application rightly belongs to the Gtk.Application class, not the Gtk.ApplicationWindow class. This is one of those "gotchas" that can be very hard to understand and apply properly. You need to think carefully when connecting signals to methods to make sure that the correct class gets the signal. This is a roundabout method to process the "clicked" signal. The normal way is to create your own method, like on_button_clicked, in the Gtk.ApplicationWindow class and connect the signal to that method. We are only showing this example to make the point that you can send signals to either the Gtk.ApplicationWindow instance or the Gtk.Application instance.

Line 14 sets the relief style for the button. You should always use the Gtk.ReliefStyle.NORMAL style unless you have good reasons for doing otherwise.

Line 16 adds the button to the Gtk.ApplicationWindow container. This works just like adding a label, as shown in Listing 3-2.

Lines 19–20 process the "clicked" signal emitted from our button. Our only action is to destroy the Gtk.ApplicationWindow instance.

We should note that when the last Gtk.ApplicationWindow instance is destroyed, the Gtk.Application causes the application to exit.

Test Your Understanding

In this chapter, you learned about the window, button, and label widgets. It is time to put that knowledge into practice. In the following exercise, you employ your knowledge of the structure of GTK+ applications, signals, and the GObject property system.

Exercise 1: Using Events and Properties

This exercise expands on the first two examples in this chapter by creating a Gtk.ApplicationWindow class that has the ability to destroy itself. You should set your first name as the title of the window. A selectable Gtk.Label with your last name as the default text string should be added as the child of the window.

Let's consider other properties of this window: it should not be resizable and the minimum size should be 300×100 pixels. The methods to perform these tasks were discussed in this chapter.

Next, by looking at the API documentation, connect the key-press-event signal to the window. In the "key-press-event" callback function, switch the window title and the label text. For example, the first time the callback method is called, the window title should be set to your last name and the label text to your first name.

Once you have completed exercise 1, you can find a description of the solution in Appendix D. The solution's complete source code can be downloaded from www. gtkbook.com.

Once you have completed this exercise, you are ready to move on to the next chapter, which covers container widgets. These widgets allow your main window to contain more than just a single widget, which was the case in all the examples in this chapter.

However, before you continue, you should know about www.gtkbook.com, which can supplement *Foundations of PyGTK Development*. This web site is filled with downloads, links to further GTK+ information, C and Python refresher tutorials, API documentation, and more. You can use it as you go through this book to aid in your quest to learn GTK+.

Summary

In this chapter, we introduced some simple GTK+ 3.x applications, along with some simple widgets, which also introduced concepts that will be beneficial in later chapters. Here are some of the concepts you learned in this chapter.

- The Gtk.Label class was introduced with an example program.

- The Gtk.Button class was introduced with an example program.

- The signals and methods to catch the signals were introduced. This concept is covered in more depth in a later chapter.

- The concept of containers was introduced. This concept is covered in more depth in Chapter 4.

In Chapter 4, we cover the Gtk.Container class and the vast array of container types available.

CHAPTER 4

Containers

Chapter 3 introduced the basic essentials needed for creating basic GTK+ applications. It also introduced signals, callback methods, the Gtk.label class, the Gtk.Button class, and the Gtk.Container class.

In this chapter, you expand our knowledge of the Gtk.Container class. Then we show the two kinds of contained widgets: layout and decorator containers. Additionally, we cover a number of derived widgets, including boxes, notebooks, handle boxes, and expanders.

The last widget covered, Gtk.EventBox, allows widgets to take advantage of GDK events. The following topics are covered.

- The purpose of the Gtk.Container class and its descendants
- How to use layout containers, including boxes, tables, grid, and panes
- When to used fixed containers
- How to provide events to all widgets using event boxes

GTK.Container

The Gtk.Container class has been covered briefly in past sections, But we now cover the class in more depth. This is necessary so that you have the necessary base knowledge about containers so we may cover all the derived classes in subsequent sections.

The Gtk.Container class is an abstract class. Therefore you should never attempt to create an instance of this class, only of the derived classes.

The main purpose of a container class is to allow a parent widget to contain one or more child widgets. There are two type of container widgets in GTK+, those used for laying out children and decorators and those that add some sort of functionality beyond positioning children.

© W. David Ashley and Andrew Krause 2019
W. D. Ashley and A. Krause, *Foundations of PyGTK Development*,
https://doi.org/10.1007/978-1-4842-4179-0_4

Decorator Containers

In Chapter 3, you were introduced to Gtk.ApplicationWindow, a window derived from Gtk.Window, which is derived from Gtk.Bin—a type of container class that has the capability of holding only one child widget. Widgets derived from this class are called decorator containers because they add some type of functionality to the child widget.

For example, a Gtk.Window provides it child with some extra functionality of being placed in a top level widget. Other example decorators include the Gtk.Frame widget, which draws a frame around it child, a Gtk.Button, which makes its child a clickable button, and a Gtk.Expander which can hide or show its child from the user. All there widgets use the add method for adding a child widget.

The Gtk.Bin only exposes one method, get_child. The only purpose of the Gtk.Bin class is to provide an instantiable widget from which all subclasses that only require one child widget can be derived. It is a central class for common base.

```
binwin = Gtk.Bin()
```

Widgets that derive from Gtk.Bin include windows, alignments, frames, buttons, combo boxes, event boxes, expanders, handle boxes, scrolled windows, and tool items. Many of these containers are covered in subsequent section of this chapter.

Layout Containers

Another type of container widget provided by GTK+ is called a layout container. These are widgets that are used to arrange multiple widgets. Layout containers can be recognized by the fact that they are derived directly from Gtk.Container.

As the name implies, the purpose of layout containers is to correctly arrange their children according to the user's preferences, your instructions, and built-in rules. User preferences include the use of themes and font preferences. These can be overridden, but in most cases, you should honor the user's preferences. There are also resizing rules that govern all container widgets, which is covered in the next section.

Layout containers include boxes, fixed containers, paned widgets, icon views, layouts, menu shells, notebooks, sockets, tables, text views, toolbars, and tree views. We are covering most of the layout widgets throughout this chapter and the rest of the book. More information on those we do not cover is available in the PyGObject API Reference (http://lazka.github.io/pgi-docs/#Gtk-3.0) documentation.

Resizing Children

In addition to arranging and decorating children, containers are tasked with resizing child widgets. Resizing is performed in two phases: size requisition and size allocation. In short, these two steps negotiate the size that is available to a widget. This is a recursive process of communication between the widget, its ancestors, and its children.

Size requisition refers to the desired size of the child. The process begins at the top-level widget, which asks its children for their preferred sizes. The children ask their children and so on, until the last child is reached.

At this point, the last child decides what size it wants to be based on the space it needs to be shown correctly on the screen and any size requests from the programmer. For example, a Gtk.Label widget asks for enough space to fully display its text on the screen or more space if you requested it to have a larger size.

The child then passes this size to its ancestors until the top-level widget receives the amount of space needed based on its children's requisitions.

Each widget stores its size preferences as width and height values in a Gtk. Requisition object. Keep in mind that a requisition is only a request; it does not have to be honored by the parent widget.

When the top-level widget has determined the amount of space it wants, size allocation begins. If you have set the top-level widget as nonresizable, the widget will never be resized; no further action occurs and requisitions are ignored; otherwise, the top-level widget resizes itself to the desired size. It then pass the amount of available space to its child widget. This process is repeated until all widgets have resized themselves.

Size allocations for every widget are stored in one instance of the Gtk.Allocation structure for each child. This structure is passed to child widgets for resizing with size_ allocate(). This function can be called explicitly by the programmer as well, but doing so is not a good idea in the majority of cases.

In most situations, children are given the space they request, but there are certain circumstances when this cannot happen. For example, a requisition is not honored when the top-level widget cannot be resized.

Conversely, once a widget has been given a size allocation by its parent, the widget has no choice but to redraw itself with the new size. Therefore, you should be careful where you call size_allocate(). In most cases, set_size_request() is best to use for resizing widgets.

Container Signals

The Gtk.Container class currently provides four signals. These are "add", "check_resize", "remove", and "set_focus_child".

- "add": A child widget was added or packed into the container. This signal is emitted even if you do not explicitly call add() but use the widget's built-in packing functions instead.

- "check_resize": The container is checking whether it needs to resize for its children before taking further action.

- "remove": A child has been removed from the container.

- "set_focus_child": A child of the container has received focus from the window manager. Now that you know the purpose of the Gtk.Container class, we will progress onto other types of container widgets. You have already learned about windows, a type of Gtk.Bin widget, so we will begin this chapter with a layout container called Gtk.Box.

Horizontal and Vertical Boxes

Gtk.Box is a container widget that allows multiple children to be packed in a one-dimensional, rectangular area. There are two types of boxes: a vertical box which packs children into a single column, and a horizontal box which packs them into a single row.

Note   In GTK+ 2.x, the Gtk.Box was an abstract class. The two subclasses Gtk.HBox and Gtk.VBox were used to create horizontal and vertical boxes respectively. In GTK+ 3.x these two classes have been deprecated and the Gtk.Box has become a real class from which both horizontal and vertical boxes can be created.

The graphical output of the application is shown in Listing 4-1. Notice that the names are shown in the same order as they were added to the array, even though each was packed at the start position. Notice that the names are shown in the same order as they were added to the array, even though each was packed at the start position.

Listing 4-1. Vertical Boxes with Default Packing

```python
#!/usr/bin/python3

import sys
import gi
gi.require_version('Gtk', '3.0')
from gi.repository import Gtk

names = ["Andrew", "Joe", "Samantha", "Jonathan"]

class AppWindow(Gtk.ApplicationWindow):

def __init__(self, *args, **kwargs):
    super().__init__(*args, **kwargs)
    vbox = Gtk.Box(orientation=Gtk.Orientation.VERTICAL, spacing=0)
    for name in names:
        button = Gtk.Button.new_with_label(name)
        vbox.pack_start(button, True, True, 0)
        button.connect("clicked", self.on_button_clicked)
        button.set_relief(Gtk.ReliefStyle.NORMAL)
    self.set_border_width(10)
    self.set_size_request(200, -1)
    self.add(vbox)
    self.show_all()

def on_button_clicked(self, widget):
    self.destroy()

class Application(Gtk.Application):

    def __init__(self, *args, **kwargs):
        super().__init__(*args, application_id="org.example.myapp",
                         **kwargs)
        self.window = None

    def do_activate(self):
        if not self.window:
            self.window = AppWindow(application=self, title="Boxes")
        self.window.show_all()
        self.window.present()
```

```
if __name__ == "__main__":
    app = Application()
    app.run(sys.argv)
```

Figure 4-1 shows the result of running Listing 4-1.

Figure 4-1. *Vertical boxes with default packing*

In analyzing Listing 4-2, Gtk.Box uses the same set of methods. Gtk.Box uses the same set of methods.

As with every widget, you need to initialize Gtk.Box before using the object. All the parameters that are passed are keyword parameters. The default orientation if no keyword "orientation" is passed the default is Gtk.Orientation.HORIZONTAL. Other keywords are available, such as "spacing". If the "homogeneous" keyword is set to True, all of the children are given the smallest amount of space that can fit every widget.

```
vbox = Gtk.Box(orientation=Gtk.Orientation.VERTICAL, spacing=0)
```

The "spacing" keyword parameter places a default number of pixels of spacing between each child and its neighbor. This value can be changed for individual cells as children are added, if the box is not set as equally spaced.

Since you do not need further access to the labels in Listing 4-2 after they are added to the widget, the application does not store individual pointers to each object. They are all cleaned up automatically when the parent is destroyed. Each button is then added to the box using a method called the packing.Gtk.Box widget.

By adding widgets to the box with pack_start(), the child has three properties automatically set. Expanding is set to True, which automatically provides the cell with the extra space allocated to the box. This space is distributed evenly to all of the cells that request it. The fill property is also set to True, which means the widget expands into all of the extra space provided instead of filling it with padding. Lastly, the amount of padding placed between the cell and its neighbors is set to zero pixels.

```
vbox.pack_start(button, True, True, 0)
```

Packing boxes can be slightly unintuitive because of the naming of functions. The best way to think about it is in terms of where the packing begins. If you pack at the start position, children are added with the first child appearing at the top or left. If you pack at the end position, the first child appears at the bottom or right of the box.

It should also be noted that the pack_start() and pack_end() methods not only specify the packing parameters, they also add the widget to the specified widget instance. It is not necessary to call the add() method to add the widget if you call one of packing methods. In fact, it is a runtime error if you attempt to add the same widget with a packing method and the add() method.

Listing 4-2. Vertical_Boxes Specifying Packing Parameters

```python
#!/usr/bin/python3

import sys
import gi
gi.require_version('Gtk', '3.0')
from gi.repository import Gtk

names = ["Andrew", "Joe", "Samantha", "Jonathan"]

class AppWindow(Gtk.ApplicationWindow):

    def __init__(self, *args, **kwargs):
        super().__init__(*args, **kwargs)
        vbox = Gtk.Box(orientation=Gtk.Orientation.VERTICAL, spacing=0)
        for name in names:
            button = Gtk.Button.new_with_label(name)
            vbox.pack_end(button, False, False, 5)
            button.connect("clicked", self.on_button_clicked)
            button.set_relief(Gtk.ReliefStyle.NORMAL)
```

45

```python
        self.set_border_width(10)
        self.set_size_request(200, -1)
        self.add(vbox)
        self.show_all()

    def on_button_clicked(self, widget):
        self.destroy()

class Application(Gtk.Application):

    def __init__(self, *args, **kwargs):
        super().__init__(*args, application_id="org.example.myapp",
                         **kwargs)
        self.window = None

    def do_activate(self):
        if not self.window:
            self.window = AppWindow(application=self, title="Boxes")
        self.window.show_all()
        self.window.present()

if __name__ == "__main__":
    app = Application()
    app.run(sys.argv)
```

Since we packed each of the widgets starting at the end, they are shown in reverse order in Figure 4-2). The packing began at the end of the box and packed each child before the previous one. You are free to intersperse calls to start and end packing functions. GTK+ keeps track of both reference positions. Since we packed each of the widgets starting at the end, they are shown in reverse order. The packing began at the end of the box and packed each child before the previous one. You are free to intersperse calls to start and end packing functions. GTK+ keeps track of both reference positions.

Figure 4-2. *Vertical_Boxes specifying packing parameters*

By setting the expand property to True, the cell expands so that it takes up additional space allocated to the box that is not needed by the widgets. By setting the fill property to True, the widget expands to fill extra space available to the cell. Table 4-1 offers a brief description of all possible combinations of the expand and fill properties.

Table 4-1. *Expand and Fill Properties*

expand	fill	Result
True	True	The cell expand so that it takes up additional space allocated to the box, and the child widget expand to fill that space.
True	False	The cell expand so that it takes up additional space, but the widget not expand. Instead, the extra space is empty.
False	True	Neither the cell nor the widget expand to fill extra space. This is the same thing as setting both properties to False.
False	False	Neither the cell nor the widget expand to fill extra space. If you resize the window, the cell not resize itself.

In the previous pack_end() call, each cell is told to place five pixels of spacing between itself and any neighbor cells. Also, according to Table 4-1 neither the cell nor its child widget expand to take up additional space provided to the box.

```
vbox.pack_end(button, True, True, 0)
```

> **Note**   If you have experience programming with other graphical toolkits, the size negotiation system provided by GTK+ may seem odd. However, you quickly learn its benefits. GTK+ automatically takes care of resizing everything if you change a user interface, instead of requiring you to reposition everything programmatically. You will come to view this as a great benefit as you continue learning GTK+.

While you should try to finalize the order of elements in a Gtk.Boxwidget before displaying it to the user, it is possible to reorder child widgets in a box with reorder_child().

```
vbox.reorder_child(child_widget, position)
```

By using this method, you can move a child widget to a new position in the Gtk.Box. The position of the first widget in a Gtk.Box container is indexed from zero. The widget is placed in the last position of the box if you specify a position value of –1 or a value greater than the number of children.

Horizontal and Vertical Panes

Gtk.Paned is a special type of container widget that holds exactly two widgets. A resize bar is placed between them, which allows the user to resize the two widgets by dragging the bar in one direction or the other. When the bar is moved, either by user interaction or programmatic calls, one of the two widgets shrinks while the other expands.

> **Note**   In GTK+ 2.x, the Gtk.Paned was an abstract class. The two subclasses Gtk.HPaned and Gtk.VPaned were used to create horizontal and vertical boxes respectively. In GTK+ 3.x, these two classes have been deprecated and the Gtk. Paned has become a real class from which both horizontal and vertical panes can be created.

There are two types of paned widgets: horizontal resizing and vertical resizing. As with boxes, Gtk.Paned provides all the functions for both horizontal and vertical panes. Listing 4-3 shows a simple example where two Gtk.Button widgets are placed as the children of a horizontal pane.

Listing 4-3. Horizontal Paned with Buttons

```
#!/usr/bin/python3

import sys
import gi
gi.require_version('Gtk', '3.0')
from gi.repository import Gtk

class AppWindow(Gtk.ApplicationWindow):

    def __init__(self, *args, **kwargs):
        super().__init__(*args, **kwargs)
        self.set_border_width(10)
        hpaned = Gtk.Paned.new(Gtk.Orientation.HORIZONTAL)
        button1 = Gtk.Button.new_with_label("Resize")
        button2 = Gtk.Button.new_with_label("Me!")
        button1.connect("clicked", self.on_button_clicked)
        button2.connect("clicked", self.on_button_clicked)
        hpaned.add1(button1)
        hpaned.add2(button2)
        self.add(hpaned)
        self.set_size_request(225, 150)
        self.show_all()

    def on_button_clicked(self, button):
        self.destroy()

class Application(Gtk.Application):

    def __init__(self, *args, **kwargs):
        super().__init__(*args, application_id="org.example.myapp",
                         **kwargs)
        self.window = None
```

```
    def do_activate(self):
        if not self.window:
            self.window = AppWindow(application=self, title="Panes")
        self.window.show_all()
        self.window.present()

if __name__ == "__main__":
    app = Application()
    app.run(sys.argv)
```

As you can see in Figure 4-3 the Gtk.Paned widget places a vertical bar between its two children. By dragging the bar, one widget shrinks while the other expands. In fact, it is possible to move the bar so that one child is completely hidden from the user's view. You learn how to prevent this with the pack1() and pack2() methods.

Figure 4-3. *Horizontal paned with buttons*

In Figure 4-3 we created a Gtk.Paned object with the following.

```
hpaned = Gtk.Paned.new(Gtk.Orientation.HORIZONTAL)
```

If you want to use a vertical paned widget instead, you need only to call the following.

```
vpaned = Gtk.Paned.new(Gtk.Orientation.VERTICAL)
```

All of the Gtk.Paned functions then work with either type of paned widget.

Since Gtk.Paned can only handle two children, GTK+ provides a function for packing each child. In the following example, pack1() and pack2() methods were used to add both children to Gtk.Paned. These functions use the default values for the resize and shrink properties of the Gtk.Paned widget.

```
hpaned.add1(button1);
hpaned.add2(button2);
```

The preceding add1() and add2() method calls are from Listing 4-3 and are equivalent to the following.

```
hpaned.pack1(label1, False, True);
hpaned.pack2(label2, True, True);
```

The second parameter in pack1() and pack2() specifies whether the child widget should expand when the pane is resized. If you set this to False, no matter how much larger you make the available area, the child widget does not expand.

The last parameter specifies whether the child can be made smaller than its size requisition. In most cases, you want to set this to True so that a widget can be completely hidden by the user by dragging the resize bar. If you want to prevent the user from doing this, set the third parameter to False. Table 4-2 illustrates how the resize and shrink properties interrelate.

Table 4-2. *Resize and Shrink Properties*

resize	shrink	Result
True	True	The widget takes up all available space when the pane is resized, and the user is able to make it smaller than its size requisition.
True	False	The widget takes up all available space when the pane is resized, but available space must be greater than or equal to the widget's size requisition.
False	True	The widget will not resize itself to take up additional space available in the pane, but the user is able to make it smaller than its size requisition.
False	False	The widget will not resize itself to take up additional space available in the pane, and the available space must be greater than or equal to the widget's size requisition.

You can easily set the exact position of the resize bar with set_position(). The position is calculated in pixels with respect to the top or left side of the container. If you set the position of the bar to zero, it is moved all the way to the top or left if the widget allows shrinking.

```
paned.set_position(position)
```

Most applications want to remember the position of the resize bar, so it can be restored to the same location when the user next loads the application. The current position of the resize bar can be retrieved with get_position().

```
pos = paned.get_position()
```

Gtk.Paned provides multiple signals, but one of the most useful is move-handle, which tells you when the resizing bar has been moved. If you want to remember the position of the resize bar, this tells you when you need to retrieve a new value.

Grids

So far, all the layout container widgets I have covered only allow children to be packed in one dimension.

The Gtk.Grid widget, however, allows you to pack children in two-dimensional space.

One advantage of using the Gtk.Grid widget over using multiple Gtk.Box widgets is that children in adjacent rows and columns are automatically aligned with each other, which is not the case with boxes within boxes. However, this is also a disadvantage, because you will not always want everything to be lined up in this way.

Figure 4-4 shows a simple grid that contains three widgets. Notice that the single label spans two columns. This illustrates the fact that grids allow one widget to span multiple columns and/or rows as long as the region is rectangular.

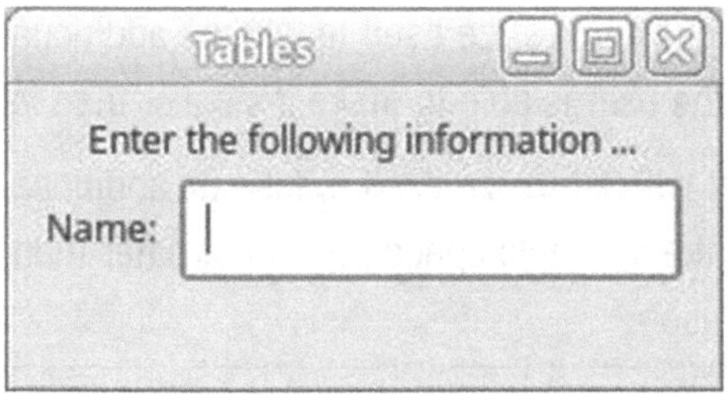

Figure 4-4. *Grid displaying name*

Listing 4-4 inserts two Gtk.Label widgets and a Gtk.Entry widget into the two-by-two area (you learn how to use the Gtk.Entry widget in Chapter 5, but this gives you a taste of what is to come).

Listing 4-4. Grids Displaying Name

```python
#!/usr/bin/python3

import sys
import gi
gi.require_version('Gtk', '3.0')
from gi.repository import Gtk

class AppWindow(Gtk.ApplicationWindow):

    def __init__(self, *args, **kwargs):
        super().__init__(*args, **kwargs)
        self.set_border_width(10)
        self.set_size_request(150, 100)
        grid = Gtk.Grid.new()
        label1 = Gtk.Label.new("Enter the following information ...")
        label2 = Gtk.Label.new("Name: ")
        entry = Gtk.Entry.new()
        grid.attach(label1, 0, 0, 2, 1)
        grid.attach(label2, 0, 1, 1, 1)
        grid.attach(entry, 1, 1, 1, 1)
        grid.set_row_spacing(5)
        grid.set_column_spacing(5)
        self.add(grid)

class Application(Gtk.Application):

    def __init__(self, *args, **kwargs):
        super().__init__(*args, application_id="org.example.myapp",
                         **kwargs)
        self.window = None
```

```
    def do_activate(self):
        if not self.window:
            self.window = AppWindow(application=self, title="Tables")
        self.window.show_all()
        self.window.present()

if __name__ == "__main__":
    app = Application()
    app.run(sys.argv)
```

Grid Spacing

If you want to set the spacing for every column in a grid, you can use set_column_spacing(). This function was used in set_row_spacing() to add padding between rows. These functions override any previous settings of the grid.set_row_spacing() to add padding between rows. These functions override any previous settings of the grid.

```
grid.set_column_spacing(5)
```

The grid.attach() method require five parameters, as follows.

```
Grid.attach(child_widget, left_pos, top_pos, width, height)
```

Fixed Containers

The Gtk.Fixed widget is a type of layout container that allows you to place widgets by the pixel. There are many problems that can arise when using this widget, but before we explore the drawbacks, let's look at a simple example.

Listing 4-5 shows the Gtk.Fixed widget that contains two buttons, one found at each of the locations (0,0) and (20,30), with respect to the top-left corner of the widget.

Listing 4-5. Specifying Exact Locations

```
#!/usr/bin/python3

import sys
import gi
gi.require_version('Gtk', '3.0')
from gi.repository import Gtk
```

```python
class AppWindow(Gtk.ApplicationWindow):

    def __init__(self, *args, **kwargs):
        super().__init__(*args, **kwargs)
        self.set_border_width(10)
        fixed = Gtk.Fixed.new()
        button1 = Gtk.Button.new_with_label("Pixel by pixel ...")
        button2 = Gtk.Button.new_with_label("you choose my fate.")
        button1.connect("clicked", self.on_button_clicked)
        button2.connect("clicked", self.on_button_clicked)
        fixed.put(button1, 0, 0)
        fixed.put(button2, 22, 35)
        self.add(fixed)
        self.show_all()

    def on_button_clicked(self, widget):
        self.destroy()

class Application(Gtk.Application):

    def __init__(self, *args, **kwargs):
        super().__init__(*args, application_id="org.example.myapp",
                         **kwargs)
        self.window = None

    def do_activate(self):
        if not self.window:
            self.window = AppWindow(application=self, title="Fixed")
        self.window.show_all()
        self.window.present()

if __name__ == "__main__":
    app = Application()
    app.run(sys.argv)
```

The Gtk.Fixed widget initialized with Gtk.Fixed.new() allows you to place widgets with a specific size in a specific location. Placing widgets is performed with put() at specified horizontal and vertical positions.

```python
fixed.put(child, x, y)
```

55

The top-left corner of the fixed container is referred to by location (0,0). You should only be able to specify real locations for widgets or locations in positive space. The fixed container resizes itself, so every widget is completely visible.

If you need to move a widget after it has been placed within a The Gtk.Fixed container, you can use move(). You need to be careful not to overlap a widget that has already been placed. The Gtk.Fixed widget does not provide notification in the case of overlap. Instead, it tries to render the window with unpredictable results.

```
fixed.move(child, x, y)
```

This brings us to the inherent problems with using the Gtk.Fixed widget. The first problem is that your users are free to use whatever theme they want. This means that the size of text on the user's machine may differ from the size of text on your machine unless you explicitly set the font. The sizes of widgets vary among different user themes as well. This can cause misalignment and overlap. This is illustrated in Figure 4-5, which shows two screenshots, one with a small font size and one with a larger font size.

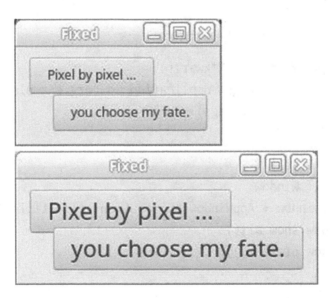

Figure 4-5. *Problems caused by different font sizes in a Gtk.Fixed container*

You can explicitly set the size and font of text to avoid overlap, but this is not advised in most cases. Accessibility options are provided for users with low vision. If you change their fonts, some users may not be able to read the text on the screen.

Another problem with using Gtk.Fixed arises when your application is translated into other languages. A user interface may look great in English, but the displayed strings in other languages may cause display problems, because the width is not constant. Furthermore, languages that are read right to left, such as Hebrew and Arabic, cannot be properly mirrored with the Gtk.Fixed widget. It is best to use a variable-sized container, such as Gtk.Box or Gtk.Grid in this case.

Finally, it can be quite a pain adding and removing widgets from your graphical interface when using a Gtk.Fixed container. Changing the user interface requires you to reposition all of your widgets. If you have an application with a lot of widgets, this presents a long-term maintenance problem.

On the other hand, you have grids, boxes, and various other automatically formatting containers. If you need to add or remove a widget from the user interface, it is as easy as adding or removing a cell. This makes maintenance much more efficient, which is something you should consider in large applications.

Therefore, unless you know that none of the presented problems will plague your application, you should use variable-sized containers instead of Gtk.Fixed. This container was presented only so you know it is available if a suitable situation arises. Even in suitable situations, flexible containers are almost always a better solution and are the proper way of doing things.

Expanders

The Gtk.Expander container can handle only one child. The child can be shown or hidden by clicking the triangle to the left of the expander's label. A before-and-after screenshot of this action can be viewed in Figure 4-6.

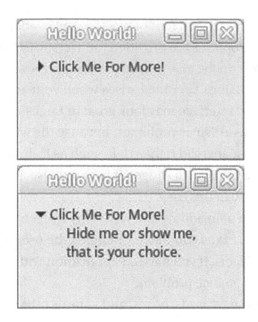

Figure 4-6. *A Gtk.Expander container*

Listing 4-6 introduces you to the most important Gtk.Expander methods.

Listing 4-6. Gtk.Expander Container

```python
#!/usr/bin/python3

import sys
import gi
gi.require_version('Gtk', '3.0')
from gi.repository import Gtk

class AppWindow(Gtk.ApplicationWindow):

    def __init__(self, *args, **kwargs):
        super().__init__(*args, **kwargs)
        self.set_border_width(10)
        self.set_size_request(200, 100)
        expander = Gtk.Expander.new_with_mnemonic("Click _Me For More!")
        label = Gtk.Label.new ("Hide me or show me,\nthat is your choice.")
        expander.add(label)
        expander.set_expanded(True)
        self.add(expander)
```

```
class Application(Gtk.Application):

    def __init__(self, *args, **kwargs):
        super().__init__(*args, application_id="org.example.myapp",
                         **kwargs)
        self.window = None

    def do_activate(self):
        if not self.window:
            self.window = AppWindow(application=self, title="Hello World!")
        self.window.show_all()
        self.window.present()

if __name__ == "__main__":
    app = Application()
    app.run(sys.argv)
```

Activating a Gtk.Expander widget cause it to be expanded or retracted depending on its current state.

Tip   Mnemonics are available in almost every widget that displays a label. Where available, you should always use this feature, because some users prefer to navigate through applications with the keyboard.

If you wish to include an underscore character in the expander label, you should prefix it with a second underscore. If you do not want to take advantage of the mnemonic feature, you can use Gtk.Expander.new() to initialize the Gtk.Expander with a standard string as the label, but providing mnemonics as an option to the user is always a good idea. In normal expander labels, underscore characters are not parsed but are treated as just another character.

The Gtk.Expander widget itself is derived from Gtk.Bin, which means that it can only contain one child. As with other containers that hold one child, you need to use expander.add() to add the child widget.

The child widget of a Gtk.Expander container can be shown or hidden by calling expander.set_expanded().expander.set_expanded().

```
expander.set_expanded(boolean)
```

By default, GTK+ does not add any spacing between the expander label and the child widget. To add pixels of spacing, you can use `expander.set_spacing()` to add padding.

```
expander.set_spacing(spacing)
```

Notebook

The `Gtk.Notebook` widget organizes child widgets into a number of pages. The user can switch between these pages by clicking the tabs that appear along one edge of the widget.

You are able to specify the location of the tabs, although they appear along the top by default. You can also hide the tabs altogether. Figure 4-7 shows a `Gtk.Notebook` widget with two tabs that was created with the code in Listing 4-7.

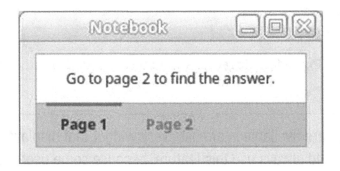

Figure 4-7. *A notebook container with multiple pages*

When creating a notebook container, you must specify a tab label widget and a child widget for each tab. Tabs can be added to the front or back, inserted, reordered, and removed.

Listing 4-7. Container with Multiple Pages

```
#!/usr/bin/python3

import sys
import gi
gi.require_version('Gtk', '3.0')
from gi.repository import Gtk
```

```python
class AppWindow(Gtk.ApplicationWindow):

    def __init__(self, *args, **kwargs):
        super().__init__(*args, **kwargs)
        self.set_border_width(10)
        self.set_size_request(250, 100)
        notebook = Gtk.Notebook.new()
        label1 = Gtk.Label.new("Page 1")
        label2 = Gtk.Label.new("Page 2")
        child1 = Gtk.Label.new("Go to page 2 to find the answer.")
        child2 = Gtk.Label.new("Go to page 1 to find the answer.")
        notebook.append_page(child1, label1)
        notebook.append_page(child2, label2)

        notebook.set_tab_pos(Gtk.PositionType.BOTTOM)
        self.add(notebook)

class Application(Gtk.Application):

    def __init__(self, *args, **kwargs):
        super().__init__(*args, application_id="org.example.myapp",
                         **kwargs)
        self.window = None

    def do_activate(self):
        if not self.window:
            self.window = AppWindow(application=self, title="Notebook")
        self.window.show_all()
        self.window.present()

if __name__ == "__main__":
    app = Application()
    app.run(sys.argv)
```

After you create a Gtk.Notebook, it is not very useful until you add tabs to it. To add a tab to the end or beginning of the list of tabs, you can use notebook.append_page() or notebook.prepend_page(), respectively. Each of these methods accepts a child widget, and a widget to display in the tab, as shown next.

Tip   The tab label does not have to be a Gtk.Label widget. For example, you could use a Gtk.Box widget that contains a label and a close button. This allows you to embed other useful widgets, such as buttons and images, into the tab label.

Each notebook page can only display one child widget. However, each of the children can be another container, so each page can display many widgets. In fact, it is possible to use Gtk.Notebook as the child widget of another Gtk.Notebook tab.

Caution   Placing notebooks within notebooks is possible but should be done with caution, because it can easily confuse the user. If you must do this, make sure that you place the child notebook's tabs on a different side of the notebook than its parent's tabs. By doing this, the user is able to figure out what tabs belong to which notebook.

If you want to insert a tab in a specific location, you can use notebook.insert_page(). This function allows you to specify the integer location of the tab. The index of all tabs located after the inserted tab increase by one.

notebook.insert_page (child, tab_label, position)

All three of the functions used to add tabs to a Gtk.Notebook return the integer location of the tab you added or –1 if the action has failed.

Notebook Properties

In Listing 4-7, the tab-position property was set for the Gtk.Notebook, which was done with the following call.

notebook.set_tab_pos(position)

Tab position can be set in notebook.set_tab_pos() by using the Gtk.PositionType enumeration. These include Gtk.PositionType.TOP, Gtk.PositionType.BOTTOM, Gtk.PositionType.LEFT, and Gtk.PositionType.RIGHT.

Notebooks are useful if you want to give the user multiple options, but you want to show them in multiple stages. If you place a few in each tab and hide the tabs with `notebook.set_show_tabs()`, you can progress the user back and forth through the options. An example of this concept would be many of the wizards you see throughout your operating system, similar to the functionality provided by the `Gtk.Assistant` widget.

```
notebook.set_show_tabs(show_tabs)
```

At some point, the `Gtk.Notebook` runs out of room to store tabs in the allocated space. To remedy this problem, you can set notebook tabs as scrollable with `notebook.set_scrollable()`.

```
notebook.set_scrollable(scrollable)
```

This property forces tabs to be hidden from the user. Arrows are provided so that the user is able to scroll through the list of tabs. This is necessary because tabs are only shown in one row or column.

If you resize the window so that all of the tabs cannot be shown, the tabs are made scrollable. Scrolling also occurs if you make the font size large enough that the tabs cannot all be drawn. You should always set this property to `True` if there is any chance that the tabs will take up more than the allotted space.

Tab Operations

GTK+ provides multiple functions that allow you to interact with tabs that already exist. Before learning about these methods, it is useful to know that most of these cause the change-current-page signal to be emitted. This signal is emitted when the current tab that is in focus is changed.

If you can add tabs, there has to be a method to remove tabs as well. By using `notebook.remove_page()`, you can remove a tab based on its index reference. If you did not increase the reference count before adding the widget to the `Gtk.Notebook`, this function releases the last reference and destroys the child.

```
notebook.remove_page(page_number)
```

You can manually reorder the tabs by calling `notebook.reorder_child()`. You must specify the child widget of the page you want to move and the location to where it should be moved. If you specify a number that is greater than the number of tabs or a negative number, the tab is moved to the end of the list.

```
notebook.reorder_child(child, position)
```

There are three methods provided for changing the current page. If you know the specific index of the page you want to view, you can use `notebook.set_current_page()` to move to that page.

```
notebook.set_current_page(page_number)
```

At times, you may also want switch to the next or previous tab, which can be done with call `notebook.next_page()` or `notebook.prev_page()`. If a call to either of these functions would cause the current tab to drop below zero or go above the current number of tabs, nothing occurs; the call is ignored.

When deciding what page to move to, it is often useful to know the current page and the total number of tabs. These values can be obtained with `notebook.get_current_page()`, respectively.

Event Boxes

Various widgets, including `Gtk.Label`, do not respond to GDK events, because they do not have an associated GDK window. To fix this, GTK+ provides a container widget called `Gtk.EventBox`. Event boxes catch events for the child widget by providing a GDK window for the object.

Listing 4-8 captures the `button-press-event` signal by using an event box. The text in the label is changed based on its current state when the label is double-clicked. Nothing visible happens when a single click occurs, although the signal is still emitted in that case (`Gtk.Label`) by using an event box. The text in the label is changed based on its current state when the label is double-clicked. Nothing visible happens when a single click occurs, although the signal is still emitted in that case.

Listing 4-8. Adding Events to Gtk.Label

```python
#!/usr/bin/python3

import sys
import gi
gi.require_version('Gtk', '3.0')
from gi.repository import Gtk, Gdk

class AppWindow(Gtk.ApplicationWindow):

    def __init__(self, *args, **kwargs):
        super().__init__(*args, **kwargs)
        self.set_border_width(10)
        self.set_size_request(200, 50)
        eventbox = Gtk.EventBox.new()
        label = Gtk.Label.new("Double-Click Me!")
        eventbox.set_above_child(False)
        eventbox.connect("button_press_event", self.on_button_pressed, label)
        eventbox.add(label)
        self.add(eventbox)
        eventbox.set_events(Gdk.EventMask.BUTTON_PRESS_MASK)
        eventbox.realize()

    def on_button_pressed(self, eventbox, event, label):
        if event.type == Gdk.EventType._2BUTTON_PRESS:
            text = label.get_text()
            if text[0] == 'D':
                label.set_text("I Was Double-Clicked!")
            else:
                label.set_text("Double-Click Me Again!")
        return False

class Application(Gtk.Application):

    def __init__(self, *args, **kwargs):
        super().__init__(*args, application_id="org.example.myapp",
                         **kwargs)
        self.window = None
```

```
    def do_activate(self):
        if not self.window:
            self.window = AppWindow(application=self, title="Hello World!")
        self.window.show_all()
        self.window.present()

if __name__ == "__main__":
    app = Application()
    app.run(sys.argv)
```

When using an event box, you need to decide whether the event box's Gdk.Window should be positioned above the windows of its child or below them. If the event box window is above, all events inside the event box go to the event box. If the window is below, events in windows of child widgets first go to that widget and then to its parents.

Note   If you set the window's position as below, events do go to child widgets first. However, this is only the case for widgets that have associated GDK windows. If the child is a Gtk.Label widget, it does not have the ability to detect events on its own. Therefore, it does not matter whether you set the window's position as above or below in Listing 4-8.

The location of the event box window can be moved above or below its children with eventbox.set_above_child(). By default, this property is set to False for all event boxes. This means that all events are handled by the widget for which the signal was first emitted. The event is then passed to its parent after the widget is finished.

```
eventbox.set_above_child(above_child)
```

Next, you need to add an event mask to the event box so that it knows what type of events the widget receives. Values for the Gdk.EventMask enumeration that specify event masks are shown in Table 4-3. A bitwise list of Gdk.EventMask values can be passed to eventbox.set_events() if you need to set more than one.

Table 4-3. *Gdk.EventMask Values*

Value	Description
Gdk.EventMask.EXPOSURE_MASK	Accepts events when a widget is exposed.
Gdk.EventMask.POINTER_MOTION_MASK	Accepts events emitted when the proximity of the window is left.
Gdk.EventMask.POINTER_MOTION_HINT_MASK	Limits the number of GDK_MOTION_NOTIFY events, so they are not emitted every time the mouse moves.
Gdk.EventMask.BUTTON_MOTION_MASK	Accepts pointer motion events while any button is pressed.
Gdk.EventMask.BUTTON1_MOTION_MASK	Accepts pointer motion events while button 1 is pressed.
Gdk.EventMask.BUTTON2_MOTION_MASK	Accepts pointer motion events while button 2 is pressed.
Gdk.EventMask.BUTTON3_MOTION_MASK	Accepts pointer motion events while button 3 is pressed.
Gdk.EventMask.BUTTON_PRESS_MASK	Accepts mouse button press events.
Gdk.EventMask.BUTTON_RELEASE_MASK	Accepts mouse button release events.
Gdk.EventMask.KEY_PRESS_MASK	Accepts key press events from a keyboard.
Gdk.EventMask.KEY_RELEASE_MASK	Accepts key release events from a keyboard.
Gdk.EventMask.ENTER_NOTIFY_MASK	Accepts events emitted when the proximity of the window is entered.
Gdk.EventMask.LEAVE_NOTIFY_MASK	Accepts events emitted when the proximity of the window is left.
Gdk.EventMask.FOCUS_CHANGE_MASK	Accepts change of focus events.
Gdk.EventMask.STRUCTURE_MASK	Accepts events emitted when changes to window configurations occur.
Gdk.EventMask.PROPERTY_CHANGE_MASK	Accepts changes to object properties.

(continued)

Table 4-3. (*continued*)

Value	Description
Gdk.EventMask.VISIBILITY_NOTIFY_MASK	Accepts change of visibility events.
Gdk.EventMask.PROXIMITY_IN_MASK	Accepts events emitted when the mouse cursor enters the proximity of the widget.
Gdk.EventMask.PROXIMITY_OUT_MASK	Accepts events emitted when the mouse cursor leaves the proximity of the widget.
Gdk.EventMask.SUBSTRUCTURE_MASK	Accepts events that change the configuration of child windows.
Gdk.EventMask.SCROLL_MASK	Accepts all scroll events.
Gdk.EventMask.ALL_EVENTS_MASK	Accepts all types of events.

You *must* call eventbox.set_events() before you call eventbox.realize() on the widget. If a widget has already been realized by GTK+, you have to instead use eventbox.add_events() to add event masks.

Before calling eventbox.realize(), your Gtk.EventBox does not yet have an associated Gdk.Window or any other GDK widget resources. Normally, realization occurs when the parent is realized, but event boxes are an exception. When you call window.show() on a widget, it is automatically realized by GTK+. Event boxes are not realized when you call window.show_all(), because they are set as invisible. Calling eventbox.realize() on the event box is an easy way to work around this problem.

When you realize your event box, you need to make sure that it is already added as a child to a top-level widget, or it will not work. This is because, when you realize a widget, it automatically realizes its ancestors. If it has no ancestors, GTK+ is not happy, and realization fails.

After the event box is realized, it has an associated Gdk.Window. Gdk.Window is a class that refers to a rectangular region on the screen where a widget is drawn. It is not the same thing as a Gtk.Window, which refers to a top-level window with a title bar and so on. A Gtk.Window contains many Gdk.Window objects, one for each child widget. They are used for drawing widgets on the screen.

Test Your Understanding

This chapter has introduced you to a number of container widgets that are included in GTK+. The following two exercises allow you to practice what you have learned about a few of these new widgets.

Exercise 1: Using Multiple Containers

One important characteristic of containers is that each container can hold other containers. To really drive this point home, in this example, you use a large number of containers. The main window shows a Gtk.Notebook and two buttons along the bottom.

The notebook should have four pages. Each notebook page should hold a Gtk. Button that moves to the next page (the Gtk.Button on the last page should wrap around to the first page).

Create two buttons along the bottom of the window. The first should move to the previous page in the Gtk.Notebook, wrapping to the last page if necessary. The second button should close the window and exit the application when clicked.

Exercise 1 is a simple application to implement, but it illustrates a few important points. First, it shows the usefulness of Gtk.Box, and how vertical and horizontal boxes can be used together to create complex user interfaces.

It is true that this same application could be implemented with a Gtk.Grid as the direct child of the window, but it is significantly easier to align the buttons along the bottom with a horizontal box. You notice that the buttons were packed at the end of the box, which aligns them to the right side of the box, and this is easier to implement with boxes.

Also, you saw that containers can, and should, be used to hold other containers. For example, in Exercise 1, a Gtk.Window holds a vertical Gtk.Box, which holds a horizontal Gtk.Box and a Gtk.Notebook. This structure can become even more complex as your application grows in size.

Once you have completed Exercise 1, move on to Exercise 2. In the next problem, you use the paned container instead of a vertical box.

Exercise 2: Even More Containers

In this exercise, you expand upon the code you wrote in Exercise 1. Instead of using a vertical Gtk.Box to hold the notebook and horizontal box of buttons, create a vertical Gtk.Paned widget.

In addition to this change, you should hide the Gtk.Notebook tabs, so the user is not able to switch between pages without pressing buttons. In this case, you not be able to know when a page is being changed. Therefore, each button that is in a Gtk.Notebook page should be contained by its own expander. The expander labels allow you to differentiate between notebook pages.

Once you have completed Exercise 2, you will have had practice with Gtk.Box, Gtk. Paned, Gtk.Notebook, and Gtk.Expander—four important containers used throughout the rest of this book.

Before continuing on to the next chapter, you may want to test out a few of the containers covered in this chapter that you did not need for Exercises 1 and 2. This gives you practice using all of the containers, because later chapters do not review past information.

Summary

In this chapter, you learned about the two types of container widgets: decorators and layout containers. Types of decorators covered were expanders, and event boxes. Types of layout containers covered were boxes, panes, grids, fixed containers, and notebooks.

The event box container is seen in later chapters, because there are other widgets besides Gtk.Label that cannot handle GDK events. This is specified when you learn about these widgets. You will see most of the containers in later chapters as well.

While these containers are necessary for GTK+ application development, merely displaying Gtk.Label and Gtk.Button widgets in containers is not very useful (or interesting) in most applications. This type of application does little to accommodate anything beyond basic user interaction.

Therefore, in the next chapter, you are going to learn about many widgets that allow you to interact with the user. These widgets include types of buttons, toggles, text entries, and spin buttons.

CHAPTER 5

Basic Widgets

So far, you have not learned about any widgets that are designed to facilitate user interaction—except `Gtk.Button`. That changes in this chapter, as we cover many types of widgets that allow the user to make choices, change settings, or input information.

These widgets include push buttons, toggle buttons, check buttons, radio buttons, color selection buttons, file chooser buttons, font selection buttons, text entries, and number selection buttons.

In this chapter, you learn

- How to use clickable buttons with stock items.

- How to use types of toggle buttons, including check buttons and radio buttons.

- How to use the entry widget for one-line, free-form text input.

- How to use the spin button widget for integer or floating-point number selection.

- What sort of specialized buttons are available.

Using Push Buttons

Previously, this section was titled "Using Stock Items." But GTK+ 3.x stock items have been deprecated, so I will show you how to create look-alike stock items out of standard items.

Figure 5-1 shows how to create a look-alike stock Close button.

71

© W. David Ashley and Andrew Krause 2019
W. D. Ashley and A. Krause, *Foundations of PyGTK Development*,
https://doi.org/10.1007/978-1-4842-4179-0_5

Figure 5-1. *Look-alike stock button*

Use the code in Listing 5-1 to produce the look-alike stock button.

Listing 5-1. Look-alike Stock Button

```python
#!/usr/bin/python3

import sys
import gi
gi.require_version('Gtk', '3.0')
from gi.repository import Gtk

class AppWindow(Gtk.ApplicationWindow):

    def __init__(self, *args, **kwargs):
        super().__init__(*args, **kwargs)
        self.set_border_width(10)
        button = Gtk.Button.new()
        hbox = Gtk.Box(orientation=Gtk.Orientation.HORIZONTAL, spacing=0)
        icon_theme = Gtk.IconTheme.get_default()
        icon = icon_theme.load_icon("window-close", -1,
                                    Gtk.IconLookupFlags.FORCE_SIZE)
        image = Gtk.Image.new_from_pixbuf(icon)
        hbox.add(image)
        label = Gtk.Label.new_with_mnemonic("_Close")
        hbox.add(label)
        hbox.set_homogeneous(True)
        button.add(hbox)
        button.connect("clicked", self.on_button_clicked)
        button.set_relief(Gtk.ReliefStyle.NORMAL)
```

```
        self.add(button)
        self.set_size_request(230, 100)

    def on_button_clicked(self, param):
        self.destroy()

class Application(Gtk.Application):

    def __init__(self, *args, **kwargs):
        super().__init__(*args, application_id="org.example.myapp",
                         **kwargs)
        self.window = None

    def do_activate(self):
        if not self.window:
            self.window = AppWindow(application=self,
                                    title="Look-alike Stock Item")
        self.window.show_all()
        self.window.present()

if __name__ == "__main__":
    app = Application()
    app.run(sys.argv)
```

The first task to create a custom button is to make a standard button and then make a horizontal box. The next task is to create an image for the button. The following statements accomplish that task.

```
icon_theme = Gtk.IconTheme.get_default()
icon = icon_theme.load_icon("window-close", -1,
Gtk.IconLookupFlags.FORCE_SIZE)
image = Gtk.Image.new_from_pixbuf(icon)
hbox.add(image)
```

The first statement gets the default GTK+ theme. Next we load the PixBuf icon from the theme by name.

Next, we turn the PixBuf icon into an image and then add it to the horizontal box.

Now we create a label an then add it to the horizontal box.

```
label = Gtk.Label.new_with_mnemonic("_Close")
hbox.add(label)
```

Now we can connect the button to our custom method, set the relief style for the button, and then add the button to the Gtk.ApplicationWindow.

```
button.connect("clicked", self.on_button_clicked)
button.set_relief(Gtk.ReliefStyle.NORMAL)
self.add(button)
```

Tip   The icon image you want may or may not be in the default theme. You may have to look at other themes to find an image you can use. You may need to install a GTK+ theme in order to obtain access to a theme that fits your purpose.

Toggle Buttons

The Gtk.ToggleButton widget is a type of Gtk.Button that holds its active or inactive state after it is clicked. It is shown as pressed down when active. Clicking an active toggle button causes it to return to its normal state. There are two widgets derived from Gtk.ToggleButton: Gtk.CheckButton and Gtk.RadioButton.

You can create a new The Gtk.ToggleButton with one of three functions. To create an empty toggle button, use Gtk.ToggleButton.new(). If you want the toggle button to include a label by default, use Gtk.ToggleButton.new_with_label(). Lastly, Gtk.ToggleButton also supports mnemonic labels with Gtk.ToggleButton.new_with_mnemonic().

Figure 5-2 shows two Gtk.ToggleButton widgets that were created with two mnemonic labels by calling the Gtk.ToggleButton.new_with_mnemonic() initializer. The widgets in the screenshot were created with the code in Listing 5-2.

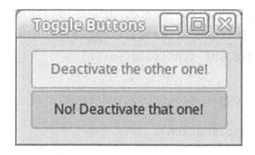

Figure 5-2. *Two Gtk.ToggleButton widgets*

In Listing 5-2, when one toggle button is activated, the other is disabled. The only way to make it sensitive is to deactivate the original toggle button.

Listing 5-2. Two Gtk.ToggleButton Widgets

```
#!/usr/bin/python3

import sys
import gi
gi.require_version('Gtk', '3.0')
from gi.repository import Gtk

class AppWindow(Gtk.ApplicationWindow):

    def __init__(self, *args, **kwargs):
        super().__init__(*args, **kwargs)
        self.set_border_width(10)
        vbox = Gtk.Box.new(orientation=Gtk.Orientation.VERTICAL, spacing=0)
        toggle1 = Gtk.ToggleButton.new_with_mnemonic("_Deactivate the other
        one!")
        toggle2 = Gtk.ToggleButton.new_with_mnemonic("_No! Deactivate that
        one!")
        toggle1.connect("toggled", self.on_button_toggled, toggle2)
        toggle2.connect("toggled", self.on_button_toggled, toggle1)
        vbox.pack_start(toggle1, True, True, 1)
        vbox.pack_start(toggle2, True, True, 1)
        self.add(vbox)
```

```python
    def on_button_toggled(self, toggle, other_toggle):
        if (Gtk.ToggleButton.get_active(toggle)):
            other_toggle.set_sensitive(False)
            else:
                other_toggle.set_sensitive(True)

class Application(Gtk.Application):

    def __init__(self, *args, **kwargs):
        super().__init__(*args, application_id="org.example.myapp",
                            **kwargs)
        self.window = None

    def do_activate(self):
        if not self.window:
            self.window = AppWindow(application=self, title="Toggle Buttons")
        self.window.show_all()
        self.window.present()

if __name__ == "__main__":
    app = Application()
    app.run(sys.argv)
```

The only signal added by the Gtk.ToggleButton class is "toggled", which is emitted when the user activates or deactivates the button. This signal was triggered in Listing 5-2 by one toggle button in order to disable the other.

In Listing 5-2 another important piece of information was shown: multiple widgets can use the same callback method. We did not need to create a separate callback method for each toggle button, since each required the same functionality. It is also possible to connect one signal to multiple callback methods, although this is not recommended. Instead, you should just implement the whole functionality in a single callback method.

Check Buttons

In most cases, you will not want to use the Gtk.ToggleButton widget, because it looks exactly like a normal Gtk.Button. Instead, GTK+ provides the Gtk.CheckButton widget, which places a discrete toggle next to the display text. Gtk.CheckButton is derived from the Gtk.ToggleButton class. Two instances of this widget are shown in Figure 5-3.

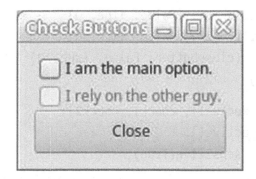

Figure 5-3. *Two Gtk.CheckButton widgets*

As with toggle buttons, three functions are provided for Gtk.CheckButton initialization. These include Gtk.CheckButton.new(), Gtk.CheckButton.new_with_label(), and Gtk.CheckButton.new_with_mnemonic(). Gtk.CheckButton also inherits the important "toggled" signal, which is used in Listing 5-3.

Listing 5-3. Gtk.CheckButtons

```
#!/usr/bin/python3

import sys
import gi
gi.require_version('Gtk', '3.0')
from gi.repository import Gtk

class AppWindow(Gtk.ApplicationWindow):

    def __init__(self, *args, **kwargs):
        super().__init__(*args, **kwargs)
        self.set_border_width(10)
        check1 = Gtk.CheckButton.new_with_label("I am the main option.")
        check2 = Gtk.CheckButton.new_with_label("I rely on the other guy.")
        check2.set_sensitive(False)
        check1.connect("toggled", self.on_button_checked, check2)
        closebutton = Gtk.Button.new_with_mnemonic("_Close")
        closebutton.connect("clicked", self.on_button_close_clicked)
        vbox = Gtk.Box.new(orientation=Gtk.Orientation.VERTICAL, spacing=0)
```

```
        vbox.pack_start(check1, False, True, 0)
        vbox.pack_start(check2, False, True, 0)
        vbox.pack_start(closebutton, False, True, 0)
        self.add(vbox)

    def on_button_checked(self, check1, check2):
        if check1.get_active():
            check2.set_sensitive(True);
        else:
            check2.set_sensitive(False)

    def on_button_close_clicked(self, button):
        self.destroy()

class Application(Gtk.Application):

    def __init__(self, *args, **kwargs):
        super().__init__(*args, application_id="org.example.myapp",
                         **kwargs)
        self.window = None

def do_activate(self):
    if not self.window:
        self.window = AppWindow(application=self, title="Check Buttons")
    self.window.show_all()
    self.window.present()

if __name__ == "__main__":
    app = Application()
    app.run(sys.argv)
```

Excluding the initialization methods, all functionality for check boxes is implemented in the Gtk.ToggleButton class and its ancestors. Gtk.CheckButton is merely a convenience widget, which provides the graphical differences from standard Gtk.Button widgets.

Radio Buttons

The second type of widget derived from Gtk.ToggleButton is the radio button widget. In fact, Gtk.RadioButton is actually derived from Gtk.CheckButton. Radio buttons are toggles that are generally grouped together.

In a group, when one radio button is selected, all others are deselected. The group forbids selecting multiple radio buttons at once. This allows you to provide multiple options to the user where only one should be selected.

Note   GTK+ does not provide a way to deselect a radio button, so one radio button is not desirable. The user is not able to deselect the option! If you only need one button, you should use a Gtk.CheckButton or Gtk.ToggleButton widget.

Radio buttons are drawn as a discrete circular toggle on the side of the label widget, so that they can be differentiated from other types of toggle buttons. It is possible to draw radio buttons with the same toggle as Gtk.CheckButton, but this should not be done because it can confuse and frustrate the user. A group of four radio buttons in a vertical box is shown in Figure 5-4.

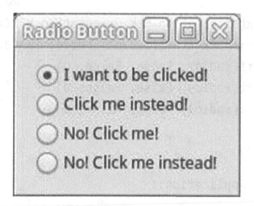

Figure 5-4. *Four Gtk.RadioButton widgets*

For radio buttons to work correctly, they must all be referenced to another radio button in the group. Otherwise, all of the buttons would act as independent toggle buttons. An example of how to use multiple radio buttons is shown in Listing 5-4.

Listing 5-4. Gtk.RadioButton

```python
#!/usr/bin/python3

import sys
import gi
gi.require_version('Gtk', '3.0')
from gi.repository import Gtk

class AppWindow(Gtk.ApplicationWindow):

    def __init__(self, *args, **kwargs):
        super().__init__(*args, **kwargs)
        self.set_border_width(10)

        radio1 = Gtk.RadioButton.new_with_label(None, "I want to be clicked!")
        radio2 = Gtk.RadioButton.new_with_label_from_widget(radio1,
                                                "Click me instead!)
        radio3 = Gtk.RadioButton.new_with_label_from_widget(radio1,
                                                "No! Click me!")
        radio4 = Gtk.RadioButton.new_with_label_from_widget(radio3,
                                                "No! Click me!")
        vbox = Gtk.Box(orientation=Gtk.Orientation.VERTICAL,
        spacing=0) vbox.pack_start(radio1, False, False, 0)
        vbox.pack_start(radio2, False, False, 0)
        vbox.pack_start(radio3, False, False, 0)
        vbox.pack_start(radio4, False, False, 0)
        self.add(vbox)
        self.show_all()

class Application(Gtk.Application):

    def __init__(self, *args, **kwargs):
        super().__init__(*args, application_id="org.example.myapp",
                        **kwargs)
        self.window = None
```

```
def do_activate(self):
    if not self.window:
        self.window = AppWindow(application=self, title="Radio Buttons")
    self.window.show_all()
    self.window.present()

if __name__ == "__main__":
    app = Application()
    app.run(sys.argv)
```

The first radio button in a group can be created with any of the following three functions. However, if you want to use a Gtk.Label widget as the child, it is also possible to use a mnemonic widget, so the toggle can be activated from the keyboard.

```
radiobutton = Gtk.RadioButton.new(list)
radiobutton = Gtk.RadioButton.new_with_label(list, "My label")
radiobutton = Gtk.RadioButton.new_with_mnemonic(list, "_My label")
```

However, there is a fourth way to both create multiple radio buttons and a list at the same time. You do this by creating your first radio button without specifying a list. Subsequent radio buttons are created referencing the first radio button created or any other radio button that is a part of the internal group.

```
radio1 = Gtk.RadioButton.new_with_label(None, "I want to be clicked!")
radio2 = Gtk.RadioButton.new_with_label_from_widget(radio1, "Click me
instead!")
radio3 = Gtk.RadioButton.new_with_label_from_widget(radio1, "No! Click me!")
radio4 = Gtk.RadioButton.new_with_label_from_widget(radio3, "No! Click me
instead!
```

None is specified for the radio group in each call. This is because the simplest way to create a group of radio buttons is to associate them to another widget in the group. By using this method, you avoid having to use the GLib with singly linked lists, since the list is created and managed for you automatically.

Referring the initialization function to a radio button that already exists creates each of these. GTK+ adds the new radio button to the group from the specified widget. Because of this, you need only refer to any widget that already exists within the desired radio group.

Lastly, every radio button in the group must be connected to the toggled signal. When a radio button is selected, exactly two radio buttons emit the toggled signal, because one is selected and another is deselected. You will not be able to catch all radio button signals if you do not connect every radio button to toggled.

Text Entries

The Gtk.Entry widget is a single line, free-form text entry widget. It is implemented in a general manner, so that it can be molded to fit many types of solutions. It can be used for text entry, password entry, and even number selections.

Gtk.Entry also implements the Gtk.Editable interface, which provides a large number of functions that are created to handle selections of text. An example Gtk.Entry widget is shown in Figure 5-5. This text entry is used for password entry.

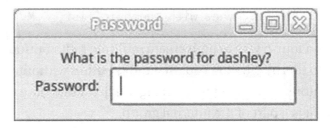

Figure 5-5. *Gtk.Entry widget for passwords*

Note   Gtk.Editable is a special type of object called an interface. An interface is a set of APIs that are implemented by multiple widgets and used for consistency. You learn how to implement and utilize interfaces in your own widgets in Chapter 12.

The Gtk.Entry widget considers all text to be standard strings. The only way it differentiates between normal text and passwords is that a special character called an *invisibility character* is shown instead of password content. Listing 5-5 shows you how to use a Gtk.Entry widget for password entry. If you want to use a Gtk.Entry widget for normal text entry, you need only to turn visibility on.

Listing 5-5. Gtk.Entry

```python
#!/usr/bin/python3

import sys
import gi
gi.require_version('Gtk', '3.0')
from gi.repository import Gtk
import os

class AppWindow(Gtk.ApplicationWindow):

    def __init__(self, *args, **kwargs):
        super().__init__(*args, **kwargs)
        self.set_border_width(10)
        prompt_str = "What is the password for " + os.getlogin() + "?"
        question = Gtk.Label(prompt_str)
        label = Gtk.Label("Password:")
        passwd = Gtk.Entry()
        passwd.set_visibility(False)
        passwd.set_invisible_char("*")
        hbox = Gtk.Box(orientation=Gtk.Orientation.HORIZONTAL, spacing=0)
        hbox.pack_start(label, False, False, 5)
        hbox.pack_start(passwd, False, False, 5)
        vbox = Gtk.Box(orientation=Gtk.Orientation.VERTICAL, spacing=0)
        vbox.pack_start(question, False, False, 0)
        vbox.pack_start(hbox, False, False, 0)
        self.add(vbox)

class Application(Gtk.Application):

    def __init__(self, *args, **kwargs):
        super().__init__(*args, application_id="org.example.myapp",
                         **kwargs)
        self.window = None
```

```
    def do_activate(self):
        if not self.window:
            self.window = AppWindow(application=self, title="Password")
        self.window.show_all()
        self.window.present()

if __name__ == "__main__":
    app = Application()
    app.run(sys.argv)
```

Entry Properties

The Gtk.Entry widget is a highly flexible widget, because it was designed to be employed in the maximum number of instances. This can be seen from the wide array of properties provided by the class. A sampling of the most important of those is included in this section. For a full list of properties, you should reference Appendix A.

Oftentimes, you want to restrict the length of the free-form text entered into an entry widget because of string limitations of the value. In the following function prototype, entry.set_max_length() limits the text of the entry to a maximum number of characters. This can be useful when you want to limit the length of user names, passwords, or other length-sensitive information.

```
entry.set_max_length(max_chars)
```

Invisibility characters facilitate password entries in GTK+. The invisibility character is the character that replace the actual password content in the entry, which can be set with entry.set_invisible_char(). The default character for the entry is an asterisk.

```
entry.set_invisible_char(single_char)
entry.set_visibility(boolean)
```

After specifying the invisibility character, you can hide all entered text by setting visibility to False with entry.set_visibility(). You are still able to retrieve the actual content of the entry programmatically, even though it is hidden from view.

Inserting Text into a Gtk.Entry Widget

In GTK+ 3.x there is only one way to replace all the text in a Gtk.Entry widget. The method entry.set_text() overwrites the whole content of the text entry with the given string. However, this is only useful if you no longer care about the current text displayed by the widget.

```
entry.set_text(text)
```

The current text displayed by Gtk.Entry can be retrieved with entry.get_text(). This string is used internally by the widget and must never be freed or modified in any way. It is also possible to use entry.insert_text() to insert text into a Gtk.Entry widget. The parameter to entry.insert_text() specify both the text to insert and the character position to insert the text.

Spin Buttons

The Gtk.SpinButton widget is a number selection widget that is capable of handling integers and floating-point numbers. It is derived from Gtk.Entry, so Gtk.SpinButton inherits all of its functions and signals.

Adjustments

Before covering the Gtk.SpinButton widget, you must understand the Gtk.Adjustment class. Gtk.Adjustment is one of the few classes in GTK+ that is not considered a widget, because it is derived directly from Gtk.Object. It is used for several widgets, including spin buttons, view ports, and the multiple widgets derived from Gtk.Range.

New adjustments are created with Gtk.Adjustment.new(). Once added to a widget, memory management of the adjustment is handled by the widget, so you do not have to worry about this aspect of the object.

```
Gtk.Adjustment.new(initial_value, lower_range, upper_range,
                step_increment, page_increment, page_size)
```

New adjustments are initialized with six parameters. A list of these parameters follows.

- `initial_value`: The value stored by the adjustment when it is initialized. This corresponds to the `value` property of the `Gtk.Adjustment` class.

- `lower_range`: The minimum value the adjustment is allowed to hold. This corresponds to the `lower` property of the `Gtk.Adjustment` class.

- `lower_range`: The maximum value the adjustment is allowed to hold. This corresponds to the `upper` property of the `Gtk.Adjustment` class.

- `step_increment`: The increment to make the smallest change possible. If you want to count all integers between 1 and 10, the increment would be set to 1.

- `page_increment`: The increment to make when Page Up or Page Down is pressed. This is almost always larger than the step_increment.

- `page_size`: The size of a page. This value does not have much use in a `Gtk.SpinButton`, so it should be set to the same value as page_increment or to 0.

There are two useful signals provided by the `Gtk.Adjustment` class: `changed` and `value-changed`. The `"changed"` signal is emitted when one or more properties of the adjustment have been altered, excluding the value property. The `"value-changed"` signal is emitted when the current value of the adjustment has been altered.

A Spin Button Example

The spin button widget allows the user to select an integer or floating-point number by incrementing or decrementing with the up or down arrows. The user can still type in a value with the keyboard, and it is displayed as the nearest acceptable value if it is out of range. Figure 5-6 shows two spin buttons in action that display an integer and a floating-point number.

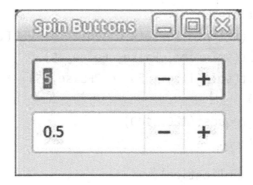

Figure 5-6. *Spin buttons*

Spin buttons show integer or floating-point numbers. In actuality, numbers are stored as double values. The spin button handles rounding the number to the correct number of decimal places. Listing 5-6 is a simple example that creates both integer and floating-point number spin buttons.

Listing 5-6. Integer and Floating-Point Number Selection

```python
#!/usr/bin/python3

import sys
import gi
gi.require_version('Gtk', '3.0')
from gi.repository import Gtk

class AppWindow(Gtk.ApplicationWindow):

    def __init__(self, *args, **kwargs):
        super().__init__(*args, **kwargs)
        self.set_border_width(10)
        integer = Gtk.Adjustment(5.0, 0.0, 10.0, 1.0, 2.0, 2.0)
        float_pt = Gtk.Adjustment(5.0, 0.0, 1.0, 0.1, 0.5, 0.5)
        spin_int = Gtk.SpinButton()
        spin_int.set_adjustment(integer)
        spin_int.set_increments(1.0, 0)
        spin_int.set_digits(0)
        spin_float = Gtk.SpinButton()
        spin_float.set_adjustment(float_pt)
        spin_float.set_increments(0.1, 0)
```

```
        spin_float.set_digits(1)
        vbox = Gtk.Box(orientation=Gtk.Orientation.VERTICAL, spacing=0)
        vbox.pack_start(spin_int, False, False, 5)
        vbox.pack_start(spin_float, False, False, 5)
        self.add(vbox)
        self.set_size_request(180, 100)
        self.show_all()

class Application(Gtk.Application):

    def __init__(self, *args, **kwargs):
        super().__init__(*args, application_id="org.example.myapp",
                            **kwargs)
        self.window = None

    def do_activate(self):
        if not self.window:
            self.window = AppWindow(application=self, title="Spin Buttons")
        self.window.show_all()
        self.window.present()

if __name__ == "__main__":
    app = Application()
    app.run(sys.argv)
```

Before creating the spin buttons, you should create the adjustments. You can also initialize the spin button with a None adjustment, but it is set as insensitive. After your adjustments are initialized, you can create new spin buttons with Gtk.SpinButton.new(). The other two parameters in the initialization function specify the climb rate of the spin button and the number of decimal places to display. The climb rate is how much the value should be incremented or decremented when a (+) or (-) sign is pressed.

```
Gtk.SpinButton.new(climb_rate, digits)
```

Alternatively, you can create a new spin button with Gtk.SpinButton.new_with_range(), which automatically creates a new adjustment based on the minimum, maximum, and step values you specify. The initial value is set to the minimum value plus a page increment of ten times the step_increment by default. The precision of the widget is automatically set to the value of step_increment.

```
Gtk.SpinButton.new_with_range (minimum_value, maximum_value, step_increment)
```

You can call `spinbutton.set_digits()` to set a new precision of the spin button and `spinbutton.set_value()` to set a new value. The value is automatically altered if it is out of bounds of the spin button.

```
spin_button.set_value(value)
```

Horizontal and Vertical Scales

Another type of widget called a scale allows you to provide a horizontal or vertical slider that can choose an integer or a floating-point number. `Gtk.Scale` is both a horizontal scale widget and a vertical scale widget. In GTK+ 2.x the `Gtk.Scale` was an abstract class. The two subclasses `Gtk.HScale` and `Gtk.VScale` were used to create horizontal and vertical scales respectively. In GTK+ 3.x these two classes have been deprecated and the `Gtk.Scale` has become a real class from which both horizontal and vertical boxes can be created.

The functionality of the `Gtk.Scale` widget is not much different from `Gtk.SpinButton`. It is often used when you want to restrict the user from entering values, since the value is chosen by moving the slider. Figure 5-7 shows a screenshot of two horizontal scale widgets.

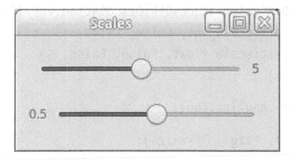

Figure 5-7. *Horizontal scale widgets*

Scales provide essentially the same functionality as spin buttons, except using a slider chooses the number. To show the similarities between the widgets, Listing 5-7 implements the same functionality as Listing 5-6: two sliders allow the user to select an integer and a floating-point number.

Listing 5-7. Integer and Floating-Point Number Selection

```python
#!/usr/bin/python3

import sys
import gi
gi.require_version('Gtk', '3.0')
from gi.repository import Gtk

class AppWindow(Gtk.ApplicationWindow):

    def __init__(self, *args, **kwargs):
        super().__init__(*args, **kwargs)
        self.set_border_width(10)
        self.set_size_request(250, -1)
        scale_int = Gtk.Scale.new_with_range(Gtk.Orientation.HORIZONTAL,
        0.0, 10.0, 1.0)
        scale_float = Gtk.Scale.new_with_range(Gtk.Orientation.HORIZONTAL,
        0.0, 1.0, 0.1)
        scale_int.set_digits(0)
        scale_float.set_digits(1)
        scale_int.set_value_pos(Gtk.PositionType.RIGHT)
        scale_float.set_value_pos(Gtk.PositionType.LEFT)
        vbox = Gtk.Box(orientation=Gtk.Orientation.VERTICAL, spacing=0)
        vbox.pack_start(scale_int, False, False, 5)
        vbox.pack_start(scale_float, False, False, 5)
        self.add(vbox)

class Application(Gtk.Application):

    def __init__(self, *args, **kwargs):

        super().__init__(*args, application_id="org.example.myapp",
                        **kwargs)
        self.window = None

    def do_activate(self):
        if not self.window:
            self.window = AppWindow(application=self, title="Scales")
```

```
        self.window.show_all()
        self.window.present()
if __name__ == "__main__":
    app = Application()
    app.run(sys.argv)
```

There are multiple ways to create new scale widgets. The first is with Gtk. Scale.new(), which accepts a Gtk.Adjustment that defines how the scale works.

```
Gtk.Scale.new(adjustment)
```

Alternatively, you can create scales with Gtk.Scale.new_with_range(). This function accepts the minimum value, the maximum value, and the step increment of the scale.

```
Gtk.Scale.new_with_range(minimum, maximum, step)
```

Since the value of the scale is always stored as a double , you need to define the number of decimal places to show with scale.set_digits() if the default value is not what you want. The default number of decimal places is calculated based on the number of decimal places provided for the step increment. For example, if you provide a step increment of 0.01, two decimal places are displayed by default.

```
scale.set_digits (digits)
```

Depending on what type of scale widget you are using, you may want to change where the value is displayed with scale.set_value_pos(). Positions are defined by the Gtk.PositionType enumeration, and they are Gtk.PositionType.LEFT, Gtk. PositionType.RIGHT. Gtk.PositionType.TOP, and Gtk.PositionType.BOTTOM. You can also use scale.set_draw_value() to hide the value from the user's view altogether.

```
scale.set_value_pos(pos)
```

Gtk.Scale is derived from a widget called Gtk.Range. This widget is an abstract type that provides the ability to handle an adjustment. You should use scale.get_value() to retrieve the current value of the scale. Gtk.Range also provides the "value-changed" signal, which is emitted when the user changes the position of the scale.

Gtk.Adjustment widgets may also be shared with other widgets. A single Gtk. Adjustment may be shared with the Gtk.SpinButton and a Gtk.Scale widgets. See the GTK documentation for more information.

Additional Buttons

While the Gtk.Button widget allows you to create your own custom buttons, GTK+ provides three additional button widgets that are at your disposal: the color selection button, file chooser button, and font selection button.

Each of the sections covering these three widgets also cover other important concepts, such as the Gtk.Color class, file filters, and Pango fonts. These concepts are used in later chapters, so it is a good idea to get a grasp of them now.

Color Button

The Gtk.ColorButton widget provides a simple way for you to allow your users to select a specific color. These colors can be specified as six-digit hexadecimal values or the RGB value. The color button itself displays the selected color in a rectangular block set as the child widget of the button. Figure 5-8 is an example of this.

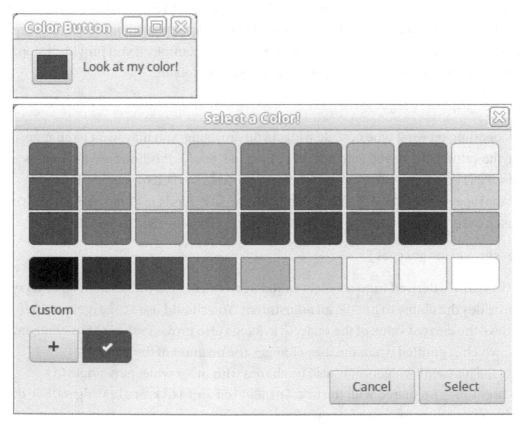

Figure 5-8. *Color selection dialog*

A Gtk.ColorButton Example

When clicked, the color button opens a dialog that allows the user to enter in the color value or browse for a choice on the color wheel. The color wheel is provided so the user is not required to know the numeric values of the colors. Listing 5-8 shows how to use the Gtk.ColorButton widget in an application.

Listing 5-8. Gtk.ColorButton and Gdk.Color

```python
#!/usr/bin/python3

import sys
import gi
gi.require_version('Gtk', '3.0')
from gi.repository import Gtk
from gi.repository import Gdk

class AppWindow(Gtk.ApplicationWindow):

    def __init__(self, *args, **kwargs):

        super().__init__(*args, **kwargs)
        self.set_border_width(10)
        color = Gdk.RGBA(red=0, green=.33, blue=.66, alpha=1.0)
        color = Gdk.RGBA.to_color(color)
        button = Gtk.ColorButton.new_with_color(color)
        button.set_title("Select a Color!")
        label = Gtk.Label("Look at my color!")
        label.modify_fg(Gtk.StateType.NORMAL, color)
        button.connect("color_set", self.on_color_changed, label)
        hbox = Gtk.Box(orientation=Gtk.Orientation.HORIZONTAL, spacing=0)
        hbox.pack_start(button, False, False, 5)
        hbox.pack_start(label, False, False, 5)
        self.add(hbox)

    def on_color_changed(self, button, label):
        color = button.get_color()
        label.modify_fg(Gtk.StateType.NORMAL, color)
```

```
class Application(Gtk.Application):

    def __init__(self, *args, **kwargs):
        super().__init__(*args, application_id="org.example.myapp",
                         **kwargs)
        self.window = None

    def do_activate(self):
        if not self.window:
            self.window = AppWindow(application=self, title="Color Button")
        self.window.show_all()
        self.window.present()

if __name__ == "__main__":
    app = Application()
    app.run(sys.argv)
```

In most cases, you want to create a `Gtk.ColorButton` with an initial color value, which is done by specifying a `Gdk.Color` object to `button = Gtk.ColorButton.new_with_color()`. The default color, if none is provided, is opaque black with the alpha option disabled.

Storing Colors in Gdk.Color

`Gdk.Color` is a class that stores red, green, and blue values for a color. These values can be retrieved or set using the method shown next. The fourth available value is the pixel object. It automatically stores the index of the color when it is allocated in a color map, so there is usually no need for you to alter this value.

After creating a new `Gdk.Color` object, if you already know the red, green, and blue values of the color, you can specify them in the following manner. Red, green, and blue values are stored as unsigned integer values ranging from 0 to 65,535, where 65,535 indicates full-color intensity. For example, the following color refers to white.

```
mycolorobj = Gdk.Color.new()
mycolorobj.red = 65535
mycolorobj.green = 65535
mycolorobj.blue = 65535
```

Using the Color Button

After setting your initial color, you can choose the title that is given to the color selection dialog with button.set_title(). By default, the title is "Pick a Color", so it is not necessary to set this value if you are content with this title.

```
button.get_color()
label.modify_fg(Gtk.StateType.NORMAL, color)
```

In Listing 5-8, the foreground color was set in the normal widget state, which is what state all labels are in, by and large, unless they are selectable. There are five options for the Gtk.StateType enumeration that can be used in label.modify_fg(). You can reset the widget's foreground color to the default value by passing a None color.

File Chooser Buttons

The Gtk.FileChooserButton widget provides an easy method for you to ask users to choose a file or a folder. It implements the functionality of the file selection framework provided by GTK+. Figure 5-9 shows a file chooser button set to select a folder and a button set to select a file.

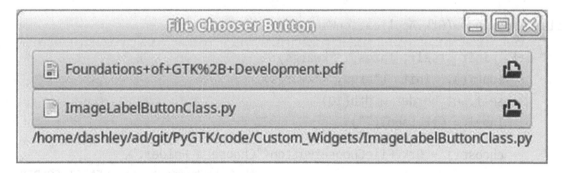

Figure 5-9. *File chooser buttons*

When the user clicks a Gtk.FileChooserButton, an instance of Gtk.FileChooserDialog is opened that allows the user to browse and select one file or one folder, depending on the type of button you created.

Note   You do not learn how to use the Gtk.FileChooserDialog widget until Chapter 6, but you do not need to directly interface with it at this point, because Gtk.FileChooserButton handles all interactions with the dialog.

A Gtk.FileChooserButton Example

You are able to change basic settings, such as the currently selected file, the current folder, and the title of the file selection window. Listing 5-9 shows you how to use both types of file chooser buttons.

Listing 5-9. Using the File Chooser Button

```python
#!/usr/bin/python3

import sys
import gi
gi.require_version('Gtk', '3.0')
from gi.repository import Gtk
from pathlib import Path

class AppWindow(Gtk.ApplicationWindow):

    def __init__(self, *args, **kwargs):
        super().__init__(*args, **kwargs)
        self.set_border_width(10)
        label = Gtk.Label("")

        chooser1 = Gtk.FileChooserButton("Choose a Folder.",
                                    Gtk.FileChooserAction.SELECT_FOLDER)
        chooser2 = Gtk.FileChooserButton("Choose a Folder.",
                                    Gtk.FileChooserAction.OPEN)
        chooser1.connect("selection_changed",
                        self.on_folder_changed, chooser2)
        chooser2.connect("selection_changed",
                        self.on_file_changed, label)
```

```python
        chooser1.set_current_folder(str(Path.home()))
        chooser2.set_current_folder(str(Path.home()))
        filter1 = Gtk.FileFilter()
        filter2 = Gtk.FileFilter()
        filter1.set_name("Image Files")
        filter2.set_name("All Files")
        filter1.add_pattern("*.png")
        filter1.add_pattern("*.jpg")
        filter1.add_pattern("*.gif")
        filter2.add_pattern("*")
        chooser2.add_filter(filter1)
        chooser2.add_filter(filter2)
        vbox = Gtk.Box(orientation=Gtk.Orientation.VERTICAL, spacing=0)
        vbox.pack_start(chooser1, False, False, 0)
        vbox.pack_start(chooser2, False, False, 0)
        vbox.pack_start(label, False, False, 0)
        self.add(vbox)
        self.set_size_request(240, -1)

    def on_folder_changed(self,
        chooser1, chooser2): folder =
        chooser1.get_filename()
        chooser2.set_current_folder(folder)

    def on_file_changed(self, chooser2, label):
        file = chooser2.get_filename()
        label.set_text(file)

class Application(Gtk.Application):

    def __init__(self, *args, **kwargs):
        super().__init__(*args, application_id="org.example.myapp",
                        **kwargs)
        self.window = None
```

```
    def do_activate(self):
        if not self.window:
            self.window = AppWindow(application=self, title="File Chooser
            Button")
        self.window.show_all()
        self.window.present()
if __name__ == "__main__":
    app = Application()
    app.run(sys.argv)
```

File chooser button widgets are created with Gtk.FileChooserButton.new(). This widget is able to serve two purposes: selecting a single file or a single folder. There are four types of file choosers that can be created (the remaining two are covered in Chapter 6), but file chooser buttons support only Gtk.FileChooserAction.OPEN and Gtk. FileChooserAction.SELECT_FOLDER.

Gtk.FileChooser

The Gtk.FileChooserButton widget is an implementation of the functionality provided by the Gtk.FileChooser class. This means that, while the button is not derived from Gtk.FileChooser, it can still utilize all the methods defined by Gtk.FileChooser. Quite a few of the methods in Listing 5-9 utilize functions provided by Gtk.FileChooser.

In Listing 5-9, chooser1.set_current_folder() was used to set the current folder of each file chooser button to the user's home directory. The contents of this folder is shown when the user initially clicks a file chooser button unless it is changed through some other means. This method returns True if the folder was successfully changed.

```
chooser1.set_current_folder(filename)
```

The Path.home() method is a utility module provided by Python that returns the current user's home directory. As with most features in pathlib, this method is platform independent.

This brings up a useful characteristic of the file chooser interface; it can be used to browse many types of file structures, whether it is on a UNIX or Windows machine. This is especially useful if you want your application to be designed for multiple operating systems.

Since the file chooser button only allows one file to be selected at a time, you can use `chooser1.get_filename()` to retrieve the currently selected file or folder, depending on the type of file chooser button. If no file is selected, this function returns None.

```
filename = chooser1.get_filename()
```

At this point, you have enough information about the `Gtk.FileChooser` class to implement file chooser buttons. `Gtk.FileChooser` is covered in more depth in the next chapter when you learn about the `Gtk.FileChooserDialog` widget.

File Filters

`Gtk.FileFilter` objects allow you to restrict the files shown in the file chooser. For example, in Listing 5-9, only PNG, JPG, and GIF files could be viewed and chosen by the user when the Image Files filter was selected.

File filters are created with `Gtk.FileFilter.new()`. Therefore, you need to use `filefilter.set_name()` to set a displayed name for the filter type. If you provide more than one filter, this name allows the user to switch between them.

```
filefilter = Gtk.FileFilter.new ();
filefilter.set_name (name)
```

Lastly, for a filter to be complete you need to add types of files to show. The standard way of doing this is with `filefilter.add_pattern()` as shown in the following code snippet. This function allows you to specify a format for the filenames that are to be shown. Usually identifying file extensions that should be shown does this. You can use the asterisk character as a wildcard for any type of filtering function.

```
filefilter.add_pattern (pattern)
```

Tip   As in Listing 5-9, you may want to provide an `All Files` filter that shows every file in the directory. To do this, you should create a filter with only one pattern set to the wildcard character. If you do not provide this filter, the user will never be able to view any files that do not match a pattern provided by another filter.

You can also specify filter patterns with `filefilter.add_mime_type()` by specifying the Multipurpose Internet Mail Extensions (MIME) type. For example, `image/*` shows all files that are an image MIME type. The problem with this function is that you need to be familiar with MIME types. However, the advantage of using MIME types is that you do not need to specify every file extension for a filter. It allows you to generalize to all files in a specific MIME category.

```
filefilter.add_mime_type(mime_type)
```

After you create the filter, it needs to be added to the file chooser, which can be done with `filechooser.add_filter()`. Once you supply the filters, the first specified filters is used by default in the file chooser. The user is able to switch between types if you have specified multiple filters.

```
filechooser.add_filter (filter)
```

Font Buttons

`Gtk.FontButton` is another type of specialized button that allows the user to select font parameters that correspond to fonts currently residing on the user's system. Font options are chosen in a font selection dialog that is displayed when the user clicks the button. These options include the font name, style options, and font size. An example `Gtk.FontButton` widget is displayed in Figure 5-10.

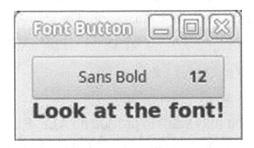

Figure 5-10. *Font selection buttons*

Font button widgets are initialized with `Gtk.FontButton.new_with_font()`, which allows you to specify the initial font. The font is provided as a string in the following format: `Family Style Size`. Each of the parameters is optional; the default font for `Gtk.FontButton` is Sans 12, which provides no style parameters.

"Family" refers to the formal font name, such as Sans, Serif, or Arial. Style options can vary between fonts, but they normally include Italic, Bold, and Bold Italic. If you choose a Regular font style, no font style is specified. The size is the point size of the text, such as 12 or 12.5.

A Gtk.FontButton Example

Listing 5-10 creates a Gtk.FontButton widget that is initialized with a Sans Bold 12 font. When the chosen font in the button is changed, the new font is applied to a Gtk.Label widget packed below the font button.

Listing 5-10. Using the Font Button

```python
#!/usr/bin/python3

import sys
import gi
gi.require_version('Gtk', '3.0')
from gi.repository import Gtk
from gi.repository import Pango

class AppWindow(Gtk.ApplicationWindow):

    def __init__(self, *args, **kwargs):
        super().__init__(*args, **kwargs)
        self.set_border_width(10)
        label = Gtk.Label("Look at the font!")
        initial_font = Pango.font_description_from_string("Sans Bold 12")
        label.modify_font(initial_font)
        button = Gtk.FontButton.new_with_font("Sans Bold 12")
        button.set_title("Choose a Font")
        button.connect("font_set", self.on_font_changed, label)
        vbox = Gtk.Box(orientation=Gtk.Orientation.VERTICAL, spacing=0)
        vbox.pack_start(button, False, False, 0)
        vbox.pack_start(label, False, False, 0)
        self.add(vbox)
```

```
    def on_font_changed(self, button, label):
        font = button.get_font()
        desc = Pango.font_description_from_string(font)
        buffer = "Font: " + font
        label.set_text(buffer)
        label.modify_font(desc)

class Application(Gtk.Application):

    def __init__(self, *args, **kwargs):
        super().__init__(*args, application_id="org.example.myapp",
                         **kwargs)
        self.window = None

    def do_activate(self):
        if not self.window:
            self.window = AppWindow(application=self, title="Font Button")
        self.window.show_all()
        self.window.present()

if __name__ == "__main__":
    app = Application()
    app.run(sys.argv)
```

Using Font Selection Buttons

The code in Listing 5-10 gives the first sampling of the Pango.FontDescription class that you have run across. The Pango.FontDescription class is used to parse font style strings. You can create and use a new font description from a font string, such as Sans Bold 12, by calling Pango.font_description_from_string() as follows.

```
initial_font = Pango.font_description_from_string("Sans Bold 12")
label.modify_font(initial_font)
```

After creating a font description, modify_font() can be called to set the font of the widget's text. This function edits the font description object stored by the widget's Gtk.StyleContext property.

In Listing 5-10, the label's text was set to the font stored by the Gtk.FontButton when the "font-set" signal was emitted. You can retrieve the whole font description string stored by the font button with fontbutton.get_font_name(), which was used to retrieve the font string displayed by the label.

```
fontbutton.get_font_name()
```

In Listing 5-10, the new font style was applied to the Gtk.Label. However, if you set fontbutton.set_use_font() and fontbutton.set_use_size() to True, the font button uses the font family and size when rendering its text. This allows the user to preview the text in the font button. This is turned off for font buttons by default.

```
fontbutton.set_use_font(boolean)
fontbutton.set_use_size(boolean)
```

Test Your Understanding

In this chapter, you learned about a number of basic widgets, such as Gtk.Entry, Gtk.SpinButton, and various types of toggles and buttons. In the following two exercises, you are creating two applications to practice using these widgets.

Exercise 1: Renaming Files

In this exercise, use a Gtk.FileChooserButton widget to allow the user to choose a file on the system. Next, use a Gtk.Entry widget that allows the user to specify a new name for the file. (Note that you can find functions for the file utilities required by this exercise in the Python documentation.)

If the file was successfully renamed, you should disable the Gtk.Entry widget and button until the user chooses a new file. If the user does not have permission to rename the file that is selected, then the Gtk.Entry widget and button should be set as insensitive as well. When you complete this exercise, you can find the solution in Appendix D.

This exercise makes use of two widgets covered in this chapter: Gtk.Entry and Gtk.FileChooserButton. It also requires you to use multiple utility functions provided by Python, including functions to rename a file and retrieve information about the permissions of an existing file.

Although you are not learning about any Python file functions, you may also want to experiment with some other file-related utility functions, such as the ability to create directories, change file permissions, and move throughout a directory structure. Python provides a lot of functionality, and it is worthwhile to explore the API documentation in your free time.

Exercise 2: Spin Buttons and Scales

In this exercise, create three widgets: a spin button, a horizontal scale, and a check button. The spin button and horizontal scale should be set with the same initial value and bounds. If the check button is selected, the two adjustment widgets should be synchronized to the same value. This means that when the user changes the value of one widget, the other is changed to the same value.

Since both widgets support integers and floating-point numbers, you should implement this exercise with various numbers of decimal places. You should also practice creating spin buttons and scales both with adjustments and by using the convenience initializers.

Summary

In this chapter, you have learned about the following nine new widgets that provide you with a meaningful way to interact with your users.

- Gtk.ToggleButton: A type of Gtk.Button widget that holds its active or inactive state after it is clicked. It is shown as pressed down when it is active.

- Gtk.CheckButton: Derived from Gtk.ToggleButton, this widget is drawn as a discrete toggle next to the displayed text. This allows it to be differentiated from a Gtk.Button.

- Gtk.RadioButton: You can group multiple radio button widgets together so that only one toggle in the group can be activated at once.

- Gtk.Entry: This widget allows the user to enter free-form text on a single line. It also facilitates password entry.

- `Gtk.SpinButton`: Derived from `Gtk.Entry`, spin buttons allow the user to select or enter an integer or floating-point number within a predefined range.

- `Gtk.Scale`: Similar to the spin button, this widget allows the user to select an integer or floating-point number by moving a vertical or horizontal slider.

- `Gtk.ColorButton`: This special type of button allows the user to select a specific color along with an optional alpha value.

- `Gtk.FileChooserButton`: This special type of button allows the user to select a single file or folder that already exists on the system.

- `Gtk.FontButton`: This special type of button allows the user to select a font family, style, and size.

In the next chapter, you learn how to create your own custom dialogs using the `Gtk.Dialog` class and about a number of dialogs that are built into GTK+. By the end of Chapter 6, you have a decent grasp of the most important simple widgets available to you in GTK+. From there, we continue on to more complex topics.

CHAPTER 6

Dialogs

This chapter introduces you to a special type of window called a *dialog*. Dialogs are windows that supplement the top-level window. The dialog is provided by `Gtk.Dialog`, a child class of `Gtk.Window`, extended with additional functionality. This means that it is possible to implement your entire interface in one or more dialogs, while leaving the main window hidden.

You can do anything with a dialog, such as display a message or prompt the user to select an option. Their purpose is to enhance user experience by providing some type of transient functionality.

In the first part of the chapter, you learn how to use `Gtk.Dialog` to create your own custom dialogs. The next section introduces the large number of built-in dialogs provided by GTK+. Lastly, you learn about a widget called `Gtk.Assistant` that allows you to create dialogs with multiple pages; assistants are meant to help the user through a multistage process.

In this chapter, you learn the following.

- How to create your own custom dialogs using the `Gtk.Dialog` widget

- How to give general information, error messages, and warnings to the user with the `Gtk.MessageDialog` widget

- How to provide information about your application with `Gtk.AboutDialog`

- What types of file chooser dialogs are available

- The ways to collect information with font and color selection dialogs

- How to create dialogs with multiple pages using the `Gtk.Assistant` widget

© W. David Ashley and Andrew Krause 2019
W. D. Ashley and A. Krause, *Foundations of PyGTK Development*,
https://doi.org/10.1007/978-1-4842-4179-0_6

Creating Your Own Dialogs

A dialog is a special type of Gtk.Window that supplements the top-level window. It can give the user a message, retrieve information from the user, or provide some other transient type of action.

Dialog widgets are split in half by an invisible horizontal separator. The top part is where you place the main part of the dialog's user interface. The bottom half is called the *action area*, and it holds a collection of buttons. When clicked, each button emits a unique response identifier that tells the programmer which button was clicked.

In most ways, the dialog widget can be treated as a window, because it is derived from the Gtk.Window class. However, when you have multiple windows, a parent-child relationship should be established between the dialog and the top-level window when the dialog is meant to supplement the top-level window.

```
vbox = mydialog.get_content_area()
```

Gtk.Dialog provides access a vertical box that has the action area defined at bottom of the box. The content area has yet to be defined. To define it you begin packing widgets at start of the vertical box. Therefore you must always use the pack_start() to add widgets to a Gtk.Dialog class. Buttons can easily be added to the action area with the add_button(button_text, response_id) method call.

Note   It is possible to manually implement the functionality of Gtk.Dialog by creating a Gtk.Window with all of the same widgets and establishing window relationships with set_transient_for() in addition to other functions provided by Gtk.Window. Gtk.Dialog is simply a convenience widget that provides standard methods.

Both the action area and a separator are packed at the end of the dialog's vertical box. The provided by Gtk.Box (vbox) holds all the dialog content. Because the action area is packed at the end, you should use pack_start() to add widgets to a Gtk.Dialog as follows.

```
vbox = mydialog.get_ac_area()
vbox.pack_start (child, expand, fill, padding)
```

By packing widgets at the start of the box, the action area and the separator always remains at the bottom of the dialog.

Creating a Message Dialog

One advantage of Gtk.Dialog is that, no matter how complex the content of your dialog is, the same basic concepts can be applied to every dialog. To illustrate this, we begin by creating a very simple dialog that gives the user a message. Figure 6-1 is a screenshot of this dialog.

Figure 6-1. *A message dialog created programmatically*

Listing 6-1 creates a simple dialog that notifies the user when the clicked signal is emitted by the button. This functionality is provided by the Gtk.MessageDialog widget, which is covered in a later section of this chapter.

Listing 6-1. Your First Custom Dialog

```
#!/usr/bin/python3

import sys
import gi
gi.require_version('Gtk', '3.0')
from gi.repository import Gtk

class AppWindow(Gtk.ApplicationWindow):

    def __init__(self, *args, **kwargs):
        super().__init__(*args, **kwargs)
        self.set_border_width(10)
        button = Gtk.Button.new_with_mnemonic("_Click Me")
        button.connect("clicked", self.on_button_clicked, self)
        self.add(button)
        self.set_size_request(150, 50)
```

```python
    def on_button_clicked(self, button, parent):
        dialog = Gtk.Dialog(title="Information", parent=parent,
                            flags=Gtk.DialogFlags.MODAL)
        dialog.add_button("Ok", Gtk.ResponseType.OK)
        label = Gtk.Label("The button was clicked.")
        image = Gtk.Image.new_from_icon_name("dialog-information",
                                             Gtk.IconSize.DIALOG)
        hbox = Gtk.Box(orientation=Gtk.Orientation.HORIZONTAL, spacing=0)
        hbox.pack_start(image, False, False, 0)
        hbox.pack_start(label, False, False, 0)
        dialog.vbox.pack_start(hbox, False, False, 0)
        dialog.show_all()
        dialog.run()
        dialog.destroy()

class Application(Gtk.Application):

    def __init__(self, *args, **kwargs):
        super().__init__(*args, application_id="org.example.myapp",
                         **kwargs)
        self.window = None

    def do_activate(self):
        if not self.window:
            self.window = AppWindow(application=self, title="Dialogs")
        self.window.show_all()
        self.window.present()

if __name__ == "__main__":
    app = Application()
    app.run(sys.argv)
```

Creating the Dialog

The first thing you need to do when the button in the main window is clicked is create
the Gtk.Dialog widget with Gtk.Dialog.new_with_buttons(). The first two parameters
of this function specify the title of the dialog, a pointer to the parent window, and the
modality flag.

```
dialog = Gtk.Dialog(title="Information", parent=parent, flags=Gtk.
DialogFlags.MODA
```

The dialog is set as the transient window of the parent window, which allows the window manager to center the dialog over the main window and keep it on top if necessary. This can be achieved for arbitrary windows by calling `window.set_transient_for()`. You can also provide `None` if you do not want the dialog to have or recognize a parent window.

Next, you can specify one or more dialog flags. Options for this parameter are given by the `Gtk.DialogFlags` enumeration. There are three available values, which are shown in the following list.

- `Gtk.DialogFlags.MODAL`: Force the dialog to remain in focus on top of the parent window until closed. The user is prevented from interacting with the parent.

- `Gtk.DialogFlags.DESTROY_WITH_PARENT`: Destroy the dialog when the parent is destroyed, but do not force the dialog to be in focus. This creates a nonmodal dialog unless you call `dialog.run()`.

- `Gtk.DialogFlags.USE_HEADER_BAR`: Create a dialog with actions in the header bar instead of the action area.

In Listing 6-1, specifying `Gtk.DialogFlags.MODAL` created a modal dialog. It is not necessary to specify a title or parent window; the values can be set to `None`. However, you should always set the title, so it can be drawn in the window manager; otherwise, the user has difficulty choosing the desired window.

In Listing 6-1, an OK button with a response of `Gtk.ResponseType.OK` was added to the dialog.

In GTK+ 2.x, all dialogs placed a horizontal separator between the main content and the action area of the dialog by default. That separator has been deprecated in GTK+ 3.x.

After the child widgets are created, they need to be added to the dialog. As I previously stated, child widgets are added to the dialog by calling `box.pack_start()`. The dialog is packed as follows.

```
image = Gtk.Image.new_from_icon_name("dialog-information", Gtk.IconSize.
DIALOG)
hbox = Gtk.Box(orientation=Gtk.Orientation.HORIZONTAL, spacing=0)
```

```
hbox.pack_start(image, False, False, 0)
hbox.pack_start(label, False, False, 0)
dialog.vbox.pack_start(hbox, False, False, 0)
```

At this point, you need to show the dialog and its child widgets, because `dialog.run()` only calls `dialog.show()` on the dialog itself. To do this, call `dialog.show_all()` on the dialog. If you do not show the widgets, only the separator and action area is visible when `dialog.run()` is called.

Response Identifiers

When a dialog is fully constructed, one method of showing the dialog is by calling `dialog.run()`. This function returns an integer called a *response identifier* when complete. It also prevents the user from interacting with anything outside of the dialog until it is destroyed or an action area button is clicked.

```
dialog.run()
```

Internally, `dialog.run()` creates a new main loop for the dialog, which prevents you from interacting with its parent window until a response identifier is emitted or the user closes the dialog. Regardless of what dialog flags you set, the dialog is always modal when you call this method, because it calls `dialog.set_modal()`.

If the dialog is manually destroyed by using a method provided by the window manager, `Gtk.ResponseType.NONE` is returned; otherwise, `dialog.run()` returns the response identifier referring to the button that was clicked. A full list of available response identifiers from the `Gtk.ResponseType` enumeration is shown in Table 6-1. You should always use the identifier's available values instead of random integer values, since they could change in future versions of GTK+.

Table 6-1. *Gtk.ResponseType Enumeration Values*

Identifiers	Value	Description
Gtk.ResponseType.NONE	−1	Returned if an action widget has no response ID, or if the dialog is programmatically hidden or destroyed.
Gtk.ResponseType.APPLY	−10	Returned by Apply buttons in GTK+ dialogs.
Gtk.ResponseType.HELP	−11	Returned by Help buttons in GTK+ dialogs.
Gtk.ResponseType.REJECT	−2	Generic response ID, not used by GTK+ dialogs.
Gtk.ResponseType.ACCEPT	−3	Generic response ID, not used by GTK+ dialogs.
Gtk.ResponseType.DELETE_EVENT	−4	Returned if the dialog is deleted.
Gtk.ResponseType.OK	−5	Returned by OK buttons in GTK + dialogs.
Gtk.ResponseType.CANCEL	−6	Returned by Cancel buttons in GTK+ dialogs.
Gtk.ResponseType.CLOSE	−7	Returned by Close buttons in GTK+ dialogs.
Gtk.ResponseType.YES	−8	Returned by Yes buttons in GTK + dialogs.
Gtk.ResponseType.No	−9	Returned by No buttons in GTK+ dialogs.

Of course, when you create your own dialogs and when using many of the built-in dialogs covered in the next few pages, you are free to choose which response identifier to use. However, you should try to resist the urge to apply a Gtk.ResponseType.CANCEL identifier to an OK button, or some other type of absurdity along those lines.

Note   You are free to create your own response identifiers, but you should use positive numbers, since all of the built-in identifiers are negative. This allows you to avoid conflicts when more identifiers are added in future versions of GTK+.

After the dialog returns a response identifier, you need to make sure to call dialog.destroy(), or it will cause a memory leak. GTK+ makes sure all of the dialog's children are destroyed, but you need to remember to initiate the process.

By calling dialog.destroy(), all of the parent's children are destroyed and its reference count drops. When an object's reference count reaches zero, the object is finalized, and its memory freed.

The Gtk.Image Widget

Listing 6-1 introduces another new widget called Gtk.Image. Images can be loaded in a wide variety of ways, but one advantage of Gtk.Image is that it displays the named image "image-missing" if the loading has failed. It is also derived from Gtk.Widget, so it can be added as a child of a container unlike other image objects, such as Gdk.Pixbuf.

In our example, new_from_icon_name() created the Gtk.Image widget from a named theme item.

```
image = Gtk.Image.new_from_icon_name("dialog-information", Gtk.IconSize.DIALOG)
```

When loading an image, you also need to specify a size for the image. GTK+ automatically looks for a stock icon for the given size and resizes the image to that size if none is found. Available size parameters are specified by the Gtk.IconTheme enumeration, as seen in the following list.

- Gtk.IconSize.INVALID: Unspecified size

- Gtk.IconSize.MENU: 16×16 pixels

- Gtk.IconSize.SMALL_TOOLBAR: 18×18 pixels

- Gtk.IconSize.LARGE_TOOLBAR: 24×24 pixels

- Gtk.IconSize.BUTTON: 24×24 pixels

- Gtk.IconSize.DND: 32×32 pixels

- Gtk.IconSize.DIALOG: 48×48 pixels

As you can see, theme Gtk.Image objects are usually used for smaller images, such as those that appear in buttons, menus, and dialogs, since theme images are provided in a discrete number of standard sizes. In Listing 6-1, the image was set to Gtk.IconSize. DIALOG or 48×48 pixels.

Multiple initialization functions for Gtk.Image are provided, which are described in the API documentation, but new_from_file() and new_from_pixbuf() are especially important to future examples in this book.

```
Gtk.Image.new_from_file(filename)
```

Gtk.Image automatically detects the image type of the file specified to new_from_ file(). If the image cannot be loaded, it displays a broken-image icon. Therefore, this function never returns a None object. Gtk.Image also supports animations that occur within the image file.

Calling new_from_pixbuf() creates a new Gtk.Image widget out of a previously initialized Gdk.Pixbuf. Unlike new_from_file(), you can use this function to easily figure out whether the image is successfully loaded since you first have to create a Gdk.Pixbuf.

```
Gdk.Image.new_from_pixbuf(pixbuf)
```

You need to note that the Gtk.Image creates its own references to the Gdk.Pixbuf, so you need to release your reference to the object if it should be destroyed with the Gtk.Image.

Nonmodal Message Dialog

By calling dialog.run(), your dialog is always set as modal, which is not always desirable. To create a nonmodal dialog, you need to connect to Gtk.Dialog's response signal.

In Listing 6-2, the message dialog from Figure 6-1 is reimplemented as a nonmodal dialog. You should try clicking the button in the main window multiple times in a row. This shows how you can not only create multiple instances of the same dialog but also access the main window from a nonmodal dialog.

Listing 6-2. A Nonmodal Message Dialog

```
#!/usr/bin/python3

import sys
import gi
gi.require_version('Gtk', '3.0')
from gi.repository import Gtk

class AppWindow(Gtk.ApplicationWindow):

    def __init__(self, *args, **kwargs):
        super().__init__(*args, **kwargs)
        self.set_border_width(10)
        button = Gtk.Button.new_with_mnemonic("_Click Me")
```

```python
            button.connect("clicked", self.on_button_clicked, self)
            self.add(button)
            self.set_size_request(150, 50)
            self.show_all()

    def on_button_clicked(self, button, parent):
        dialog = Gtk.Dialog(title="Information", parent=parent)
        dialog.add_button("Ok", Gtk.ResponseType.OK)
        label = Gtk.Label("The button was clicked.")
        image = Gtk.Image.new_from_icon_name("dialog-information",
                                             Gtk.IconSize.DIALOG)
        hbox = Gtk.Box(orientation=Gtk.Orientation.HORIZONTAL, spacing=0)
        hbox.pack_start(image, False, False, 0)
        hbox.pack_start(label, False, False, 0)
        dialog.vbox.pack_start(hbox, False, False, 0)
        dialog.connect("response", self.on_dialog_button_clicked)
        dialog.show_all()

    def on_dialog_button_clicked(self, dialog, response):
        dialog.destroy()

class Application(Gtk.Application):

    def __init__(self, *args, **kwargs):
        super().__init__(*args, application_id="org.example.myapp",
                         **kwargs)
        self.window = None

    def do_activate(self):
        if not self.window:
            self.window = AppWindow(application=self, title="Dialogs")
        self.window.show_all()
        self.window.present()

if __name__ == "__main__":
    app = Application()
    app.run(sys.argv)
```

Creating a nonmodal dialog is very similar to the previous example, except you do not want to call `dialog.run()`. By calling this function, a modal dialog is created by blocking the parent window's main loop regardless of the dialog flags.

Tip   You can still create a modal dialog without using `dialog.run()` by setting the `Gtk.DialogFlags.MODAL` flag. You can then connect to the response signal. This function simply provides a convenient way to create modal dialogs and handle response identifiers within one function.

By connecting to `Gtk.Dialog`'s response signal, you can wait for a response identifier to be emitted. By using this method, the dialog is not automatically unreferenced when a response identifier is emitted. The response callback method receives the dialog, the response identifier that was emitted, and the optional data parameter.

One of the most important decisions you have to make when designing a dialog is whether it is modal or nonmodal. As a rule of thumb, if the action needs to be completed before the user can continue working with the application, then the dialog should be modal. Examples of this would be message dialogs, dialogs that ask the user a question, and dialogs to open a file.

If there is no reason why the user cannot continue working while the dialog is open, you should use a nonmodal dialog. You also need to remember that multiple instances of nonmodal dialogs can be created unless you prevent this programmatically, so dialogs that must have only one instance should be created as modal.

Another Dialog Example

Now that you have created a simple message dialog from scratch, it is time to produce a more complex dialog. In Listing 6-3, a few pieces of basic information about the user are propagated using Python's utility functions. A dialog, which is shown in Figure 6-2, allows you to edit each piece of information.

Figure 6-2. *A simple Gtk.Dialog widget*

This information is, of course, not actually changed within the user's system; the new text is simply output to the screen. This example illustrates the fact that, regardless of the complexity of the dialog, the basic principles of how to handle response identifiers are still the only ones that are necessary.

You could easily implement this as a nonmodal dialog as well, although this would not be of much use since the dialog itself is the application's top-level window.

Listing 6-3. Editing Information in a Dialog

```python
#!/usr/bin/python3

import sys
import gi
gi.require_version('Gtk', '3.0')
from gi.repository import Gtk
import os
import getpass
import socket
import pwd

class AppWindow(Gtk.ApplicationWindow):

    def __init__(self, *args, **kwargs):
        super().__init__(*args, **kwargs)
        self.set_border_width(10)
        button = Gtk.Button.new_with_mnemonic("_Click Me")
```

```python
        button.connect("clicked", self.on_button_clicked, self)
        self.add(button)
        self.set_size_request(180, 50)
        self.show_all()

    def on_button_clicked(self, button, parent):
        dialog = Gtk.Dialog(title="Edit User Information",
                            parent=parent, flags=Gtk.DialogFlags.MODAL)
        dialog.add_button("Ok", Gtk.ResponseType.OK)
        dialog.add_button("Cancel", Gtk.ResponseType.CANCEL)
        dialog.set_default_response(Gtk.ResponseType.OK)
        lbl1 = Gtk.Label("User Name:")
        lbl2 = Gtk.Label("Real Name:")
        lbl3 = Gtk.Label("Home Dir:")
        lbl4 = Gtk.Label("Host Name:")
        user = Gtk.Entry()
        real_name = Gtk.Entry()
        home = Gtk.Entry()
        host = Gtk.Entry()
        user.set_text(getpass.getuser())
        real_name.set_text(pwd.getpwuid(os.getuid())[4])
        home.set_text(os.environ['HOME'])
        host.set_text(socket.gethostname())
        grid = Gtk.Grid()
        grid.attach(lbl1, 0, 0, 1, 1)
        grid.attach(lbl2, 0, 1, 1, 1)
        grid.attach(lbl3, 0, 2, 1, 1)
        grid.attach(lbl4, 0, 3, 1, 1)
        grid.attach(user, 1, 0, 1, 1)
        grid.attach(real_name, 1, 1, 1, 1)
        grid.attach(home, 1, 2, 1, 1)
        grid.attach(host, 1, 3, 1, 1)
        dialog.vbox.pack_start(grid, False, False, 5)
        dialog.show_all()
        result = dialog.run()
```

```
        if result == Gtk.ResponseType.OK:
            print("User Name: " + user.get_text())
            print("Real Name: " +
            real_name.get_text()) print("Home: " +
            home.get_text()) print("Host: " +
            host.get_text())
        dialog.destroy()

class Application(Gtk.Application):

    def __init__(self, *args, **kwargs):
        super().__init__(*args, application_id="org.example.myapp",
                        **kwargs)
        self.window = None

    def do_activate(self):
        if not self.window:
            self.window = AppWindow(application=self, title="Simple Dialog")
        self.window.show_all()
        self.window.present()

if __name__ == "__main__":
    app = Application()
    app.run(sys.argv)
```

The proper way to handle any modal dialog is to use the response identifiers, deriving the correct response based on the clicked button. Since there was only one response that needed to be deliberately detected, a conditional if statement was used in Listing 6-3.

However, let's assume that you need to handle multiple response identifiers. In this case, an if statement would be a better solution, since it was created to compare a single variable to multiple selections, as shown in the following code snippet.

```
result = dialog.run()
if result == Gtk.ResponseType.OK:
    # ... Handle result ...
elif result == Gtk.ResponseType.APPLY:
    # ... Handle result ...
```

```
else:
    # ... Handle default result ...

dialog.destroy()
```

Built-in Dialogs

There are many types of dialogs already built into GTK+. Although not all of the available dialogs are covered in this chapter, you are given a strong understanding of the concepts needed to use any built-in dialog. This section covers Gtk.MessageDialog, GtkAboutDialog, Gtk.FileChooserDialog, Gtk.FontChooserDialog, and Gtk.ColorChooserDialog.

Message Dialogs

Message dialogs give one of four types of informational messages: general information, error messages, warnings, and questions. This type of dialog decides the icon to display, the title of the dialog, and the buttons to add.

There is also a general type provided that makes no assumption as to the content of the message. In most cases, you will not want to use this, since the four provided types would fill most of your needs.

It is very simple to re-create the Gtk.MessageDialog widget. The first two examples implemented a simple message dialog, but Gtk.MessageDialog already provides this functionality, so you should not need to re-create the widget. Using Gtk.MessageDialog saves on typing and avoids the need to re-create this widget many times, since most applications make heavy use of Gtk.MessageDialog. It also provides a uniform look for message dialogs across all GTK+ applications.

Figure 6-3 shows an example of a Gtk.MessageDialog (compare this to Figure 6-1), which gives the user visual notification of a button's clicked signal.

Figure 6-3. *A Gtk.MessageDialog widget*

Since the content of the message is not critical, its type is set to a general message. This message dialog can be produced using the code shown in Listing 6-4.

Listing 6-4. Using a Gtk.MessageDialog

```python
#!/usr/bin/python3

import sys
import gi
gi.require_version('Gtk', '3.0')
from gi.repository import Gtk

class AppWindow(Gtk.ApplicationWindow):

    def __init__(self, *args, **kwargs):
        super().__init__(*args, **kwargs)
        self.set_border_width(10)
        button = Gtk.Button.new_with_mnemonic("_Click Me")
        button.connect("clicked", self.on_button_clicked, self)
        self.add(button)
        self.set_size_request(150, 50)

    def on_button_clicked(self, button, parent):
        dialog = Gtk.MessageDialog(type=Gtk.MessageType.INFO, parent=parent,
                                   flags=Gtk.DialogFlags.MODAL,
                                   buttons=("Ok", Gtk.ResponseType.OK),
                                   text="The button was clicked.",
                                   title="Information")
        dialog.run()
        dialog.destroy()
```

```
class Application(Gtk.Application):

    def __init__(self, *args, **kwargs):
        super().__init__(*args, application_id="org.example.myapp",
                         **kwargs)
        self.window = None

    def do_activate(self):
        if not self.window:
            self.window = AppWindow(application=self, title="Dialogs")
        self.window.show_all()
        self.window.present()

if __name__ == "__main__":
    app = Application()
    app.run(sys.argv)
```

After the button in the main window is clicked, this example creates a new Gtk. MessageDialog.

The parent window can be set to None if necessary, but in most cases, a parent-child relationship should be established. If you do not set a parent widget, the message dialog will not be centered above the parent window.

Message dialogs should be addressed by the user immediately, because they present some type of important message or critical question that needs the user's attention. By not setting a parent window, the message dialog can be easily ignored, which is not the desired action in most cases.

```
dialog = Gtk.MessageDialog.(type=Gtk.MessageType.INFO, parent=parent, \
                 flags=Gtk.DialogFlags.MODAL, \
                 buttons=("Ok", Gtk.ResponseType.OK), \
                 text="The button was clicked.", \
                 title="Information")
```

You specify one or more dialog flags. Options for this parameter are given by the Gtk. DialogFlags enumeration that was used when creating custom dialogs in the previous three examples.

Unlike GTK+ 2.x, the 3.x Gtk.MessageDialog does not use any positional parameters. Instead, it uses keyword parameters exclusively. Also note that Gtk.MessageDialog does not use a new method. This is because Gtk.MessageDialog creates a subclass of Gtk. MessageDialog and the keywords determine what kind subclass is created.

Also note that the light bulb icon image is missing from the message dialog. This is due to philosophy changes in GTK+ 3.x. If you must have icons in your dialogs then you need to use Gtk.Dialog to hand create your dialogs.

Multiple buttons are supported by including a comma-separated list of buttons/ response ids using the "buttons" keyword.

You have no control over the visual formatting of the message provided to Gtk. MessageDialog. If you would like to use the Pango Text Markup Language to format the message dialog's text, you can leave out the "text" keyword from the Gtk.MessageDialog call. Then call set_markup(str) method with a string of Pango markup to set the text of the message.

It is possible to add a secondary text to the message dialog, which causes the first message to be set as bold with format_secondary_text(). The text string provided to this function should be similar to the format supported by the C printf().

This feature is very useful, because it allows you to give a quick summary in the primary text and go into detail with the secondary text.

About Dialogs

The Gtk.AboutDialog widget provides you with a simple way to provide the user with information about an application. This dialog is usually displayed when the item in the Help menu is chosen. However, since menus are not covered until Chapter 10, our example dialog is used as the top-level window.

Various types of information are shown with Gtk.AboutDialog, including the name of the application, copyright, current version, license content, authors, documenters, artists, and translators. Because an application won't have all of this information, every property is optional. The main window displays only the basic information, which is seen along with the author credits in Figure 6-4.

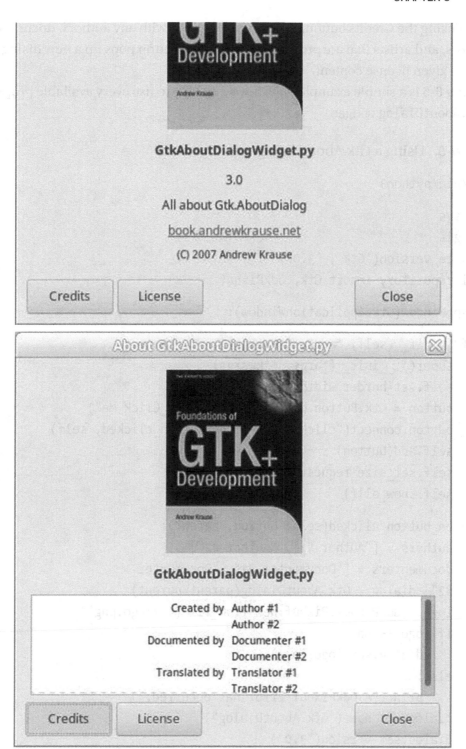

Figure 6-4. *An About credit dialog and author credit*

By clicking the Credits button, the user is presented with any authors, documenters, translators, and artists that are provided. The License button pops up a new dialog that shows the given license content.

Listing 6-5 is a simple example that shows you how to use every available property of the Gtk.AboutDialog widget.

Listing 6-5. Using a Gtk.AboutDialog

```
#!/usr/bin/python3

import sys
import gi
gi.require_version('Gtk', '3.0')
from gi.repository import Gtk, GdkPixbuf

class AppWindow(Gtk.ApplicationWindow):

    def __init__(self, *args, **kwargs):
        super().__init__(*args, **kwargs)
        self.set_border_width(10)
        button = Gtk.Button.new_with_mnemonic("_Click Me")
        button.connect("clicked", self.on_button_clicked, self)
        self.add(button)
        self.set_size_request(150, 50)
        self.show_all()

    def on_button_clicked(self, button, parent):
        authors = ["Author #1", "Author #2"]
        documenters = ["Documenter #1", "Documenter
        #2"] dialog = Gtk.AboutDialog(parent=parent)
        logo = GdkPixbuf.Pixbuf.new_from_file("./logo.png")
        if logo != None:
            dialog.set_logo(logo)
        else:
            print("A GdkPixbuf Error has occurred.")
        dialog.set_name("Gtk.AboutDialog")
        dialog.set_version("3.0")
        dialog.set_copyright("(C) 2007 Andrew Krause")
```

```
        dialog.set_comments("All about Gtk.AboutDialog")
        dialog.set_license("Free to all!")
        dialog.set_website("http://book.andrewKrause.net")
        dialog.set_website_label("book.andrewkrause.net")
        dialog.set_authors(authors)
        dialog.set_documenters(documenters)
        dialog.set_translator_credits("Translator #1\nTranslator #2")
        dialog.connect("response", self.on_dialog_button_clicked)
        dialog.run()

    def on_dialog_button_clicked(self, dialog, response):
        dialog.destroy()

class Application(Gtk.Application):

    def __init__(self, *args, **kwargs):
        super().__init__(*args, application_id="org.example.myapp",
                         **kwargs)
        self.window = None

    def do_activate(self):
        if not self.window:
            self.window = AppWindow(application=self, title="About Dialog")
        self.window.show_all()
        self.window.present()

if __name__ == "__main__":
    app = Application()
    app.run(sys.argv)
```

Many properties are available for you to set when creating your own Gtk. AboutDialog instance. Table 6-2 summarizes those options that were used in Listing 6-5. If the license is not specified, the License button is not visible. The Credits button is not visible if there are no credits.

Table 6-2. *Gtk.AboutDialog Option Values*

Property	Description
program_name	The application's name.
version	The current version of the application the user is running.
copyright	A short copyright string that should not span more than one or two lines.
comments	A short description of the application that should not span more than one or two lines.
license	License information that is displayed in a secondary dialog. Setting this to None hides the License button.
web site	The home page URL of the application.
web site_label	A label that is displayed instead of the URL.
authors	A Python list of authors who have contributed code to the project.
artists	A Python list of artists who have created graphics for the project.
documenters	A Python list of documenters who have written documentation for the project.
translator_credits	A string that specifies the translator(s) of the current language.
logo	Usually loaded from a file, this `Gdk.Pixbuf` object is the application's logo.

Unlike author, artist, and documenter credits, the translator credits are only a single string. This is because the translator string should be set to the person that translated the language currently in use. Internationalization and `gettext` are not topics for this book. For more information, you should visit `www.gnu.org/software/gettext`.

Gdk.Pixbuf

`GdkPixbuf` is a class that contains information about an image stored in memory. It allows you to build images manually by placing shapes or pixels or to load a pre-built image from a file. The latter is preferred in most cases, so that is what is covered in this book.

Since `GdkPixbuf` is derived from `GObject`, it supports referencing. This means that the same image can be used in multiple locations in a program by increasing the reference count with `ref()`. Dereferencing `GdkPixbuf` objects (pixbufs) is performed automatically in almost all cases.

To load a pixbuf from a file, you can use GdkPixbuf.new_from_file(), which was used in Listing 6-5. This function loads the image with an initial size set to the actual size of the image.

```
logo = GdkPixbuf.Pixbuf.new_from_file("./logo.png")
```

After you load the image, you can resize it with scale_simple(). This function accepts the new size parameters of the Gdk.Pixbuf and the interpolation mode to use for the scaling.

```
pixbuf.scale_simple(dest_width, dest_height, interp_type)
```

The following are the four GdkPixbuf.InterpType modes.

- GdkPixbuf.InterpType.NEAREST: Sampling is performed on the nearest neighboring pixel. This mode is very fast, but it produces the lowest quality of scaling. It should never be used for scaling an image to a smaller size!

- GdkPixbuf.InterpType.TILES: This mode renders every pixel as a shape of color and uses antialiasing for the edges. This is similar to using GdkPixbuf.InterpType.NEAREST for making an image larger or GdkPixbuf.InterpType.BILINEAR for reducing its size.

- GdkPixbuf.InterpType.BILINEAR: This mode is the best mode for resizing images in both directions, because it has a balance between its speed and the quality of the image.

- GdkPixbuf.InterpType.HYPER: While it is very high quality, this method is also very slow. It should only be used when speed is not a concern. Therefore, it should never be used for any application that the user would expect a fast display time. In one function call, GdkPixbuf.new_from_file_at_size() conveniently resizes the image immediately after it loads from the file.

Many other features are provided in the GdkPixbuf class, but only a few of these are covered, as needed. For further information on GdkPixbuf, you should reference the API documentation.

Gtk.FileChooser Dialogs

In the last chapter, you learned about Gtk.FileChooser and the Gtk.FileChooserButton widget. Recall that Gtk.FileChooser is not a widget, but an abstract class. Abstract classes differ from real classes, because they may not implement the methods they declare.

GTK+ provides the following three widgets that subclass the Gtk.FileChooser class.

- Gtk.FileChooserButton: The file chooser button was covered in the previous chapter. It allows the user to choose one file or folder by displaying a Gtk.FileChooser dialog when clicked.

- Gtk.FileChooserDialog: This is the actual widget that allows the user to choose a file folder. It can also facilitate the creation of a folder or saving of a file. When you use Gtk.FileChooserDialog, you are actually using a file chooser widget packed into a Gtk.Dialog.

- Gtk.FileChooserWidget: This is the actual widget that allows the user to choose a file folder. It can also facilitate the creation of a folder or saving of a file. When you use Gtk.FileChooserDialog, you are actually using a file chooser widget packed into a Gtk.Dialog.

You have already learned about Gtk.FileChooserButton and have used a file chooser to open one file and to select a directory. There are three other abilities provided by the file chooser widget. In the next three examples, you learn how to use a file chooser dialog to save a file, create a directory, and choose multiple files.

Saving Files

Figure 6-5 shows a Gtk.FileChooserDialog widget that is saving a file. You will notice that it is similar to the next two figures as well, because all types of file chooser dialogs have a consistent look so that it is minimally confusing to new users and maximally efficient to all. The widget also uses the same code to implement each dialog type to minimize the amount of necessary code.

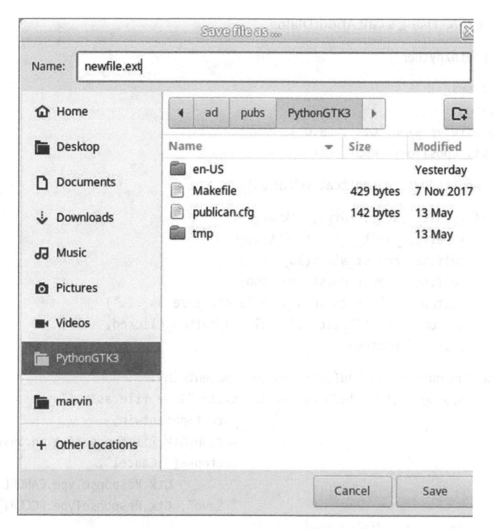

Figure 6-5. *A file chooser dialog for saving*

File chooser dialogs are used in the same way as the previous two dialogs covered in this chapter, except you need to handle the response code returned by Gtk.Dialog. new(). Listing 6-6 allows the user to choose a file name and sets the button's text to that file name if the correct response identifier is returned.

Listing 6-6. Using a Gtk.AboutDialog

```python
#!/usr/bin/python3

import sys
import gi
gi.require_version('Gtk', '3.0')
from gi.repository import Gtk

class AppWindow(Gtk.ApplicationWindow):

    def __init__(self, *args, **kwargs):
        super().__init__(*args, **kwargs)
        self.set_border_width(10)
        self.set_size_request(200, 100)
        button = Gtk.Button.new_with_label("Save as ...")
        button.connect("clicked", self.on_button_clicked, self)
        self.add(button)

    def on_button_clicked(self, button, parentwin):
        dialog = Gtk.FileChooserDialog(title="Save file as ...",
                                       parent=parentwin,
                                       action=Gtk.FileChooserAction.SAVE,
                                       buttons=("_Cancel",
                                                Gtk.ResponseType.CANCEL,
                                       "_Save", Gtk.ResponseType.ACCEPT))
        response = dialog.run()
        if response == Gtk.ResponseType.ACCEPT:
            filename = dialog.get_filename()
            button.set_label(filename)
        dialog.destroy()

class Application(Gtk.Application):

    def __init__(self, *args, **kwargs):
        super().__init__(*args, application_id="org.example.myapp",
                         **kwargs)
        self.window = None
```

```
    def do_activate(self):
        if not self.window:
            self.window = AppWindow(application=self, title="Save a File")
        self.window.show_all()
        self.window.present()

if __name__ == "__main__":
    app = Application()
    app.run(sys.argv)
```

All file chooser dialogs are created with the Gtk.FileChooserDialog() regardless of what options you choose. As with other dialogs, you begin by setting the title of the dialog and the parent window. The parent window should always be set, because file chooser dialogs should be modal.

```
dialog = Gtk.FileChooserDialog(title="Save file as ...", \
                               parent=parentwin, \
                               action=Gtk.FileChooserAction.SAVE, \
                               buttons=("_Cancel", Gtk.ResponseType.CANCEL, \
                               "_Save", Gtk.ResponseType.ACCEPT))
```

Next, as with file chooser buttons, you have to choose the action of file chooser that is created. All four action types provided by the Gtk.FileChooser abstract class are available to Gtk.FileChooserDialog. These are described in the following list.

- Gtk.FileChooserAction.SAVE: The user is prompted to enter a file name and browse throughout the file system for a location. The returned file is the chosen path with the new file name appended to the end. Gtk.FileChooser provides methods that allow you to ask for confirmation if the user enters a file name that already exists.

- Gtk.FileChooserAction.OPEN: The file chooser only allows the user to select one or more files that already exist on the user's system. The user is able to browse throughout the file system or choose a bookmarked location.

- `Gtk.FileChooserAction.SELECT_FOLDER`: This is very similar to the save action, because it allows the user to choose a location and specify a new folder name. The user can enter a new folder name that is created when the file chooser returns or click the Create Folder button, shown in Figure 5-6, which creates a new folder in the current directory.

- `Gtk.FileChooserAction.CREATE_FOLDER`: This is very similar to the save action, because it allows the user to choose a location and specify a new folder name. The user can enter a new folder name that is created when the file chooser returns or click the Create Folder button, shown in Figure 5-6, which creates a new folder in the current directory.

Lastly, you have to provide a name/response ID list of buttons to add to the action area. In Listing 6-6, when the Cancel button is clicked, `Gtk.ResponseType.CANCEL` is emitted, and when the Save button is clicked, `GTK_RESPONSE_ACCEPT` is emitted.

Creating a Folder

GTK+ allows you not only to select a folder but also to create a folder. A `Gtk.FileChooserDialog` widget using this type can be seen in Figure 6-6, which is a screenshot of Listing 6-7.

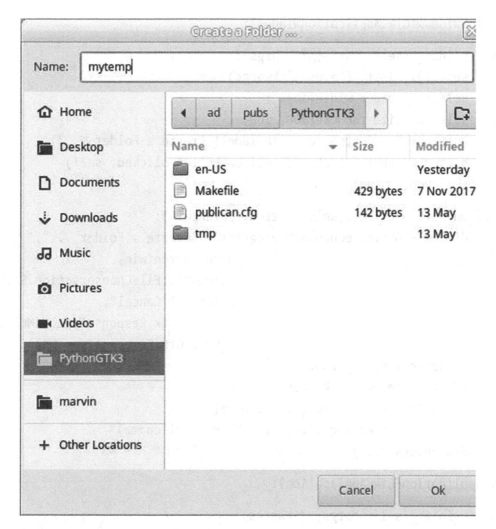

Figure 6-6. *A file chooser dialog for creating a folder*

The dialog in Listing 6-7 handles creating the new folder when accepted by the user, so you do not need to take any further action beyond destroying the dialog.

Listing 6-7. Using a Gtk.AboutDialog

```
#!/usr/bin/python3

import sys
import gi
gi.require_version('Gtk', '3.0')
from gi.repository import Gtk
```

```python
class AppWindow(Gtk.ApplicationWindow):

    def __init__(self, *args, **kwargs):
        super().__init__(*args, **kwargs)
        self.set_border_width(10)
        self.set_size_request(200, 100)
        button = Gtk.Button.new_with_label("Create a Folder ...")
        button.connect("clicked", self.on_button_clicked, self)
        self.add(button)

    def on_button_clicked(self, button, parentwin):
        dialog = Gtk.FileChooserDialog(title="Create a Folder ...",
                                       parent=parentwin,
                                       action=Gtk.FileChooserAction.SAVE,
                                       buttons=("_Cancel",
                                                    Gtk.ResponseType.CANCEL,
                                       "_Ok", Gtk.ResponseType.OK))
        response = dialog.run()
        if response == Gtk.ResponseType.OK:
            filename = dialog.get_filename()
            print("Creating directory: %s\n" % filename)
        dialog.destroy()

class Application(Gtk.Application):

    def __init__(self, *args, **kwargs):
        super().__init__(*args, application_id="org.example.myapp",
                         **kwargs)
        self.window = None

    def do_activate(self):
        if not self.window:
            self.window = AppWindow(application=self, title="Create Folder")
        self.window.show_all()
        self.window.present()

if __name__ == "__main__":
    app = Application()
    app.run(sys.argv)
```

The full folder name of the dialog can be retrieved by using the same function that retrieved the file name in the previous example, get_filename(). The standard os. mkdir() method from the os module creates a folder in the specified location on all supported operating systems.

Selecting Multiple Files

Figure 6-7 shows a standard file chooser dialog that allows the user to choose a file. The difference between Gtk.FileChooserDialog and Gtk.FileChooserButton using the Gtk.FileChooserAction.OPEN type is that dialogs are capable of selecting multiple files while buttons are restricted to one file.

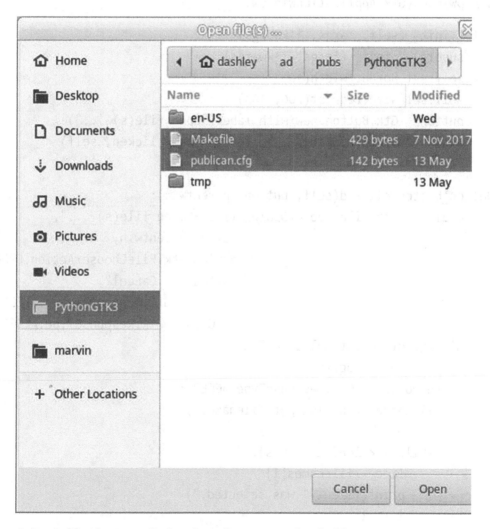

Figure 6-7. *A file chooser dialog for selecting multiple files*

Listing 6-8 shows you how to handle multiple file selections. It is very similar to single file selections except for the fact that selections are returned in a Python list.

Listing 6-8. Using A Gtk.FileChooserDialog to Select Multiple Files

```python
#!/usr/bin/python3

import sys
import gi
gi.require_version('Gtk', '3.0')
from gi.repository import Gtk

class AppWindow(Gtk.ApplicationWindow):

    def __init__(self, *args, **kwargs):
        super().__init__(*args, **kwargs)
        self.set_border_width(10)
        self.set_size_request(200, 100)
        button = Gtk.Button.new_with_label("Open file(s) ...")
        button.connect("clicked", self.on_button_clicked, self)
        self.add(button)

    def on_button_clicked(self, button, parentwin):
        dialog = Gtk.FileChooserDialog(title="Open file(s) ...",
                                       parent=parentwin,
                                       action=Gtk.FileChooserAction.OPEN,
                                       buttons=("_Cancel",
                                                Gtk.ResponseType.CANCEL,
                                        "_Open", Gtk.ResponseType.ACCEPT))
        dialog.set_select_multiple(True)
        response = dialog.run()
        if response == Gtk.ResponseType.ACCEPT:
            filenames = dialog.get_filenames()
            i = 0
            while i < len(filenames):
                file = filenames[i]
                print(file + " was selected.")
                i += 1
        dialog.destroy()
```

```
class Application(Gtk.Application):

    def __init__(self, *args, **kwargs):
        super().__init__(*args, application_id="org.example.myapp",
                          **kwargs)
        self.window = None

    def do_activate(self):
        if not self.window:
            self.window = AppWindow(application=self, title="Open Nultiple
            Files")
        self.window.show_all()
        self.window.present()

if __name__ == "__main__":
    app = Application()
    app.run(sys.argv)
```

The get_filenames() function returns a Python list of the selected file(s).

```
filenames = dialog.get_filenames()
```

Color Selection Dialogs

In the previous chapter, you learned about the Gtk.ColorButton widget, which allowed
the user to select a color. After clicking that button, the user was presented with a dialog.
Although not specified at the time, that dialog was a Gtk.ColorSelectionDialog widget.

Similar to Gtk.FileChooserDialog, the color selection dialog is actually a Gtk.
Dialog container with a Gtk.ColorSelection widget packed as its child widget. Gtk.
ColorSelection can easily be used on its own. However, since a dialog is a natural way
of presenting the widget, GTK+ provides Gtk.ColorSelectionDialog. A color selection
dialog is shown in Figure 6-8.

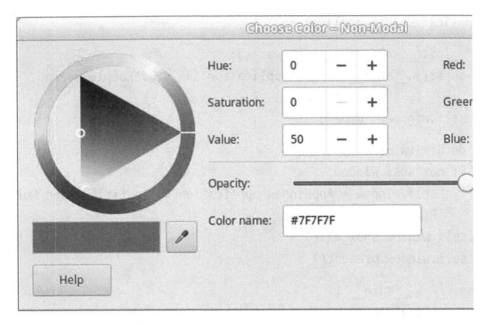

Figure 6-8. *A file chooser dialog for selecting multiple files*

Listing 6-9 contains a top-level window that has two buttons. When the first button is clicked, a modal Gtk.ColorSelectionDialog is created. The other button creates a nonmodal Gtk.ColorSelectionDialog. Each chooses global color and opacity values.

This example also loops through program arguments, setting the initial color value if provided. This allows you to pass an initial color when launching the application.

Listing 6-9. Using a Gtk.ColorSelectionDialog

```
#!/usr/bin/python3

import sys
import gi
gi.require_version('Gtk', '3.0')
from gi.repository import Gtk, Gdk

global_color = Gdk.RGBA(red=.50, green=.50, blue=.50,
alpha=1.0).to_color() global_alpha = 65535

class AppWindow(Gtk.ApplicationWindow):
```

```python
    def __init__(self, *args, **kwargs):
        super().__init__(*args, **kwargs)
        self.set_border_width(10)
        self.set_size_request(200, 100)
        modal = Gtk.Button.new_with_label("Modal")
        nonmodal = Gtk.Button.new_with_label("Non-Modal")
        modal.connect("clicked", self.on_run_color_selection_dialog,
                        self, True)
        nonmodal.connect("clicked", self.on_run_color_selection_dialog,
                        self, False)
        hbox = Gtk.Box(orientation=Gtk.Orientation.HORIZONTAL, spacing=0)
        hbox.pack_start(modal, False, False, 5)
        hbox.pack_start(nonmodal, False, False, 5)
        self.add(hbox)

    def on_dialog_response(self, dialog, result):
        if result == Gtk.ResponseType.OK:
            colorsel = dialog.get_color_selection()
            alpha = colorsel.get_current_alpha()
            color = colorsel.get_current_color()
            print(color.to_string())
            global_color = color
            global_alpha = alpha
        dialog.destroy()

    def on_run_color_selection_dialog(self, button, window, domodal):
        if domodal:
            title = ("Choose Color -- Modal")
        else:
            title = ("Choose Color -- Non-Modal")
        dialog = Gtk.ColorSelectionDialog(title=title, parent=window,
                                            modal=domodal)
        colorsel = dialog.get_color_selection()
        colorsel.set_has_opacity_control(True)
        colorsel.set_current_color(global_color)
        dialog.connect("response", self.on_dialog_response)
        dialog.show_all()
```

```
class Application(Gtk.Application):

    def __init__(self, *args, **kwargs):
        super().__init__(*args, application_id="org.example.myapp",
                         **kwargs)
        self.window = None

    def do_activate(self):
        if not self.window:
            self.window = AppWindow(application=self,
                                    title="Color Selection Dialog")
            self.window.show_all()
            self.window.present()

if __name__ == "__main__":
    app = Application()
    app.run(sys.argv)
```

The only function provided by the Gtk.ColorSelectionDialog class is Gtk. ColorSelectionDialog(). The following code can get the selected color.

```
alpha = colorsel.get_current_alpha()
color = colorsel.get_current_color()
print(color.to_string())
```

Gtk.ColorSelectionDialog provides direct access to its four available child widgets. The first, colorsel is the Gtk.ColorSelection widget that facilitates color selection. The other three are an OK button, a Cancel button, and a Help button. By default, the Help button is hidden. You can use show() or the show_all() method to set it visible.

As with Listing 6-2, this example connects to the response signal, which receives all of the response identifiers regardless of whether the dialog is modal or nonmodal. The dialog is set as modal or nonmodal with the "modal" keyword on the insanitation of the Gtk.ColorSelectionDialog class.

```
Gtk.ColorSelectionDialog(title=title, parent=window, modal=domodal)
```

Listing 6-9 shows a fourth color property apart from its RGB values, its opacity (alpha value). Ranging between 0 and 65,535, this value regulates how transparent the color is drawn, where 0 is fully transparent and 65,535 is opaque. By default, the opacity control is turned off within color selection widgets. You can call the method set_has_opacity_ control() to enable the feature.

colorsel.set_has_opacity_control(boolean)

When opacity is turned on, the hexadecimal color value is sixteen digits long, four digits for each of the values: red, green, blue, and alpha. You must use colorsel.get_ current_alpha() to retrieve its value from the color selection widget.

Font Selection Dialogs

The font selection dialog is a dialog that allows the user to select a font and is the dialog shown when a Gtk.FontButton button is clicked. As with Gtk. ColorSelectionDialog, direct access to the action area buttons is provided through the Gtk.FontSelectionDialog structure. An example font selection dialog is shown in Figure 6-9, which should look similar to the one you saw in the last chapter.

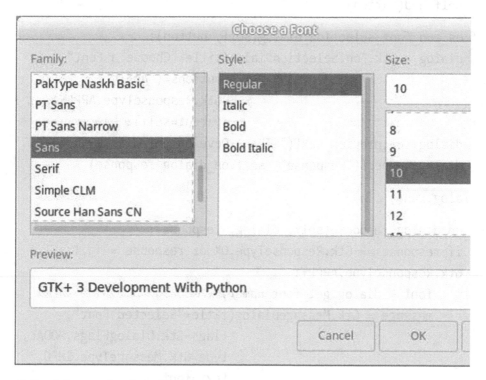

Figure 6-9. *A font selection dialog*

Figure 6-9 is the result of running Listing 6-10.

Listing 6-10. Using a Gtk.FontSelectionDialog

```python
#!/usr/bin/python3

import sys
import gi
gi.require_version('Gtk', '3.0')
from gi.repository import Gtk

class AppWindow(Gtk.ApplicationWindow):

    def __init__(self, *args, **kwargs):
        super().__init__(*args, **kwargs)
        self.set_border_width(10)
        self.set_size_request(200, 100)
        button = Gtk.Button.new_with_label("Run Font Selection Dialog")
        button.connect("clicked", self.on_run_font_selection_dialog)
        self.add(button)

    def on_run_font_selection_dialog(self, button):
        dialog = Gtk.FontSelectionDialog(title="Choose a Font",
                                         buttons=("Apply",
                                         Gtk.ResponseType.APPLY),
                                         parent=self)
        dialog.set_preview_text("GTK+ 3 Development With Python")
        dialog.connect("response", self.on_dialog_response)

      dialog.run()

    def on_dialog_response(self, dialog, response):
        if response == Gtk.ResponseType.OK or response ==
        Gtk.ResponseType.APPLY:
            font = dialog.get_font_name()
            message = Gtk.MessageDialog(title="Selected Font",
                                        flags=Gtk.DialogFlags.MODAL,
                                        type=Gtk.MessageType.INFO,
                                        text=font,
                                        buttons=("Ok", Gtk.ResponseType.OK),
                                        parent=dialog);
```

```
            message.run()
            message.destroy()
            if response == Gtk.ResponseType.OK:
                dialog.destroy()
        else:
            dialog.destroy()

class Application(Gtk.Application):

    def __init__(self, *args, **kwargs):
        super().__init__(*args, application_id="org.example.myapp",
                         **kwargs)
        self.window = None

    def do_activate(self):
        if not self.window:
            self.window = AppWindow(application=self,
                                title="Font Selection Dialog")
        self.window.show_all()
        self.window.present()

if __name__ == "__main__":
    app = Application()
    app.run(sys.argv)
```

The font selection dialog initialization function, `Gtk.FontSelectionDialog()`, returns a new `Gtk.FontSelectionDialog` widget with the specified title.

The dialog itself contains three buttons: OK, Apply, and Cancel. They emit the `Gtk.ResponseType.OK`, `Gtk.ResponseType.APPLY`, and `Gtk.ResponseType.CANCEL` signals respectively.

There is no need to create a modal dialog, because the font selection dialog is connected to a response signal.

If the user clicks the OK button, the user is presented with the selected font, and the dialog is destroyed. By clicking Apply, the selected font is presented to the user, but the dialog is not destroyed. This allows you to apply the new font so the user can view the changes without closing the dialog.

The font selection widget contains a `Gtk.Entry` widget that allows the user to preview the font. By default, the preview text is set to "abcdefghijk ABCDEFGHIJK". This is somewhat boring, so I decided to reset it to "GTK+ 3 Development With Python", the title of this book.

The last methods provided by `Gtk.FontSelectionDialog()` allow you to set and retrieve the current font string. The font string used by `dialog.set_font_name()` and `dialog.get_font_name()` is in the same format that we parsed with `Pango.FontDescription` in the previous chapter.

Dialogs with Multiple Pages

With the release of GTK+ 2.10, a widget called `Gtk.Assistant` was introduced. `Gtk.Assistant` makes it easier to create dialogs with multiple stages, because you do not have to programmatically create the whole dialog. This allows you to split otherwise complex dialogs, into steps that guide the user. This functionality is implemented by what are often referred to as *wizards* in various applications.

Figure 6-10 shows the first page of a simple `Gtk.Assistant` widget, which was created using the code in Listing 6-11. This example begins by giving the user general information. The next page will not allow the user to proceed until text is entered in a `Gtk.Entry` widget. The third page will not allow the user to proceed until a `Gtk.CheckButton` button is activated. The fourth page will not let you do anything until the progress bar is filled, and the last page gives a summary of what has happened. This is the general flow that every `Gtk.Assistant` widget should follow.

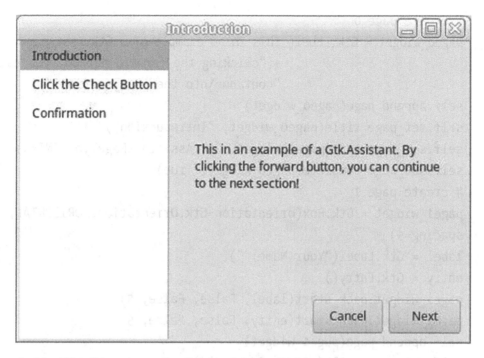

Figure 6-10. *The first page of a Gtk.Assistant widget*

Listing 6-11. The Gtk.Assistant Widget

```python
#!/usr/bin/python3

import sys
import gi
gi.require_version('Gtk', '3.0')
from gi.repository import Gtk
import time

class assistant(Gtk.Assistant):
    progress = None

    def __init__(self, *args, **kwargs):
        super().__init__(*args, **kwargs)
        self.set_size_request(450, 300)
        self.set_title("Gtk.Assistant Example")
        self.connect("destroy", Gtk.main_quit, None)
```

```
# create page 0
page0_widget = Gtk.Label("This in an example of a Gtk.Assistant. By\n"
                         + "clicking the forward button, you can " +
                         "continue\nto the next section!")
self.append_page(page0_widget)
self.set_page_title(page0_widget, "Introduction")
self.set_page_type(page0_widget, Gtk.AssistantPageType.INTRO)
self.set_page_complete(page0_widget, True)
# create page 1
page1_widget = Gtk.Box(orientation=Gtk.Orientation.HORIZONTAL,
spacing=5)
label = Gtk.Label("Your Name: ")
entry = Gtk.Entry()
page1_widget.pack_start(label, False, False, 5)
page1_widget.pack_start(entry, False, False, 5)
self.append_page(page1_widget)
self.set_page_title(page1_widget, "")
self.set_page_type(page1_widget, Gtk.AssistantPageType.CONTENT)
self.set_page_complete(page1_widget, False)
# create page 2
page2_widget = Gtk.CheckButton.new_with_label("Click me to Continue!")
self.append_page(page2_widget)
self.set_page_title(page2_widget, "Click the Check Button")
self.set_page_type(page2_widget, Gtk.AssistantPageType.CONTENT)
self.set_page_complete(page2_widget, False)
# create page 3
page3_widget = Gtk.Alignment.new(0.5, 0.5, 0.0, 0.0)
button = Gtk.Button.new_with_label("Click Me!")
self.progress = Gtk.ProgressBar()
hbox = Gtk.Box(orientation=Gtk.Orientation.HORIZONTAL, spacing=5)
hbox.pack_start(self.progress, True, False, 5)
hbox.pack_start(button, False, False, 5)
page3_widget.add(hbox)
self.append_page(page3_widget)
self.set_page_title(page3_widget, "Click the Check Button")
self.set_page_type(page3_widget, Gtk.AssistantPageType.PROGRESS)
```

```
        self.set_page_complete(page3_widget, False)
        # create page 4
        page4_widget = Gtk.Label("Text has been entered in the label and
        the\n" + "combo box is clicked. If you are done, then\n"
                                    + "it is time to leave!")
        self.append_page(page4_widget)
        self.set_page_title(page4_widget, "Confirmation")
        self.set_page_type(page4_widget, Gtk.AssistantPageType.CONFIRM)
        self.set_page_complete(page4_widget, True)
        # set up the callbacks
        entry.connect("changed",self.entry_changed)
        # page2_widget.connect("toggled",self.button_toggle)
        button.connect("clicked", self.button_clicked)
        self.connect("cancel", self.assistant_canceled)
        self.connect("close", self.assistant_close)

    def entry_changed(self, entry):
        text = entry.get_text()
        num = self.get_current_page()
        page = self.get_nth_page(num)
        self.set_page_complete(page, len(text) > 0)

    def button_toggled(self, toggle):
        active = toggle.get_active()
        self.set_page_complete(toggle, active)

    def button_clicked(self, button):
        percent = 0.0
        button.set_sensitive(False)
        page = self.get_nth_page(3)
        while (percent <= 100.0):
            message = str(percent) + " complete"
            print(message)
            self.progress.set_fraction(percent / 100.0)
            self.progress.set_text(message)
```

```
            while (Gtk.events_pending()):
                Gtk.main_iteration()
            time.sleep(1)
            percent += 5.0
        self.set_page_complete(page, True)

    def assistant_canceled(self, response):
        self.destroy()

    def assistant_close(self, response):
        print("You would apply your changes
        now!") self.destroy()

class AppWindow(Gtk.ApplicationWindow):
    def __init__(self, *args, **kwargs): super().__init__(*args, **kwargs)
        self.set_border_width(25)
        button = Gtk.Button.new_with_mnemonic("_Open Assistant")
        button.connect("clicked", self.on_start_button_clicked)
        button.set_relief(Gtk.ReliefStyle.NORMAL)
        self.add(button)
        self.set_size_request(200, 100)

    def on_start_button_clicked(self, button):
        assistant()

class Application(Gtk.Application):

    def __init__(self, *args, **kwargs):
        super().__init__(*args, application_id="org.example.myapp", **kwargs)
        self.window = None

def do_activate(self):
    if not self.window:
        self.window = AppWindow(application=self, title="Gtk.Assistant")
    self.window.show_all()
    self.window.present()

if __name__ == "__main__":
    app = Application()
    app.run(sys.argv)
```

Creating Gtk.Assistant Pages

A Gtk.Assistant widget is a dialog with multiple pages, although it is actually not derived from Gtk.Dialog. By calling Gtk.Assistant(), you create a new Gtk.Assistant widget with no initial pages.

```
index = assistant.append_page(widget)
```

There is no actual page widget for assistants, because each page is actually a child widget that is added with assistant.prepend_page(), assistant.append_page(), or assistant.insert_page(). Each of these functions accepts the child widget (added as the contents of the page) and returns the new page's index. Each page has a number of properties that can be set, each of which is optional. A list of these options follows.

- *Page title*: Every page should have a title, so the user knows what it is for. Your first page should be an introductory page that tells the user information about the assistant. The last page must be a summary or confirmation page that makes sure the user is ready to apply the previous changes.

- *Header image*: In the top panel, you can display an optional image to the left of the title. This is often the application's logo or an image that complements the assistant's purpose.

- *Side image*: This optional image is placed along the left side of the assistant beside the main page content. It is used for aesthetic appeal.

- *Page type*: The page type must always be set, or it defaults to Gtk.AssistantPageType.CONTENT. The last page must always be a confirmation or summary page. You should also make the first page an introductory page that gives the user information about what task the assistant performs.

After you have set the page's properties, you must choose what type of page it is. There are five types of pages. The first page should always be Gtk.AssistantPageType. INTRO. The last page should always be Gtk.AssistantPageType.CONFIRM or Gtk.AssistantPageType.SUMMARY—if your assistant does not end with one of those two types of pages, it will not work correctly. All the available page types are described in the following list.

- Gtk.AssistantPageType.CONTENT: This type of page has general content, which means it is used for almost every page in the assistant. It should never be used for the last page in an assistant.

- Gtk.AssistantPageType.INTRO: This type of page has introductory information for the user. This should only be set for the first page in the assistant. Although not required, introductory pages give the user direction; they should be used in most assistants.

- Gtk.AssistantPageType.CONFIRM: The page allows the user to confirm or deny a set of changes. It is typically used for changes that cannot be undone or may cause something to break if not set correctly. This should only be set for the last page of the assistant.

- Gtk.AssistantPageType.SUMMARY: The page gives a summary of the changes that have occurred. This should only be set for the last page of the assistant.

- Gtk.AssistantPageType.PROGRESS: When a task takes a long time to complete, this blocks the assistant until the page is marked as complete. The difference between this page and a normal content page is that all of the buttons are disabled and the user is prevented from closing the assistant.

Caution   If you do not set the last page type as Gtk.AssistantPageType. CONFIRM or Gtk.AssistantPageType.SUMMARY, your application will abort with a GTK+ error when computing the last button state.

Since Gtk.Assistant is not derived from Gtk.Dialog, you cannot use dialog.run() (or any other Gtk.Dialog method) on this widget. Instead, the following four signals are provided for you to handle button-clicked signals.

- "apply": This signal is emitted when the Apply button or Forward button clicks any assistant page.

- "cancel": This signal is emitted when the Cancel button clicks any assistant page.

- "close": This signal is emitted when the Close button or Apply button on the last page in the assistant is clicked.

- "prepare": Before making a new page visible, this signal is emitted so that you can do any preparation work before it is visible to the user.

You can connect to all Gtk.Assistant signals with assistant.connect() or any other signal connection function provided by GLib. Excluding "prepare", the callback methods for Gtk.Assistant signals receive the assistant and the user data parameter. The callback method for the prepare signal also accepts the child widget of the current page.

By default, every page is set as incomplete. You have to manually set each page as complete when the time is right with assistant.set_page_complete() or the Gtk.Assistant will not be able to proceed to the next page.

```
assistant.set_page_complete(page, boolean)
```

On every page, a Cancel button is displayed in addition to a few others. On pages other than the first one, a Back button is displayed that is always sensitive. This allows you to visit the previously displayed page and make changes.

Note   The page that is visited when the user clicks the Back button is not always the previous page according to the page index. It is the previously displayed page, which may be different based on how you defined the page flow of your assistant.

On every page except the last, a Forward button is placed, which allows the user to move to the next page. On the last page, an Apply button is displayed that allows the user to apply the changes. However, until the page is set as complete, the assistant sets the Forward or Apply button as insensitive. This allows you to prevent the user from proceeding until some action is taken.

In Listing 6-11, the first and last pages of the assistant were set as complete, because they were merely informative pages. This is the case in most assistants, since they should begin with an introduction page and end with a confirmation or summary page.

The other two pages are where it becomes interesting. On the second page, we want to make sure that the user cannot proceed until text is entered in the Gtk.Entry widget. It would seem that we should just check when text has been inserted and be done with it.

However, what happens if the user deletes all of the text? In this case, the forward button should be disabled yet again. To handle both of these actions, you can use Gtk.Editable's changed signal. This allows you to check the current state of the text in the entry upon every change, as in Listing 6-11.

On the third page, we want to enable the forward button only when the check button is active. To do this, we used the toggled signal of Gtk.ToggleButton to check the current state of the check button. Based on this state, the forward button's sensitivity was set.

The fourth page has a type of Gtk.AssistantPageType.PROGRESS, which disables all actions until the page is set as complete. The user is instructed to click a button, which begins the process of filling a Gtk.ProgressBar widget 10 percent every second. When the progress bar is filled, the page is set as complete.

Gtk.ProgressBar

The Gtk.Assistant example introduced another new widget called Gtk.ProgressBar. Progress bars are a simple way to show how much of a process has been completed and is useful for processes that take a long time to handle. Progress bars give the user a visual cue that progress is being made, so they do not think the program has frozen.

New progress bars are created with Gtk.ProgressBar(). The implementation of Gtk.ProgressBar was made a lot simpler with the release of GTK+ 2.0, so be careful when using the API documentation, because a number of the displayed functions and properties are depreciated. The two examples following show you how to correctly use the Gtk.ProgressBar widget.

```
percent = 0.0
button.set_sensitive(False)
page = self.get_nth_page(3)
while (percent <= 100.0):
    message = str(percent) + " complete"
    print(message)
```

```
self.progress.set_fraction(percent / 100.0)
self.progress.set_text(message)
while (Gtk.events_pending()):
    Gtk.main_iteration()
time.sleep(1)
percent += 5.0
```

You may also want to display text that can complement the progress bar. In the preceding example, `progress.set_text()` displayed the percent complete statistic, which is superimposed on the progress bar widget.

If you are not able to detect the progress of the process, you can use pulses. In the preceding example, `progress.pulse()` moved the progress bar one step for every pending event that was processed. You can set the pulse step with `progress.set_pulse_step()`.

```
progress.set_pulse_step(0.1)
while (Gtk.events_pending ()):
    Gtk.main_iteration()
    progress.pulse()
```

By setting the pulse step to 0.1, the progress bar fills up in the first ten steps and clears itself in the next ten. This process continues for as long as you continue pulsing the progress bar.

Page Forward Methods

There are times that you may want to skip to specific assistant pages if conditions are correct. For example, let's assume your application is creating a new project. Depending on the chosen language, you want to jump to either the third or fourth page. In this case, you want to define your own `Gtk.AssistantPageFunc` method for forward motion.

You can use `assistant.set_forward_page_func()` to define a new page forward function for the assistant. By default, GTK+ increments directly through the pages in order, one page at a time. By defining a new forward function, you can define the flow.

```
assistant.set_forward_page_func(page_func, data)
```

For example, `assistant_forward()` is a simple `Gtk.AssistantPageFunc` implementation that moves from page two to either three or four, depending on the condition returned by `decide_next_page()`.

```
def assistant_forward(self, current_page, data):
    next_page = 0;
    if current_page == 0:
        next_page = 1
    elif current_page == 1:
        next_page = (decide_next_page() ? 2 : 3)
    elif current_page == 2 or current_page == 3:
        next_page = 4
    else:
        next_page = -1
    return next_page
```

Note   By returning −1 from a page forward function, the user is presented with a critical error and the assistant will not move to another page. The critical error message will tell the user that the page flow is broken.

In the `assistant.forward()` method, flow is changed based on the Boolean value returned by the fictional function `decide_next_page()`. In either case, the last page is page 4. If the current page is not within bounds, −1 is returned, so an exception is thrown by GTK+.

While this `Gtk.Assistant` example is very simple, implementations of this widget can become very complex as they expand in number of pages. This widget could be re-created with a dialog, a `Gtk.Notebook` with hidden tabs, and a few buttons. (I have had to do that very thing multiple times!), but it makes the process a lot easier.)

Test Your Understanding

In the exercise for this chapter, you are creating custom dialogs of your own. Each of the dialogs is an implementation of a type of file chooser dialog. However, you are embedding a `Gtk.FileChooserWidget` into a `Gtk.Dialog` to re-create the functionality of the built-in dialogs.

Exercise 1: Implementing File Chooser Dialogs

In this exercise, you create a window with four buttons. Each button opens a different dialog when clicked, which implements one of the four Gtk.FileChooser actions. You should use Gtk.FileChooserWidget added to Gtk.Dialog instead of the prebuilt Gtk.FileChooserDialog.

- Your dialog implements a Gtk.FileChooserAction.SAVE file chooser dialog. The chosen file name should be printed to the screen.

- Your dialog implements a Gtk.FileChooserAction.CREATE_FOLDER file chooser dialog. The new folder name should be printed to the screen. You have to manually create the new folder with a Python function.

- Your dialog implements a Gtk.FileChooserAction.OPEN file chooser dialog. The chosen file names should be printed to the screen.

- Your dialog implements a Gtk.FileChooserAction.SELECT_FOLDER file chooser dialog. The chosen folder path should be printed to the screen.

You need to set each of the dialogs to a decent size so that the entire content is visible to the user. If you get stuck during this exercise, you can find a solution in Appendix D.

Summary

In this chapter, you learned how to create your own custom dialogs. To do this, you need to first initialize the dialog. Then, action area buttons need to be added as well as the main content to the dialog's vertical Gtk.Box.

Dialogs can be created as modal or nonmodal. A modal dialog created with dialog.run() blocks the user from interacting with the parent window until it is destroyed by creating a main loop for the dialog. It also centers the dialog above its parent window. Nonmodal dialogs allow the user to interact with any other window in the application and will not force focus on the dialog.

After learning about the built-in dialogs, you learned about multiple types of built-in dialogs provided by GTK+.

- *Message dialog* (Gtk.MessageDialog): Provides a general message, error message, warning, or simple yes/no question to the user.

- *About dialog* (Gtk.AboutDialog): Shows information about the application, including version, copyright, license, authors, and others.

- *File chooser dialog* (Gtk.FileChooserDialog): Allows the user to choose a file, choose multiple files, save a file, choose a directory, or create a directory.

- *Color selection dialog* (Gtk.ColorSelectionDialog): Allows the user to choose a color along with an optional opacity value.

- *Font selection dialog* (Gtk.FontSelectionDialog): Allows the user to choose a font and its size and style properties.

The last section of this chapter showed you a widget called Gtk.Assistant, which was introduced in GTK+ 2.10. It allows you to create dialogs with multiple stages. It is important to note that assistants are not actually a type of Gtk.Dialog widget but are directly derived from the Gtk.Window class. This means that you have to handle these by connecting signals in the main loop instead of calling dialog.run().

You now have a firm understanding of many important aspects of GTK+. The Chapter 9 explains the multiline text entry widget called Gtk.TextView. Other topics include the clipboard and the Gtk.SourceView library.

CHAPTER 7

Python and GTK+

Now that you have a reasonable grasp of GTK+ and a number of simple widgets, it is time to move to the details of how Python and GTK+ work together. We also cover other Python aspects that will be useful for your projects, as well as some useful PGObject libraries.

Although this book is not a comprehensive guide to Python, we examine several topics used by GTK+ that are not usually covered by basic Python programming guides.

Arguments and Keyword Arguments

Keyword parameters and arguments are used throughout the GTK+ library to pass class instance property values from class to subclass to subclass, and so on. So let's examine this phenomenon closely.

The most important thing to understand about GTK+ class properties is that they are implemented as Python properties in PyGTK. This means that a reference to a property class and methods should be replaced as a standard Python class and methods when accessed. The following example shows how to access the Gtk.Window property named title.

```
win = Gtk.Window()
title = win.props.title
```

The property can also be set using standard Python methods.

```
win = Gtk.Window()
win.props.title = "My Main Window"
```

Of course, the Gtk.Window class also supplies the get_title() and set_title() methods to perform the same tasks, but the shortcut Python methods also perform the same tasks. The choice as to which methods you use is entirely up to you.

© W. David Ashley and Andrew Krause 2019
W. D. Ashley and A. Krause, *Foundations of PyGTK Development*,
https://doi.org/10.1007/978-1-4842-4179-0_7

Now that you understand that GTK+ properties are implemented as Python properties, we can move on to describing how to use and pass keyword arguments to classes. Let's continue looking at Gtk.Window and how you create instances of that class. The class definition for Gtk.Window looks like this:

```
class Gtk.Window(Gtk.Bin):
    def __init__(self, *args, **kwargs):
        super().__init__(*args, **kwargs)
```

So, what are these *args and **kwargs arguments/parameters and what do they do? PyGTK uses this methodology to pass property names and values to class instances. When a class instance receives these arguments, it has the choice to use them, pass them on to the super class, or simply throw them away. Most of the time, it uses the ones that match the properties that the class defines. It then locates the corresponding value and assigns it to the corresponding property name. It does this task using code similar to the code in Listing 7-1.

Listing 7-1. Keyword Arguments

```
class MyWindow(Gtk.Window):
    def __init__(self, *args, **kwargs):
        super().__init__(*args, **kwargs)
        for arg in argv:
            print("Another arg through *argv :",arg) for kw in keywords:
            print(kw, ":", keywords[kw])
```

Not shown in the example are formal arguments. There is a required order for arguments: formal arguments must all appear first in the argument list, followed by all args arguments, and finally, by all the keyword arguments. The following example shows the formal declaration for how this must work.

```
function(formal_args, args, kwargs)
```

The following are calling statements that use formal arguments, variable arguments, and keyword arguments.

```
# function using formal and variable args def function1(title, modal, *args):
```

```
# calling function1
function1("My title", False, # variable args follow
         "Peaches", "and", "Cream")
function1("My Window", True) # Only formal args, no variable args
function1(True)                # Invalid!!! Missing one formal arg
```

```
# function using formal and keyword args def function2(title, modal, **kwargs)
```

```
# calling function2
function2("My title", True, parent=window, accept_focus=True) function2("My
Window", False) # Only formal args, no keyword args
function2(parent=window)      # Invalid, no formal args
```

There are many other variations of these examples, but if you follow these three simple rules, you should have no problem coping with all the variations:

- Formal arguments must all appear in the argument list first. If there are no formal arguments, then they can be absent from the argument list. There can be as many formal arguments as you need.

- Variable arguments must all appear next in the argument list. If there are no variable arguments, then they can be absent from the argument list. There can be as many variable arguments as you need.

- Keyword arguments must all appear last in the argument list. If there are no keyword arguments, then they can be absent from the argument list. There can be as many keyword arguments as you need.

PyGTK rarely uses formal arguments; it uses variable and keyword arguments almost exclusively. This makes it a little easier to cope with instantiating all the GTK+ classes. Just remember that GTK+ ignores any keyword arguments that are *not* also property names. This is very useful when you want to establish and manage your own properties.

Logging

Logging tracks events that happen when software runs. The software developer adds logging calls to their code to indicate that certain events have occurred. An event is described by a descriptive message that can optionally contain variable data (i.e., data that is potentially different for each occurrence of the event). Events also have an importance that the developer ascribes to the event; the importance can also be called the *level* or *severity*.

When to Use Logging

Logging provides a set of convenience functions for simple logging usage. These are debug(), info(), warning(), error(), and critical(). Table 7-1 describes when to use logging for common tasks and the best tool to use for each task.

Table 7-1. *Logging Tasks*

Task You Want to Perform	Best Tool for the Task
Display console output for ordinary use of a command-line script or program	`print()`
Report events that occur during normal operation of a program (e.g., status monitoring or fault investigation)	`logging.info()` (or `logging.debug()` for very detailed output for diagnostic purposes)
Issue a warning for a particular runtime event	`logging.warning()` if there is nothing the client application can do about the situation, but the event should still be noted
Report an error for a particular runtime event	Raise an exception
Report suppression of an error without raising an exception (e.g., error handler in a long-running server process)	`logging.error()`, `logging.exception()` or `logging.critical()` as appropriate for the specific error and application domain

The logging functions are named after the level or severity of the events that they track. The standard levels and their applicability are described in Table 7-2 (in increasing order of severity).

Table 7-2. *Logging Levels*

Level	When It's Used
DEBUG	Detailed information, typically of interest only when diagnosing problems.
INFO	Confirmation that things are working as expected.
WARNING	An indication that something unexpected happened, or indicative of some problem in the near future (e.g., disk space low). The software is still working as expected.
ERROR	Due to a more serious problem, the software has not been able to perform a function.
CRITICAL	A serious error indicating that the program itself may be unable to continue running.

The default level is WARNING, which means that only events of this level and above will be tracked, unless the logging package is configured to do otherwise.

Events that are tracked can be handled in different ways. The simplest way of handling tracked events is to print them to the console. Another common way is to write them to a disk file.

Some Simple Examples

The following is a very simple example.

```
import logging

logging.warning('Watch out!') # will print a message to the console
logging.info('I told you so') # will not print anything
```

If you type these lines into a script and run it, you see the following printed on the console.

```
WARNING:root:Watch out!
```

The INFO message doesn't appear because the default level is WARNING. The printed message includes the indication of the level and the description of the event provided in the logging call (i.e., Watch out!). Don't worry about the "root" part for now; it is explained later. The actual output can be formatted quite flexibly if you need that; formatting options are also explained later.

Logging to a File

Recording logging events in a file is a very common, so let's look at that next. Be sure to try the following in a newly started Python interpreter; don't just continue from the session described earlier.

```python
import logging

logging.basicConfig(filename='example.log',level=logging.DEBUG)
logging.debug('This message should go to the log file')
logging.info('So should this')
logging.warning('And this, too')
```

And now if we open the file and look at what we have, we should find the log messages.

```
DEBUG:root:This message should go to the log file INFO:root:So should this
WARNING:root:And this, too
```

This example also shows how you can set the logging level, which acts as the threshold for tracking. In this case, because we set the threshold to DEBUG, all of the messages were printed.

If you want to set the logging level from a command-line option, such as

```
--log=INFO
```

and you have the value of the parameter passed for `--log` in a `loglevel` variable, you can use

```
getattr(logging, loglevel.upper())
```

to get the value, which you pass to `basicConfig()` via the level argument.

You may want to error check any user input value, perhaps as in the following example.

```python
# assuming loglevel is bound to the string value obtained from the
# command line argument. Convert to upper case to allow the user to
# specify --log=DEBUG or --log=debug
numeric_level = getattr(logging, loglevel.upper(), None)
if not isinstance(numeric_level, int):
    raise ValueError('Invalid log level: %s' % loglevel)
logging.basicConfig(level=numeric_level, ...)
```

The call to `basicConfig()` should come before any calls to `debug()`, `info()`, and so forth. As it's intended as a one-off simple configuration facility, only the first call actually does anything; subsequent calls are effectively no-ops.

If you run the preceding script several times, the messages from successive runs are appended to the `example.log` file. If you want each run to start afresh, not remembering the messages from earlier runs, you can specify the `filemode` argument, by changing the call in the example to this:

```
logging.basicConfig(filename='example.log', filemode='w', level=logging.DEBUG)
```

The output is the same as before, but the log file is no longer appended, so the messages from earlier runs are lost.

Logging from Multiple Modules

If your program consists of multiple modules, the following is an example of how you could organize logging in it.

```
# myapp.py
# import logging
# import mylib

def main():
    logging.basicConfig(filename='myapp.log', level=logging.INFO)
    logging.info('Started')
    mylib.do_something()
    logging.info('Finished')

if __name__ == '__main__':
    main()

# mylib.py
import logging

def do_something():
logging.info('Doing something')
```

If you run `myapp.py`, you should see this in `myapp.log`:

```
INFO:root:Started INFO:root:Doing something INFO:root:Finished
```

This is hopefully what you were expecting to see. You can generalize this to multiple modules using the pattern in `mylib.py`. Note that for this simple usage pattern, apart from looking at the event description, you won't know where in your application your messages came from by looking in the log file. If you want to track the location of your messages, you'll need to refer to the documentation beyond this tutorial level.

Logging Variable Data

To log variable data, use a format string for the event description message and append the variable data as arguments; for example,

```
import logging

logging.warning('%s before you %s', 'Look', 'leap!')
```

displays

```
WARNING:root:Look before you leap!
```

As you can see, merging variable data into the event description message uses the old, %-style of string formatting. This is for backward compatibility; the logging package predates newer formatting options, such as `str.format()` and `string.Template`. These newer formatting options are supported, but exploring them is outside the scope of this book. See the Python documentation for more information.

Changing the Format of Displayed Messages

To change the format that is used to display messages, you need to specify the format you want to use.

```
import logging

logging.basicConfig(format='%(levelname)s:%(message)s', level=logging.DEBUG)
logging.debug('This message should appear on the console')
logging.info('So should this')
logging.warning('And this, too')
```

This should print something like the following.

```
2010-12-12 11:41:42,612 is when this event was logged.
```

The default format for date/time display is ISO8601 or [RFC 3339]. If you need more control over the formatting of the date/time, provide a `datefmt` argument to `basicConfig()`, as follows.

```
import logging
```

```
logging.basicConfig(format='%(asctime)s %(message)s', datefmt='%m/%d/%Y
%I:%M:%S % logging.warning('is when this event was logged.')
```

This displays something like the following.

```
12/12/2010 11:46:36 AM is when this event was logged.
```

The format of the `datefmt` argument is the same as supported by `time.strftime()`.

Exceptions

Running exceptions in GTK+, application are the same as running any standard Python program. Since the GTK module is simply a standard Python module that wraps the GTK+ APIs, the library implementation morphs all GTK+ exceptions into standard Python exceptions. The result of this is that you do not need to worry about catching `Glib.Error` errors. None will ever be thrown by the GTK module.

That does not mean that you can ignore standard Python exceptions. You should plan for any exceptions in your application, just the way you would for any Python application. Let's review some principals of Python exceptions.

Raising Exceptions

Exceptions are raised automatically when something goes wrong in your application. Before we take a look at how to handle an exception, let's take a look at how you can raise exceptions manually—and even create your own kinds of exceptions.

The Raise Statement

You raise an exception with the `raise` statement, which takes an argument that is either a class (which should subclass the `Exception` class) or an instance. When using a class as an argument, an instance of the class is automatically created. The following is an example of using the built-in `Exception` class.

```
>>> raise Exception
Traceback (most recent call last):
  File "<stdin>", line 1, in <module>
Exception
> raise Exception('overload') Traceback (most recent call last):
  File "<stdin>", line 1, in <module> Exception: overload
```

The first example raises a generic exception with no information about what went wrong. The second example added the error message overload.

Many built-in classes are available. A full description of all the exception classes are available in the Python Library Reference in the "Built-in Exceptions" section. The following lists the class hierarchy for all the Python 3.x exceptions.

```
BaseException
 +-- SystemExit
 +-- KeyboardInterrupt
 +-- GeneratorExit
 +-- Exception
      +-- StopIteration
      +-- StopAsyncIteration
      +-- ArithmeticError
      |    +-- FloatingPointError
      |    +-- OverflowError
      |    +-- ZeroDivisionError
      +-- AssertionError
      +-- AttributeError
      +-- BufferError
      +-- EOFError
      +-- ImportError
      |    +-- ModuleNotFoundError
      +-- LookupError
      |    +-- IndexError
      |    +-- KeyError
      +-- MemoryError
      +-- NameError
      |    +-- UnboundLocalError
```

```
+-- OSError
|     +-- BlockingIOError
|     +-- ChildProcessError
|     +-- ConnectionError
|     |     +-- BrokenPipeError
|     |     +-- ConnectionAbortedError
|     |     +-- ConnectionRefusedError
|     |     +-- ConnectionResetError
|     +-- FileExistsError
|     +-- FileNotFoundError
|     +-- InterruptedError
|     +-- IsADirectoryError
|     +-- NotADirectoryError
|     +-- PermissionError
|     +-- ProcessLookupError
|     +-- TimeoutError
+-- ReferenceError
+-- RuntimeError
|     +-- NotImplementedError
|     +-- RecursionError
+-- SyntaxError
|
      +-- IndentationError
|           +-- TabError
+-- SystemError
+-- TypeError
+-- ValueError
|     +-- UnicodeError
|           +-- UnicodeDecodeError
|           +-- UnicodeEncodeError
|           +-- UnicodeTranslateError
```

```
+-- Warning
      +-- DeprecationWarning
      +-- PendingDeprecationWarning
      +-- RuntimeWarning
      +-- SyntaxWarning
      +-- UserWarning
      +-- FutureWarning
      +-- ImportWarning
      +-- UnicodeWarning
      +-- BytesWarning
      +-- ResourceWarning
```

Custom Exception Classes

There are a lot of built-in exceptions that cover a lot of ground. But there times when you might want to create your own exception class. For example, there is no GTK+ exception class, so you might have a need to create your own. This gives you a chance to selectively handle exceptions based on their class. Thus, if you wanted to handle GTK runtime errors, you would need a separate class for the exceptions.

You create such an exception just like you would any other class, but be sure to subclass the Exception class (either directly or indirectly, which means that subclassing any other built-in exception is okay). The following shows how to write a custom exception class.

```
class GtkCustomException)Exception): pass
```

Feel free to add your own methods to class as you need them.

Catching Exceptions

Of course, raising an exception is only the first part of exceptions. The really useful part is catching (or trapping) and handling exceptions in your own application code. You do this with the try and except statements. Let's take a look at a simple example.

```
x = input('Enter the first number: ')
y = input('Enter the second number: ')
print(x/y)
```

This works nicely until the user enters zero as the second number.

```
Enter the first number: 10
Enter the second number: 0
Traceback (most recent call last):
  File "<stdin>", line 3, in <module>
ZeroDivisionError: division by zero
```

To catch the exception and perform some error handling (like printing a more friendly error message), you could rewrite the program like this:

```
try:
    x = input('Enter the first number: ')
    y = input('Enter the second number: ')
    print(x/y)
except ZeroDivisionError:
    print('The second number can not be zero!')
```

Although this solution might seem overblown for such a simple case, when hundreds of division statements are used throughout an application, this would be a more reasonable case.

Note   Exceptions propagate out of functions and methods to where they are called, and if they are not caught there either, the exceptions will "bubble up" to the top level of the program. This means that you can use try and except statements to catch exceptions that are raised in your own and other people's code (modules, function, classes, etc.).

Raising and Reraising Exceptions

Exceptions can be raised inside other exceptions, passing the exception on to a higher level of code. To do this, the subsequent exception must be called without any arguments via the raise statement.

The following is an example of this very useful technique. The example passes the ZeroDivisionException to a higher level of code if the exception is not suppressed.

```python
class SuppressedDivision:
    suppressed = False
    def calc(self, expr):
        try:
            return eval(expr)
        except ZeroDivisionError:
            if self.suppressed:
                print('Division by zero is illegal!')
            else:
                raise
```

As you can see, when the calculation is not suppressed, the ZeroDivisionException is caught but passed on to the higher level of code, where it will be caught and handled.

Catching Multiple Exceptions

The try and except block can also catch and process more than one exception. To see how this works, let's enhance the previous example to catch the TypeError exception.

```python
class SuppressedDivision:
    suppressed = False
    def calc(self, expr):
        try:
            return eval(expr)
        except ZeroDivisionError:
            if self.suppressed:
                print('Division by zero is illegal!')
            else:
                raise
        except TypeError:
            if self.suppressed:
                print('One of the operands was not a valid number!')
            else:
                raise
```

Now we begin to see the power of the `try` and `except` code block and using exceptions. In the preceding example, we are using the interpreter's ability to examine all the variables of the calculation, instead of writing essentially the same code ourselves to process all the variables to find out if the calculation works before we process it.

We can also combine both exceptions into a single block of code, as follows.

```
class SuppressedDivision:
    suppressed = False
    def calc(self, expr):
        try:
            return eval(expr)
        except ZeroDivisionError, TypeError:
            if self.suppressed:
                print('One or both operands is illegal!')
            else:
                raise
```

We can also capture the object that causes the exception.

```
class SuppressedDivision:
    suppressed = False
    def calc(self, expr):
        try:
            return eval(expr)
        except (ZeroDivisionError, TypeError_, e:
            if self.suppressed:
                print('The value "' + str(e) '" is illegal!')
            else:
                raise
```

There is much more to processing exceptions but this information is enough to whet your appetite.

You should consult with your Python resources for more complete information on exceptions.

CHAPTER 8

Text View Widget

This chapter teaches you how to use the Gtk.TextView widget. The text view widget is similar to a Gtk.Entry widget, except it is capable of holding text that spans multiple lines. Scrolled windows allow the document to exist beyond the bounds of the screen.

Before you learn about Gtk.TextView, this chapter begins by introducing a few new widgets. The first two widgets are scrolled windows and viewports. Scrolled windows are composed of two scrollbars that scroll the child widget. A few widgets support scrolling already, including Gtk.Layout, Gtk.TreeView, and Gtk.TextView. For all other widgets that you want to scroll, you need to add them first to a Gtk.Viewport widget, which gives its child widget scrolling abilities.

In this chapter, you learn the following:

- How to use scrolled windows and viewports

- How to use the Gtk.TextView widget and apply text buffers

- The functions that text iterators and text marks perform when dealing with buffers

- Methods for applying styles to the whole or part of a document

- How to cut, copy, and paste to and from the clipboard

- How to insert images and child widgets into a text view

Scrolled Windows

Before you can learn about the Gtk.TextView widget, you need to learn about two container widgets called Gtk.ScrolledWindow and Gtk.Viewport. Scrolled windows use two scrollbars to allow a widget to take up more space than is visible on the screen. This widget allows the Gtk.TextView widget to contain documents that expand beyond the bounds of the window.

© W. David Ashley and Andrew Krause 2019
W. D. Ashley and A. Krause, *Foundations of PyGTK Development*,
https://doi.org/10.1007/978-1-4842-4179-0_8

Both scrollbars in the scrolled window have associated Gtk.Adjustment objects. These adjustments track the current position and range of a scrollbar; however, you will not need to directly access the adjustments in most cases.

A scrollbar's Gtk.Adjustment holds information about scroll bounds, steps, and its current position. The value variable is the current position of the scrollbar between the bounds. This variable must always be between the lower and upper values, which are the bounds of the adjustment. The page_size is the area that can be visible on the screen at one time, depending on the size of the widget. The step_increment and page_increment variables are used for stepping when an arrow is pressed or when the Page Down key is pressed.

Figure 8-1 is a screenshot of the window created with the code in Listing 8-1. Both scrollbars are enabled because the table containing the buttons is larger than the visible area.

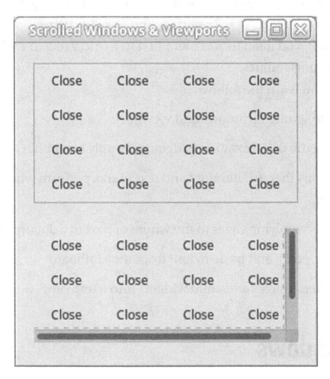

Figure 8-1. *A synchronized scrolled window and viewport*

Listing 8-1 shows how to use scrolled windows and viewports. As a scrollbar moves, the viewport scrolls as well because the adjustments are synchronized. Try to resize the window to see how the scrollbars react to becoming larger and smaller than the child widget.

Listing 8-1. Using Scrolled Windows

```python
#!/usr/bin/python3
import sys
import gi
gi.require_version('Gtk', '3.0')
from gi.repository import Gtk
class AppWindow(Gtk.ApplicationWindow):
    def __init__(self, *args, **kwargs):
        super().__init__(*args, **kwargs)
        self.set_border_width(10)
        grid1 = Gtk.Grid.new()
        grid2 = Gtk.Grid.new()
        grid1.set_column_homogeneous = True
        grid2.set_column_homogeneous = True
        grid1.set_row_homogeneous = True
        grid2.set_row_homogeneous = True
        grid1.set_column_spacing = 5
        grid2.set_column_spacing = 5
        grid1.set_row_spacing = 5
        grid2.set_row_spacing = 5
        i = 0
        while i < 10:
            j = 0
            while j < 10:
                button = Gtk.Button.new_with_label("Close")
                button.set_relief(Gtk.ReliefStyle.NONE)
                button.connect("clicked", self.on_button_clicked)
                grid1.attach(button, i, j, 1, 1)
                button = Gtk.Button.new_with_label("Close")
                button.set_relief(Gtk.ReliefStyle.NONE)
                button.connect("clicked", self.on_button_clicked)
                grid2.attach(button, i, j, 1, 1)
                j += 1
            i += 1
```

```
        swin = Gtk.ScrolledWindow.new(None, None)
        horizontal = swin.get_hadjustment()
        vertical = swin.get_vadjustment()
        viewport = Gtk.Viewport.new(horizontal, vertical)
        swin.set_border_width(5)
        swin.set_propagate_natural_width(True)
        swin.set_propagate_natural_height(True)
        viewport.set_border_width(5)
        swin.set_policy (Gtk.PolicyType.AUTOMATIC, Gtk.PolicyType.AUTOMATIC)
        swin.add_with_viewport(grid1)
        viewport.add(grid2)
        vbox = Gtk.Box.new(Gtk.Orientation.VERTICAL, 5)
        vbox.set_homogeneous = True
        vbox.pack_start(viewport, True, True, 5)
        vbox.pack_start(swin, True, True, 5)
        self.add (vbox)
        self.show_all()
    def on_button_clicked(self, button):
        self.destroy()
class Application(Gtk.Application):
    def __init__(self, *args, **kwargs):
        super().__init__(*args, application_id="org.example.myapp",
                        **kwargs)
        self.window = None
    def do_activate(self):
        if not self.window:
        self.window = AppWindow(application=self,
                title="Scrolled Windows & Viewports")
        self.window.show_all()
        self.window.present()
    if __name__ == "__main__":
        app = Application()
        app.run(sys.argv)
```

Newly scrolled windows are created with `Gtk.ScrolledWindow.new()`. In Listing 8-1 each parameter is set to `None` , which causes the scrolled window to create two default adjustments for you. In most cases, you want to use the default adjustments, but it is also possible to specify your own horizontal and vertical adjustments for the scroll bars.

The adjustments in this example are used when the new viewport is created with `Gtk.Viewport.new()`. The viewport adjustments are initialized with those from the scrolled window, which makes sure that both containers are scrolled at the same time.

As you set up a scrollable window, the first decision you need to make is when the scrollbars will be visible. In this example, `Gtk.PolicyType.AUTOMATIC` was used for both scrollbars so that each is only shown when needed. `Gtk.PolicyType.ALWAYS` is the default policy for both scrollbars. The following are three enumeration values provided by `Gtk.PolicyType`.

- `Gtk.PolicyType.ALWAYS`: The scrollbar is always visible. It is displayed as disabled or grayed out if scrolling is not possible.

- `Gtk.PolicyType.AUTOMATIC`: The scrollbar is only visible if scrolling is possible. If it is not needed, the scrollbar temporarily disappears.

- `Gtk.PolicyType.NEVER`: The scrollbar is never shown.

Another property, although not used by very many applications, is the placement of the scrollbars. In most applications, you want the scrollbars to appear along the bottom and the right side of the widget, which is the default functionality.

However, if you want to change this, you can call `set_placement()`. This function receives a `Gtk.CornerType` value, which defines where the content is placed with respect to the scrollbars. For example, the default value is `Gtk.CornerType.TOP_LEFT`, because the content normally appears above and to the left of the scrollbars.

```
swin.set_placement(window_placement)
```

Available `Gtk.CornerType` values include `Gtk.CornerType.TOP_LEFT`, `Gtk.CornerType.BOTTOM_LEFT`, `Gtk.CornerType.TOP_RIGHT`, and `Gtk.CornerType.BOTTOM_RIGHT`, which define where the content is placed with respect to the scrollbars.

Caution   It is a very rare occasion when `set_placement()` should be used! In almost every possible case, you should not use this function, because it can confuse the user. Unless you have a good reason for changing the placement, use the default value.

It is possible to set the shadow type of the widget with respect to the child widget by calling `set_shadow_type()`.

```
swin.set_shadow_type(type)
```

In Chapter 4, you learned how to use the `Gtk.ShadowType` enumeration along with handle boxes to set the type of border to place around the child widget. The same values as before set the shadow type of a scrolled window.

After you have set up a scrolled window, you should add a child widget for it to be of any use. There are two possible ways to do this, and the method is chosen based on the type of child widget. If you are using a `Gtk.TextView`, `Gtk.TreeView`, `Gtk.IconView`, `Gtk.Viewport`, or `Gtk.Layout` widget, you should use the default `add()` method, since all five of these widgets include native scrolling support.

All other GTK+ widgets do not have native scrolling support. For those widgets, `add_with_viewport()` should be used. This function gives the child scrolling support by first packing it into a container widget called a `Gtk.Viewport`. This widget implements scrolling ability for the child widget that lacks its own support. The viewport is then automatically added to the scrolled window.

Caution   You should never pack `Gtk.TextView`, `Gtk.TreeView`, `Gtk.IconView`, `Gtk.Viewport`, or `Gtk.Layout` widgets into a scrolled window with `add_with_viewport()`, because scrolling may not be performed correctly on the widget!

It is possible to manually add a widget to a new `Gtk.Viewport` and then add that viewport to a scrolled window with `add()`, but the convenience function allows you to ignore the viewport completely.

The scrolled window is simply a container with scrollbars. Neither the container nor the scrollbars perform any action by themselves. Scrolling is handled by the child widget, which is why the child must already have native scrolling support to work correctly with the `Gtk.ScrolledWindow` widget.

When you add a child widget that has scrolling support, a function is called to add adjustments for each axis. Nothing is done unless the child widget has scrolling support, which is why a viewport is required by most widgets. When the scrollbar is clicked and dragged by the user, the value in the adjustment changes, which causes the value-changed signal to be emitted. This action also causes the child widget to render itself accordingly.

Because the Gtk.Viewport widget did not have any scrollbars of its own, it relied completely on the adjustments to define its current position on the screen. The scrollbars are used in the Gtk.ScrolledWindow widget as an easy mechanism for adjusting the current value of the adjustment.

Text Views

The Gtk.TextView widget displays multiple lines of text of a document. It provides many ways to customize the whole of a document or individual portions of it. It is even possible to insert GdkPixbuf objects and child widgets into a document. Gtk.TextView is the first reasonably involved widget you have encountered up to this point, so the rest of this chapter is dedicated to many aspects of the widget. It is a very versatile widget that you need to use in many GTK+ applications.

The first few examples of this chapter may lead you to believe that Gtk.TextView can only display simple documents, but that is not the case. It can also display many types of rich text, word processing, and interactive documents that are used by a wide variety of applications. You learn how to do this in the sections that follow.

Figure 8-2 introduces you to a simple text view window that allows you to enter text and do some basic layout design. But it also does not have many features and is lacking features found in many word processors.

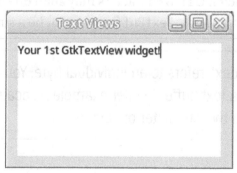

Figure 8-2. *A Gtk.TextView widget*

Text views are used in every type of text and document editing application that uses GTK+. If you have ever used AbiWord, gedit, or most other text editors created for GNOME, you have used the Gtk.TextView widget. It is also used in the Gaim application in instant message windows. (In fact, all the examples in this book were created in the OpenLDev application, which uses Gtk.TextView for source code editing!)

Text Buffers

Each text view displays the contents of a class called Gtk.TextBuffer. Text buffers store the current state of the content within a text view. They hold text, images, child widgets, text tags, and all other information necessary for rendering the document.

A single text buffer is capable of being displayed by multiple text views, but each text view has only one associated buffer. Most programmers do not take advantage of this feature, but it becomes important when you learn how to embed child widgets into a text buffer in a later section.

As with all text widgets in GTK+, text is stored as UTF-8 strings. UTF-8 is a type of character encoding that uses from 1 byte to 4 bytes for every character. To differentiate the number of bytes that a character takes up, "0" always precedes a character that is 1 byte, "110" precedes 2-byte characters, "1110" comes before 3-byte sequences, and so on. UTF-8 characters that span multiple bytes have "10" in the two most significant bits of the rest of the bytes.

By doing this, the basic 128 ASCII characters are still supported, because an additional 7 bits are available in a single-byte character after the initial "0". UTF-8 also provides support for characters in many other languages. This method also avoids small byte sequences occurring within larger byte sequences.

When handling text buffers, you need to know two terms: offset and index. The word "offset" refers to one character. UTF-8 characters may span one or more bytes within the buffer, so a character offset in a Gtk.TextBuffer may not be a single byte long.

Caution   The word "index" refers to an individual byte. You need to be careful when stepping through a text buffer in later examples, because you cannot refer to an index that is between two character offsets.

Listing 8-2 illustrates one of the simplest text view examples you could create. A new Gtk.TextView widget is created. Its buffer is retrieved, and text is inserted into the buffer. A scrolled window then contains the text view.

Listing 8-2. A Simple Gtk.TextView Example

```python
#!/usr/bin/python3
import sys
import gi
gi.require_version('Gtk', '3.0')
from gi.repository import Gtk
class AppWindow(Gtk.ApplicationWindow):
    def __init__(self, *args, **kwargs):
        super().__init__(*args, **kwargs)
        self.set_border_width(10)
        self.set_size_request(250, 150)
        textview = Gtk.TextView.new()
        buffer = textview.get_buffer()
        text = "Your 1st GtkTextView widget!"
        buffer.set_text(text, len(text))
        scrolled_win = Gtk.ScrolledWindow.new (None, None)
        scrolled_win.add(textview)
        self.add(scrolled_win)
class Application(Gtk.Application):
    def __init__(self, *args, **kwargs):
        super().__init__(*args, application_id="org.example.myapp",
                        **kwargs)
        self.window = None
    def do_activate(self):
        if not self.window:
            self.window = AppWindow(application=self, title="Text Views")
        self.window.show_all()
        self.window.present()
    if __name__ == "__main__":
        app = Application()
        app.run(sys.argv)
```

Most new `Gtk.TextView` widgets are created with `Gtk.TextView.new()`. By using this function, an empty buffer is created for you. This default buffer can be replaced later with `set_buffer()` or retrieved with `get_buffer()`.

If you want to set the initial buffer to one that you have already created, you can create the text view with `Gtk.TextView.new_with_buffer()`. In most cases, it is easier to simply use the default text buffer.

Once you have access to a `Gtk.TextBuffer` object, there are many ways to add content, but the easiest method is to call `set_text()`. This function receives a text buffer, a UTF-8 text string to set as the buffer's new text, and the length of the text.

```
set_text(text, length)
```

If the text string is NULL-terminated, you can use –1 as the length of the string. This function silently fails if a null character is found before the specified length of text.

The current contents of the buffer are completely replaced by the new text string. In the "Text Iterators and Marks" section, you are introduced to functions that allow you to insert text into a buffer without overwriting the current content that are more suitable for inserting large amounts of text.

Recall from the previous section that there are five widgets that have native scrolling abilities, including the `Gtk.TextView` widget. Because text views already have the facilities to manage adjustments, `container.add()` should always add them to scrolled windows.

Text View Properties

`Gtk.TextView` was created to be a very versatile widget. Because of this, many properties are provided for the widget. In this section, you learn about a number of these widget properties.

One feature that makes the text view widget extremely useful is that you are able to apply changes to the whole or only an individual part of the widget. Text tags change the properties of a segment of text. Customizing only a part of the document is covered in a later section of this chapter.

Listing 8-3 shows many of the properties that can customize the contents of `Gtk.TextBuffer`. You should note that many of these properties could be overridden in individual sections of a document with text tags.

Listing 8-3. Using Gtk.TextView Properties

```python
#!/usr/bin/python3
import sys
import gi
gi.require_version('Gtk', '3.0')
from gi.repository import Gtk, Pango
class AppWindow(Gtk.ApplicationWindow):
    def __init__(self, *args, **kwargs):
        super().__init__(*args, **kwargs)
        self.set_border_width(10)
        self.set_size_request(260, 150)
        font = Pango.font_description_from_string("Monospace Bold 10")
        textview = Gtk.TextView.new()
        textview.modify_font(font)
        textview.set_wrap_mode(Gtk.WrapMode.WORD)
        textview.set_justification(Gtk.Justification.RIGHT)
        textview.set_editable(True)
        textview.set_cursor_visible(True)
        textview.set_pixels_above_lines(5)
        textview.set_pixels_below_lines(5)
        textview.set_pixels_inside_wrap(5)
        textview.set_left_margin(10)
        textview.set_right_margin(10)
        buffer = textview.get_buffer()
        text = "This is some text!\nChange me!\nPlease!"
        buffer.set_text(text, len(text))
        scrolled_win = Gtk.ScrolledWindow.new(None, None)
        scrolled_win.set_policy(Gtk.PolicyType.AUTOMATIC,
                                Gtk.PolicyType.ALWAYS)
        scrolled_win.add(textview)
        self.add(scrolled_win)
```

```
class Application(Gtk.Application):
    def __init__(self, *args, **kwargs):
        super().__init__(*args, application_id="org.example.myapp",
                         **kwargs)
        self.window = None
    def do_activate(self):
        if not self.window:
            self.window = AppWindow(application=self,
                                    title="Text Views Properties")
        self.window.show_all()
        self.window.present()
    if __name__ == "__main__":
        app = Application()
        app.run(sys.argv)
```

The best way to explain what each of Gtk.TextView's properties does is to show you a screenshot of the result, which can be viewed in Figure 8-3. You should compile the application on your own machine and try changing the values used in Listing 8-3 to get a feel for what they do as well.

Figure 8-3. *Gtk.TextView with nondefault properties*

It is possible to change the font and colors of individual parts of the text view content, but as shown in Listing 8-3 it is still possible to use the functions from past chapters to change the content of the whole widget. This is useful when editing documents that have a consistent style, such as text files.

When dealing with a widget that displays text on multiple lines, you need to decide if and how text is wrapped. In Listing 8-3 the wrap mode was set to Gtk.WrapMode.WORD with set_wrap_mode(). This setting wraps the text but does not split a word over two lines. There are four types of wrap modes available in the Gtk.WrapMode enumeration.

- Gtk.WrapMode.NONE: No wrapping occurs. If a scrolled window contains the view, the scrollbar expands; otherwise, the text view expands on the screen. If a scrolled window does not contain the Gtk.TextView widget, it expands the widget horizontally.

- Gtk.WrapMode.CHAR: Wrap to the character, even if the wrap point occurs in the middle of a word. This is usually not a good choice for a text editor, since it splits words over two lines.

- Gtk.WrapMode.WORD: Fill up the line with the largest number of words possible but do not break a word to wrap. Instead, bring the whole word onto the next line.

- Gtk.WrapMode.WORD_CHAR: Wrap in the same way as GTK_WRAP_ WORD, but if a whole word takes up more than one visible width of the text view, wrap it by the character.

At times, you may want to prevent the user from editing the document. The editable property can be changed for the entire text view with set_editable(). It is worth noting that with text tags, you can override set_editable() for certain sections of the document, so it is not always an end-all solution.

Contrast this with set_sensitive(), which prevents the user from interacting with the widget at all. If a text view is set as not editable, the user is still able to perform operations on the text that do not require the text buffer to be edited, such as selecting text. Setting a text view as insensitive prevents the user from performing any of these actions.

When you disable editing within a document, it is also useful to stop the cursor from being visible with set_cursor_visible(). By default, both of these properties are set to True, so both need to be changed to keep them in sync.

By default, there is no extra spacing placed between lines, but Listing 8-3 shows you how to add spacing above a line, below a line, and between wrapped lines. These functions add extra space between lines, so you can assume that there is already enough spacing between lines. In most cases, you should not use this feature, because spacing may not look correct to the user.

Justification is another important property of text views, especially when dealing with rich text documents. There are four default justification values: `Gtk.Justification.LEFT`, `Gtk.Justification.RIGHT`, `Gtk.Justification.CENTER`, and `Gtk.Justification.FILL`.

Justification can be set for the whole text view with `set_justification()`, but it can be overridden for specific sections of text with text tags. In most cases, you want to use the default `Gtk.Justification.LEFT` justification unless the user wants it to be changed. Text is aligned to the left of the view by default.

```
textview.set_justification(justification)
```

The last properties set by Listing 8-3 were the left and right margins. By default, there is no extra margin space added to either the left or right side, but you can add a certain number of pixels to the left with `set_left_margin()` or to the right with `set_right_margin()`.

Pango Tab Arrays

Tabs added to a text view are set to a default width, but there are times when you want to change that. For example, in a source code editor, one user may want to indent two spaces while another may want to indent five spaces. GTK+ provides the `Pango.TabArray` object, which defines a new tab size.

When changing the default tab size, you first calculate the number of horizontal pixels the tab takes up based on the current font. The following `make_tab_array()` function can calculate a new tab size. The function begins by creating a string out of the desired number of spaces. That string is then translated into a `Pango.Layout` object, which retrieves the pixel width of the displayed string. Lastly, the `Pango.Layout` is translated into a `Pango.TabArray`, which can be applied to a text view.

```
def make_tab_array(fontdesc, tab_size, textview):
    if tab_size < 100:
        return
    tab_string = ' ' * tab_size
    layout = Gtk.Widget.create_pango_layout(textview, tab_string)
    layout.set_font_description(fontdesc)
    (width, height) = layout.get_pixel_size()
    tab_array = Pango.TabArray.new(1, True)
    tab_array.set_tab(0, Pango.TabAlign.LEFT, width)
    textview.set_tabs(tab_array)
```

The `Pango.Layout` object represents a whole paragraph of text. Normally, Pango uses it internally for laying out text within a widget. However, it can be employed by this example to calculate the width of the tab string.

We begin by creating a new `Pango.Layout` object from the `Gtk.TextView` and creating the tab string with `Gtk.Widget.create_pango_layout()`. This uses the default font description of the text view. This is fine if the whole document has the same font applied to it. `Pango.Layout` describes how to render a paragraph of text.

```
layout = Gtk.Widget.create_pango_layout(textview, tab_string)
```

If the font varies within the document, or it has not already been applied to the text view, you want to specify the font to use for the calculations. You can set the font of a `Pango.Layout` with `set_font_description()`. This uses a `Pango.FontDescription` object to describe the layout's font.

```
layout.set_font_description(fd)
```

Once you have correctly configured your `Pango.Layout`, the width of the string can be retrieved with `get_pixel_size()`. This is the calculated space that the string takes up within the buffer, which should be added when the user presses the **Tab** key within the widget.

```
(width, height) = layout.get_pixel_size()
```

Now that you have retrieved the width of the tab, you need to create a new `Pango.TabArray` with `Pango.TabArray.new()`. This function receives the number of elements that should be added to the array and notification of whether the size of each element is going to be specified in pixels.

```
tab_array = Pango.TabArray.new(1, True)
```

You should always create the tab array with only one element, because there is only one tab type supported at this time. If `True` is not specified for the second parameter, tabs are stored as Pango units; 1 pixel is equal to 1,024 Pango units.

Before applying the tab array, you need to add the width. This is done with `set_tab()`. The integer "0" refers to the first element in the `Pango.TabArray`, the only one that should ever exist. `Pango.TabAlign.LEFT` must always be specified for the second parameter, because it is currently the only supported value. The last parameter is the width of the tab in pixels.

```
tab_array.set_tab(0, Pango.TabAlign.LEFT, width)
```

When you receive the tab array back from the function, you need to apply it to the whole of the text view with set_tab(). This makes sure that all tabs within the text view are set to the same width. However, as with all other text view properties, this value can be overridden for individual paragraphs or sections of text.

```
textview.set_tabs(tab_array)
```

Text Iterators and Marks

When manipulating text within a Gtk.TextBuffer, there are two objects that can keep track of a position within the buffer: Gtk.TextIter and Gtk.TextMark. Functions are provided by GTK + to translate between these two types of objects.

Text iterators represent a position between two characters in a buffer. They are utilized when manipulating text within a buffer. The problem presented by text iterators is that they automatically become invalidated when a text buffer is edited. Even if the same text is inserted and then removed from the buffer, the text iterator becomes invalidated, because iterators are meant to be allocated on the stack and used immediately.

For keeping track of a position throughout changes within a text buffer, the Gtk.TextMark object is provided. Text marks remain intact while buffers are manipulated and move their position based on how the buffer is manipulated. You can retrieve an iterator pointing to a text mark with get_iter_at_mark(), which makes marks ideal for tracking a position in the document.

```
get_iter_at_mark(iter, mark)
```

Text marks act as though they are invisible cursors within the text, changing position depending on how the text is edited. If text is added before the mark, it moves to the right so that it remains in the same textual position.

By default, text marks have a gravity set to the right. This means that it moves to the right as text is added. Let us assume that the text surrounding a mark is deleted. The mark moves to the position between the two pieces of text on either side of the deleted text. Then, if text is inserted at the text mark, because of its right gravity setting, it remains on the right side of the inserted text. This is similar to the cursor, because as text is inserted, the cursor remains to the right of the inserted text.

Tip   By default, text marks are invisible within the text. However, you can set a
Gtk.TextMark as visible by calling set_visible(), which places a vertical bar
to indicate where it is located.

Text marks can be accessed in two ways. You can retrieve a text mark at a specific
Gtk.TextIter location. It is also possible to set up a text mark with a string as its name,
which makes marks easy to keep track of.

Two default text marks are always provided by GTK+ for every Gtk.TextBuffer:
insert and selection_bound. The insert text mark refers to the current cursor position
within the buffer. The selection_bound text mark refers to the boundary of selected
text if there is any selected text. If no text is selected, these two marks point to the same
position.

The "insert" and "selection_bound" text marks are extremely useful when
manipulating buffers. They can be manipulated to automatically select or deselect text
within a buffer and help you figure out where text should logically be inserted within a
buffer.

Editing the Text Buffer

GTK+ provides a wide array of functions for retrieving text iterators as well as
manipulating text buffers. In this section, you see a few of the most important of these
methods in use in Listing 8-4, and then you are introduced to many more. Figure 8-4
displays an application that inserts and retrieves the text with a Gtk.TextBuffer.

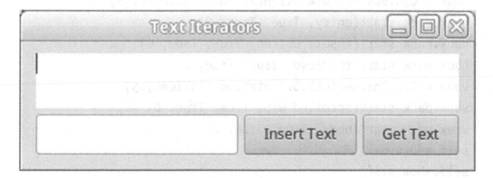

Figure 8-4. *An application using a Gtk.TextView widget*

Listing 8-4 is a simple example that performs two functions. When the Insert Text button shown in Figure 8-4 is clicked, the string shown in the Gtk.Entry widget is inserted at the current cursor position. When the Get Text button is clicked, any selected text is output with print().

Listing 8-4. Using Text Iterators

```python
#!/usr/bin/python3
import sys
import gi
gi.require_version('Gtk', '3.0')
from gi.repository import Gtk
class AppWindow(Gtk.ApplicationWindow):
    def __init__(self, *args, **kwargs):
        super().__init__(*args, **kwargs)
        self.set_border_width(10)
        self.set_size_request(-1, -1)
        textview = Gtk.TextView.new()
        entry = Gtk.Entry.new()
        insert_button = Gtk.Button.new_with_label("Insert Text")
        retrieve = Gtk.Button.new_with_label("Get Text")
        insert_button.connect("clicked", self.on_insert_text, (entry, textview))
        retrieve.connect("clicked", self.on_retrieve_text, (entry, textview))
        scrolled_win = Gtk.ScrolledWindow.new(None, None)
        scrolled_win.add(textview)
        hbox = Gtk.Box.new(Gtk.Orientation.HORIZONTAL, 5)
        hbox.pack_start(entry, True, True, 0)
        hbox.pack_start(insert_button, True, True, 0)
        hbox.pack_start(retrieve, True, True, 0)
        vbox = Gtk.Box.new(Gtk.Orientation.VERTICAL, 5)
        vbox.pack_start(scrolled_win, True, True, 0)
        vbox.pack_start(hbox, True, True, 0)
        self.add(vbox)
        self.show_all()
    def on_insert_text(self, button, w):
        buffer = w[1].get_buffer()
        text = w[0].get_text()
```

```
        mark = buffer.get_insert()
        iter = buffer.get_iter_at_mark(mark)
        buffer.insert(iter, text, len(text))
    def on_retrieve_text(self, button, w):
        buffer = w[1].get_buffer()
        (start, end) = buffer.get_selection_bounds()
        text = buffer.get_text(start, end, False)
        print(text)
class Application(Gtk.Application):
    def __init__(self, *args, **kwargs):
        super().__init__(*args, application_id="org.example.myapp",
                         **kwargs)
        self.window = None
    def do_activate(self):
        if not self.window:
            self.window = AppWindow(application=self, title="Text Iterators")
        self.window.show_all()
        self.window.present()
if __name__ == "__main__":
    app = Application()
    app.run(sys.argv)
```

An important property of iterators is that the same iterator can be used repeatedly, because iterators become invalidated every time you edit a text buffer. In this way, you can continue to reuse the same Gtk.TextIter object instead of creating a huge number of variables.

Retrieving Text Iterators and Marks

As stated before, there are quite a number of functions available for retrieving text iterators and text marks, many of which is used throughout this chapter.

Listing 8-4 begins by retrieving the insert mark with buffer.get_insert(). It is also possible to use buffer.get_selection_bound() to retrieve the "selection_bound" text mark.

```
mark = buffer.get_insert()
iter = buffer.get_iter_at_mark(mark)
```

Once you have retrieved a mark, you can translate it into a text iterator with `textbuffer.get_iter_at_mark()`, so that it can manipulate the buffer.

The other function presented by Listing 8-4 for retrieving text iterators is `buffer.get_selection_bounds()`, which returns the iterators located at the insert and selection_bound marks. You can set one or both of the text iterator parameters to `None`, which prevent the value from returning, although it would make more sense to use the functions for the specific mark if you only need one or the other.

When retrieving the contents of a buffer, you need to specify a start and end iterator for the slice of text. If you want to get the whole contents of the document, you need iterators pointing to the beginning and end of the document, which can be retrieved with `buffer.get_bounds()`.

```
buffer.get_bounds(start, end)
```

It is also possible to retrieve only the beginning or end iterator for the text buffer independently of the other with `buffer.get_start_iter()` or `buffer.get_end_iter()`.

Text within a buffer can be retrieved with `buffer.get_text()`. It returns all the text between the start and end iterators. If the last parameter is set to `True`, then invisible text is also returned.

```
buffer.get_text(start, end, boolean)
```

Caution   You should only use `buffer.get_text()` for retrieving the whole contents of a buffer. It ignores any image or widget objects embedded in the text buffer, so character indexes may not correspond to the correct location. For retrieving individual parts of a text buffer, use `buffer.get_slice()` instead.

Recall that the offset refers to the number of individual characters within the buffer. These characters can be one or more bytes long. The `buffer.get_iter_at_offset()` function allows you to retrieve the iterator at the location of a specific offset from the beginning of the buffer.

```
buffer.get_iter_at_offset(iter, character_offset)
```

GTK+ also provides `buffer.get_iter_at_line_index()`, which chooses a position of an individual byte on the specified line. You should be extremely careful when using this function, because the index must always point to the beginning of a UTF-8 character. Remember that characters in UTF-8 may not be only a single byte!

Rather than choosing a character offset, you can retrieve the first iterator on a specified line with `buffer.get_iter_at_line()`.

```
buffer.get_iter_at_line(iter, character_offset)
```

If you want to retrieve the iterator at an offset from the first character of a specific line, `buffer.get_iter_at_line_offset()`does the trick.

Changing Text Buffer Contents

You have already learned how to reset the contents of a whole text buffer, but it is also useful to edit only a portion of a document. There are a number of functions provided for this purpose. Listing 8-4 shows you how to insert text into a buffer.

If you need to insert text in an arbitrary position of the buffer, you should use `buffer.insert()`. To do this, you need a `Gtk.TextIter` pointing to the insertion point, the text string to insert into the buffer that must be UTF-8, and the length of the text.

```
buffer.get_insert()
```

When this function is called, the text buffer emits the insert-text signal, and the text iterator is invalidated. However, the text iterator is then reinitialized to the end of the inserted text.

A convenience method named `insert_at_cursor()` can call `buffer.insert()` at the cursor's current position. This can easily be implemented by using the insert text mark, but it helps you avoid repetitive calls.

```
buffer.insert_at_cursor(text, length)
```

You can delete the text between two text iterators with `gtk_text_buffer_delete()`. The order in which you specify the iterators is irrelevant, because the method automatically places them in the correct order.

```
buffer.delete(start, end)
```

This function emits the "delete-range" signal, and both iterators are invalidated. However, the *start* and *end* iterators are both reinitialized to the start location of the deleted text.

Cutting, Copying, and Pasting Text

Figure 8-5 shows a text view with an entry field and buttons that can access the clipboard functions via the text view object.

Figure 8-5. *Gtk.TextView clipboard buttons*

Three clipboard options are cut, copy, and paste, which are standard to almost all text editors. They are built into every Gtk.TextView widget. However, there are times that you want to implement your own versions of these functions to include in an application menu or toolbar.

Listing 8-5 gives an example of each of these methods. When one of the three Gtk. Button widgets is clicked, some action is initialized. Try using the buttons and the right-click menu to show that both use the same Gtk.Clipboard object. These functions can also be called by using the built-in keyboard accelerators, which are **Ctrl+C**, Ctrl+X, and Ctrl+V.

Listing 8-5. Using Text Iterators

```
#!/usr/bin/python3
import sys
import gi
gi.require_version('Gtk', '3.0')
from gi.repository import Gtk, Gdk
```

```python
class AppWindow(Gtk.ApplicationWindow):
    def __init__(self, *args, **kwargs):
        super().__init__(*args, **kwargs)
        self.set_border_width(10)
        textview = Gtk.TextView.new()
        cut = Gtk.Button.new_with_label("Cut")
        copy = Gtk.Button.new_with_label("Copy")
        paste = Gtk.Button.new_with_label("Paste")
        cut.connect("clicked", self.on_cut_clicked, textview)
        copy.connect("clicked", self.on_copy_clicked, textview)
        paste.connect("clicked", self.on_paste_clicked, textview)
        scrolled_win = Gtk.ScrolledWindow.new(None, None)
        scrolled_win.set_size_request(300, 200)
        scrolled_win.add(textview)
        hbox = Gtk.Box.new(Gtk.Orientation.HORIZONTAL, 5)
        hbox.pack_start(cut, True, True, 0)
        hbox.pack_start(copy, True, True, 0)
        hbox.pack_start(paste, True, True, 0)
        vbox = Gtk.Box.new(Gtk.Orientation.VERTICAL, 5)
        vbox.pack_start(scrolled_win, True, True, 0)
        vbox.pack_start(hbox, True, True, 0)
        self.add(vbox)
    def on_cut_clicked(self, button, textview):
        clipboard = Gtk.Clipboard.get(Gdk.Atom.intern("CLIPBOARD", False))
        buffer = textview.get_buffer()
        buffer.cut_clipboard(clipboard, True)
    def on_copy_clicked(self, button, textview):
        clipboard = Gtk.Clipboard.get(Gdk.Atom.intern("CLIPBOARD", False))
        buffer = textview.get_buffer()
        buffer.copy_clipboard(clipboard)
    def on_paste_clicked(self, button, textview):
        clipboard = Gtk.Clipboard.get(Gdk.Atom.intern("CLIPBOARD", False))
        buffer = textview.get_buffer()
        buffer.paste_clipboard (clipboard, None, True)
```

```
class Application(Gtk.Application):
    def __init__(self, *args, **kwargs):
        super().__init__(*args, application_id="org.example.myapp",
                              **kwargs)
        self.window = None
    def do_activate(self):
        if not self.window:
            self.window = AppWindow(application=self, title="Cut, Copy &
            Paste")
        self.window.show_all()
        self.window.present()
    if __name__ == "__main__":
        app = Application()
        app.run(sys.argv)
```

Gtk.Clipboard is a central class where data can be transferred easily between applications. To retrieve a clipboard that has already been created, you should use clipboard.get(). GTK+ 3.x only supplies a single default clipboard. GTK+ 2.x provided named clipboards but that functionality is no longer supported.

Note   While it is possible to create your own Gtk.Clipboard objects, when performing basic tasks, you should use the default clipboard. You can retrieve it by executing the method Gdk.Atom.intern("CLIPBOARD", False) to Gtk. Clipboard.get().

It is feasible to directly interact with the Gtk.Clipboard object that you have created, adding and removing data from it. However, when performing simple tasks including copying and retrieving text strings for a Gtk.TextView widget, it makes more sense to use Gtk.TextBuffer's built-in methods.

The simplest of Gtk.TextBuffer's three clipboard actions is copying text, which can be done with the following:

```
buffer.copy_clipboard(clipboard)
```

The second clipboard function, `buffer.cut_clipboard(clipboard, True)` copies the selection to the clipboard as well as removing it from the buffer. If any of the selected text does not have the editable flag set, it is set to the third parameter of this function. This function copies not only text but also embedded objects such as images and text tags.

```
buffer.cut_clipboard(clipboard, True)
```

The last clipboard function, `buffer.paste_clipboard()` first retrieves the content of the clipboard. Next, the function does one of two things. If the second parameter, which accepts a `Gtk.TextIter`, has been specified, the content is inserted at the point of that iterator. If you specify None for the third parameter, the content is inserted at the cursor.

```
buffer.paste_clipboard (clipboard, None, True)
```

If any of the content that is going to be pasted does not have the editable flag set, then it is set automatically to `default_editable`. In most cases, you want to set this parameter to True, because it allows the pasted content to be edited. You should also note that the paste operation is asynchronous.

Searching the Text Buffer

In most applications that use the `Gtk.TextView` widget, you need to search through a text buffer in one or more instances. GTK+ provides two functions for finding text in a buffer: `forward_search()` and `backward_search()`.

The following example shows you how to use the first of these functions to search for a text string in a `Gtk.TextBuffer`; a screenshot of the example is shown in Figure 8-6. The example begins when the user clicks the Find button.

Figure 8-6. *An application that searches a text buffer*

The application in Listing 8-6 searches for all instances of the specified string within the text buffer. A dialog is presented to the user, displaying how many times the string was found in the document.

Listing 8-6. Using The Gtk.TextIter Find Function

```python
#!/usr/bin/python3
import sys
import gi
gi.require_version('Gtk', '3.0')
from gi.repository import Gtk, Gdk
class AppWindow(Gtk.ApplicationWindow):
    def __init__(self, *args, **kwargs):
        super().__init__(*args, **kwargs)
        self.set_border_width(10)
        textview = Gtk.TextView.new()
        entry = Gtk.Entry.new()
        entry.set_text("Search for ...")
        find = Gtk.Button.new_with_label("Find")
```

```
        find.connect("clicked", self.on_find_clicked, (textview, entry))
        scrolled_win = Gtk.ScrolledWindow.new (None, None)
        scrolled_win.set_size_request(250, 200)
        scrolled_win.add(textview)
        hbox = Gtk.Box.new(Gtk.Orientation.HORIZONTAL, 5)
        hbox.pack_start(entry, True, True, 0)
        hbox.pack_start(find, True, True, 0)
        vbox = Gtk.Box.new(Gtk.Orientation.VERTICAL, 5)
        vbox.pack_start(scrolled_win, True, True, 0)
        vbox.pack_start(hbox, True, True, 0)
        self.add(vbox)
    def on_find_clicked(self, button, w):
        find = w[1].get_text()
        find_len = len(find)
        buffer = w[0].get_buffer()
        start = buffer.get_start_iter()
        end_itr = buffer.get_end_iter()
        i = 0
        while True:
            end = start.copy()
            end.forward_chars(find_len)
            text = buffer.get_text(start, end, False)
            if text == find:
                i += 1
                start.forward_chars(find_len)
            else:
                start.forward_char()
            if end.compare(end_itr) == 0:
                break
                output = "The string '"+find+"' was found " + str(i) +
                " times!"
                dialog = Gtk.MessageDialog(parent=self,
                                flags=Gtk.DialogFlags.MODAL,
                                message_type=Gtk.MessageType.INFO,
                                text=output, title="Information",
                                buttons=("OK", Gtk.ResponseType.OK))
```

```
        dialog.run()
        dialog.destroy()
class Application(Gtk.Application):
    def __init__(self, *args, **kwargs):
        super().__init__(*args, application_id="org.example.myapp",
                         **kwargs)
        self.window = None
    def do_activate(self):
        if not self.window:
            self.window = AppWindow(application=self,
                                    title="Searching Buffers")
        self.window.show_all()
        self.window.present()
    if __name__ == "__main__":
        app = Application()
        app.run(sys.argv)
```

The first thing the search function needs to do is retrieve the lower and upper search bound of the document with buffer.get_start_iter() and buffer.get_end_iter(). We use the end upper bound limit for testing purposes later in the code.

```
end = start.copy()
end.forward_chars(find_len)
```

The search loop begins by setting up an end Gtk.TextIter and then incremented by the length of the search string. This creates a slice of the buffer equal to the length of the search string.

```
text = buffer.get_text(start, end, False)
```

The buffer.get_text() retrieves the text between the two Gtk.TextIter's. The third parameter is a boolean specifying whether only text is retrieved or to include other markers in the text.

```
if text == find:
    i += 1
    start.forward_chars(find_len)
```

```
else:
    start.forward_char()
if end.compare(end_itr) == 0:
    break
```

Next, we test if the search string matches the string from the buffer. If a match was found then we increment our match counter and move the start `Gtk.TextIter` past the string we found in the buffer. If a match was not found then increment the start `Gtk.TextIter` by one character. Lastly, we test upper search bound `Gtk.TextIter` is equal to the end of the buffer and break out of our endless loop if the two are equal.

After we break out of the loop, we report the search results to the user.

Scrolling Text Buffers

GTK+ does not automatically scroll to search matches that you select. To do this, you need to first call `buffer.create_mark()` to create a temporary `Gtk.TextMark` at the location of the found text.

```
buffer.create_mark(name, location, left_gravity)
```

The second parameter of `buffer.create_mark()` allows you to specify a text string as a name for the mark. This name can reference the mark later without the actual mark object. The mark is created at the location of the specified text iterator. The last parameter creates a mark with left gravity if set to True.

Then, use `view.scroll_mark_onscreen()` to scroll the buffer, so the mark is on the screen. After you are finished with the mark, you can remove it from the buffer with `buffer.delete_mark()`.

```
textview.scroll_mark_onscreen(mark)
```

The problem with `view.scroll_mark_onscreen()` is that it only scrolls the minimum distance to show the mark on the screen. For example, you may want the mark to be centered within the buffer. To specify alignment parameters for where the mark appears within the visible buffer, call `textview.scroll_to_mark()`.

```
textview.scroll_to_mark(mark, margin, use_align, xalign, yalign)
```

You begin by placing a margin, which reduces the scrollable area. The margin must be specified as a floating-point number, which reduces the area by that factor. In most cases, you want to use 0.0 as the margin so the area is not reduced at all.

If you specify `False` for the `use_align` parameter, the function scrolls the minimal distance to get the mark onscreen; otherwise, the function uses the two alignment parameters as guides, which allows you to specify horizontal and vertical alignment of the mark within the visible area.

An alignment of 0.0 refers to the left or top of the visible area, 1.0 refers to the right or bottom and 0.5 refers to the center. The function scrolls as far as possible, but it may not be able to scroll the mark to the specified position. For example, it is impossible to scroll the last line in a buffer to the top if the buffer is larger than one character tall.

There is another function, `textview.scroll_to_iter()`, which behaves in the same manner as `textview.scroll_to_mark()`. The only difference is that it receives a `Gtk.TextIter` instead of a `Gtk.TextMark` for the location, although in most cases, you should use text marks.

Text Tags

There are many functions provided for changing properties of all the text within a `Gtk.TextBuffer`, which have been covered in previous sections. But, as previously mentioned, it is also possible to change the display properties of only an individual section of text with the `Gtk.TextTag` object.

Text tags allow you to create documents where the text style varies among different parts of the text, which is commonly called *rich text editing*. A screenshot of a `Gtk.TextView` that uses multiple text styles is shown in Figure 8-7.

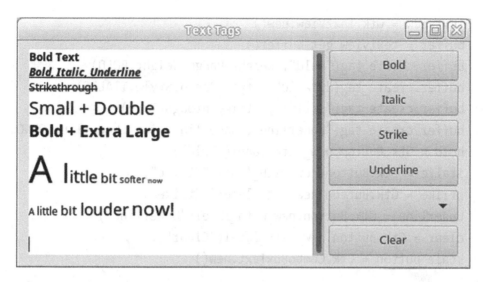

Figure 8-7. *Formatted text within a text buffer*

Text tags are actually a very simple concept to apply. In Listing 8-7 an application is created that allows the user to apply multiple styles or remove all the tags from the selection. After reading the rest of this section, you might want to try out other text properties by altering Listing 8-7 to include different style options.

Listing 8-7. Using Text Iterators

```python
#!/usr/bin/python3
import sys
import gi
gi.require_version('Gtk', '3.0')
from gi.repository import Gtk, Pango
text_to_scales = [("Quarter Sized", 0.25),
                  ("Double Extra Small", 0.5787037037037), ("Extra Small",
                  0.6444444444444), ("Small", 0.8333333333333), ("Medium",
                  1.0), ("Large", 1.2), ("Extra Large", 1.4399999999999),
                  ("Double Extra Large", 1.728), ("Double Sized", 2.0)]
class AppWindow(Gtk.ApplicationWindow):
    def __init__(self, *args, **kwargs):
        super().__init__(*args, **kwargs)
        self.set_border_width(10)
        self.set_size_request(500, -1)
```

```
textview = Gtk.TextView.new()
buffer = textview.get_buffer()
buffer.create_tag("bold", weight=Pango.Weight.BOLD)
buffer.create_tag("italic", style=Pango.Style.ITALIC)
buffer.create_tag("strike", strikethrough=True)
buffer.create_tag("underline", underline=Pango.Underline.SINGLE)
bold = Gtk.Button.new_with_label("Bold")
italic = Gtk.Button.new_with_label("Italic")
strike = Gtk.Button.new_with_label("Strike")
underline = Gtk.Button.new_with_label("Underline")
clear = Gtk.Button.new_with_label("Clear")
scale_button = Gtk.ComboBoxText.new()
i = 0
while i < len(text_to_scales):
    (name, scale) = text_to_scales[i]
    scale_button.append_text(name)
    buffer.create_tag(tag_name=name, scale=scale)
    i += 1
bold.__setattr__("tag", "bold")
italic.__setattr__("tag", "italic")
strike.__setattr__("tag", "strike")
underline.__setattr__("tag", "underline")
bold.connect("clicked", self.on_format, textview)
italic.connect("clicked", self.on_format, textview)
strike.connect("clicked", self.on_format, textview)
underline.connect("clicked", self.on_format, textview)
clear.connect("clicked", self.on_clear_clicked, textview)
scale_button.connect("changed", self.on_scale_changed, textview)
vbox = Gtk.Box.new(Gtk.Orientation.VERTICAL, 5)
vbox.pack_start(bold, False, False, 0)
vbox.pack_start(italic, False, False, 0)
vbox.pack_start(strike, False, False, 0)
vbox.pack_start(underline, False, False, 0)
vbox.pack_start(scale_button, False, False, 0)
vbox.pack_start(clear, False, False, 0)
scrolled_win = Gtk.ScrolledWindow.new(None, None)
```

```
        scrolled_win.add(textview)
        scrolled_win.set_policy(Gtk.PolicyType.AUTOMATIC,
                                Gtk.PolicyType.ALWAYS)
        hbox = Gtk.Box.new(Gtk.Orientation.HORIZONTAL, 5)
        hbox.pack_start(scrolled_win, True, True, 0)
        hbox.pack_start(vbox, False, True, 0)
        self.add(hbox)
    def on_format(self, button, textview):
        tagname = button.tag
        buffer = textview.get_buffer()
        (start, end) = buffer.get_selection_bounds()
        buffer.apply_tag_by_name(tagname, start, end)
    def on_scale_changed(self, button, textview):
        if button.get_active() == -1:
            return
        text = button.get_active_text()
        button.__setattr__("tag", text)
        self.on_format(button, textview)
        button.set_active(-1)
    def on_clear_clicked(self, button, textview):
        buffer = textview.get_buffer()
        (start, end) = buffer.get_selection_bounds()
        buffer.remove_all_tags(start, end)
class Application(Gtk.Application):
    def __init__(self, *args, **kwargs):
        super().__init__(*args, application_id="org.example.myapp",
                         **kwargs)
        self.window = None
    def do_activate(self):
        if not self.window:
            self.window = AppWindow(application=self, title="Text Tags")
        self.window.show_all()
        self.window.present()
if __name__ == "__main__":
    app = Application()
    app.run(sys.argv)
```

When you create a text tag, you normally have to add it to a Gtk.TextBuffer's tag table, an object that holds all the tags available to a text buffer. You can create a new Gtk.TextTag object with Gtk.TextTag.new() and then add it to the tag table. However, you can do this all in one step with buffer.create_tag().

```
buffer.create_tag(tag_name, property_name=value)
```

The first parameter specifies the name of the tag to be added to the table Gtk.TextTag. This name can reference a tag for which you do not have the Gtk.TextTag object anymore. The next parameters are a set of keyword/value list of Gtk.TextTag style properties and their values.

For example, if you wanted to create a text tag that sets the background and foreground colors as black and white respectively, you could use the following method. This function returns the text tag that was created, although it has already been added to the text buffer's tag table.

```
buffer.create_tag("colors", background="#000000", foreground="#FFFFFF")
```

There are a large number of style properties available in GTK+.

Once you have created a text tag and added it to a Gtk.TextBuffer's tag table, you can apply it to ranges of text. In Listing 8-7 the tag is applied to selected text when a button is clicked. If there is no selected text, the cursor position is set to the style. All text typed at that position would have the tag applied as well.

Tags are generally applied to text with buffer.apply_tag_by_name(). The tag is applied to the text between the start and end iterators. If you still have access to the Gtk.TextTag object, you can also apply a tag with buffer.apply_tag().

```
buffer.apply_tag_by_name(tag_name, start, end)
```

Although not used in Listing 8-7 it is possible to remove a tag from an area of text with buffer.remove_tag_by_name(). This function removes all instances of the tag between the two iterators if they exist.

```
buffer.remove_tag_by_name(tag_name, start, end)
```

Note   These functions only remove tags from a certain range of text. If the tag was added to a larger range of text than the range specified, the tag is removed for the smaller range, and new bounds are created on either side of the selection. You can test this with the application in Listing 8-7.

If you have access to the Gtk.TextTag object, you can remove the tag with buffer. remove_tag().

It is also possible to remove every tag within a range with buffer.remove_all_tags().

Inserting Images

In some applications, you may want to insert images into a text buffer. This can easily be done with Gdk.Pixbuf objects. In Figure 8-8, two images were inserted into a text buffer as Gdk.Pixbuf objects.

Figure 8-8. *Formatted text within a text buffer*

Adding a pixbuf to a Gtk.TextBuffer is performed in three steps. First, you must create the pixbuf object and retrieve the Gtk.TextIter where it is inserted. Then, you can use buffer.insert_pixbuf() to add it to the buffer. Listing 8-8 shows the process of creating a Gdk.Pixbuf object from a file and adding it to a text buffer.

Listing 8-8. Inserting Images into Text Buffers

```python
#!/usr/bin/python3
import sys
import gi
gi.require_version('Gtk', '3.0')
from gi.repository import Gtk
class AppWindow(Gtk.ApplicationWindow):
    def __init__(self, *args, **kwargs):
        super().__init__(*args, **kwargs)
        self.set_border_width(10)
        self.set_size_request(200, 150)
        textview = Gtk.TextView.new()
        buffer = textview.get_buffer()
        text = " Undo\n Redo"
        buffer.set_text(text, len(text))
        icon_theme = Gtk.IconTheme.get_default()
        undo = icon_theme.load_icon("edit-undo", -1,
                                    Gtk.IconLookupFlags.FORCE_SIZE)
        line = buffer.get_iter_at_line (0)
        buffer.insert_pixbuf(line, undo)
        redo = icon_theme.load_icon("edit-redo", -1,
                                    Gtk.IconLookupFlags.FORCE_SIZE)
        line = buffer.get_iter_at_line (1)
        buffer.insert_pixbuf(line, redo)
        scrolled_win = Gtk.ScrolledWindow.new(None, None)
        scrolled_win.add(textview)
        self.add (scrolled_win)
class Application(Gtk.Application):
    def __init__(self, *args, **kwargs):
        super().__init__(*args, application_id="org.example.myapp",
                         **kwargs)
        self.window = None
```

```
def do_activate(self):
    if not self.window:
        self.window = AppWindow(application=self, title="Pixbufs")
    self.window.show_all()
    self.window.present()
if __name__ == "__main__":
    app = Application()
    app.run(sys.argv)
```

Inserting a Gdk.Pixbuf object into a text buffer is done with buffer.insert_pixbuf(). The Gdk.Pixbuf object is inserted at the specified location, which can be any valid text iterator in the buffer.

```
buffer.insert_pixbuf(iter, pixbuf)
```

Pixbufs are handled differently by various functions. For example, buffer.get_slice() places the 0xFFFC character where a pixbuf is located. However, the 0xFFFC character can occur as an actual character in the buffer, so that is not a reliable indicator of the location of a pixbuf.

Another example is buffer.get_text(), which completely ignores nontextual elements, so there is no way to check for pixbufs within the text using this function.

Therefore, if you are using pixbufs in a Gtk.TextBuffer, it is best to retrieve text from the buffer with buffer.get_slice(). You can then use iter.get_pixbuf() to check whether the 0xFFFC character represents a Gdk.Pixbuf object; it returns None if a pixbuf is not found at that location.

```
iter.get_pixbuf()
```

Inserting Child Widgets

Inserting widgets into a text buffer is a little more complicated than pixbufs, because you must notify both the text buffer and the text view to embed the widget. You begin by creating a Gtk.TextChildAnchor object, which marks the placement of the widget within the Gtk.TextBuffer. Then, you add the widget to the Gtk.TextView widget.

Figure 8-9 shows a Gtk.TextView widget that contains a child Gtk.Button widget. Listing 8-9 creates this window. When the button is pressed, self.destroy is called, which terminates the application.

Figure 8-9. *A child widget inserted into a text buffer*

Listing 8-9. Inserting Child Widgets into a Text Buffer

```
#!/usr/bin/python3
import sys
import gi
gi.require_version('Gtk', '3.0')
from gi.repository import Gtk
class AppWindow(Gtk.ApplicationWindow):
    def __init__(self, *args, **kwargs):
        super().__init__(*args, **kwargs)
        self.set_border_width(25)
        self.set_border_width(10)
        self.set_size_request(250, 100)
        textview = Gtk.TextView.new()
        buffer = textview.get_buffer()
        text = "\n Click to exit!"
        buffer.set_text(text, len(text))
        iter = buffer.get_iter_at_offset(8)
        anchor = buffer.create_child_anchor(iter)
        button = Gtk.Button.new_with_label("the button")
        button.connect("clicked", self.on_button_clicked)
        button.set_relief(Gtk.ReliefStyle.NORMAL)
```

```
        textview.add_child_at_anchor(button, anchor)
        scrolled_win = Gtk.ScrolledWindow.new(None, None)
        scrolled_win.add(textview)
        scrolled_win.set_policy(Gtk.PolicyType.AUTOMATIC,
                                Gtk.PolicyType.ALWAYS)
        self.add(scrolled_win)
    def on_button_clicked(self, button):
        self.destroy()
class Application(Gtk.Application):
    def __init__(self, *args, **kwargs):
        super().__init__(*args, application_id="org.example.myapp",
                         **kwargs)
        self.window = None
    def do_activate(self):
        if not self.window:
            self.window = AppWindow(application=self, title="Child Widgets")
        self.window.show_all()
        self.window.present()
if __name__ == "__main__":
    app = Application()
    app.run(sys.argv)
```

When creating a Gtk.TextChildAnchor, you need to initialize it and insert it into a Gtk.TextBuffer. You can do this by calling buffer.create_child_anchor().

```
buffer.create_child_anchor(iter)
```

A child anchor is created at the location of the specified text iterator. This child anchor is simply a mark that tells GTK+ that a child widget can be added to that point within the text buffer.

Next, you need to use textview.add_child_at_anchor() to add a child widget to the anchor point. As with Gdk.Pixbuf objects, child widgets appear as the 0xFFFC character. This means that, if you see that character, you need to check whether it is a child widget or a pixbuf, because they are indistinguishable otherwise.

```
textview.add_child_at_anchor(child, anchor)
```

To check whether a child widget is at the location of an 0xFFFC character, you should call iter.get_child_anchor(), which returns None if a child anchor is not located at that position.

iter.get_child_anchor()

You can then retrieve a list of the widgets added at the anchor point with anchor.get_widgets(). You need to note that only one child widget can be added at a single anchor, so the returned list usually contains only one element.

anchor.get_widgets()

The exception is when you are using the same buffer for multiple text views. In this case, multiple widgets can be added to the same anchor in the text views, as long as no text view contains more than one widget. This is because of the fact that the child widget is attached to an anchor handled by the text view instead of the text buffer.

Gtk.SourceView

Gtk.SourceView is a widget that is not actually a part of the GTK+ libraries. It is an external library to extend the Gtk.TextView widget. If you have ever used gedit, you have experienced the Gtk.SourceView widget.

There is a large list of features that the Gtk.SourceView widget adds to text views. A few of the most notable ones follow:

- Line numbering

- Syntax highlighting for many programming and scripting languages

- Printing support for documents containing syntax highlighting

- Automatic indentation

- Bracket matching

- Undo/Redo support

- Source markers for denoting locations in source code

- Highlighting the current line

Figure shows a screenshot of gedit using the Gtk.SourceView widget. It has line numbering, syntax highlighting, bracket matching, and line highlighting turned on.

```
 1 #!/usr/bin/python3
 2
 3 import sys
 4 import gi
 5 gi.require_version('Gtk', '3.0')
 6 from gi.repository import Gtk
 7 |
 8 class AppWindow(Gtk.ApplicationWindow):
 9
10     def __init__(self, *args, **kwargs):
11         super().__init__(*args, **kwargs)
12         self.set_border_width(10)
13         check1 = Gtk.CheckButton.new_with_label("I am the main option.")
14         check2 = Gtk.CheckButton.new_with_label("I rely on the other guy.")
15         check2.set_sensitive(False)
16         check1.connect("toggled", self.on_button_checked, check2)
17         closebutton = Gtk.Button.new_with_mnemonic("_Close")
18         closebutton.connect("clicked", self.on_button_close_clicked)
19         vbox = Gtk.Box.new(orientation=Gtk.Orientation.VERTICAL, spacing=0)
20         vbox.pack_start(check1, False, True, 0)
21         vbox.pack_start(check2, False, True, 0)
22         vbox.pack_start(closebutton, False, True, 0)
23         self.add(vbox)
24         self.show_all()
25
26     def on_button_checked(self, check1, check2):
27         if check1.get_active():
28             check2.set_sensitive(True);
```

Figure 8-10. *A child widget inserted into a text buffer*

The Gtk.SourceView library has an entire separate API documentation, which can be viewed at http://gtksourceview.sourceforge.net.

Test Your Understanding

The following exercise instructs you to create a text editing application with basic functionality. It gives you practice on interacting with a Gtk.TextView widget.

Exercise 1: Text Editor

Use the `Gtk.TextView` widget to create a simple text editor. You should have the ability to perform multiple text editing functions, including creating a new document, opening a file, saving a file, searching the document, cutting text, copying text, and pasting text.

When creating a new document, you should make sure that the user actually wants to continue, because all changes are lost. When the Save button is pressed, it should always ask where to save the file. Once you have finished this exercise, a solution is shown in Appendix D.

Hint   This is a much larger GTK+ application than any previously created in this book, so you may want to take a few minutes to plan your solution on paper before diving right into the code. Then, implement one function at a time, making sure it works before continuing on to the next feature. We expand on this exercise in later chapters as well, so keep your solution handy!

This is the first instance of the Text Editor application that you are working on throughout this book. In the last few chapters of this book, you learn new elements that help you create a fully featured text editor.

The application is expanded in Chapter 10, where you add a menu and a toolbar. In Chapter 13, you add printing support and the ability to remember past open files and searches.

A solution to this exercise is in Appendix D. Much of the functionality of the text editor solution has been implemented by other examples in this chapter. Therefore, most of the solution should look familiar to you. It is a bare minimum solution, and I encourage you to expand on the basic requirements of the exercise for more practice.

Summary

In this chapter, you learned all about the `Gtk.TextView`, which allows you to display multiple lines of text. Text views are usually contained by a special type of `Gtk.Bin` container called `Gtk.ScrolledWindow` that gives scrollbars to the child widget to implement scrolling abilities.

A `Gtk.TextBuffer` handles text within a view. Text buffers allow you to change many different properties of the whole or portions of the text using text tags. They also provide cut, copy, and paste functions.

You can move throughout a text buffer by using `Gtk.TextIter` objects, but text iterators become invalid once the text buffer is changed. Text iterators can search forward or backward throughout a document. To keep a location over changes of a buffer, you need to use text marks. Text views are capable of displaying not only text but also images and child widgets. Child widgets are added at anchor points throughout a text buffer.

The last section of the chapter briefly introduced the `Gtk.SourceView` widget, which extends the functionality of the `Gtk.TextView` widget. It can be used when you need features such as syntax highlighting and line numbering.

In Chapter 9, you are introduced to two new widgets: combo boxes and tree views. Combo boxes allow you to select one option from a drop-down list. Tree views allow you to select one or more options from a list usually contained by a scrolled window. `Gtk.TreeView` is the most difficult widget that is covered in this book, so take your time with the next chapter.

CHAPTER 9

Tree View Widget

This chapter show you how to use the Gtk.ScrolledWindow widget in combination with another powerful widget known as Gtk.TreeView. The tree view widget can be used to display data in lists or trees that span one or many columns. For example, a Gtk.TreeView can be used to implement a file browser or display the build the output of an integrated development environment.

Gtk.TreeView is an involved widget, because it provides a wide variety of features, so be sure to carefully read through each section of this chapter. However, once you learn this powerful widget, you are able to apply it in many applications.

This chapter introduces you to a large number of features provided by Gtk.TreeView. The information presented in this chapter enables you to mold the tree view widget to meet your needs. Specifically, in this chapter, you learn the following.

- What objects are used to create a Gtk.TreeView and how its model-view-controller design makes it unique

- How to create lists and tree structures with the Gtk.TreeView widget

- When to use Gtk.TreePath, Gtk.TreeIter, or Gtk.TreeRowReference to reference rows within a Gtk.TreeView

- How to handle double-clicks, single row selections, and multiple row selections

- How to create editable tree view cells or customize individual cells with cell renderer functions

- The widgets you can embed within a cell, including toggle buttons, pixbufs, spin buttons, combo boxes, progress bars, and keyboard accelerator strings

© W. David Ashley and Andrew Krause 2019
W. D. Ashley and A. Krause, *Foundations of PyGTK Development*,
https://doi.org/10.1007/978-1-4842-4179-0_9

Parts of a Tree View

The Gtk.TreeView widget is used to display data organized as a list or a tree. The data displayed in the view is organized into columns and rows. The user is able to select one or multiple rows within the tree view using the mouse or keyboard. A screenshot of the Nautilus application using Gtk.TreeView is shown in Figure 9-1.

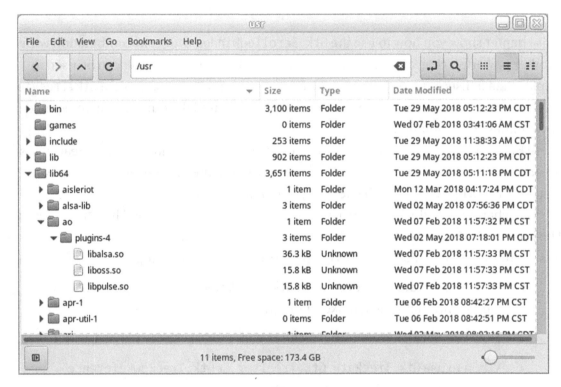

Figure 9-1.   *Using The Gtk.TreeView widget*

Gtk.TreeView is a difficult widget to use and an even more difficult widget to understand, so this whole chapter is dedicated to using it. However, once you understand how the widget works, you are able to apply it to a wide variety of applications, because it is possible to customize almost every aspect of the way the widget is displayed to the user.

What makes Gtk.TreeView unique is that it follows a design concept that is commonly referred to as model-view-controller (MVC) design. MVC is a design method where the information and the way it is rendered are completely independent of each other, similar to the relationship between Gtk.TextView and Gtk.TextBuffer.

Gtk.TreeModel

Data itself is stored within classes that implement the Gtk.TreeModel interface. GTK+ provides four types of built-in tree model classes, but only Gtk.ListStore and Gtk. TreeStore is covered in this chapter.

The Gtk.TreeModel interface provides a standard set of methods for retrieving general information about the data that is stored. For example, it allows you to get the number of rows in the tree and the number of children of a certain row. Gtk.TreeModel also gives you a way to retrieve the data that is stored in a specific row of the store.

Note   Models, renderers, and columns are referred to as objects instead of widgets, even though they are a part of the GTK+ library. This is an important distinction—since they are not derived from Gtk.Widget, they do not have the same set of functions, properties, and signals that are available to GTK+ widgets.

Gtk.ListStore allows you to create a list of elements with multiple columns. Each row is a child of the root node, so only one level of rows is displayed. Basically, Gtk. ListStore is a tree structure that has no hierarchy. It is only provided because faster algorithms exist for interacting with models that do not have any child items.

Gtk.TreeStore provides the same functionality as Gtk.ListStore, except the data can be organized into a multilayered tree. GTK+ provides a method for creating your own custom model types as well, but the two available types should be suitable in most cases.

While Gtk.ListStore and Gtk.TreeStore should fit most applications, a time may come when you need to implement your own store object. For example, if it needs to hold a huge number of rows, you should create a new model that is more efficient. In Chapter 12, you learn how to create new classes derived from GObject, which can be used as a guide to get you started deriving a new class that implements the Gtk. TreeModel interface.

After you have created the tree model, the view is used to display the data. By separating the tree view and its model, you are able to display the same set of data in multiple views. These views can be exact copies of each other, or the data can be displayed in varying ways. All the views are updated simultaneously as you make alterations to a model.

Tip   While it may not immediately seem beneficial to display the same set of data in multiple tree views, consider a file browser. If you need to display the same set of files in multiple file browsers, using the same model for each view would save memory as well as make your program run considerably faster. This is also useful when you want to provide multiple display options for the file browser. When switching between display modes, you do not need to alter the data itself.

Models are composed of columns that contain the same data type and rows that hold each set of data. Each model column can hold a single type of data. A tree model column should not be confused with a tree view column, which is composed of a single header but may be rendered with data from multiple model columns. For example, a tree column may display a text string that has a foreground color defined by a model column that is not visible to the user. Figure 9-2 illustrates the difference between model columns and tree columns.

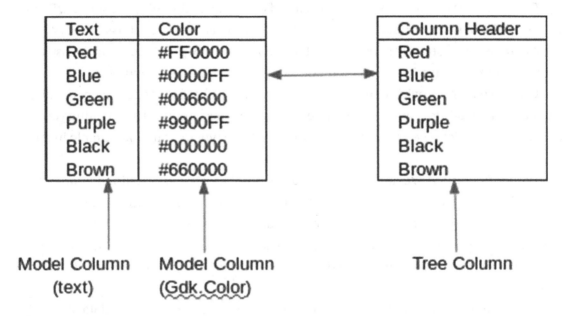

Figure 9-2. *The relationship between model and tree columns*

Each row within a model contains one piece of data corresponding to each model column. In Figure 9-2, each row contains a text string and a Gdk.Color value. These two values are used to display the text with the corresponding color in the tree column. You learn how to implement this in code later in this chapter. For now, you should simply understand the differences between the two types of columns and how they relate.

New list and tree stores are created with a number of columns, each defined by an existing GObject.TYPE. Usually, you need to use only those already implemented in GLib. For example, if you want to display text you can use GObject.TYPE_STRING, GObject.TYPE_BOOLEAN, and a few of the number types like GObject.TYPE_INT.

Tip Since it is possible to store an arbitrary data type with GObject. TYPE_POINTER, one or more tree model columns can be used to simply store information about every row. You just need to be careful when there are a large number of rows, because memory usage quickly escalates. You also have to take care of freeing the pointers yourself.

Gtk.TreeViewColumn and Gtk.CellRenderer

As previously mentioned, a tree view displays one or more Gtk.TreeViewColumn objects. Tree columns are composed of a header and cells of data that are organized into one column. Each tree view column also contains one or more visible columns of data. For example, in a file browser, a tree view column may contain one column of images and one column of file names.

The header of the Gtk.TreeViewColumn widget contains a title that describes what data is held in the cells below. If you make the column sortable, the rows are sorted when one of the column headers is clicked.

Tree view columns do not actually render anything to the screen. This is done with an object derived from Gtk.CellRenderer. Cell renderers are packed into tree view columns similar to how you add widgets into a horizontal box. Each tree view column can contain one or more cell renderers, which are used to render the data. For example, in a file browser, the image column would be rendered with

Gtk.CellRendererPixbuf and the file name with Gtk.CellRendererText. An example of this was shown in Figure 9-1.

Each cell renderer is responsible for rendering a column of cells, one for every row in the tree view. It begins with the first row, rendering its cell and then proceeding to the next row down until the whole column, or part of the column, is rendered.

In GTK+ 3 the g_object_set() function is no longer available. So you must add attributes to the renderer. Column attributes correspond to tree model columns and are associated with cell renderer properties, as shown in Figure 9-3. These properties are applied to each cell as it is rendered.

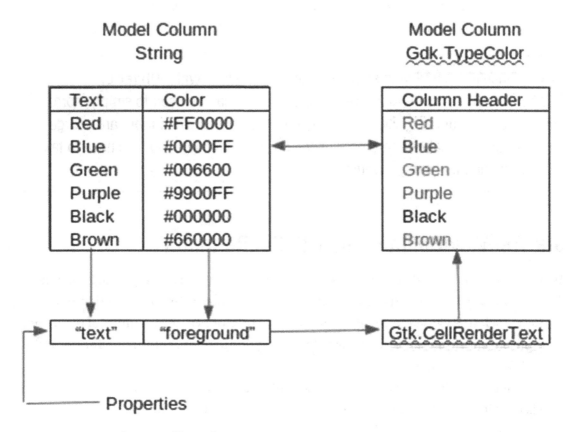

Figure 9-3. *Applying cell renderer properties*

In Figure 9-3, there are two tree model columns with the types GObject.TYPE_STRING and Gdk.RGBA. These are applied to Gtk.CellRendererText's text and foreground properties and used to render the tree view column accordingly.

An additional way to change cell renderer properties is by defining a cell data function. This function is called for every row in the tree view before it is rendered. This allows you to customize how every cell is rendered without the need for the data to be stored in a tree model. For example, a cell data function can be used to define how many decimal places of a floating-point number to display. Cell data functions are covered in detail in the "Cell Data Methods" section of this chapter.

This chapter also covers cell renderers that are used to display text (strings, numbers, and Boolean values), toggle buttons, spin buttons, progress bars, pixbufs, combo boxes, and keyboard accelerators. In addition, you can create custom cell renderer types, but this is usually not needed, since GTK+ now provides such a wide variety of types.

This section has taught you what objects are needed to use the `Gtk.TreeView` widget, what they do, and how they interrelate. Now that you have a basic understanding of the `Gtk.TreeView` widget, the next section has a simple example of the `Gtk.ListStore` tree model.

Using Gtk.ListStore

Recall from the previous section that `Gtk.TreeModel` is simply an interface implemented by data stores, such as `Gtk.ListStore`. `Gtk.ListStore` is used to create lists of data that have no hierarchical relationship among rows.

In this section, a simple Grocery List application is implemented that contains three columns, all of which use `Gtk.CellRendererText`. Figure 9-4 is a screenshot of this application. The first column is a boolean value displaying `True` or `False` that defines whether or not the product should be purchased.

Tip   You usually do not want to display Boolean values as text, because if you have many Boolean columns, it becomes unmanageable for the user. Instead, you want to use toggle buttons. You learn how to do this with `Gtk.CellRendererToggle` in a later section. Boolean values are often also used as column attributes to define cell renderer properties.

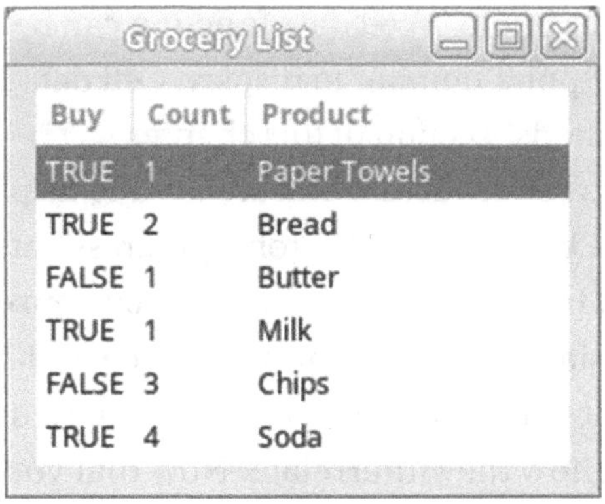

Figure 9-4. *A tree view widget using a Gtk.ListStore tree model*

Listing 9-1 creates a Gtk.ListStore object, which displays a list of groceries. In addition to displaying the products, the list store also displays whether to buy the product and how many of them to buy.

This Grocery List application is used for many examples throughout the rest of the chapter. Therefore, the content of some functions may be excluded later on if it is presented in previous examples. Also, to keep things organized, in every example, setup_tree_view() is used to set up columns and renderers. Full code listings for every example can be downloaded at www.gtkbook.com.

Listing 9-1. Using a Gtk.FontSelectionDialog

```
#!/usr/bin/python3
import sys
import gi
gi.require_version('Gtk', '3.0')
from gi.repository import Gtk, GObject

BUY_IT = 0
QUANTITY = 1
PRODUCT = 2

GroceryItem = (( True, 1, "Paper Towels" ),
               ( True, 2, "Bread" ),
               ( False, 1, "Butter" ),
               ( True, 1, "Milk" ),
               ( False, 3, "Chips" ),
               ( True, 4, "Soda" ))
```

```python
class AppWindow(Gtk.ApplicationWindow):

    def __init__(self, *args, **kwargs):
        super().__init__(*args, **kwargs)
        self.set_border_width(10)
        self.set_size_request(250, 175)
        treeview = Gtk.TreeView.new()
        self.setup_tree_view(treeview)
        store = Gtk.ListStore.new((GObject.TYPE_BOOLEAN,
                                   GObject.TYPE_INT,
                                   GObject.TYPE_STRING))
        for row in GroceryItem:
            iter = store.append(None)
            store.set(iter, BUY_IT, row[BUY_IT], QUANTITY,
                        row[QUANTITY], PRODUCT, row[PRODUCT])
        treeview.set_model(store)
        scrolled_win = Gtk.ScrolledWindow.new(None, None)
        scrolled_win.set_policy(Gtk.PolicyType.AUTOMATIC,
                                Gtk.PolicyType.AUTOMATIC)
        scrolled_win.add(treeview)
        self.add(scrolled_win)
    def setup_tree_view(self, treeview):
        renderer = Gtk.CellRendererText.new()
        column = Gtk.TreeViewColumn("Buy", renderer, text=BUY_IT)
        treeview.append_column(column)
        renderer = Gtk.CellRendererText.new()
        column = Gtk.TreeViewColumn("Count", renderer, text=QUANTITY)
        treeview.append_column(column)
        renderer = Gtk.CellRendererText.new()
        column = Gtk.TreeViewColumn("Product", renderer, text=PRODUCT)
        treeview.append_column(column)

class Application(Gtk.Application):
    def __init__(self, *args, **kwargs):
        super().__init__(*args, application_id="org.example.myapp",
                        **kwargs)
        self.window = None
```

```
    def do_activate(self):
        if not self.window:
            self.window = AppWindow(application=self, title="Grocery List")
        self.window.show_all()
        self.window.present()
    if __name__ == "__main__":
        app = Application()
        app.run(sys.argv)
```

Creating the Tree View

Creating the Gtk.TreeView widget is the easiest part of the process. You need only to call Gtk.TreeView.new(). A tree model can easily be applied to a Gtk.TreeView after initialization with treeview.set_model(store).

Until GTK+ 3 came along, there were functions to hide/unhide the column header for a Gtk.TreeViewColumn. Those functions have been deprecated in GTK+ 3 and now all column headers are always visible.

Gtk.TreeViewColumn headers provide more functionality beyond column titles for some tree views. In sortable tree models, clicking the column header can initiate sorting of all of the rows according to the data held in the corresponding column. It also gives a visual indication of the sort order of the column if applicable. You should not hide the headers if the user needs them to sort the tree view rows.

As a GTK+ developer, you should be very careful about changing visual properties. Users have the ability to choose themes that fit their needs, and you can make your application unusable by changing how widgets are displayed.

Renderers and Columns

After creating the Gtk.TreeView, you need to add one or more columns to the view for it to be of any use. Each Gtk.TreeViewColumn is composed of a header, which displays a short description of its content, and at least one cell renderer. Tree view columns do not actually render any content. Tree view columns hold one or more cell renderers that are used to draw the data on the screen.

All cell renderers are derived from the Gtk.CellRenderer class and are referred to as objects in this chapter, because Gtk.CellRenderer is derived directly from GObject, not from Gtk.Widget. Each cell renderer contains a number of properties that determine how the data is drawn within a cell.

The Gtk.CellRenderer class provides common properties to all derivative renderers, including background color, size parameters, alignments, visibility, sensitivity, and padding. A full list of Gtk.CellRenderer properties can be found in Appendix A. It also provides the editing-canceled and editing-started signals, which allow you to implement editing in custom cell renderers.

In Listing 9-1, you were introduced to Gtk.CellRendererText, which is capable of rendering strings, numbers, and boolean values as text. Textual cell renderers are initialized with Gtk.CellRendererText.new().

Gtk.CellRendererText provides a number of additional properties that dictate how each cell is rendered. You should always set the text property, which is the string that is displayed in the cell. The rest of the properties are similar to those used with text tags.

Gtk.CellRendererText contains a large number of properties that dictate how every row is rendered. renderer.foreground-rgba() was used in the following example to set the foreground color of every piece of text in the renderer to orange. Some properties have a corresponding set property as well, which must be set to True if you want the value to be used. For example, you should set foreground-set to True for the changes takes effect.

```
renderer.props.foreground-rgba = Gdk.RGBA(red=1.0, green=0.65, blue=0.0,
                                          alpha=1.0)
```

After you create a cell renderer, it needs to be added to a Gtk.TreeViewColumn. Tree view columns can be created with Gtk.TreeViewColumn() if you only want the column to display one cell renderer. In the following code, a tree view column is created with the title "Buy" and a renderer with one attribute. This attribute is referred to as BUY_IT (with a value of 0) when the Gtk.ListStore is populated.

```
column = Gtk.TreeViewColumn("Buy", renderer, text=BUY_IT)
```

The preceding function accepts a string to display in the column header, a cell renderer, and a list of attributes. Each attribute contains a string that refers to the renderer property and the tree view column number. The important thing to realize is that the column number provided to Gtk.TreeViewColumn() refers to the tree model column, which may not be the same as the number of tree model columns or cell renderers used by the tree view.

It turns out that the Gtk.TreeViewColumn() is very hard to implement piecemeal in Python 3. It is not just convenience method, but the preferred method for creating a Gtk.TreeViewColumn(). The following code snippet is the correct way to create a Gtk. TreeViewColumn() in Python 3 and assign at least one attribute.

```
renderer = Gtk.CellRendererText.new()
column = Gtk.TreeViewColumn("Buy", renderer, text=BUY_IT)
treeview.append_column(column)
```

If you want to add multiple renderers to the tree view column, you need to pack each renderer and set its attributes separately. For example, in a file manager, you might want to include a text and an image renderer in the same column. However, if every column only needs one cell renderer, it is easiest to use Gtk.TreeViewColumn().

Note   If you want a property, such as the foreground color, set to the same value for every row in the column, you should apply that property directly to the cell renderer with renderer.foreground-rgba(). However, if the property varies depending on the row, you should add it as an attribute of the column for the given renderer.

After you have finished setting up a tree view column, it needs to be added to the tree view with treeview.append_column(column). Columns may also be added into an arbitrary position of the tree view with treeview.insert_column(column) or removed from the view with treeview.remove_column(column).

Creating the Gtk.ListStore

The tree view columns are now set up with the desired cell renderers, so it is time to create the tree model that interfaces between the renderers and the tree view. For the example found in Listing 9-1, we used Gtk.ListStore so that the items would be shown as a list of elements.

New list stores are created with `Gtk.ListStore.new()`. This function accepts the number of columns and the type of the data each column holds. In Listing 9-1, the list store has three columns that store boolean, integer, and string data types.

```
Gtk.ListStore.new((GObject.TYPE_BOOLEAN, GObject.TYPE_INT,
                   GObject.TYPE_STRING))
```

In Python 3, the column type parameters are formed into a tuple. That tells the method not only the column type but also the number of columns.

After creating the list store, you need to add rows with `store.append(None)` for it to be of any use. This method appends a new row to the list store, and the iterator is set to point to the new row. You learn more about tree iterators in a later section of this chapter. For now, it is adequate for you to know that it points to the new tree view row.

```
iter = store.append(None)
store.set(iter, BUY_IT, row[BUY_IT], QUANTITY, row[QUANTITY],
          PRODUCT, row[PRODUCT])
```

Next, we need to set which column and what values are to be loaded with data. This is done with the `store.set()` method. One or more rows can be set with this method. The preceding example stores values in each column of the row from left to right, but the column can be listed in any order since we are also specifying the column number where the value is loaded.

Note   `Gtk.CellRendererText` automatically converts Boolean values and numbers into text strings that can be rendered on the screen. Therefore, the type of data applied to a text attribute column does not have to be text itself, but just has to be consistent with the list store column type that was defined during initialization of the `Gtk.ListStore`.

There are multiple other functions for adding rows to a list store, including `store.prepend()` and `store.insert()`. A full list of available functions can be found in the `Gtk.ListStore` API documentation.

In addition to adding rows, you can also remove them with `store.remove()`. This function removes the row that `Gtk.TreeIter` refers to. After the row is removed, the iterator points to the next row in the list store, and the function returns `True`. If the last row was just removed, the iterator becomes invalid, and the function returns `False`.

```
store.remove(iter)
```

In addition, `store.clear()` is provided, which can be used to remove all rows from a list store. You are left with a `Gtk.ListStore` that contains no data.

After the list store is created, you need to call `treeview.set_model()` to add it to the tree view. By calling this method, the reference count of the tree model is incremented by one.

Using Gtk.TreeStore

There is one other type of built-in tree model called `Gtk.TreeStore`, which organizes rows into a multilevel tree structure. It is possible to implement a list with a `Gtk.TreeStore` tree model as well, but this is not recommended because some overhead is added when the object assumes that the row may have one or more children.

Figure 9-5 shows an example tree store, which contains two root elements, each with children of its own. By clicking the expander to the left of a row with children, you can show or hide its children. This is similar to the functionality provided by the `Gtk.Expander` widget.

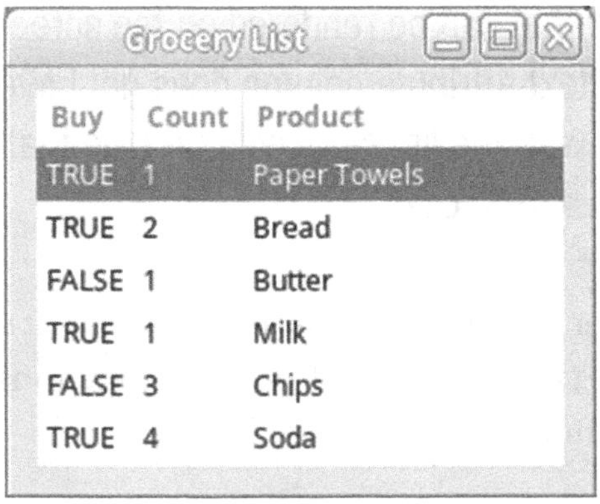

Figure 9-5. *A tree view widget using a Gtk.TreeStore tree model*

The only difference between a Gtk.TreeView implemented with a Gtk.TreeStore instead of a Gtk.ListStore is in the creation of the store. Adding columns and renderers is performed in the same manner with both models, because columns are a part of the view not the model. Executing Listing 9-2 will produce the dialog in Figure 9-5.

Listing 9-2. Creating a Gtk.TreeStore

```python
#!/usr/bin/python3
import sys
import gi
gi.require_version('Gtk', '3.0')
from gi.repository import Gtk, GObject

BUY_IT = 0
QUANTITY = 1
PRODUCT = 2

PRODUCT_CATEGORY = 0
PRODUCT_CHILD = 1

GroceryItem = (( PRODUCT_CATEGORY, True, 0, "Cleaning Supplies"),
               ( PRODUCT_CHILD, True, 1, "Paper Towels" ),
               ( PRODUCT_CHILD, True, 3, "Toilet Paper" ),
               ( PRODUCT_CATEGORY, True, 0, "Food"),
               ( PRODUCT_CHILD, True, 2, "Bread" ),
               ( PRODUCT_CHILD, False, 1, "Butter" ),
               ( PRODUCT_CHILD, True, 1, "Milk" ),
               ( PRODUCT_CHILD, False, 3, "Chips" ),
               ( PRODUCT_CHILD, True, 4, "Soda" ))
class AppWindow(Gtk.ApplicationWindow):
    def __init__(self, *args, **kwargs):
        super().__init__(*args, **kwargs)
        self.set_border_width(10)
        self.set_size_request(275, 270)
        treeview = Gtk.TreeView.new()
        self.setup_tree_view(treeview)
```

```
        store = Gtk.TreeStore.new((GObject.TYPE_BOOLEAN,
                                   GObject.TYPE_INT,
                                   GObject.TYPE_STRING))
    iter = None
    i = 0
    for row in GroceryItem:
        (ptype, buy, quant, prod) = row
        if ptype == PRODUCT_CATEGORY:
            j = i + 1
            (ptype1, buy1, quant1, prod1) = GroceryItem[j]
            while j < len(GroceryItem) and ptype1 == PRODUCT_CHILD:
                if buy1:
                    quant += quant1
                j += 1;
                if j < len(GroceryItem):
                    (ptype1, buy1, quant1, prod1) = GroceryItem[j]
                    iter = store.append(None)
            store.set(iter, BUY_IT, buy, QUANTITY, quant, PRODUCT, prod)
        else:
            child = store.append(iter)
            store.set(child, BUY_IT, buy, QUANTITY, quant, PRODUCT, prod)
        i += 1
    treeview.set_model(store)
    treeview.expand_all()
    scrolled_win = Gtk.ScrolledWindow.new(None, None)
    scrolled_win.set_policy(Gtk.PolicyType.AUTOMATIC,
                            Gtk.PolicyType.AUTOMATIC)
    scrolled_win.add(treeview)
    self.add(scrolled_win)
def setup_tree_view(self, treeview):
    renderer = Gtk.CellRendererText.new()
    column = Gtk.TreeViewColumn("Buy", renderer, text=BUY_IT)
    treeview.append_column(column)
    renderer = Gtk.CellRendererText.new()
    column = Gtk.TreeViewColumn("Count", renderer, text=QUANTITY)
```

```
    treeview.append_column(column)
    renderer = Gtk.CellRendererText.new()
    column = Gtk.TreeViewColumn("Product", renderer, text=PRODUCT)
    treeview.append_column(column)

class Application(Gtk.Application):

    def __init__(self, *args, **kwargs):
        super().__init__(*args, application_id="org.example.myapp",
                         **kwargs)
        self.window = None
    def do_activate(self):
        if not self.window:
            self.window = AppWindow(application=self, title="Grocery List")
        self.window.show_all()
        self.window.present()
    if __name__ == "__main__":
        app = Application()
        app.run(sys.argv)
```

Tree stores are initialized with Gtk.TreeStore.new(), which accepts the same parameters as Gtk.ListStore.new(). The column type parameters are formed into a tuple. That tells the method not only the column type but also the number of columns.

Adding rows to a tree store is a little different than adding rows to a list store. You add rows to a tree store with store.append(), which accepts one iterator or None. The iterator should point to the parent row of the new row. The method returns an iterator that points to the inserted row when the function returns, and the second.

```
iter = store.append(None)
```

In the preceding call to store.append(), a root element was appended to the list by passing None as the parent iterator. The iter tree iterator returned by the method was set to the location of the new row.

In the second call to store.append(), which follows, the row is added as a child of iter. Next, the child tree iterator is returned set to the current location of the new row within the tree store when the method returns.

```
child = store.append(iter)
```

As with list stores, there are many methods available for adding rows to a tree store. These include `store.insert()`, `store.prepend()`, and `store.insert_before()` to name a few. For a full list of methods, you should reference the `Gtk.TreeStore` API documentation.

After you add a row to the tree store, it is simply an empty row with no data. To add data to the row, call `store.set()`. This function works in the same way as `store.set()`. It accepts the tree store, a tree iterator pointing to the location of the row, and a list of column-data pairs. These column numbers correspond to those you used when setting up the cell renderer attributes.

```
store.set(child, BUY_IT, buy, QUANTITY, quant, PRODUCT, prod)
```

In addition to adding rows to a tree store, you can also remove them with `store.remove()`. This function removes the row that is referred to by `Gtk.TreeIter`. After the row is removed, `iter` points to the next row in the tree store, and the function returns `True`. If the row that you removed was the last in the tree store, the iterator becomes invalid, and the function returns `False`.

```
store.remove(iter)
```

In addition, `store.clear()` is provided, which can be used to remove all rows from a tree store. You are left with a `Gtk.TreeStore` that contains no data.

In Listing 9-2, `treeview.expand_all()` is called to expand all of the rows. This is a recursive function that expands every possible row, although it only affects tree models that have child-parent row relationships. In addition, you can collapse all of the rows with `treeview.collapse_all()`. By default, all rows are collapsed.

Referencing Rows

Three objects are available for referring to a specific row within a tree model; each has its own unique advantages. They are `Gtk.TreePath`, `Gtk.TreeIter`, and `Gtk.TreeRowReference`. In the following sections, you learn how each object works and how to use them within your own programs.

Tree Paths

For example, if you are presented with the string 3:7:5, you would start at the fourth root element (recall that indexing begins at zero, so element three is actually the fourth element in the level). You would next proceed to the eighth child of that root element. The row in question is that child's sixth child.

To illustrate this graphically, Figure 9-6 shows the tree view created in Figure 9-5 with the tree paths labeled. Each root element is referred to as only one element, 0 and 1. The first root element has two children, referred to as 0:0 and 0:1.

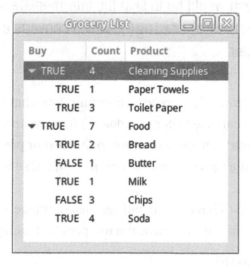

Figure 9-6. *Tree paths for a tree view using Gtk.TreeStore*

Two functions are provided that allow you to convert back and forth between a path and its equivalent string: `treepath.to_string()` and `Gtk.TreePath.new_from_string()`. You usually do not have to deal with the string path directly unless you are trying to save the state of a tree view, but using it helps in understanding the way tree paths work.

Listing 9-3 gives a short example of using tree paths. It begins by creating a new path that points to the Bread product row. Next, `treepath.up()` moves up one level in the path. When you convert the path back into a string, you see that the resulting output is 1, pointing to the Food row.

Listing 9-3. Converting Between Paths and Strings

```
treepath = Gtk.TreePath.new_from_string("1:0")
treepath.up(path)
str = treepath.to_string(path)
print(str)
```

Tip   If you need to get a tree iterator and only have the path string available, you can convert the string into a Gtk.TreePath and then to a Gtk.TreeIter. However, a better solution would be to skip the intermediate step with treemodel.get_iter_from_string(), which converts a tree path string directly into a tree iterator.

In addition to treepath.up(), there are other functions that allow you to navigate through a tree model. You can use treepath.down() to move to the child row and treepath.next() or treepath.prev() to move to the next or previous row in the same level. When you move to the previous row or parent row, False is returned if it was not successful.

At times, you may need to have a tree path as a list of integers instead of a string. The treepath.get_indices() function returns the integers that compose the path string.

```
treepath.get_indices(path)
```

Problems can arise with tree paths when a row is added or removed from the tree model. The path could end up pointing to a different row within the tree or, worse, a row that does not exist anymore! For example, if a tree path points to the last element of a tree and you remove that row, it now points beyond the limits of the tree. To get around this problem, you can convert the tree path into a tree row reference.

Tree Row References

Gtk.TreeRowReference objects are used to watch a tree model for changes. Internally, they connect to the "row-inserted", "row-deleted", and "rows-reordered" signals, updating the stored path based on the changes.

New tree row references are created with Gtk.TreeRowReference.new() from an existing Gtk.TreeModel and Gtk.TreePath. The tree path copied into the row reference is updated as changes occur within the model.

```
treerowref.new(model, path)
```

When you need to retrieve the path, you can use treerowref.get_path(), which returns None if the row no longer exists within the model. Tree row references are able to update the tree path based on changes within the tree model, but if you remove all elements from the same level as the tree path's row, it no longer has a row to point to.

You should be aware that tree row references do add a small bit of overhead processing when adding, removing, or sorting rows within a tree model, since the references have to handle all of the signals emitted by these actions. This overhead does not matter for most applications, because there will not be enough rows for the user to notice. However, if your application contains a large number of rows, you should use tree row references wisely.

Tree Iterators

GTK+ provides the Gtk.TreeIter object, which can be used to reference a specific row within a Gtk.TreeModel. These iterators are used internally by models, which means that you should never directly alter the content of a tree iterator.

You have already seen multiple instances of Gtk.TreeIter, from which you can discern that tree iterators are used in a similar way to Gtk.TreeIter. Tree iterators are used for manipulation of tree models. Tree paths, however, are used to point to rows within a tree model in a way that provides a human-readable interface. Tree row references can be used to make sure that tree paths adjust where they point throughout changes of a tree model.

GTK+ provides a number of built-in methods to perform operations on the tree iterators. Typically, iterators are used to add rows to a model, set the content of a row, and retrieve the content of a model. In Figure 9-1 and Figure 9-2, tree iterators were used to add rows to Gtk.ListStore and Gtk.TreeStore models and then set the initial content of each row.

Gtk.TreeModel provides a number of iter_*() methods, which can be used to move iterators and retrieve information about them. For example, to move to the next iterator position, you could use treemodel.iter_next(), which returns True if the action was successful. A full list of available functions can be found in the Gtk.TreeModel API documentation.

It is easy to convert between tree iterators and tree paths with the use of `treemodel.get_path()` and `treemodel.get_iter()`. The tree path or iterator must be valid for either of these functions to work correctly. Listing 9-4 gives a short example of how to convert between `Gtk.TreeIter` and `Gtk.TreePath`.

Listing 9-4. Converting Between Paths and Iterators

```
path = treemodel.get_path(model, iter)
iter = treemodel.get_iter(model, path)
```

The first method in Listing 9-4, `treemodel.get_path()` converts a valid tree iterator into a tree path. That path is then sent to `treemodel.get_iter()`, which converts it back into an iterator. Notice that the second method accepts two parameters.

One problem presented by `Gtk.TreeIter` is that the iterator is not guaranteed to exist after a model is edited. This is not true in all cases, and you can use `treemodel.get_flags()` to check the `Gtk.TreeModelFlags.ITERS_PERSIST` flag, which is turned on by default for `Gtk.ListStore` and `Gtk.TreeStore`. If this flag is set, the tree iterator is always valid as long as the row exists.

```
treemodel.get_flags()
```

Even if the iterator is set to persist, it is not a good idea to store tree iterator objects, since they are used internally by tree models. Instead, you should use tree row references to keep track of rows over time, since references will not become invalidated when the tree model changes.

Adding Rows and Handling Selections

Both of the examples that you have been given up to this point define the tree model during startup. The content does not change after it is initially set. In this section, the Grocery List application is expanded to allow the user to add and remove products. Before the example is introduced, you learn how to handle single and multiple selections.

Single Selections

Selection information is held for each tree view by a Gtk.TreeSelection object. You can retrieve this object with treeview.get_selection(). A Gtk.TreeSelection object is automatically created for you for every Gtk.TreeView, so there is never a need to create your own tree selection.

Caution   Gtk.TreeSelection provides one signal, "changed", which is emitted when the selection has changed. You should be careful when using this signal, because it is not always reliable. It can be emitted when no changes occur by the user selecting a row that is already selected. Therefore, it is best to use the signals provided by Gtk.TreeView for selection handling, which is in Appendix B.

Tree views support multiple types of selections. You can change the selection type with treeselection.set_mode(). Selection types are defined by the Gtk.SelectionMode enumeration, which includes the following values.

- Gtk.SelectionMode.NONE: The user is prohibited from selecting any rows.

- Gtk.SelectionMode.SINGLE: The user may select up to one row, though it is possible that no row is selected. By default, tree selections are initialized with Gtk.SelectionMode.SINGLE.

- Gtk.SelectionMode.BROWSE: The user is able to select exactly one row. In some rare cases, there may not be a selected row. This option actually prohibits the user from deselecting a row except when the selection is moved to another row.

- Gtk.SelectionMode.MULTIPLE: The user may select any number of rows. The user is able to use the Ctrl and Shift keys to select additional elements or ranges of elements.

If you have defined the selection type as Gtk.SelectionMode.SINGLE or Gtk.SelectionMode.BROWSE, you can be sure that only one row is selected. For tree views with one selection, you can use treeselection.get_selected() to retrieve the selected row.

```
treeselection.get_selected(model, iter)
```

The `treeselection.get_selected()` method can be used to retrieve the tree model associated with the `Gtk.TreeSelection` object and a tree iterator pointing to the selected row. `True` is returned if the model and iterator were successfully set. This function will not work with a selection mode of `Gtk.SelectionMode.MULTIPLE`!

If no row has been selected, the tree iterator is set to `None`, and `False` is returned from the function. Therefore, `treeselection.get_selected()` can also be used as a test to check whether or not there is a selected row.

Multiple Selections

If your tree selection allows multiple rows to be selected (`Gtk.SelectionMode.MULTIPLE`), you have two options for handling selections, calling a function for every row or retrieving all of the selected rows as a Python list. Your first option is to call a function for every selected row with `treeselection.selected_foreach()`.

```
treeselection.selected_foreach(selected, foreach_func, None)
```

This function allows you to call `selected_foreach_func()` for every selected row, passing an optional data parameter. In the preceding example, `None` was passed to the function. The function must be either a Python function or method, an example of which is seen in Listing 9-5. The function in Listing 9-5 retrieves the product string and prints it to the screen.

Listing 9-5. Selected for-each Function

```
foreach_func(model, path, iter, data)
    (text,) = model.get(iter, PRODUCT)
    print ("Selected Product: %s" % text)
```

Note   You should not modify the tree model or selection from within the `foreach_func` implementation! GTK+ gives critical errors to the user if you do so, because invalid tree paths and iterators may result.

Also note the method `model.get()` always return a tuple, even if you only ask for a single column.

One problem with using tree selection `foreach_func` functions is that you are not able to manipulate the selection from within the function. To remedy this problem, a better solution would be to use `treeselection.get_selected_rows()`, which returns a Python list of `Gtk.TreePath` objects, each pointing to a selected row.

```
treeselection.get_selected_rows(model)
```

You can then perform some operation on each row within the list. However, you need to be careful. If you need to edit the tree model within the List, you want to first convert all of the tree paths to tree row references, so they continue to be valid throughout the duration of your actions.

If you want to loop through all of the rows manually, you are also able to use `treeselection.count_selected_rows()`, which returns the number of rows that are currently selected.

Adding New Rows

Now that you have been introduced to selections, it is time to add the ability to add new products to the list.

The only difference in this example in comparison to the previous Grocery List application is visible in Figure 9-7, which shows that an Add and Remove buttons were added along the bottom of the tree view. Also, the selection mode was changed to allow the user to select multiple rows at a time.

Figure 9-7. *Editing an item in the grocery list*

Listing 9-6 is the implementation of the callback function that is run when the user clicks the Add button. It presents the user with a Gtk.Dialog that asks the user to choose a category, enter a product name and quantity of products to buy, and select whether or not to purchase the product.

If all of the fields are valid, the row is added under the chosen category. Also, if the user specified that the product should be purchased, the quantity is added to the total quantity of the category.

Listing 9-6. Adding a New Product

```python
#!/usr/bin/python3
import sys
import gi
gi.require_version('Gtk', '3.0')
from gi.repository import Gtk, GObject

BUY_IT = 0
QUANTITY = 1
PRODUCT = 2

PRODUCT_CATEGORY = 0
PRODUCT_CHILD = 1

GroceryItem = (( PRODUCT_CATEGORY, True, 0, "Cleaning Supplies"), (
            PRODUCT_CHILD, True, 1, "Paper Towels" ),
            ( PRODUCT_CHILD, True, 3, "Toilet Paper" ), ( PRODUCT_CATEGORY,
            True, 0, "Food"), ( PRODUCT_CHILD, True, 2, "Bread" ),
            ( PRODUCT_CHILD, False, 1, "Butter" ),
            ( PRODUCT_CHILD, True, 1, "Milk" ),
            ( PRODUCT_CHILD, False, 3, "Chips" ),
            ( PRODUCT_CHILD, True, 4, "Soda" ))
class AddDialog(Gtk.Dialog):

    def __init__(self, *args, **kwargs):
        super().__init__(*args, **kwargs)
        parent = kwargs['parent']
        # set up buttons
        self.add_button("Add", Gtk.ResponseType.OK)
```

```python
self.add_button("Cancel", Gtk.ResponseType.CANCEL)
# set up dialog widgets
combobox = Gtk.ComboBoxText.new()
entry = Gtk.Entry.new()
spin = Gtk.SpinButton.new_with_range(0, 100, 1)
check = Gtk.CheckButton.new_with_mnemonic("_Buy the Product")
spin.set_digits(0)
# Add all of the categories to the combo box. for row in GroceryItem:
    (ptype, buy, quant, prod) = row
    if ptype == PRODUCT_CATEGORY:
        combobox.append_text(prod)
# create a grid
grid = Gtk.Grid.new()
grid.set_row_spacing (5)
grid.set_column_spacing(5)
# fill out the grid
grid.attach(Gtk.Label.new("Category:"), 0, 0, 1, 1)
grid.attach(Gtk.Label.new("Product:"), 0, 1, 1, 1)
grid.attach(Gtk.Label.new("Quantity:"), 0, 2, 1, 1)
grid.attach(combobox, 1, 0, 1, 1)
grid.attach(entry, 1, 1, 1, 1)
grid.attach(spin, 1, 2, 1, 1)
grid.attach(check, 1, 3, 1, 1)
self.get_content_area().pack_start(grid, True, True, 5)
self.show_all()

# run the dialog and check the results
if self.run() != Gtk.ResponseType.OK:
    self.destroy()
    return
quantity = spin.get_value()
product = entry.get_text()
category = combobox.get_active_text()
buy = check.get_active()
```

```
        if product == "" or category == None:
            print("All of the fields were not correctly filled out!")
            return
        model = parent.get_treeview().get_model();
        iter = model.get_iter_from_string("0")
        # Retrieve an iterator pointing to the selected category. while iter:
            (name,) = model.get(iter, PRODUCT)
            if name == None or name.lower() == category.lower():
                break
            iter = model.iter_next(iter)
        #
        #
        # Convert the category iterator to a path so that it  # will not
        become invalid and add the new product as a child of the category.

        path = model.get_path(iter)

        child = model.append(iter)
        model.set(child, BUY_IT, buy, QUANTITY, quantity, PRODUCT, product)
        # Add the quantity to the running total if it is to be purchased.
        if buy:
            iter = model.get_iter(path)
            (i,) = model.get(iter, QUANTITY) i += quantity
            model.set(iter, QUANTITY, i)
        self.destroy()
class AppWindow(Gtk.ApplicationWindow):

    def __init__(self, *args, **kwargs):
        super().__init__(*args, **kwargs)
        self.set_border_width(10)
        self.set_size_request(275, 270)
        self.treeview = Gtk.TreeView.new()
        self.setup_tree_view(self.treeview)
        store = Gtk.TreeStore.new((GObject.TYPE_BOOLEAN,
                            GObject.TYPE_INT,
                            GObject.TYPE_STRING))
```

```
iter = None
i = 0
for row in GroceryItem:
    (ptype, buy, quant, prod) = row
    if ptype == PRODUCT_CATEGORY:
        j = i + 1
        (ptype1, buy1, quant1, prod1) = GroceryItem[j]
        while j < len(GroceryItem) and ptype1 == PRODUCT_CHILD:
            if buy1:
                quant += quant1
            j += 1;
            if j < len(GroceryItem):
                (ptype1, buy1, quant1, prod1) = GroceryItem[j]
                iter = store.append(None)
        store.set(iter, BUY_IT, buy, QUANTITY, quant, PRODUCT, prod)
    else:
        child = store.append(iter)
        store.set(child, BUY_IT, buy, QUANTITY, quant, PRODUCT, prod)
    i += 1
self.treeview.set_model(store)
self.treeview.expand_all()
scrolled_win = Gtk.ScrolledWindow.new(None, None)
scrolled_win.set_policy(Gtk.PolicyType.AUTOMATIC,
                        Gtk.PolicyType.AUTOMATIC)
scrolled_win.add(self.treeview)
button_add = Gtk.Button.new_with_label("Add")
button_add.connect("clicked", self.on_add_button_clicked, self)
button_remove = Gtk.Button.new_with_label("Remove")
hbox = Gtk.Box(orientation=Gtk.Orientation.HORIZONTAL, spacing=0)
hbox.pack_end(button_remove, False, True, 5)
hbox.pack_end(button_add, False, True, 5)
vbox = Gtk.Box(orientation=Gtk.Orientation.VERTICAL, spacing=0)
vbox.pack_end(hbox, False, True, 5)
vbox.pack_end(scrolled_win, True, True, 5)
self.add(vbox)
```

```python
    def setup_tree_view(self, treeview):
        renderer = Gtk.CellRendererText.new()
        column = Gtk.TreeViewColumn("Buy", renderer, text=BUY_IT)
        self.treeview.append_column(column)
        renderer = Gtk.CellRendererText.new()
        column = Gtk.TreeViewColumn("Count", renderer, text=QUANTITY)
        treeview.append_column(column)
        renderer = Gtk.CellRendererText.new()
        column = Gtk.TreeViewColumn("Product", renderer, text=PRODUCT)
        treeview.append_column(column)

    def on_add_button_clicked(self, button, parent):
        dialog = AddDialog(title="Add a Product", parent=parent,
                           flags=Gtk.DialogFlags.MODAL)

    def get_treeview(self):
        return self.treeview

class Application(Gtk.Application):

    def __init__(self, *args, **kwargs):
        super().__init__(*args, application_id="org.example.myapp",
                         **kwargs)
        self.window = None

    def do_activate(self):
        if not self.window:
            self.window = AppWindow(application=self, title="Grocery List")
        self.window.show_all()
        self.window.present()
if __name__ == "__main__":
    app = Application()
    app.run(sys.argv)
```

Retrieving Row Data

Retrieving the values stored in a tree model row is very similar to adding a row. In Listing 9-6 model.get_iter_from_string() is first used to retrieve a tree iterator that points to the first row in the tree view. This corresponds to the first category.

Next, model.iter_next() is used to loop through all of the root-level rows. For each root-level row, the following code is run. First, the product name is retrieved with model. get(). This function works like treestore.set(), which accepts a Gtk.TreeModel, an iterator pointing to a row, and a list of one or more column numbers. This method always returns a tuple even if you supply a single column as a parameter.

```
(name,) = model.get(iter, PRODUCT)
if name.lower() == category.lower():
    break
```

Then the current product is compared to the chosen category name. If the two strings match, the loop is exited, because the correct category was found. The iter variable now points to the selected category.

Adding a New Row

Adding new rows to the tree model is done in the same way as they were originally added during startup. In the following code, the Gtk.TreeIter that points to the chosen category is first converted into a tree path, since it becomes invalidated when the tree store is changed. Note that it does not have to be converted to a tree row reference, because its location will not possibly change.

```
path = model.get_path(iter)
child = model.append(iter)
model.set(child, BUY_IT, buy, QUANTITY, quantity, PRODUCT, product)
```

Next, a new row is appended with treestore.append(), where iter is the parent row. That row is populated with treestore.set(), using the data entered by the user in the dialog.

Combo Boxes

Listing 9-6 introduces a new widget called Gtk.ComboBox.

Gtk.ComboBox is a widget that allows the user to choose from a number of options in a drop-down list.

The combo box displays the selected choice in its normal state. Combo boxes can be used in two different ways, depending on what method you use to instantiate the widget, either with a custom Gtk.TreeModel or with a default model with only a single column of strings.

In Listing 9-6 a new Gtk.ComboBox was created with Gtk.ComboBoxText.new(), which creates a specialized combo box that contains only one column of strings. This is simply a convenience method, because the drop-down list of a combo box is internally handled with a Gtk.TreeModel. This allows you to easily append and prepend options and insert new options with the following methods.

```
combobox.append_text(text)
combobox.prepend_text(text)
combobox.insert_text(position, text)
```

The first function combobox.get_active_text() returns an integer that refers to the index of the current row or -1 if there is no selection. This can be converted into a string and then into a Gtk.TreePath. Also, combobox.get_active_iter() retrieves an iterator pointing to the selected row, returning True if the iterator was set.

Removing Multiple Rows

The next step is to add the ability to remove products from the list. Since we have added the ability for multiple rows to be selected, the code must also be able to remove more than one row.

Listing 9-7 implements two methods. The first method, remove_row(), is called for every selected row, removing the row if it is not a category. If the removed row was to be purchased, its quantity is removed from the category's running total. The second function, remove_products(), is the method that is run when the Remove button is clicked.

Listing 9-7. Removing One or More Products

```
def remove_row(self, ref, model):
    # Convert the tree row reference to a path and retrieve the
    iterator. path = ref.get_path()
    iter = model.get_iter(path)
    # Only remove the row if it is not a root row.
    parent = model.iter_parent(iter)
    if parent:
        (buy, quantity) = model.get(iter, BUY_IT, QUANTITY)
        (pnum,) = model.get(parent, QUANTITY)
        if (buy):
            pnum -= quantity
            model.set(parent, QUANTITY, pnum)
        iter = model.get_iter(path)
    model.remove(iter)

def remove_products(self, button, treeview):
    selection = treeview.get_selection()
    model = treeview.get_model()
    rows = selection.get_selected_rows(model)
    # Create tree row references to all of the selected rows.
    references = []
    for data in rows:
        ref = Gtk.TreeRowReference.new(model, data)
        references.append(ref)
    for ref in references:
        self.remove_row(ref, model)
```

When the Remove button is pressed, the remove_products() method is called. This function begins by calling selection.get_selected_rows() to retrieve a Python list of tree paths that point to the selected rows. Since the application is altering the rows, the list of paths is converted into a list of row references. This makes sure that all of the tree paths remain valid.

After the paths are converted to tree row references, the list is iterated via a Python for statement and the remove_row() method is called for every item. Within remove_row(), a new function is used to check whether the row is a category.

If the selected row is a category, we know that it is a root element and have no parents. Therefore, the following model.iter_parent() call performs two tasks. First, if the parent iterator is not set, this method returns False, and the category row is not removed. If the row has a parent, which means that it is a product, the parent iterator is set and used later in the function.

```
parent = model.iter_parent(iter)
```

Second, the function retrieves information about the selected product and its parent category. If the product is set to be purchased, its quantity is subtracted from the total product count displayed by the category. Since changing this data invalidates the iterator, the path is converted into an iterator, and the row is removed from the tree model.

Handling Double-clicks

Double-clicks are handled with the row-activated signal of the Gtk.TreeView. The signal is emitted when the user double-clicks a row, when the user presses the spacebar, Shift+spacebar, Return, or Enter on a noneditable row, or when you call treeview.row_activated().

Listing 9-8. Editing a Clicked Row

```
def row_activated(self, treeview, path, column, data):
    model = treeview.get_model()
    if model.get_iter(path))
        # Handle the selection ...
```

In Listing 9-8, the callback method row_activated() is called when the user activates a row within the tree view. The activated row is retrieved from the tree path object with treemodel.get_iter(). From there, you are free to use whatever functions/methods you have learned thus far to retrieve or alter the content of the row.

Editable Text Renderers

It would be very useful to allow the user to edit the contents of a tree view. This could be accomplished by presenting a dialog that contains a Gtk.Entry, in which the user would be able to edit the content of a cell. However, GTK+ provides a much simpler way to edit textual components that is integrated into the tree cell by using Gtk.CellRendererText's edited signal.

When a user clicks a cell in the selected row that is marked as editable, a Gtk.Entry is placed in the cell that contains the current contents of the cell. An example of a cell being edited is shown in Figure 9-8.

Figure 9-8. *An editable cell*

After the user presses the **Enter** key or removes focus from the text entry, the edited widget is emitted. You need to connect to this signal and apply the changes once it is emitted. Listing 9-9 shows you how to create the Gtk.ListStore Grocery List application where the product column is editable.

Listing 9-9. Editing a Cell's Text

```
def set_up_treeview(self, treeview):
    renderer = Gtk.CellRenderer.Text.new()
    column = Gtk.TreeViewColumn.new_with_attributes("Buy", renderer,
    "text", BUY_IT)
```

253

```
treeview.append_column(column)
renderer = Gtk.CellRendererText.new()
column = Gtk.TreeViewColumn.new_with_attributes("Count", renderer,
"text", QUANTITY)

treeview.append_column(column)

# Set up the third column in the tree view to be editable. renderer
= Gtk.CellRendererText.new() renderer.set_property("editable",
True) renderer.connect("edited", self.cell_edited, treeview)
column = Gtk.TreeViewColumn.new_with_attributes("Product",
renderer, "text", PRODUCT)

treeview.append_column(column)

def cell_edited(self, renderer, path, new_text, treeview):Tree View Widget
    if len(new_text) > 0:
        model = treeview.get_model()
        iter = model.get_iter_from_string(path)
        if iter:
            model.set(iter, PRODUCT, new_text)
```

Creating editable `Gtk.CellRendererText` cells is a very simple process. The first thing you need to do is set the editable and editable-set properties of the text renderer to True.

```
renderer.set_property("editable", True)
```

Remember that setting the editable property applies it to the whole column of data that is drawn by the renderer. If you want to specify row by row whether the cell should be editable, you should add it as an attribute of the column.

The next thing you need to do is connect the cell renderer to the edited signal provided by `Gtk.CellRendererText`. The callback function for this signal receives the cell renderer, a `Gtk.TreePath` string pointing to the edited row, and the new text that was entered by the user. This signal is emitted when the user presses the **Enter** key or moves focus from the cell's `Gtk.Entry` while the cell is being edited.

The edited signal is necessary, because changes are not automatically applied to the cell. This allows you to filter out invalid entries. For example, in Listing 9-9, the new text is not applied when the new string is empty.

```
iter = model.get_iter_from_string(path)
if iter:
    model.set(iter, PRODUCT, new_text)
```

Once you are ready to apply the text, you can convert the Gtk.TreePath string directly into a Gtk.TreeIter with model.get_iter_from_string(). This function returns True if the iterator was successfully set, which means that the path string points to a valid row.

Caution   You always want to check that the path is valid, even though it is supplied by GTK+, because there is a chance that the row has been removed or moved since the callback function was initialized.

After you retrieve the Gtk.TreeIter, you can use model.set() to apply the new text string to the column. In Listing 9-9, new_text was applied to the PRODUCT column of the Gtk.ListStore.

Cell Data Methods

If you need to further customize every cell before it is rendered to the screen, you can use cell data methods. They allow you to tinker with every property of each individual cell. For example, you can set the foreground color based on the content of the cell or restrict the number of decimal places a floating-point number that are shown. It can also be used to set properties that are calculated during runtime.

Figure 9-9, which creates a color list, shows an application that uses cell data functions to set the background color of each cell based on the text property of the Gtk.CellRendererText.

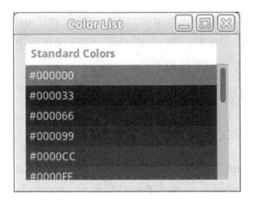

Figure 9-9. *Screenshot of Listing 9-10*

Caution   Make sure not to use cell data functions if you have a large number of rows in your tree model. Cell data functions process every cell in the column before it is rendered, so they can significantly slow down tree models with many rows.

In Listing 9-10, a cell data function is used to set the background color to the value of the color string stored by the cell. The foreground color is also set to white for every cell, although this could also be applied to the whole renderer with the model.set(). This application shows a list of the 256 web-safe colors.

Listing 9-10. Using Cell Data Functions

```python
#!/usr/bin/python3

import sys
import gi
gi.require_version('Gtk', '3.0')
from gi.repository import Gtk, Gdk, GObject

clr = ( "00", "33", "66", "99", "CC", "FF" )
COLOR = 0

class AppWindow(Gtk.ApplicationWindow):

    def __init__(self, *args, **kwargs):
        super().__init__(*args, **kwargs)
        self.set_border_width(10)
```

```
    self.set_size_request(250, 175)
    treeview = Gtk.TreeView.new()
    self.setup_tree_view(treeview)
    store = Gtk.ListStore.new((GObject.TYPE_STRING,
                        GObject.TYPE_STRING, GObject.TYPE_STRING))
    for var1 in clr:
        for var2 in clr:
            for var3 in clr:
                color = "#" + var1 + var2 + var3
                iter = store.append()
                store.set(iter, (COLOR,), (color,))
    treeview.set_model(store)
    scrolled_win = Gtk.ScrolledWindow.new(None, None)
    scrolled_win.set_policy(Gtk.PolicyType.AUTOMATIC,
                        Gtk.PolicyType.AUTOMATIC)
    scrolled_win.add(treeview)
    self.add(scrolled_win)

def setup_tree_view(self, treeview):
    renderer = Gtk.CellRendererText.new()
    column = Gtk.TreeViewColumn.new()
    column.pack_start(renderer, True)
    column.add_attribute(renderer, "text", COLOR)
    column.set_title("Standard Colors")
    treeview.append_column(column)
    column.set_cell_data_func(renderer, self.cell_data_func, None)

def cell_data_func(self, column, renderer, model, iter, data):
    # Get the color string stored by the column and make it the
    # foreground color
    (text,) = model.get(iter, COLOR)
    renderer.props.foreground_rgba = Gdk.RGBA(red=1.0, green=1.0,
                                        blue=1.0, alpha=1.0)

    red = int(text[1:3], 16) / 255
```

```
        green = int(text[3:5], 16) / 255 blue = int(text[5:7], 16) / 255
        renderer.props.background_rgba = Gdk.RGBA(red=red, green=green,
                                                  blue=blue, alpha=1.0)
        renderer.props.text = text

class Application(Gtk.Application):

    def __init__(self, *args, **kwargs):
        super().__init__(*args, application_id="org.example.myapp", **kwargs)
        self.window = None

    def do_activate(self):
        if not self.window:
            self.window = AppWindow(application=self, title="Color List")
        self.window.show_all()
        self.window.present()

if __name__ == "__main__":
    app = Application()
    app.run(sys.argv)
```

Another example of a useful cell data function is when you are using floating-point numbers, and you need to control the number of decimal places that are displayed. In fact, that example is used when you learn about spin button cell renderers in the "Spin Button Renderers" section of this chapter.

Once you have set up your cell data function, you need to connect it to a specific column by calling `column.set_cell_data_func()`. The last two parameters of this function allow you to supply data that is passed to the cell data function and an additional function that is called to destroy the data. You can set both of these parameters to None if they are not necessary.

```
column.set_cell_data_func(renderer, self.cell_data_func, None)
```

If you have added a cell data function to a column that you now want to remove, you should call `column.set_cell_data_func()` function parameter set to None.

As previously stated, cell data functions should only be used when you have a definite need for fine-tuning the rendering of the data. In most cases, you want to use additional column attributes or `column.property_set()` to change properties, depending on the scope of the settings. As a rule of thumb, cell data functions should only be used to apply settings that cannot be handled with column attributes or may not be set for every cell.

Cell Renderers

Up to this point, you have only learned about one type of cell renderer, Gtk. CellRendererText. This renderer allows you to display strings, numbers, and Boolean values as text. You are able to customize how the text is displayed with cell renderer attributes and cell data functions and allow it to be edited by the user.

GTK+ provides a large number of cell renderers that can display other types of widgets besides text. These are toggle buttons, images, spin buttons, combo boxes, progress bars, and accelerators, which are all covered in this chapter.

Toggle Button Renderers

Displaying Boolean values as "TRUE" or "FALSE" with Gtk.CellRendererText is a bit tacky, and it takes up a large amount of valuable space in each row, especially when there are a lot of visible Boolean columns. You might be thinking that it would be nice if you could display a check button for Boolean values instead of text strings. It turns out that you can — with the help of a type of cell renderer named Gtk.CellRendererToggle.

By default, toggle button cell renderers are drawn as a check button, as shown in Figure 9-10. You can also set up toggle button renderers to be drawn as radio buttons, but you need to manage the radio button functionality yourself.

Figure 9-10. *Toggle button renderers*

As with editable text renderers, you have to manually apply the changes performed by the user; otherwise, the button will not toggle visually on the screen. Because of this, Gtk.CellRendererToggle provides the toggled signal, which is emitted when the user presses the check button. Listing 9-11 presents a toggled callback function for the Grocery List application. In this version of the application, the BUY_IT column is rendered with Gtk.CellRendererToggle.

Listing 9-11. Using Cell Data Functions

```
def buy_it_toggled(renderer, path, treeview):
        model = treeview.get_model()
        iter = model.get_iter_from_string(path)
        if iter:
            (value,) = model.get(iter, BUY_IT)
            model.set_row(iter, (!value, None))
```

Toggle cell renderers are created with Gtk.CellRendererToggle.new(). After creating a toggle cell renderer, you want to set its activatable property to True so that it can be toggled; otherwise, the user will not be able to toggle the button (which can be useful if you only want to display a setting but not allow it to be edited). column.property_set() can be used to apply this setting to every cell.

Next, the active property should be added as a column attribute instead of text, which was used by Gtk.CellRendererText. This property is set to True or False, depending on the desired state of the toggle button.

Then, you should connect the Gtk.CellRendererToggle cell renderer to a callback function for the toggled signal. Listing 9-11 gives an example callback function for the toggled signal. This callback function receives the cell renderer and a Gtk.TreePath string pointing to the row that contains the toggle button.

Within the callback function, you need to manually toggle the current value displayed by the toggle button as shown in the following two lines of code. The emission of a toggled signal only tells you that the user wants the button to be toggled; it does not perform the action for you.

```
(value,) = model.get(iter, BUY_IT)
model.set_row(iter, (!value, None))
```

To toggle the value, you can use model.get() to retrieve the current value stored by the cell. Since the cell is storing a Boolean value, you can set the new value to the opposite of the current in model.set_row().

As previously mentioned, Gtk.CellRendererToggle also allows you to render the toggle as a radio button. This can be initially set to the renderer by changing the radio property with renderer.set_radio().

renderer.set_radio(radio)

You need to realize that the only thing that is changed by setting radio to True is the rendering of the toggle button! You have to manually implement the functionality of a radio button through your toggled callback function. This includes activating the new toggle button and deactivating the previously selected toggle button.

Pixbuf Renderers

Adding images in the form of GdkPixbuf objects as a column in a Gtk.TreeView is a very useful feature provided by Gtk.CellRendererPixbuf. An example of a pixbuf renderer is shown in Figure 9-11, in which there is a small icon to the left of each item.

Figure 9-11. *Pixbuf renderers*

You have already learned almost everything necessary to add GdkPixbuf images to a tree view in previous sections, but Listing 9-12 presents a simple example to guide you. There is no need to create a separate column header for pixbufs in most cases, so Listing 9-12 shows you how to include multiple renderers in one column. Pixbuf cell renderers are extremely useful in types of tree view implementations, such as file system browsers.

Listing 9-12. GdkPixbuf Cell Renderers

```
def set_up_treeview(self, treeview):
    column = Gtk.TreeViewColumn.new()
    column.set_resizable(True)
    column.set_title("Some Items")
    renderer = Gtk.CellRendererPixbuf.new()
    # it is important to pack the renderer BEFORE adding attributes!!
    column.pack_start(renderer, False) column.add_attribute(renderer,
    "pixbuf", ICON)
    renderer = Gtk.CellRendererText.new()
    # it is important to pack the renderer BEFORE adding attributes!!
    column.pack_start(renderer, True) column.add_attribute(renderer,
    "text", ICON_NAME) treeview.append_column(column)
```

New Gtk.CellRendererPixbuf objects are created with Gtk.CellRendererPixbuf. new(). You then want to add the renderer to the column. Since there is multiple renderers Gtk.CellRendererPixbuf.new() in our column, you can use column.pack_ start() to add the renderer to the column. It is important to pack the renderer into the column BEFORE adding an attributes. Failure to do this invalidates the renderer and you receive a runtime warning and no data appears in the column.

Next, you need to add attributes to the column for the Gtk.CellRendererPixbuf. In Listing 9-12, the pixbuf property was used so that we could load a custom icon from a file. However, pixbufs are not the only type of image supported by Gtk. CellRendererPixbuf.

If you are using a Gtk.TreeStore, it is useful to display a different pixbuf when the row is expanded and when it is retracted. To do this, you can specify two GdkPixbuf objects to pixbuf-expander-open and pixbuf-expander-closed. For example, you may want to do this to display an open folder when the row is expanded and a closed folder when the row is retracted.

When you create the tree model, you need to use a new type called GdkPixbuf.
Pixbuf, which stores GdkPixbuf objects in each model column. Every time you add a
GdkPixbuf to a tree model column, its reference count is incremented by one.

Spin Button Renderers

In Chapter 5, you learned how to use the Gtk.SpinButton widget. While
Gtk.CellRendererText can display numbers, a better option is to use Gtk.
CellRendererSpin. Instead of displaying a Gtk.Entry when the content is to be edited, a
Gtk.SpinButton is used. An example of a cell rendered with Gtk.CellRendererSpin that
is being edited is shown in Figure 9-12.

Figure 9-12. *Spin button renderers*

You notice that the floating-point numbers in the first column in Figure 9-12 show
multiple decimal places. You can set the number of decimal places shown in the spin
button but not the displayed text. To decrease or eliminate the number of decimal
places, you should use a cell data function. An example of a cell data function that hides
decimal places is shown in Listing 9-13.

Listing 9-13. Cell Data Function for Floating-Point Numbers

```
def cell_edited(self, renderer, path, new_text, treeview):

    # Retrieve the current value stored by the spin button renderer's
    adjustme adjustment = renderer.get_property("adjustment")
    value = "%.0f" % adjustment.get_value() model = treeview.get_model()
    iter = model.get_iter_from_string(path) if iter:
        model.set(iter, QUANTITY, value)
```

Recall that if you want to dictate the number of decimal places shown by a floating-point number in a column using Gtk.CellRendererText or another derived renderer, you need to use a cell data function. In Listing 9-13, a sample cell data function was shown that reads in the current floating-point number and forces the renderer to display no decimal places. This is necessary because Gtk.CellRendererSpin stores numbers as floating-point numbers.

Gtk.CellRendererSpin is compatible with both integers and floating-point numbers, because its parameters are stored in a Gtk.Adjustment. Listing 9-13 is an implementation of the Grocery List application in which the Quantity column is rendered with Gtk.CellRendererSpin.

Listing 9-14. Spin Button Cell Renderers

```
def setup_tree_view(self, renderer, column, adj):
    adj = Gtk.Adjustment.new(0.0, 0.0, 100.0, 1.0, 2.0, 2.0)
    renderer = Gtk.CellRendererSpin(editable=True, adjustment=adj, digits=0)
    column = Gtk.TreeViewColumn("Count", renderer, text=QUANTITY)
    treeview.append_column(column)
    renderer.connect("edited", self.cell_edited, treeview)

    # Add a cell renderer for the PRODUCT column
```

New Gtk.CellRendererSpin objects are created with Gtk.CellRendererSpin(). When you create the renderer, you should set the editable, adjustment, and digits properties of the object, as follows.

```
Gtk.CellRendererSpin(editable=True, adjustment=adj, digits=0)
```

Gtk.CellRendererSpin provides three properties: adjustment, climb rate, and digits. These are stored in a Gtk.Adjustment defining the spin button's properties, the acceleration rate when an arrow button is held down, and the number of decimal places to display in the spin button respectively. The climb rate and number of decimals to display are both set to zero by default.

After setting up the cell renderer, you should then connect to the edited signal to the cell renderer, which is used to apply the new value chosen by the user to the cell. There is usually no need to filter this value, because the adjustment already limits the values allowed by the cell. The callback function is run after the user presses the Enter key or moves focus from the spin button of a cell that is being edited.

Within the `cell_edited()`callback method in Listing 9-14 you need to first retrieve the adjustment of the spin button renderer, because it stores the new value that is to be displayed. This new value can then be applied to the given cell.

Note   Although the edited signal of a `Gtk.CellRendererText` still receives the `new_text` parameter, this should not be used. The parameter does not store a textual version of the spin button's value. Furthermore, the value used in `model.set()` that replaces the current value must be supplied as a floating-point number, so a string is not acceptable regardless of its contents.

You can retrieve the adjustment's value with `renderer.get_property("adjustment")`, applying it to the appropriate column. if the QUANTITY column is used to display a floating-point number (`GObject.TYPE_FLOAT`), you can use the returned type in its current state. We have instead chosen to convert the float value to a string value.

When creating the tree model, the column must be of the type `GObject.TYPE_FLOAT`, even if you want to store an integer. You should use cell data functions to limit the number of decimal places displayed by each cell.

Combo Box Renderers

`Gtk.CellRendererCombo` provides a cell renderer for a widget that you have just learned about, `Gtk.ComboBox`. Combo box cell renderers are useful, because they allow you to present multiple predefined options to the user. `Gtk.CellRendererCombo` renders text in a similar way to `Gtk.CellRendererText`, but instead of showing a `Gtk.Entry` widget when editing, a `Gtk.ComboBox` widget is presented to the user. An example of a `Gtk.CellRendererCombo` cell being edited is shown in Figure 9-13.

Figure 9-13. *A combo box cell renderer*

To use Gtk.CellRendererCombo, you need to create a Gtk.TreeModel for every cell in the column. In Listing 9-15, the QUANTITY column of the Grocery List application from Listing 9-1 is rendered with Gtk.CellRendererCombo.

Listing 9-15. Combo Box Cell Renderers

```
def setup_tree_view(self, treeview):
    # Create a GtkListStore that will be used for the combo box
    renderer. model = Gtk.ListStore.new((GObject.TYPE_STRING,
                              GObject.TYPE_STRING))
    iter = model.append()
    model.set(iter, 0, "None")
    iter = model.append()
    model.set(iter, 0, "One")
    iter = model.append()
    model.set(iter, 0, "Half a Dozen")
    iter = model.append()
    model.set(iter, 0, "Dozen")
    iter = model.append()
    model.set(iter, 0, "Two Dozen")
    # Create the GtkCellRendererCombo and add the tree model. Then, add the
    # renderer to a new column and add the column to the GtkTreeView.
    renderer = Gtk.CellRendererCombo(text_column=0, editable=True,
                                has_entry=True, model=model)
```

```
    column = Gtk.TreeViewColumn("Count", renderer, text=QUANTITY)
    treeview.append_column(column)
    renderer.connect("edited", self.cell_edited, treeview)
    renderer = Gtk.CellRendererText.new()
    column = Gtk.TreeViewColumn("Product", renderer, text=PRODUCT)
    treeview.append_column(column)

def cell_edited(self, renderer, path, new_text, treeview):
    # Make sure the text is not empty. If not, apply it to the tree view
    cell. if new_text != "":
        model = treeview.get_model()
        iter = model.get_iter_from_string(path)
        if iter:
            model.set(iter, QUANTITY, new_text)
```

New combo box cell renderers are created with Gtk.CellRendererCombo(). Gtk. CellRendererCombo has three properties in addition to those inherited from Gtk. CellRendererText: "has_entry", "model", and "text_column".

```
renderer = Gtk.CellRendererCombo(text_column=0, editable=True,
                                        has_entry=True, model=model)
```

The first property you need to set is "text_column", which refers to the column in the combo box's tree model that is displayed in the cell renderer. This must be a type supported by Gtk.CellRendererText, such as GObject.TYPE_STRING, GObject.TYPE_INT, or GObject.TYPE_BOOLEAN. The model property is a Gtk.TreeModel that is used as the content of the combo box. You must also set the editable property to True, so the cell content may be edited.

Lastly, there is a widget called Gtk.ComboBoxEntry that gives the user choices like a normal combo box, but it also uses a Gtk.Entry widget to allow the user to enter a custom string instead of choosing an existing option. To allow this functionality with a combo box cell renderer, you must set the has-entry property to True. This is turned on by default, which means that you must turn it off to restrict the choices to those that appear in Gtk.CellRendererCombo's tree model.

As with other cell renderers derived from Gtk.CellRendererText, you want to use the text field as the column attribute and set its initial text when creating the tree view's model. You can then use the edited signal to apply the text to the tree model. In Listing 9-15, the changes are only applied when the "new_text" string is not empty, since the user is free to enter free-form text as well.

Progress Bar Renderers

Another type of cell renderer is Gtk.CellRendererProgress, which implements the Gtk.ProgressBar widget. While progress bars support pulsing, Gtk.CellRendererProgress only allows you to set the current value of the progress bar. Figure 9-14 shows a Gtk.TreeView widget that has a progress bar cell renderer in the second column, which displays textual feedback.

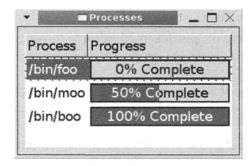

Figure 9-14. *Progress bar cell renderers*

Progress bar cell renderers are another easy feature to implement in a program. You can use Gtk.CellRendererProgress() to create new Gtk.CellRendererProgress objects. Gtk.CellRendererProgress provides two properties: "text" and "value". The progress bar state is defined by the "value" property, which is an integer with a value between 0 and 100. A value of 0 refers to an empty progress bar, and 100 refers to a full progress bar. Since it is stored as an integer, the tree model column corresponding to the value of the progress bar should have the type GObject.TYPE_INT.

The second property provided by Gtk.CellRendererProgress is text. This property is a string that is drawn over the top of the progress bar. This property can be ignored in some cases, but it is usually a good idea to give the user more information about the progress of a process. Examples of possible progress bar strings are "67% Complete", "3 of 80 Files Processed", "Installing foo . . .", and so on.

Gtk.CellRendererProgress is a useful cell renderer in some cases, but you should be careful when you deploy it. You should avoid using multiple progress bars in one row, because doing so could confuse the user and takes up a lot of horizontal space. Also, tree views with many rows appear messy. In many cases, it would be better for the user to use a textual cell renderer instead of a progress bar cell renderer.

However, there are some cases where Gtk.CellRendererProgress is a good choice. For example, if your application has to manage multiple downloads at the same time, progress bar cell renderers are an easy way to give coherent feedback about progress for each download.

Keyboard Accelerator Renderers

GTK+ 2.10 introduced a new type of cell renderer called Gtk.CellRendererAccel, which displays a textual representation of a keyboard accelerator. An example of an accelerator cell renderer is shown in Figure 9-15.

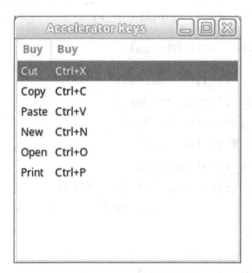

Figure 9-15. *Accelerator cell renderers*

Listing 9-16 creates a list of actions along with their keyboard accelerators. This type of tree view could be used to allow the user to edit the accelerators for an application. The accelerator is displayed as text, since the renderer is derived from Gtk.CellRendererText.

To edit the accelerator, the user needs to click the cell once. The cell then shows a string asking for a key. The new key code is added, along with any mask keys, such as Ctrl and Shift, into the cell. Basically, the first keyboard shortcut pressed is displayed by the cell.

Listing 9-16. Combo Box Cell Renderers

```python
#!/usr/bin/python3

import sys
import gi
gi.require_version('Gtk', '3.0')
from gi.repository import Gtk, Gdk, GObject

ACTION = 0
MASK = 1
VALUE = 2

list = [( "Cut", Gdk.ModifierType.CONTROL_MASK, Gdk.KEY_X ), ( "Copy",
Gdk.ModifierType.CONTROL_MASK, Gdk.KEY_C ), ( "Paste", Gdk.ModifierType.
CONTROL_MASK, Gdk.KEY_V ), ( "New", Gdk.ModifierType.CONTROL_MASK, Gdk.
KEY_N ), ( "Open", Gdk.ModifierType.CONTROL_MASK, Gdk.KEY_O ), ( "Print",
Gdk.ModifierType.CONTROL_MASK, Gdk.KEY_P )]

class AppWindow(Gtk.ApplicationWindow):

    def __init__(self, *args, **kwargs):
        super().__init__(*args, **kwargs)
        self.set_size_request(250, 250)
        treeview = Gtk.TreeView.new()
        self.setup_tree_view(treeview)
        store = Gtk.ListStore(GObject.TYPE_STRING,
                              GObject.TYPE_INT, GObject.TYPE_UINT)
        for row in list:
            (action, mask, value) = row
            iter = store.append(None)
            store.set(iter, ACTION, action, MASK, mask, VALUE, value)
        treeview.set_model(store)
          scrolled_win = Gtk.ScrolledWindow.new(None, None)
          scrolled_win.set_policy(Gtk.PolicyType.AUTOMATIC,
                                  Gtk.PolicyType.AUTOMATIC)
        scrolled_win.add(treeview)
        self.add(scrolled_win)
```

```python
def setup_tree_view(self, treeview):
    renderer = Gtk.CellRendererAccel()
    column = Gtk.TreeViewColumn("Action", renderer, text=ACTION)
    treeview.append_column(column)
    renderer = Gtk.CellRendererAccel(accel_mode=Gtk.
    CellRendererAccelMode.GTK, editable=True)
    column = Gtk.TreeViewColumn("Key", renderer, accel_mods=MASK,
    accel_key=VALUE)
    treeview.append_column(column)
    renderer.connect("accel_edited", self.accel_edited, treeview)
def accel_edited(self, renderer, path, accel_key, mask, hardware_
keycode, treeview):
    model = treeview.get_model()
    iter = model.get_iter_from_string(path)
    if iter:
            model.set(iter, MASK, mask, VALUE, accel_key)

class Application(Gtk.Application):

    def __init__(self, *args, **kwargs):
        super().__init__(*args, application_id="org.example.myapp",
                        **kwargs)
        self.window = None

    def do_activate(self):
        if not self.window:
            self.window = AppWindow(application=self, title="Accelerator
            Keys")
        self.window.show_all()
        self.window.present()
    if __name__ == "__main__":
        app = Application()
        app.run(sys.argv)
```

You can use `Gtk.CellRendererAccel()` to create new `Gtk.CellRendererAccel` objects. `Gtk.CellRendererAccel` provides the following four properties that can be accessed with `renderer.get()`.

- `Gdk.ModifierType.SHIFT_MASK`: The Shift key.

- `Gdk.ModifierType.CONTROL_MASK`: The Ctrl key.

- `Gdk.ModifierType.MOD_MASK,Gdk.ModifierType.MOD2_MASK, Gdk.ModifierType.MOD3_MASK,Gdk.ModifierType.MOD4_MASK, Gdk.ModifierType.MOD5_MASK`: The first modifier usually represents the Alt key, but these are interpreted based on your X server mapping of the keys. They can also correspond to the Meta, Super, or Hyper key.

- `Gdk.ModifierType.SUPER_MASK`: Introduced in 2.10, this allows you to explicitly state the Super modifier. This modifier may not be available on all systems!

- `Gdk.ModifierType.HYPER_MASK`: Introduced in 2.10, this allows you to explicitly state the Hyper modifier. This modifier may not be available on all systems!

- `Gdk.ModifierType.META_MODIFIER`: Introduced in 2.10, this allows you to explicitly state the **Meta** modifier. This modifier may not be available on all systems!

In most cases, you want to set the modifier mask (acel-mods) and the accelerator key value (accel-key) as two attributes of the tree view column using `Gtk.CellRendererAccel`. In this case, the modifier mask is of type `GObject.TYPE_INT`, and the accelerator key value `GObject.TYPE_UINT`. Because of this, you want to make sure to case the `Gdk.ModifierType` value to an int when setting the content of the modifier mask column.

```
store = Gtk.ListStore(GObject.TYPE_STRING, GObject.TYPE_INT, GObject.TYPE_UINT)
```

`Gtk.CellRendererAccel` provides two signals. The first, `accel-cleared`, allows you to reset the accelerator when the user removes the current value. In most cases, you will not need to do this unless you have a default value that you want the accelerator to revert to.

Of greater importance, `accel-edited` allows you to apply changes that the user makes to the keyboard accelerator, as long as you set the editable property to `True`. The callback function receives a path string to the row in question along with the accelerator key code, mask and hardware key code. In the callback function, you can apply the changes with `store.set()`, as you would with any other editable type of cell.

Test Your Understanding

In Exercise 1, you have the opportunity to practice using the `Gtk.TreeView` widget, along with multiple types of cell renderers. This is an extremely important exercise for you to try, because you need to use the `Gtk.TreeView` widget in many applications. As always, when you are finished, you can find one possible solution in Appendix D.

Exercise 1: File Browser

By now, you have probably had enough of Grocery List applications, so let's try something different. In this exercise, create a file browser using the `Gtk.TreeView` widget. You should use `Gtk.ListStore` for the file browser and allow the user to browse through the file system.

The file browser should show images to differentiate among directories and files. Images are found in the downloadable source code at `www.gtkbook.com`. You can also use the Python directory utility functions to retrieve directory content. Double-clicking a directory should move you to that location.

Summary

In this chapter, you learned how to use the `Gtk.TreeView` widget. This widget allows you to display lists and tree structures of data with `Gtk.ListStore` and `Gtk.TreeStore` respectively. You also learned the relationship among the tree view, tree model, columns, and cell renderers and how to use each of the objects.

Next, you learned about the types of objects that can be used to refer to a row within the tree view. These include tree iterators, paths, and row references. Each of these objects has its own advantages and disadvantages. Tree iterators can be used directly with models, but they become invalid when the tree model changes. Tree paths are easily understandable, because they have associated human-readable strings, but may not point to the same row if the tree model is changed. Lastly, tree row references are useful, because they remain valid for as long as the row exists, even when the model is changed.

You next learned how to handle selections of one row or multiple rows. With multiple row selections, you can use a `for-each` function, or you can get a Python list of the selected rows. A useful signal when dealing with selections is `Gtk.TreeView`'s row-activated signal, which allows you to handle double-clicks.

After that, you learned how to create editable cells with `Gtk.CellRendererText`'s edited signal, which displays a `Gtk.Entry` to allow the user to edit the content in the cell. Cell data functions can also be connected to columns. These cell data functions allow you to customize each cell before it is rendered to the screen.

Lastly, you learned about a number of cell renderers that allow you to display toggle buttons, pixbufs, spin buttons, combo boxes, progress bars, and keyboard accelerator strings. You were also introduced to the `Gtk.ComboBox` widget.

Congratulations! You are now familiar with one of the hardest and most versatile widgets provided by GTK+. In the next chapter, you learn how to create menus, toolbars, and pop-up menus. You also learn how to automate menu creation with user interface (UI) files.

CHAPTER 10

Menus and Toolbars

This chapter teaches you how to create pop-up menus, menu bars, and toolbars. You begin by creating each manually, so you learn how the widgets are constructed. This gives you a firm understanding of all of the concepts on which menus and toolbars rely.

After you understand each widget, you are introduced to `Gtk.Builder`, which allows you to dynamically create menus and toolbars through custom XML files. Each user interface file is loaded, and each element applied to a corresponding action object, which tells the item how it is displayed and how it acts.

In this chapter, you learn the following.

- How to create pop-up menus, menu bars, and toolbars

- How to apply keyboard accelerators to menu items

- What the `Gtk.StatusBar` widget is and how you can use it to provide more information to the user about a menu item

- What types of menu and toolbar items are provided by GTK+

- How to dynamically create menus and toolbars with UI files

- How to create custom stock items with `Gtk.IconFactory`

Pop-up Menus

You begin this chapter by learning how to create a pop-up menu. A pop-up menu is a `Gtk.Menu` widget that is displayed to the user when the right mouse button is clicked while hovering above certain widgets. Some widgets, such as `Gtk.Entry` and `Gtk.TextView`, already have pop-up menus built into the widget by default.

© W. David Ashley and Andrew Krause 2019
W. D. Ashley and A. Krause, *Foundations of PyGTK Development*,
https://doi.org/10.1007/978-1-4842-4179-0_10

If you want to change the pop-up menu of a widget that offers one by default, you should edit the supplied Gtk.Menu widget in the pop-up callback function. For example, both Gtk.Entry and Gtk.TextView have a populate-popup signal, which receives the Gtk.Menu that is going to be displayed. You can edit this menu in any way you see fit before displaying it to the user.

Creating a Pop-up Menu

For most widgets, you need to create your own pop-up menu. In this section, you are going to learn how to supply a pop-up menu to a Gtk.ProgressBar widget. The pop-up menu we are going to implement is presented in Figure 10-1.

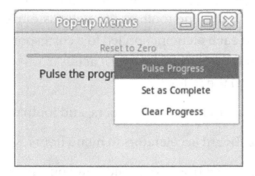

Figure 10-1. *A simple pop-up menu with three menu items*

The three pop-up menu items pulse the progress bar, set it as 100 percent complete, and clear it. In Listing 10-1, an event box contains the progress bar. Because Gtk.ProgressBar, like Gtk.Label, is not able to detect GDK events by itself, we need to catch button-press-event signals using an event box.

Listing 10-1. Simple Pop-up Menu

```python
#!/usr/bin/python3

import sys
import gi
gi.require_version('Gtk', '3.0')
from gi.repository import Gtk, Gdk
```

```python
class AppWindow(Gtk.ApplicationWindow):

    def __init__(self, *args, **kwargs):
        super().__init__(*args, **kwargs)
        self.set_border_width(10)
        self.set_size_request(250, -1)
        # Create all of the necessary widgets and initialize the pop-up
        menu.   menu = Gtk.Menu.new()
        eventbox = Gtk.EventBox.new()
        progress = Gtk.ProgressBar.new() progress.set_text("Nothing Yet
        Happened")
        progress.set_show_text(True) self.create_popup_menu(menu, progress)
        progress.set_pulse_step(0.05) eventbox.set_above_child(False)
        eventbox.connect("button_press_event", self.button_press_event,
        menu) eventbox.add(progress)
        self.add(eventbox)
        eventbox.set_events(Gdk.EventMask.BUTTON_PRESS_MASK)
        eventbox.realize()

    def create_popup_menu(self, menu, progress):
        pulse = Gtk.MenuItem.new_with_label("Pulse Progress")
        fill = Gtk.MenuItem.new_with_label("Set as Complete")
        clear = Gtk.MenuItem.new_with_label("Clear Progress")
        separator = Gtk.SeparatorMenuItem.new()
        pulse.connect("activate", self.pulse_activated, progress)
        fill.connect("activate", self.fill_activated, progress)
        clear.connect("activate", self.clear_activated, progress)
        menu.append(pulse)
        menu.append(separator)
        menu.append(fill)
        menu.append(clear)
        menu.attach_to_widget(progress, None)
        menu.show_all()
```

277

```python
    def button_press_event(self, eventbox, event, menu):
        pass

    def pulse_activated(self, item, progress):
        pass

    def fill_activated(self, item, progress):
        pass

    def clear_activated(self, item, progress):
        pass

class Application(Gtk.Application):

    def __init__(self, *args, **kwargs):
        super().__init__(*args, application_id="org.example.myapp",
                         **kwargs)
        self.window = None

    def do_activate(self):
        if not self.window:
            self.window = AppWindow(application=self, title="Pop-up Menus")
        self.window.show_all()
        self.window.present()
if __name__ == "__main__":
    app = Application()
    app.run(sys.argv)
```

In most cases, you want to use button-press-event to detect when the user wants the pop-up menu to be shown. This allows you to check whether the right mouse button was clicked. If the right mouse button was clicked, Gdk.EventButton's button member is equal to 3.

However, Gtk.Widget also provides the popup-menu signal, which is activated when the user presses built-in key accelerators to activate the pop-up menu. Most users use the mouse to activate pop-up menus, so this is not usually a factor in GTK+ applications. Nevertheless, if you would like to handle this signal as well, you should create a third function that displays the pop-up menu that is called by both callback functions.

New menus are created with Gtk.Menu.new(). The menu is initialized with no initial content, so the next step is to create menu items.

In this section, we cover two types of menu items. The first is the base class for all other types of menu items, Gtk.MenuItem. There are three initialization functions provided for Gtk.MenuItem: Gtk.MenuItem.new(), Gtk.MenuItem.new_with_label(), and Gtk.MenuItem.new_with_mnemonic().

```
pulse = Gtk.MenuItem.new_with_label("Pulse Progress")
```

In most cases, you do not need to use the Gtk.MenuItem.new(), because a menu item with no content is not of much use. If you use that function to initialize the menu item, you have to construct each aspect of the menu in code instead of allowing GTK+ to handle the specifics.

Note   Menu item mnemonics are not the same thing as keyboard accelerators. A mnemonic activates the menu item when the user presses **Alt** and the appropriate alphanumeric key while the menu has focus. A keyboard accelerator is a custom key combination that causes a callback function to be run when the combination is pressed. You learn about keyboard accelerators for menus in the next section.

The other type of basic menu item is Gtk.SeparatorMenuItem, which places a generic separator at its location. You can use Gtk.SeparatorMenuItem.new() to create a new separator menu item.

Separators are extremely important when designing a menu structure, because they organize menu items into groups so that the user can easily find the appropriate item. For example, in the File menu, menu items are often organized into groups that open files, save files, print files, and close the application. Rarely should you have many menu items listed without a separator in between them (e.g., a list of recent files might appear without a separator). In most cases, you should group similar menu items together and place a separator between adjacent groups.

After the menu items are created, you need to connect each menu item to the activate signal, which is emitted when the user selects the item. Alternatively, you can use the activate-item signal, which is also emitted when a submenu of the given menu item is displayed. There is no discernable difference between the two unless the menu item expands into a submenu.

Each activate and activate-item callback function receives the `Gtk.MenuItem` widget that initiated the action and any data you need to pass to the function. In Listing 10-2, three menu item callback functions are provided to pulse the progress bar, fill it to 100 percent complete, and clear all progress.

Now that you have created all of the menu items, you need to add them to the menu. `Gtk.Menu` is derived from `Gtk.MenuShell`, which is an abstract base class that contains and displays submenus and menu items. Menu items can be added to a menu shell with `menu.append()`. This function appends each item to the end of the menu shell.

```
menu.append(pulse)
```

Additionally, you can use `menu.prepend()` or `menu.insert()` add a menu item to the beginning of the menu or insert it into an arbitrary position respectively. Positions accepted by `menu.insert()` begin with an index of zero.

After setting all of the `Gtk.Menu`'s children as visible, you should call `menu.attach_to_widget()` so that the pop-up menu is associated to a specific widget. This function accepts the pop-up menu and the widget that it is attached to.

```
menu.attach_to_widget(progress, None)
```

The last parameter of `menu.attach_to_widget()` accepts a `Gtk.MenuDetachFunc`, which can call a specific function when the menu is detached from the widget.

Pop-up Menu Callback Methods

After creating the necessary widgets, you need to handle the `button-press-event` signal, which is shown in Listing 10-2. In this example, the pop-up menu is displayed every time the right mouse button clicks the progress bar.

Listing 10-2. Callback Functions for the Simple Pop-up Menu

```
#!/usr/bin/python3

import sys
import gi
gi.require_version('Gtk', '3.0')
from gi.repository import Gtk, Gdk
```

```python
class AppWindow(Gtk.ApplicationWindow):

    def __init__(self, *args, **kwargs):
        super().__init__(*args, **kwargs)
        self.set_border_width(10)
        self.set_size_request(250, -1)
        # Create all of the necessary widgets and initialize the pop-up
        menu. menu = Gtk.Menu.new()
        eventbox = Gtk.EventBox.new() progress =
        Gtk.ProgressBar.new()
        progress.set_text("Nothing Yet Happened")
        progress.set_show_text(True) self.create_popup_menu(menu, progress)
        progress.set_pulse_step(0.05) eventbox.set_above_child(False)
        eventbox.connect("button_press_event", self.button_press_event,
        menu) eventbox.add(progress)
        self.add(eventbox)
        eventbox.set_events(Gdk.EventMask.BUTTON_PRESS_MASK) eventbox.realize()

    def create_popup_menu(self, menu, progress):
        pulse = Gtk.MenuItem.new_with_label("Pulse Progress")
        fill = Gtk.MenuItem.new_with_label("Set as Complete")
        clear = Gtk.MenuItem.new_with_label("Clear Progress")
        separator = Gtk.SeparatorMenuItem.new()
        pulse.connect("activate", self.pulse_activated, progress)
        fill.connect("activate", self.fill_activated, progress)
        clear.connect("activate", self.clear_activated, progress)
        menu.append(pulse)
        menu.append(separator)
        menu.append(fill)
        menu.append(clear)
        menu.attach_to_widget(progress, None)
        menu.show_all()

    def button_press_event(self, eventbox, event, menu):
        if event.button == 3 and event.type == Gdk.EventType.BUTTON_PRESS: menu.
        popup(None, None, None, None, event.button, event.time) return True

        return False
```

```python
    def pulse_activated(self, item, progress):
        progress.pulse()
        progress.set_text("Pulse!")

    def fill_activated(self, item, progress):
        progress.set_fraction(1.0)
        progress.set_text("One Hundred Percent")

    def clear_activated(self, item, progress):
        progress.set_fraction(0.0)
        progress.set_text("Reset to Zero")

class Application(Gtk.Application):

    def __init__(self, *args, **kwargs):
        super().__init__(*args, application_id="org.example.myapp",
                         **kwargs)
        self.window = None

    def do_activate(self):
        if not self.window:
            self.window = AppWindow(application=self, title="Pop-up Menus")
        self.window.show_all()
        self.window.present()
    if __name__ == "__main__":
        app = Application()
        app.run(sys.argv)
```

In the button-press-event callback function in Listing 10-2, you can use menu.
popup() to display the menu on the screen.

```python
menu.popup(parent_menu_shell, parent_menu_item, func, func_data, button,
event_time)
```

In Listing 10-2 all parameters were set to None except for the mouse button that
was clicked to cause the event (event ➤ button) and the time when the event occurred
(event.time). If the pop-up menu was activated by something other than a button, you
should supply 0 to the button parameter.

Note   If the action was invoked by a popup-menu signal, the event time will not be available. In that case, you can use `Gtk.get_current_event_time()`. This function returns the timestamp of the current event or `Gdk.CURRENT_TIME` if there are no recent events.

Usually, `parent_menu_shell`, `parent_menu_item`, `func`, and `func_data` are set to None , because they are used when the menu is a part of a menu bar structure. The `parent_menu_shell` widget is the menu shell that contains the item that caused the pop-up initialization. Alternatively, you can supply `parent_menu_item`, which is the menu item that caused the pop-up initialization.

`Gtk.MenuPositionFunc` is a function that decides at what position on the screen the menu should be drawn. It accepts `func_data` as an optional last parameter. These parameters are not frequently used in applications, so they can safely be set to None. In our example, the pop-up menu was already associated with the progress bar, so it is drawn in the correct location.

Keyboard Accelerators

When creating a menu, one of the most important things to do is to set up keyboard accelerators. A keyboard accelerator is a key combination created from one accelerator key and one or more modifiers, such as **Ctrl** or **Shift**. When the user presses the key combination, the appropriate signal is emitted.

Listing 10-3 is an extension of the progress bar pop-up menu application that adds keyboard accelerators to the menu items. The progress bar is pulsed when the user presses Ctrl+P, filled with Ctrl+F, and cleared with Ctrl+C.

Listing 10-3. Adding Accelerators to Menu Items

```
#!/usr/bin/python3

import sys
import gi
gi.require_version('Gtk', '3.0')
from gi.repository import Gtk, Gdk
```

```python
class AppWindow(Gtk.ApplicationWindow):

    def __init__(self, *args, **kwargs):
        super().__init__(*args, **kwargs)
        self.set_border_width(10)
        self.set_size_request(250, -1)
        # Create all of the necessary widgets and initialize the pop-up
        menu. menu = Gtk.Menu.new()
        eventbox = Gtk.EventBox.new() progress = Gtk.ProgressBar.new()
        progress.set_text("Nothing Yet Happened") progress.set_show_
        text(True) self.create_popup_menu(menu, progress) progress.set_
        pulse_step(0.05) eventbox.set_above_child(False)
        eventbox.connect("button_press_event", self.button_press_event,
        menu) eventbox.add(progress)
        self.add(eventbox)
        eventbox.set_events(Gdk.EventMask.BUTTON_PRESS_MASK)
        eventbox.realize()

    def create_popup_menu(self, menu, progress):
        group = Gtk.AccelGroup.new()
        self.add_accel_group(group)
        menu.set_accel_group(group)
        pulse = Gtk.MenuItem.new_with_label("Pulse Progress")
        fill = Gtk.MenuItem.new_with_label("Set as Complete")
        clear = Gtk.MenuItem.new_with_label("Clear Progress")
        separator = Gtk.SeparatorMenuItem.new()
        # Add the necessary keyboard accelerators.
        pulse.add_accelerator("activate", group, Gdk.KEY_P, Gdk.
        ModifierType.CONTROL, Gtk.AccelFlags.VISIBLE)
        fill.add_accelerator("activate", group, Gdk.KEY_F, Gdk.
        ModifierType.CONTROL, Gtk.AccelFlags.VISIBLE)
        clear.add_accelerator("activate", group, Gdk.KEY_C, Gdk.
        ModifierType.CONTROL, Gtk.AccelFlags.VISIBLE)
        pulse.connect("activate", self.pulse_activated, progress)
        fill.connect("activate", self.fill_activated, progress)
        clear.connect("activate", self.clear_activated, progress)
```

```python
        menu.append(pulse)
        menu.append(separator)
        menu.append(fill)
        menu.append(clear)
        menu.attach_to_widget(progress, None)
        menu.show_all()

    def button_press_event(self, eventbox, event, menu):
        if event.button == 3 and event.type == Gdk.EventType.BUTTON_PRESS:
        menu.popup(None, None, None, None, event.button, event.time)
        return True
        return False

    def pulse_activated(self, item, progress):
        progress.pulse()
        progress.set_text("Pulse!")

    def fill_activated(self, item, progress):
        progress.set_fraction(1.0)
        progress.set_text("One Hundred Percent")

    def clear_activated(self, item, progress):
        progress.set_fraction(0.0)
        progress.set_text("Reset to Zero")

class Application(Gtk.Application):

    def __init__(self, *args, **kwargs):
        super().__init__(*args, application_id="org.example.myapp",
                         **kwargs)
        self.window = None

    def do_activate(self):
        if not self.window:
            self.window = AppWindow(application=self, title="Pop-up Menus")
        self.window.show_all()
        self.window.present()
    if __name__ == "__main__":
        app = Application()
        app.run(sys.argv)
```

Keyboard accelerators are stored as an instance of Gtk.AccelGroup. To implement accelerators in your application, you need to create a new accelerator group with Gtk. AccelGroup.new(). This accelerator group must be added to the Gtk.Window where the menu appears for it to take effect. It must also be associated with any menus that take advantage of its accelerators. In Listing 10-3, this is performed immediately after creating the Gtk.AccelGroup with self.add_accel_group() and menu.set_accel_group().

It is possible to manually create keyboard accelerators with Gtk.AccelMap, but in most cases, widget.add_accelerator() provides all of the necessary functionality. The only problem that this method presents is that the user cannot change keyboard accelerators created with this function during runtime.

```
widget.add_accelerator(signal_name, group, accel_key, mods, flags)
```

To add an accelerator to a widget, you can use widget.add_accelerator(), which emits the signal specified by signal_name on the widget when the user presses the key combination. You need to specify your accelerator group to the function, which must be associated with the window and the menu as previously stated.

An accelerator key and one or more modifier keys form the complete key combination. A list of available accelerator keys is available in the PyGObject API Reference. All the definitions for the available keys can be included by with the statement import GDK.

Modifiers are specified by the Gdk.ModifierType enumeration. The most often used modifiers are Gdk.ModifierType.SHIFT_MASK, Gdk.ModifierType.CONTROL_MASK, and Gdk.ModifierType.MOD1_MASK, which correspond to the Shift, Ctrl, and Alt keys respectively.

Tip   When dealing with key codes, you need to be careful because you many need to supply multiple keys for the same action in some cases. For example, if you want to catch the number **1** key, you need to watch for Gdk.KEY_1 and Gdk. KEY_KP_1 - they correspond to the **1** key at the top of the keyboard and the **1** key on the numeric keypad.

The last parameter of widget.add_accelerator() is an accelerator flag. There are three flags defined by the Gtk.AccelFlags enumeration. The accelerator is visible in a label if Gtk.AccelFlags.VISIBLE is set. Gtk.AccelFlags.LOCKED prevents the user from modifying the accelerator. Gtk.AccelFlags.MASK sets both flags for the widget accelerator.

Status Bar Hints

Usually placed along the bottom of the main window, the Gtk.Statusbar widget can give the user further information about what is going on in the application. A status bar can also be very useful with menus, because you can provide more information to the user about the functionality of the menu item that the mouse cursor is hovering over. A screenshot of a status bar is shown in Figure 10-2.

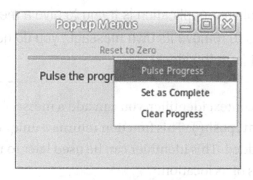

Figure 10-2. *A pop-up menu with status bar hints*

The Status Bar Widget

While the status bar can only display one message at a time, the widget actually stores a stack of messages. The currently displayed message is on the top of the stack. When you pop a message from the stack, the previous message is displayed. If there are no more strings left on the stack after you pop a message from the top, no message is displayed on the status bar.

New status bar widgets are created with Gtk.Ststusbar.new(). This creates a new Gtk.Statusbar widget with an empty message stack. Before you are able to add or remove a message from the new status bar's stack, you must retrieve a context identifier with statusbar.get_context_id().

id = statusbar.get_context_id(description)

The context identifier is a unique unsigned integer that is associated with a context description string. This identifier is used for all messages of a specific type, which allows you to categorize messages on the stack.

For example, if your status bar holds hyperlinks and IP addresses, you could create two context identifiers from the strings "URL" and "IP". When you push or pop messages to and from the stack, you have to specify a context identifier. This allows separate parts of your application to push and pop messages to and from the status bar message stack without affecting each other.

Tip   It is important to use different context identifiers for different categories of messages. If one part of your application is trying to give a message to the user while the other is trying to remove its own message, you do not want the wrong message to be popped from the stack!

After you generate a context identifier, you can add a message to the top of the status bar's stack with `statusbar.push()`. This function returns a unique message identifier for the string that was just added. This identifier can be used later to remove the message from the stack, regardless of its location.

```
statusbar.push(context_id, message)
```

There are two ways to remove a message from the stack. If you want to remove a message from the top of the stack for a specific context ID, you can use `statusbar.pop()`. This function removes the message that is highest on the status bar's stack with a context identifier of `context_id`.

```
statusbar.pop(context_id)
```

It is also possible to remove a specific message from the status bar's message stack with `statusbar.remove()`. To do this, you must provide the context identifier of the message and the message identifier of the message you want to remove, which was returned by `statusbar.push()` when it was added.

```
statusbar.remove(context_id, message_id)
```

Menu Item Information

One useful role of the status bar is to give the user more information about the menu item the mouse cursor is currently hovering over. An example of this was shown in Figure 10-2, which is a screenshot of the progress bar pop-up menu application in Listing 10-4.

To implement status bar hints, you should connect each of your menu items to Gtk. Widget's "enter-notify-event" and "leave-notify-event" signals. Listing 10-4 shows the progress bar pop-up menu application you have already learned about, except status bar hints are provided when the mouse cursor moves over a menu item.

Listing 10-4. Displaying More Information About a Menu Item

```python
#!/usr/bin/python3

import sys
import gi
gi.require_version('Gtk', '3.0')
from gi.repository import Gtk, Gdk

class AppMenuItem(Gtk.MenuItem):

    def __init__(self, *args, **kwargs):
        super().__init__(*args, **kwargs)

    def __setattr__(self, name, value):
        self.__dict__[name] = value

    def __getattr__(self, name):
        return self.__dict__[name]

class AppWindow(Gtk.ApplicationWindow):

    def __init__(self, *args, **kwargs):
        super().__init__(*args, **kwargs)
        self.set_border_width(10)
        self.set_size_request(250, -1)
        # Create all of the necessary widgets and initialize the pop-up
        menu. menu = Gtk.Menu.new()
        eventbox = Gtk.EventBox.new() progress = Gtk.ProgressBar.new()
```

```python
        progress.set_text("Nothing Yet Happened")
        progress.set_show_text(True)
        statusbar = Gtk.Statusbar.new()
        self.create_popup_menu(menu, progress, statusbar)
        progress.set_pulse_step(0.05)
        eventbox.set_above_child(False)
        eventbox.connect("button_press_event", self.button_press_event, menu)
        eventbox.add(progress)
        vbox = Gtk.Box.new(orientation=Gtk.Orientation.VERTICAL, spacing=0)
        vbox.pack_start(eventbox, False, True, 0)
        vbox.pack_start(statusbar, False, True, 0)
        self.add(vbox)
        eventbox.set_events(Gdk.EventMask.BUTTON_PRESS_MASK)
        eventbox.realize()

    def create_popup_menu(self, menu, progress, statusbar):
        pulse = AppMenuItem(label="Pulse Progress")
        fill = AppMenuItem(label="Set as Complete")
        clear = AppMenuItem(label="Clear Progress")
        separator = Gtk.SeparatorMenuItem.new()
        pulse.connect("activate", self.pulse_activated, progress)
        fill.connect("activate", self.fill_activated, progress)
        clear.connect("activate", self.clear_activated, progress)
        Connect signals to each menu item for status bar messages. pulse.
        connect("enter-notify-event", self.statusbar_hint, statusbar)
        pulse.connect("leave-notify-event", self.statusbar_hint, statusbar)
        fill.connect("enter-notify-event", self.statusbar_hint, statusbar)
        fill.connect("leave-notify-event", self.statusbar_hint, statusbar)
        clear.connect("enter-notify-event", self.statusbar_hint, statusbar)
        clear.connect("leave-notify-event", self.statusbar_hint, statusbar)
        pulse.__setattr__("menuhint", "Pulse the progress bar one step.")
        fill.__setattr__("menuhint", "Set the progress bar to 100%.")
        clear.__setattr__("menuhint", "Clear the progress bar to 0%.")
        menu.append(pulse)
```

```python
            menu.append(separator)
            menu.append(fill)
            menu.append(clear)
            menu.attach_to_widget(progress, None) menu.show_all()

    def button_press_event(self, eventbox, event, menu):
        if event.button == 3 and event.type == Gdk.EventType.BUTTON_PRESS:
        menu.popup(None, None, None, None, event.button, event.time)
        return True
        return False

    def pulse_activated(self, item, progress):
        progress.pulse()
        progress.set_text("Pulse!")

    def fill_activated(self, item, progress):
        progress.set_fraction(1.0)
        progress.set_text("One Hundred Percent")

    def clear_activated(self, item, progress): progress.set_fraction(0.0)
    progress.set_text("Reset to Zero")

    def statusbar_hint(self, menuitem, event, statusbar): id = statusbar.
    get_context_id("MenuItemHints")
        if event.type == Gdk.EventType.ENTER_NOTIFY:
            hint = menuitem.__getattr__("menuhint")
            id = statusbar.push(id, hint)
        elif event.type == Gdk.EventType.LEAVE_NOTIFY:
            statusbar.pop(id)
        return False

class Application(Gtk.Application):

    def __init__(self, *args, **kwargs):
        super().__init__(*args, application_id="org.example.myapp",
                    **kwargs)
        self.window = None
```

```
def do_activate(self):
    if not self.window:
        self.window = AppWindow(application=self, title="Pop-up Menus")
    self.window.show_all()
    self.window.present()
if __name__ == "__main__":
    app = Application()
    app.run(sys.argv)
```

When implementing status bar hints, you first need to figure out what signals are necessary. We want to be able to add a message to the status bar when the mouse cursor moves over the menu item and remove it when the mouse cursor leaves. From this description, using "enter-notify-event" and "leave-notify-event" is a good solution.

Since the GTK+ 3 interface to Python 3 does not implement the get_data() and set_data() methods on GTK+ objects, we need to subclass the Gtk.MenuItem class to implement the corresponding Python 3 attributes. This methodology is used on some other examples in this book as well.

One advantage of using these two signals is that we only need one callback function, because the prototype for each receives a Gdk.EventProximity object. From this object, we can discern between Gdk.EventType.ENTER_NOTIFY and Gdk.EventType. LEAVE_NOTIFY events. You want to return False from the callback function, because you do not want to prevent GTK+ from handling the event; you only want to enhance what is performed when it is emitted.

Within the statusbar_hint() callback method, you should first retrieve a context identifier for the menu item messages. You can use whatever string you want, as long as your application remembers what was used. Listing 10-4 described all the menu item messages added to the status bar. If other parts of the application used the status bar, using a different context identifier would leave the menu item hints untouched.

```
id = statusbar.get_context_id("MenuItemHints")
```

If the event type is Gdk.EventType.ENTER_NOTIFY, you need to show the message to the user. In the create_popup_menu() method, a data parameter was added to each menu item called "menuhint". This is a more in-depth description of what the menu item does, which is displayed to the user.

```
hint = menuitem.__getattr__("menuhint")
statusbar.push(id, hint)
```

Then, with `statusbar.push()`, the message can be added to the status bar under the `"MenuItemHints"` context identifier. This message is placed on the top of the stack and displayed to the user. You may want to consider processing all GTK+ events after calling this method, since the user interface should reflect the changes immediately.

However, if the event type is `Gdk.EventType.LEAVE_NOTIFY`, you need to remove the last menu item message that was added with the same context identifier. The most recent message can be removed from the stack with `statusbar.pop()`.

Menu Items

Thus far, you have learned about flat menus that display label and separator menu items. It is also possible to add a submenu to an existing menu item. GTK+ also provides a number of other `Gtk.MenuItem` objects. Figure 10-3 shows a pop-up menu that contains a submenu along with image, check, and radio menu items.

Figure 10-3. *Image, check, and radio menu items*

Submenus

Submenus in GTK+ are not created by a separate type of menu item widget but by calling menuitem.set_submenu(). This method calls menu.attach_to_widget() to attach the submenu to the menu item and places an arrow beside the menu item to show that it now has a submenu. If the menu item already has a submenu, it is replaced with the given Gtk.Menu widget.

```
menuitem.set_submenu(submenu)
```

Submenus are very useful if you have a list of very specific options that would clutter an otherwise organized menu structure. When using a submenu, you can use the "activate-item" signal provided by the Gtk.MenuItem widget, which is emitted when the menu item displays its submenu.

In addition to Gtk.MenuItem and menu item separators, there are three other types of menu item objects: image, check, and radio menu items; these are covered in the remainder of this section.

Image Menu Items

Warning   The Gtk.ImageMenuItem class has been deprecated since GTK+ 3.1. Do not use it in new code and be aware it could disappear completely in a newer version of GTK+.

Gtk.ImageMenuItem is very similar to its parent class Gtk.MenuItem except it shows a small image to the left of the menu item label. There are four functions provided for creating a new image menu item.

The first function, imagemenuitem.new() creates a new Gtk.ImageMenuItem object with an empty label and no associated image. You can use image menu item's image property to set the image displayed by the menu item.

```
Gtk.ImageMenuItem.new()
```

Additionally, you can create a new image menu item from a stock identifier with Gtk. ImageMenuItem.new_from_stock(). This function creates the Gtk.ImageMenuItem with the label and image associated with stock_id. This function accepts stock identifier strings.

```
Gtk.ImageMenuItem.new_from_stock(stockid, accel_group)
```

The second parameter of this function accepts an accelerator group, which is set to the default accelerator of the stock item. If you want to manually set the keyboard accelerator for the menu item as we did in Listing 10-3, you can specify None for this parameter.

Also, you can use Gtk.ImageMenuItem.new_with_label() to create a new Gtk.ImageMenuItem initially with only a label. Later, you can use the image property to add an image widget. GTK+ also provided the method imagemenuitem.set_image(), which allows you to edit the image property of the widget.

```
Gtk.ImageMenuItem.new_with_label(label)
```

Also, GTK+ provides Gtk.ImageMenuItem.new_with_mnemonic(), which creates an image menu item with a mnemonic label. As with the previous method, you have to set the image property after the menu item is created.

Check Menu Items

Gtk.CheckMenuItem allows you to create a menu item that displays a check symbol beside the label, depending on whether its Boolean active property is True or False. This would allow the user to view whether an option is activated or deactivated.

As with Gtk.MenuItem, three initialization functions are provided.

Gtk.CheckMenuItem.new(), Gtk.CheckItem.new_with_label(), and Gtk.CheckMenuItem.new_with_mnemonic(). These functions create a Gtk.CheckMenuItem with no label, with an initial label, or with a mnemonic label, respectively.

```
Gtk.CheckMenuItem.new()
Gtk.CheckMenuItem.new_with_label(label)
Gtk.CheckMenuItem.new_with_mnemonic(label)
```

As previously stated, the current state of the check menu item is held by the active property of the widget. GTK+ provides two functions, checkmenuitem.set_active() and checkmenuitem.get_active() to set and retrieve the active value.

As with all check button widgets, you are able to use the "toggled" signal, which is emitted when the user toggles the state of the menu item. GTK+ takes care of updating the state of the check button, so this signal is simply to allow you to update your application to reflect the changed value.

Gtk.CheckMenuItem also provides checkmenuitem.set_inconsistent(), which alters the inconsistent property of the menu item. When set to True, the check menu item displays a third "in between" state that is neither active nor inactive. This can show the user that a choice must be made that has yet to be set or that the property is both set and unset for different parts of a selection.

Radio Menu Items

Gtk.RadioMenuItem is a widget derived from Gtk.CheckMenuItem. It is rendered as a radio button instead of a check button by setting check menu item's draw-as-radio property to True. Radio menu items work the same way as normal radio buttons.

The first radio button should be created with one of the following functions. You can set the radio button group to None, since requisite elements are added to the group by referencing the first element. These functions create an empty menu item, a menu item with a label, and a menu item with a mnemonic, respectively.

```
Gtk.RadioMenuItem.new(group)
Gtk.RadioMenuItem.new_with_label(group, text)
Gtk.RadioMenuItem.new_with_mnemonic(group, text)
```

All other radio menu items should be created with one of the following three functions, which add it to the radio button group associated with group. These functions create an empty menu item, a menu item with a label, and a menu item with a mnemonic, respectively.

```
Gtk.RadioMenuItem.new_from_widget(group)
Gtk.RadioMenuItem.new_from_widget_with_label(group, text)
Gtk.RadioMenuItem.new_from_widget_with_mnemonic(group, text)
```

Menu Bars

Gtk.MenuBar is a widget that organizes multiple pop-up menus into a horizontal or vertical row. Each root element is a Gtk.MenuItem that pops down into a submenu. An instance of Gtk.MenuBar is usually displayed along the top of the main application window to provide access to functionality provided by the application. An example menu bar is shown in Figure 10-4.

Figure 10-4. *Menu bar with three menus*

In Listing 10-5, a Gtk.MenuBar widget is created with three menus: File, Edit, and Help. Each of the menus is actually a Gtk.MenuItem with a submenu. A number of menu items are then added to each submenu.

Listing 10-5. Creating Groups of Menus

```python
#!/usr/bin/python3

import sys
import gi
gi.require_version('Gtk', '3.0')
from gi.repository import Gtk

class AppWindow(Gtk.ApplicationWindow):

    def __init__(self, *args, **kwargs):
        super().__init__(*args, **kwargs)
        self.set_size_request(250, -1)
        menubar = Gtk.MenuBar.new()
        file = Gtk.MenuItem.new_with_label("File")
        edit = Gtk.MenuItem.new_with_label("Edit")
        help = Gtk.MenuItem.new_with_label("Help")
        filemenu = Gtk.Menu.new()
        editmenu = Gtk.Menu.new()
        helpmenu = Gtk.Menu.new()
        file.set_submenu(filemenu)
        edit.set_submenu(editmenu)
        help.set_submenu(helpmenu)
        menubar.append(file)
        menubar.append(edit)
        menubar.append(help)
```

```
        # Create the File menu content.
        new = Gtk.MenuItem.new_with_label("New")
        open = Gtk.MenuItem.new_with_label("Open")
        filemenu.append(new)
        filemenu.append(open)
        # Create the Edit menu content.
        cut = Gtk.MenuItem.new_with_label("Cut")
        copy = Gtk.MenuItem.new_with_label("Copy")
        paste = Gtk.MenuItem.new_with_label("Paste")
        editmenu.append(cut)
        editmenu.append(copy)
        editmenu.append(paste)
        # Create the Help menu content.
        contents = Gtk.MenuItem.new_with_label("Help")
        about = Gtk.MenuItem.new_with_label("About")
        helpmenu.append(contents)
        helpmenu.append(about)
    self.add(menubar)

class Application(Gtk.Application):

    def __init__(self, *args, **kwargs):
        super().__init__(*args, application_id="org.example.myapp",
                         **kwargs)
        self.window = None
    def do_activate(self):
        if not self.window:
            self.window = AppWindow(application=self, title="Menu Bars")
        self.window.show_all()
        self.window.present()
    if __name__ == "__main__":
        app = Application()
        app.run(sys.argv)
```

New Gtk.MenuBar widgets are created with Gtk.MenuBar.new(). This creates an empty menu shell into which you can add content.

After you create the menu bar, you can define the pack direction of the menu bar items with menubar.set_pack_direction(). Values for the pack_direction property are defined by the Gtk.PackDirection enumeration and include Gtk.PackDirection.LTR, Gtk.PackDirection.RTL, Gtk.PackDirection.TTB, or Gtk.PackDirection.BTT. These pack the menu items from left to right, right to left, top to bottom, or bottom to top, respectively. By default, child widgets are packed from left to right.

Gtk.MenuBar also provides another property called child-pack-direction, which sets what direction the menu items of the menu bar's children are packed. In other words, it controls how submenu items are packed. Values for this property are also defined by the Gtk.PackDirection enumeration.

Each child item in the menu bar is actually a Gtk.MenuItem widget. Since Gtk. MenuBar is derived from Gtk.MenuShell, you can use the menuitem.append() method to add an item to the bar as shown in the following line.

```
menubar.append(file)
```

You can also use file.prepend() or file.insert() to add an item to the beginning or in an arbitrary position of the menu bar.

You next need to call file.set_submenu() to add a submenu to each of the root menu items. Each of the submenus is a Gtk.Menu widget created in the same way as pop-up menus. GTK+ then takes care of showing submenus to the user when necessary.

```
file.set_submenu(filemenu)
```

Toolbars

A Gtk.Toolbar is a type of container that holds a number of widgets in a horizontal or vertical row. It is meant to allow easy customization of a large number of widgets with very little trouble. Typically, toolbars hold tool buttons that can display an image along with a text string. However, toolbars are actually able to hold any type of widget. A toolbar holding four tool buttons and a separator is shown in Figure 10-5.

Figure 10-5. *A toolbar showing both images and text*

In Listing 10-6, a simple toolbar is created that shows five tool items in a horizontal row. Each toolbar item displays an icon and a label that describes the purpose of the item. The toolbar is also set to display an arrow that provides access to toolbar items that do not fit in the menu.

In this example, a toolbar provides cut, copy, paste, and select-all functionality to a Gtk.Entry widget. The AppWindow() method creates the toolbar, packing it above the Gtk.Entry. It then calls create_toolbar(), which populates the toolbar with tool items and connects the necessary signals.

Listing 10-6. Creating a Gtk.Toolbar Widget

```
#!/usr/bin/python3

import sys
import gi
gi.require_version('Gtk', '3.0')
from gi.repository import Gtk

class AppWindow(Gtk.ApplicationWindow):

    def __init__(self, *args, **kwargs):
        super().__init__(*args, **kwargs)
        vbox = Gtk.Box(orientation=Gtk.Orientation.VERTICAL, spacing=0)
        toolbar = Gtk.Toolbar.new()
        entry = Gtk.Entry.new()
        vbox.pack_start(toolbar, True, False, 0)
        vbox.pack_start(entry, True, False, 0)
        self.create_toolbar(toolbar, entry)
        self.add(vbox)
        self.set_size_request(310, 75)
```

```python
def create_toolbar(self, toolbar, entry): icon_theme = Gtk.IconTheme.
get_default()
    icon = icon_theme.load_icon("edit-cut", -1,
                                Gtk.IconLookupFlags.FORCE_SIZE)
    image = Gtk.Image.new_from_pixbuf(icon)
    cut = Gtk.ToolButton.new(image, "Cut")
    icon = icon_theme.load_icon("edit-copy", -1,
    Gtk.IconLookupFlags.FORCE_SIZE)
    image = Gtk.Image.new_from_pixbuf(icon)
    copy = Gtk.ToolButton.new(image, "Copy")
    icon = icon_theme.load_icon("edit-paste", -1,
                                Gtk.IconLookupFlags.FORCE_SIZE)
    image = Gtk.Image.new_from_pixbuf(icon)
    paste = Gtk.ToolButton.new(image, "Paste")
    icon = icon_theme.load_icon("edit-select-all", -1,
    Gtk.IconLookupFlags.FORCE_SIZE)
    image = Gtk.Image.new_from_pixbuf(icon)
    selectall = Gtk.ToolButton.new(image, "Select All")
    separator = Gtk.SeparatorToolItem.new()
    toolbar.set_show_arrow(True)
    toolbar.set_style(Gtk.ToolbarStyle.BOTH)
    toolbar.insert(cut, 0)
    toolbar.insert(copy, 1)
    toolbar.insert(paste, 2)
    toolbar.insert(separator, 3)
    toolbar.insert(selectall, 4)
    cut.connect("clicked", self.cut_clipboard, entry)
    copy.connect("clicked", self.copy_clipboard, entry)
    paste.connect("clicked", self.paste_clipboard, entry)
    selectall.connect("clicked", self.select_all, entry)

def cut_clipboard(self, button, entry):
    entry.cut_clipboard()

def copy_clipboard(self, button, entry):
    entry.copy_clipboard()
```

```
    def paste_clipboard(self, button, entry):
        entry.paste_clipboard()

    def select_all(self, button, entry):
        entry.select_region(0, -1)

class Application(Gtk.Application):

    def __init__(self, *args, **kwargs):
        super().__init__(*args, application_id="org.example.myapp",
                            **kwargs)
        self.window = None
    def do_activate(self):
        if not self.window:
            self.window = AppWindow(application=self, title="Toolbar")
        self.window.show_all()
        self.window.present()
    if __name__ == "__main__":
        app = Application()
        app.run(sys.argv)
```

New toolbars are created with Gtk.Toolbar.new(), which was called before the create_toolbar() function shown in Listing 10-6. This creates an empty Gtk.Toolbar widget in which you can add tool buttons.

Gtk.Toolbar provides a number of properties for customizing how it appears and interacts with the user, including the orientation, button style, and the ability to give access to items that do not fit in the toolbar.

If all of the toolbar items cannot be displayed on the toolbar because there is not enough room, then an overflow menu appears if you set toolbar.set_show_arrow() to True. If all of the items can be displayed on the toolbar, the arrow is hidden from view.

```
toolbar.set_show_arrow(boolean)
```

Another Gtk.Toolbar property is the style by which all of the menu items are displayed, which is set with toolbar.set_style(). You should note that this property could be overridden by the theme, so you should provide the option of using the default style by calling toolbar.unset_style(). There are four toolbar styles, which are defined by the Gtk.ToolbarStyle enumeration.

- Gtk.ToolbarStyle.ICONS: Show only icons for each tool button in the toolbar.

- Gtk.ToolbarStyle.TEXT: how only labels for each tool button in the toolbar.

- Gtk.ToolbarStyle.BOTH: Show both icons and labels for each tool button, where the icon is located above its label.

- Gtk.ToolbarStyle.BOTH_HORIZ: Show both icons and labels for each tool button, where the icon is to the left of the label. The label text of a tool item is only shown if the "is-important" property for the item is set to True.

Another important property of the toolbar is the orientation that can be set with toolbar.set_orientation(). There are two possible values defined by the Gtk.Orientation enumeration, Gtk.Orientation.HORIZONTAL and Gtk.Orientation.VERTICAL, which can make the toolbar horizontal (default) or vertical.

Toolbar Items

Listing 10-6 introduces three important tool item types: Gtk.ToolItem, Gtk.ToolButton, and Gtk.SeparatorToolItem. All tool buttons are derived from the Gtk.ToolItem class, which holds basic properties that are used by all tool items.

If you are using the Gtk.ToolbarStyle.BOTH_HORIZ style, then an essential property installed in Gtk.ToolItem is the "is-important" setting. The label text of the toolbar item is only shown for this style if this property is set to True.

As with menus, separator tool items are provided by Gtk.SeparatorToolItem and are created with Gtk.SeparatorToolItem.new(). Separator tool items have a draw property, which draws a separator when set to True. If you set draw to False, it places padding at its location without any visual separator.

Tip   If you set the expand property of a Gtk.SeparatorToolItem to True and its draw property to False, you force all tool items after the separator to the end of the toolbar.

303

Most toolbar items are of the type Gtk.ToolButton. Gtk.ToolButton provides only the single initialization method Gtk.ToolButton.new() as all other initialization methods have been deprecated since GTK+ 3.1. Gtk.ToolButton.new() can create a Gtk.ToolButton with a custom icon and label. Each of these properties can be set to None.

```
Gtk.ToolButton.new(icon, label)
```

It is possible to manually set the label and icon after initialization with toolbutton. set_label() and toolbutton.set_icon_widget(). These functions provide access to tool button's label and icon-widget properties.

Additionally, you can define your own widget to use instead of the default Gtk.Label widget of the tool button with toolbutton.set_label_widget(). This allows you to embed an arbitrary widget, such as an entry or combo box, into the tool button. If this property is set to None, the default label is used.

```
toolbutton.set_label_widget(label_widget)
```

After you create the toolbar items, you can insert each Gtk.ToolItem into the toolbar with toolbar.insert().

```
toolbar.insert(item, pos)
```

The second parameter of toolbar.insert() accepts the position to insert the item into the toolbar. Tool button positions are indexed from zero. A negative position appends the item to the end of the toolbar.

Toggle Tool Buttons

Gtk.ToggleToolButton is derived from Gtk.ToolButton, and therefore only implements initialization and toggle abilities. Toggle tool buttons provide the functionality of a Gtk. ToggleButton widget in the form of a toolbar item. It allows the user to view whether the option is set or unset.

Toggle tool buttons are tool buttons that remain depressed when the active property is set to True. You can use the toggled signal to receive notification when the state of the toggle button has been changed.

There is only one way to create a new Gtk.ToggleToolButton. This is with Gtk. ToggleToolButton.new(), which creates an empty tool button. You can then use the methods provided by Gtk.ToolButton to add a label and image.

```
Gtk.ToggleToolButton.new()
```

Radio Tool Buttons

Gtk.RadioToolButton is derived from Gtk.ToggleToolButton, so it inherits the "active" property and "toggled" signal. Therefore, the widget only needs to give a way for you to create new radio tool buttons and add them to a radio group.

A radio tool button should be created with Gtk.RadioToolButton.new(), where the radio group is set to None. This creates a default initial radio group for the radio tool button.

Gtk.RadioToolButton.new(group)

Gtk.RadioToolButton inherits functions from Gtk.ToolButton, which provides functions and properties that can then set the label of the radio tool button, if necessary.

All requisite elements should be created with Gtk.RadioToolButton.from_ widget(). Setting group as the first radio tool button adds all requisite items added to the same group.

Gtk.RadioToolButton.new_from_widget(group)

Gtk.RadioToolButton provides one property, group, which is another radio tool button that belongs to the radio group. This allows you to link all of the radio buttons together so that only one is selected at a time.

Menu Tool Buttons

Gtk.MenuToolButton, derived from Gtk.ToggleToolButton, allows you to attach a menu to a tool button. The widget places an arrow beside the image and label that provides access to the associated menu. For example, you could use Gtk.MenuToolButton to add a list of recently opened files to a toolbar button. Figure 10-6 is a screenshot of a menu tool button that is used for this purpose.

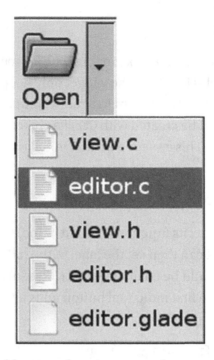

Figure 10-6. *A menu tool button showing recently opened files*

Listing 10-7 shows you how to implement a menu tool button. The actual tool button is created in a similar way as any other Gtk.ToolButton except there is an extra step of attaching a menu to the Gtk.MenuToolButton widget.

Listing 10-7. Using Gtk.MenuToolButton

```
recent = Gtk.Menu.new()
# Add a number of menu items where each corresponds to one recent file.
icon_theme = Gtk.IconTheme.get_default()
icon = icon_theme.load_icon("document-open", -1,
Gtk.IconLookupFlags.FORCE_SIZE)
image = Gtk.Image.new_from_pixbuf(icon)
open = Gtk.MenuToolButton.new(image, "Open")
open.set_menu(recent)
```

In Listing 10-7, the menu tool button was created with an image and a label with Gtk.MenuToolButton.new(image, label). You can set either of these parameters to None if you want to set them at a later time using Gtk.ToolButton properties.

```
Gtk.MenuToolButton.new(image, label)
```

What makes Gtk.MenuToolButton unique is that an arrow to the right of the tool button provides the user with access to a menu. The tool button's menu is set with menutoolbutton.set_menu() or by setting the menu property to a Gtk.Menu widget. This menu is displayed to the user when the arrow is clicked.

Dynamic Menu Creation

Note   The Gtk.UIManager was deprecated in GTK+ 3.1 so the creation and loading of UI files are not covered in this section. Instead, the new Gtk.Builder class and its associated XML files are covered. Gtk.Builder is a more powerful and flexible system for managing external user interface descriptions and actions. It also provides addition capabilities and reduces the amount of work needed to create and manage user interfaces.

While it is possible to manually create every menu and toolbar item, doing so can take up a large amount of space and cause you to have to code monotonously for longer than necessary. To automate menu and toolbar creation, GTK+ allows you to dynamically create menus from XML files.

The Gtk.Builder class can create many user interface objects, including menus, menu bars, pop-up menus, entire dialogs, main windows, and many others. This section concentrates on different types of menus, but you should keep in mind that Gtk.Builder can build many other kinds of user interface objects.

Creating XML Files

User interface files are constructed in XML format. All of the content has to be contained between <interface> and </interface> tags. One type of dynamic UI that you can create is a Gtk.Menu with the <menu> tag shown in Listing 10-8.

Listing 10-8. Menu UI File

```xml
<?xml version="1.0" encoding="UTF-8"?>
<interface>
  <menu id="menubar">
    <submenu>
      <attribute name="label">File</attribute>
    </submenu>
    <submenu>
      <attribute name="label">Edit</attribute>
    </submenu>
    <submenu>
      <attribute name="label">Choices</attribute>
    </submenu>
    <submenu>
      <attribute name="label">Help</attribute>
    </submenu>
  </menu>
</interface>
```

Every menu and item tag should have a unique ID associated with it so that you can access that item directly from your code. While not necessary, you should always add the name property to every menu and item. The name property can access the actual widget.

Each <menu> can have any number of <item> children. Both of these tags must be closed according to normal XML rules. If a tag does not have a closing tag (e.g., <menu/>), you must place a forward slash character (/) at the end of the tag so the parser knows the tag has ended.

Each <menu> and <item> tags can have other children as well, such as the <section> and <attribute> tags. The <section> tag organizes <item> tags. The <attribute> tags are used to describe (i.e., add properties) to both <menu> and <item> tags.

The <attribute> tag has multiple purposes but one purpose common to all <item> tags is the one containing the label property. This property supplies the label string that is visible on the <item>. In this case, the <item> tags correspond to a Gtk.MenuItem label attribute specifies the string that appears in the menu item.

Another <attribute> tag that appears with each <item> tags is the action attribute. This tag specifies the action to be taken when the <item> is clicked. The action specified is closely tied to the Gtk.Application and the Gtk.ApplicationWindow class (or their subclasses). The target of each action specifies which class instance—the Gtk. ApplicationWindow or the Gtk.Application—creates the Gio.SimpleAction and connects it to a method in the same class instance for processing the action. You can think of the <attribute> action tag as a kind of signal name that is an alias for the real signal to be processed.

The action attribute is applied to all elements except top-level widgets and separators. When loading the UI file to associate a Gtk.Action object to each element, Gtk.Builder uses the action attributes. Gtk.Action holds information about how the item is drawn and what callback method should be called, if any, when the item is activated.

Separators can be placed in a menu with the <separator/> tag. You do not need to provide name or action information for separators, because a generic Gtk.SeparatorMenuItem is added.

In addition to menu bars, you can create toolbars in a UI file with the <toolbar> tag, as shown in Listing 10-9.

Listing 10-9. Toolbar UI File

```
<?xml version='1.0' encoding='utf-8' ?>
<interface>
<requires lib='gtk+' version='3.4'/>
<object class='GtkToolbar' id='toolbar'>
  <property name='visible'>True</property>
  <property name='can_focus'>False</property>
  <child>
    <object class='GtkToolButton' id='toolbutton_new'>
      <property name='visible'>True</property> <property name=
      'can_focus'>False</property>
      <property name='tooltip_text' translatable='yes'>New Standard
      </property> <property name='action_name'>app.newstandard</property>
      <property name='icon_name'>document-new</property>
    </object>
    <packing>
```

```
      <property name='expand'>False</property> <property name=
      'homogeneous'>True</property>
      </packing>
   </child>
   <child>
      <object class='GtkToolButton' id='toolbutton_quit'> <property
      name='visible'>True</property> <property name='can_focus'>False</property>
         <property name='tooltip_text' translatable='yes'>Quit</property>
         <property name='action_name'>app.quit</property>
         <property name='icon_name'>application-exit</property> </object>
         <packing>
            <property name='expand'>False</property>
            <property name='homogeneous'>True</property>
         </packing>
</child>
</object>
</interface>
```

Each toolbar can contain any number of <toolitem> elements. Tool items are specified in the same manner as menu items, with an action ("action") and an ID. You can use the ID for elements in separate UI files, but you should not use the same names if, for example, the toolbar and menu bar are located in the same file.

However, you can and should use the same action for multiple elements. This causes each element to be drawn in the same way and to be connected to the same callback method. The advantage of this is that you need to define only one Gtk.Action for each item type. For example, the same action is used for the Cut element in the UI files in Listing 10-8 through 10-10.

Tip   While the toolbar, menu bar, and pop-up menu were split into separate UI files, you can include as many of these widgets as you want in one file. The only requirement is that the whole file content is contained between the <interface> and </interface> tags.

In addition to toolbars and menu bars, it is possible to define pop-up menus in a UI file, as illustrated in Listing 10-10. Notice that there are repeated actions in Listing 10-8, Listing 10-9, and Listing 10-10. Repeating actions allows you to define only a single Gtk. Action object instead of separate objects for each instance of an action.

Listing 10-10. Pop-up UI File

```
<?xml version='1.0' encoding='utf-8' ?>
<interface>
  <menu id="app-menu">
    <section>
      <item>
        <attribute name="label">About</attribute> <attribute
        name="action">app.about</attribute>
      </item>
      <item>
        <attribute name="label">Quit</attribute> <attribute
        name="action">app.quit</attribute>
      </item>
    </section>
  </menu>
</interface>
```

The last type of top-level widget supported by UI files is the pop-up menu, denoted by the <popup> tag. Since a pop-up menu is the same thing as a normal menu, you can still use <menuitem> elements as children.

Loading XML Files

After you create your UI files, you need to load them into your application and retrieve the necessary widgets. To do this, you need to utilize the functionality provided by Gtk. ActionGroup and Gtk.Builder.

Gtk.ActionGroup is a set of items with name, stock identifier, label, keyboard accelerator, tooltip, and callback methods. The name of the each action can be set to an action parameter from a UI file to associate it with a UI element.

Gtk.Builder is a class that allows you to dynamically load one or more user interface definitions. It automatically creates an accelerator group based on associated action groups and allows you to reference widgets based on the "ID" parameter from the UI file.

In Listing 10-11, Gtk.UIManager loads the menu bar and toolbar from the UI files in Listing 10-10. The resulting application is shown in Figure 10-7.

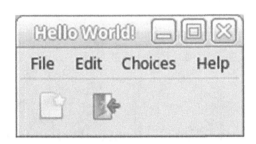

Figure 10-7. *A menu bar and a toolbar that are dynamically loaded*

Each of the menu and tool items in the application are connected to empty callback methods, because this example is only meant to show you how to dynamically load menus and toolbars from UI definitions. You implement callback methods with actual content in the two exercises found at the end of this chapter.

Listing 10-11. Loading a Menu with Gtk.Builder

```python
#!/usr/bin/python3

import sys
import gi
gi.require_version('Gtk', '3.0')
from gi.repository import Gtk

class AppWindow(Gtk.ApplicationWindow):

    def __init__(self, *args, **kwargs):
        super().__init__(*args, **kwargs)

    def change_label(self):
        pass

    def maximize(self):
        pass
```

```
    def about(self):
        pass

    def quit(self):
        self.destroy()

    def newstandard(self):
        pass

class Application(Gtk.Application):

    def __init__(self, *args, **kwargs):
        super().__init__(*args, application_id="org.example.myapp",
                         **kwargs)
        self.window = None

    def do_activate(self):
        if not self.window:
            self.window = AppWindow(application=self, title="Hello World!")
            builder = Gtk.Builder()
            builder.add_from_file("./Menu_XML_File.ui")
            builder.add_from_file("./Toolbar_UI_File.xml")
            builder.connect_signals(self.window)
            self.set_menubar(builder.get_object("menubar"))
            self.window.add(builder.get_object("toolbar"))
        self.window.present()
    if __name__ == "__main__":
        app = Application()
        app.run(sys.argv)
```

Test Your Understanding

The following two exercises give an overview of what you have learned about menus and toolbars throughout the chapter.

In addition to completing them, you may want to create examples of pop-up menus with other widgets that do not support them by default. Also, after finishing both of these exercises, you should expand them by creating your own stock icons that are used in place of the default items.

Exercise 1: Toolbars

In Chapter 8, you created a simple text editor using the Gtk.TextView widget. In this exercise, expand on that application and provide a toolbar for actions instead of a vertical box filled with Gtk.Button widgets.

Although manual toolbar creation is possible, in most applications, you want to utilize the Gtk.Builder method for toolbar creation. Therefore, use that method in this exercise. You should also create your own with Gtk.IconFactory.

Oftentimes, it is advantageous for an application to provide the toolbar as a child of a handle box. Do this for your text editor, placing the toolbar above the text view. Also, set up the toolbar so that the textual descriptor is shown below every tool button.

This first exercise taught you how to build your own toolbars. It also showed you how to use the Gtk.HandleBox container. In the next exercise, you reimplement the Text Editor application with a menu bar.

Exercise 2: Menu Bars

In this exercise, implement the same application as in Exercise 1, except use a menu bar this time. You should continue to use Gtk.Builder, but the menu does not need to be contained by a Gtk.HandleBox.

Since tooltips are not shown for menu items automatically, use a status bar to provide more information about each item. The menu bar should contain two menus: File and Edit. You should also provide a Quit menu item in the File menu.

Summary

In this chapter, you learned two methods for creating menus, toolbars, and menu bars. The first method was the manual method, which was more difficult but introduced you to all of the necessary widgets.

The first example showed you how to use basic menu items to implement a pop-up menu for a progress bar. This example was expanded on to provide keyboard accelerators and more information to the user with the Gtk.Statusbar widget. You also learned about submenus as well as image, toggle, and radio menu items.

The next section showed you how to use menu items with submenus to implement a menu bar with a `Gtk.MenuShell`. This menu bar could be displayed horizontally or vertically and forward or backward.

Toolbars are simply a horizontal or vertical list of buttons. Each button contains an icon and label text. You learned about three additional types of toolbar buttons: toggles, radio buttons, and tool buttons with a supplemental menu.

Then, after much hard work, you were taught how to create dynamically loadable menus. Each menu or toolbar is held in a UI definition file, which is loaded by the `Gtk.Builder` class. The Builder associates each object with the appropriate action and creates the widgets according to the UI definition.

Last, you learned how to create your own custom icons. It is necessary to create your own icons, because arrays of actions require an identifier to add an icon to an action.

In the next chapter, we are going to take a short break from coding and cover the design of graphical user interfaces with the Glade user interface builder. This application creates user interface XML files, which can be dynamically loaded when your application starts. You then learn how to handle these files programmatically with `Gtk.Builder`.

CHAPTER 11

Dynamic User Interfaces

By now, you have learned a great deal about GTK+ and its supporting libraries, and you are able to create fairly complex applications. However, manually writing all of the code to create and configure the widgets and behavior for these applications can quickly become tedious.

The Glade user interface builder removes the need for you to write all of that code by allowing you to design your UI graphically. It supports the GTK+ library of widgets as well as various widgets from the GNOME libraries. User interfaces are saved as XML files, which can dynamically build your application's user interface.

The last part of this chapter covers Gtk.Builder, a library that can dynamically load the XML files. Gtk.Builder creates all the necessary widgets and allows you to connect any signals defined in Glade.

Note This chapter covers the user interface of Glade that is current at the time of this writing. It is possible that this may change in the future, but any changes should be an easy transition from the instructions provided in this chapter.

In this chapter, you learn the following.

- Issues you should keep in mind when designing graphical user interfaces (GUIs)

- How to design custom graphical user interfaces with Glade

- How to dynamically load Glade user interfaces with Gtk.Builder

© W. David Ashley and Andrew Krause 2019
W. D. Ashley and A. Krause, *Foundations of PyGTK Development*,
https://doi.org/10.1007/978-1-4842-4179-0_11

User Interface Design

In this chapter, you are going to learn how to use Glade 3 and `Gtk.Builder` to implement dynamic user interfaces. However, it is prudent to first learn a few concepts that you should keep in mind when designing graphical user interfaces. These concepts can help you to avoid confusing and frustrating users in the future.

You also have to realize that, while you know how to use your application because you designed it, you need to do as much as possible to help the user make sense of it. Whether the user is an expert or a novice, each user should be able to use your application with the shortest possible learning curve. That said, the following sections include many tips and design decisions to help you achieve this level of intuitiveness. They also improve the maintainability of your application.

Know Your Users

When designing a user interface, the most important thing to consider is your audience. Are they all experienced with the task at hand, or will some need more help than others? Can you model your user interface after one that they are already familiar with, or is this something completely new?

One of the biggest possible mistakes is to make rash generalizations about your users' skill level. You may think that the way you lay out your application makes sense, but that is because you designed it. You should place yourself in the users' position, understanding they will have no prior knowledge about how to use your application.

To avoid confusion, take time to study similar applications, taking note of what design decisions seem successful and which cause problems. For example, if you are creating an application to be used in the GNOME desktop environment, you should check out the GNOME Human Interface Guidelines (`http://developer.gnome.org`), which can help you lay out a design that is used for other compliant applications.

Another thing to consider when designing a user interface is accessibility. Users may have vision problems that could inhibit them from using an application. The Accessibility Toolkit provides many facilities for GTK+ applications to make them compatible with screen readers. GTK+ also relies heavily on themes, which is why you should avoid setting the font, when possible, or provide the user with a way to change it.

Your language is another consideration when designing the user interface. First, you should always use jargon that is familiar to the users. For example, you are free to use mathematical terms in an engineering application, but you should not do so in a web browser.

Many applications are translated into other languages when they become popular, which may cause problems if you use words or images that could be offensive in other cultures.

Keep the Design Simple

Once you know your audience, it becomes a lot simpler to design an effective user interface, but you can still run into problems if the interface is too difficult or cluttered. Always try to reduce the number of widgets on the screen to a reasonable number.

For example, if you need to provide many choices to the user where only one can be selected, you might be tempted to use a lot of radio buttons. However, a better solution may be to use a Gtk.ComboBox, which significantly decreases the number of required widgets.

The Gtk.Notebook container is extremely useful for grouping similar option groups that would otherwise clutter a huge page. In many applications, this widget groups widgets that relate or depend on each other into a preferences dialog.

Menu layout is also another problematic area, because it is not always done in a sensible manner. When possible, you should use standard menus, such as File, Edit, View, Help, Format, and Window. These menus are familiar to users who are experienced with computing, and users expect them. Because of this, these menus should contain standard items as well. For example, the File menu should contain items for manipulating files, printing, and exiting the application. You should investigate how other applications lay out their menu items if you are not sure where to place a particular item.

Repetitive jobs, or those that the user performs often, should always be made quick and easy. There are multiple ways to do this. The most important is to provide keyboard accelerators for many actions —pressing Ctrl+O on the keyboard is a lot faster than clicking the File menu and the Open menu item.

Note   Whenever possible, you should always use standard keyboard accelerators, such as Ctrl+X for cutting and Ctrl+N for creating something new. This significantly decreases the initial learning curve for users of your application. In fact, some keyboard accelerators are already built into many widgets, such as Ctrl+X for cutting the selection in text widgets.

It may take some time for your users to become accustomed to keyboard accelerators, which is why toolbars are also extremely useful for repetitive options. You need to find a balance between placing too few and too many items on a toolbar, though. A cluttered toolbar scares and confuses the user, but a toolbar with too few items is useless. If you have a large number of items that users might want on toolbars, it would make sense to allow the users to customize the toolbars themselves.

Always Be Consistent

Consistency is important when designing a graphical user interface, and GTK+ makes this extremely easy. First, GTK+ provides many stock items that should always be used in favor of homegrown items where possible. The user will already be familiar with the icons for the stock items and will know how to use them.

Caution   Stock items can be very dangerous if you do not use them correctly. You should never use a stock item for an action for which it was not originally intended. For example, you should not use GTK_STOCK_REMOVE icon for a subtraction operation just because it looks like a "minus sign." The icons are defined by the user's theme; they may not always look the way you assume.

Speaking of themes, you should fall back on the settings provided by a theme whenever possible. This helps you create a consistent look—not only throughout your application but across the entire desktop environment. Since themes are applied to all applications throughout a desktop, your application is consistent with most other applications that the user runs.

In those few cases where you do need to deviate from the defaults provided by the user's theme, you should always give the user a way to change the settings or to just use the system defaults. This is especially important when dealing with fonts and colors, because your changes can render your application unusable with some themes.

Another advantage of consistency is that the user learns how to use your application much faster. The user needs to learn only one design instead of many. If you do not use a consistent layout for your application and supplemental dialogs, the user is presented with a brand-new adventure with every new window.

Keep the User in the Loop

One thing that can turn off a user of your application very quickly is if it is not responsive for a long period of time. Most computer users are accustomed to a bug or two, but if your application is processing information and remains unresponsive for quite a while, the user may give up.

To avoid this, there are two possible solutions. The first is to make your application more efficient. However, if your application is not to blame, or there is no way to make it more efficient, you should use progress bars. A progress bar tells the user that your application is still working. Just make sure to update your progress bar! If you do not know how long the process will take, another option would be to pulse the progress bar and provide messages that update the user on the process's progress.

Also, remember the following loop from Chapter 3.

```
while Gtk.events_pending():
    Gtk.main_iteration()
```

This loop makes sure that the user interface is updated, even when the processor is busy processing another task. If you do not update the user interface during a CPU-intensive process, the application may be unresponsive to the user until it is finished!

You should also provide your users with feedback when actions are performed. If a document is being saved, you should mark it as unmodified or display a message in the status bar. If you do not provide feedback to the user when an action is performed, it may be assumed that the action was not performed.

Message dialogs are a very useful way to provide feedback, but they should be used only when necessary. The user will become frustrated if message dialogs appear too often, which is why only critical errors and warnings should be reported this way.

We All Make Mistakes

Whether you are an expert or a novice, we all make mistakes. Because of this, you should always forgive your users. After all, everyone has at one time or another pressed an incorrect button that resulted in losing a large amount of work. In a properly designed application, this should never occur.

For basic actions that cannot be easily undone by the user, you should provide the ability to undo the action. For example, these basic actions could include deleting an item from our Grocery List application or moving text within a text view.

For actions that cannot be undone, you should always provide a confirmation dialog. It should explicitly state that this action cannot be undone and ask whether the user wants to continue. For example, you should always ask the user whether the application should be closed when there are documents with unsaved changes. People have been using software for years and have come to expect a confirmation dialog box for actions that cannot be undone.

The Glade User Interface Builder

One factor that can make or break a GUI toolkit is whether it can rapidly deploy applications. While the user interface is extremely important to the success of an application, it should not be the most consuming aspect of the development process.

Glade is a tool that allows you to quickly and efficiently design graphical user interfaces so that you can move onto other aspects of your code. User interfaces are saved as an XML file that describes the widget structure, the properties of each widget, and any signal handlers you associated with each. Gtk.Builder can then load the user interface file to dynamically build it on application load. This allows you to alter the user interface aesthetically without the need to recompile the application.

Note   Older versions of Glade allowed you to generate source code instead of saving the user interface in an XML file. This method is deprecated, because it is difficult to manage when you want to change your user interface. Therefore, you should follow the method provided in this chapter.

You need to realize from the start what Glade is and what it is not. Glade designs the user interface of an application, set up signals that are associated with callback methods implemented in your code, and take care of common widget properties. However, Glade is not a code editor or an integrated development environment. The files it outputs must be loaded by your application, and you must implement all of the callback methods in your code. Glade is just meant to simplify the process of initializing your application's graphical user interface and connecting signals.

Tip   Glade 3.22.1, the version used in this book, now allows integrated development environments, such as Anjuta, to embed it into their user interfaces. These IDEs provide a complete, start-to-finish solution for deploying GTK+ applications.

Another advantage of Glade is that, since the user interfaces are stored as XML files, they are independent of the language. Any language that has wrapped the functionality provided by `Gtk.Builder` can load user interfaces. This means that the same graphical user interface designer can be used regardless of the programming language you choose.

Before continuing with the rest of this chapter, you should install Glade and the development package for `Gtk.Builder` from your operating system's package manager. Alternatively, you can download and compile the sources from `glade.gnome.org`.

Also, you should make sure to follow along and create this application while reading the rest of the chapter. This gives you a chance to learn your way around the Glade 3 application, so you can get as much practice as possible while you have this book to guide you.

The Glade Interface

When you launch Glade for the first time, you see a main window with three panes: the main window tree view, the widget palette, and the widget property editor. Figure 11-1 is a screenshot of the main Glade application window with a project opened from the `FileBrowser.glade`.

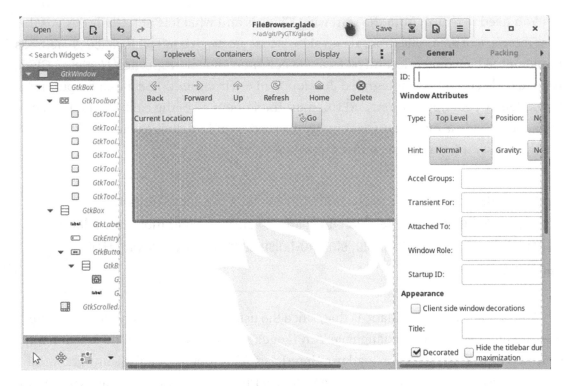

Figure 11-1. *The Glade main window*

The main tree view window facilitates Glade project management. The Main Window Title Bar shows a list of the currently open projects, allowing you to switch among them. The left pane also includes the widget tree view, which shows the widget containment of the project with focus.

The widget tree view shows the parent-to-child container relationships within a project. It is possible to have multiple top-level widgets. However, in Figure 11-1 window is the only top-level widget of the FileBrowser.glade.

This pane is where you specify project options, save the project, and load existing projects. The Popup menus in this window also provide many other options that can help you when working with projects, such as undoing and redoing actions.

Note   If you decide to work with Glade 2 instead of Glade 3, make sure to save often. Undo and redo support was not implemented in the older versions of Glade, and it is very frustrating if you accidentally overwrite an hour of work with one wrong mouse click!

The middle pane shown when you launch Glade 3 has buttons for selecting widgets from a widget palette, which lists all of the widgets available to you for designing your applications. A screenshot of the one of the widget palettes is shown in Figure 11-2.

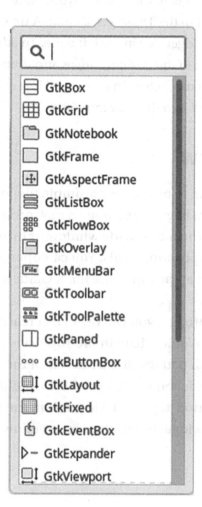

Figure 11-2. *A Glade widget palette*

By default, there are five categories of widgets that can be displayed: top-level widgets, containers, widgets used for control, display widgets, and composite and depreciated widgets. You should not use any widgets in the GTK+ Obsolete list in new applications, because they are depreciated and may be removed in future releases.

In addition to the default categories of widgets, you may find other categories that include additional widget libraries. These include widgets added for the GNOME libraries or other custom widget libraries.

Through the View menu, you can change the layout of the widget palette. Figure 11-2 shows a widget palette that is set to show both icons and text. However, you can show only text or only icons depending on what style you are most comfortable with.

To add a new top-level widget to the widget layout pane, all you need to do is click the icon of the desired widget in the Toplevels section. A new top-level widget is then displayed and added to the widget tree in the left pane. To add non-top-level widgets, you need to first click the icon of the desired widget and then click your mouse where the widget should be placed. You must click an empty cell in a container widget for the non-top-level widget to be inserted into the user interface.

Creating the Window

In this chapter, you are going to be creating a simple file browser application with Glade and `Gtk.Builder`. You begin by creating a new project by clicking on the new project button at the top of the main Glade window or by using the blank project created for you when the application loads. You can open an existing project by clicking on the Open button at the top of the main Glade window if you return to this tutorial at a later time.

After you have a blank project, you can begin by creating a new top-level `Gtk.Window` by clicking the Window icon in the Toplevels widget palette. In the new window, you see a mesh pattern in the interior of the widget, as displayed in Figure 11-3. This pattern designates a region where a child widget can be added to a container. After selecting a non-top-level widget from the widget palette, you must click this region to add the widget to the container. Follow this method for adding all non-top-level widgets.

Figure 11-3. *The Default Gtk.Window widget*

After you create the top-level window, you notice changes in the content of the widget Properties pane, shown in Figure 11-4. In this pane, you can customize all of the properties of each widget that is supported in Glade.

Note While Glade allows you to edit many widget properties, some actions simply have to be performed in the code. Therefore, you should not view Glade as a replacement for everything that you have learned thus far in the book. You are still doing a lot of GTK+ development in most applications.

The widget Properties window displayed in Figure 11-4 has a complete list of the various options. The pane is divided into sections, which categorize the basic options that are specific to the widget type that is currently selected. For example, the Gtk. Window widget allows you to specify the window's type, title, ability to be resized, default size, and so on.

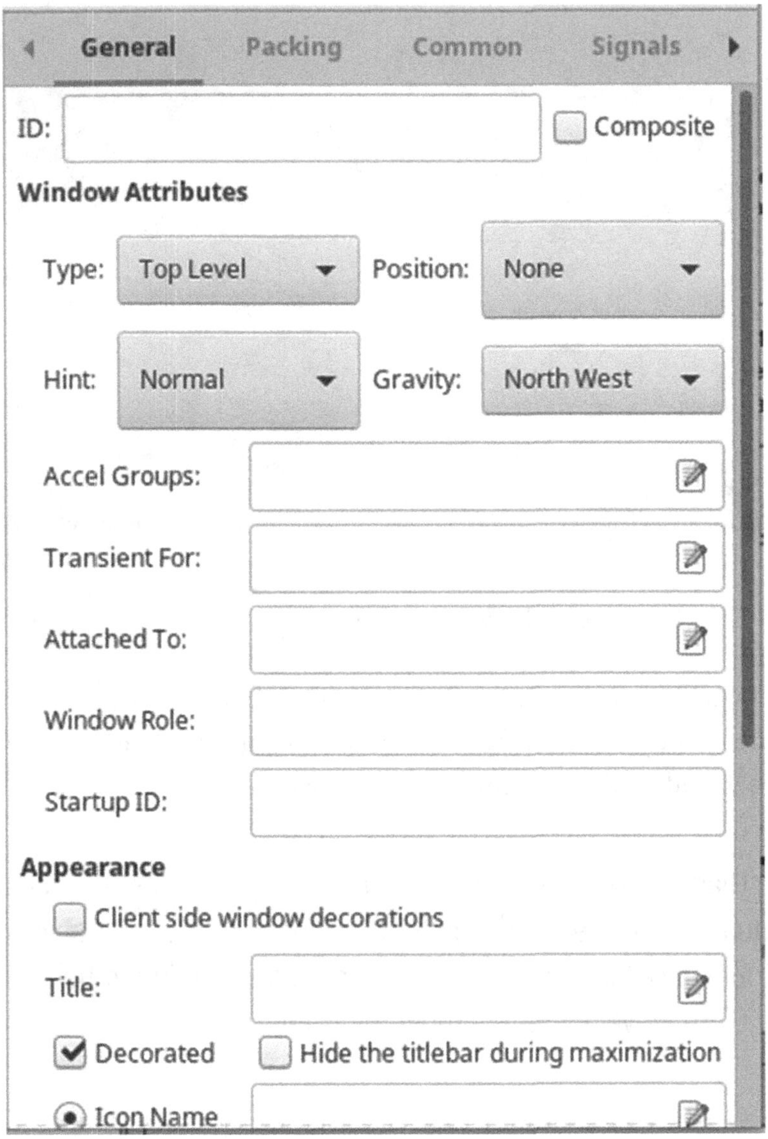

Figure 11-4. *The widget properties pane*

The ID field, which is scrolled beyond the bounds of the scrolled window in Figure 11-4 gives a unique name to the widget. Glade automatically assigns a name to each widget that is unique for the current project, but these are generic names. If you plan to reference a widget from within your application, you should give it an ID that means something. It can easily become confusing when you have to load three Gtk. TreeView3 widgets named treeview1, treeview2, and treeview3!

The Packing tab provides basic information about how the widget reacts to changes in the size of its parent widget, such as expanding and filling. Common properties are those provided by Gtk.Widget and are available to all widgets. For example, you can provide a size request in this tab.

Note   Packing options are a bit unintuitive when first working with Glade, because properties are set by the child instead of the parent container. For example, packing options for the children of a Gtk.Box are provided in the Packing tab of the children themselves instead of the parent container.

The Signals tab allows you to define signals for each widget that is connected by Gtk.Builder. Lastly, the Accessibility tab, designated by the handicapped symbol, gives options that are used for accessibility support.

As you will recall from the first example in this book, an empty Gtk.Window widget is not of any use except for illustrating how to create one. Since the file browser needs multiple widgets packed into the main window for this application, the next step is to add a vertical box container. Select the Box widget from the palette and click inside the grid pattern of window to insert a Gtk.Box widget into the window. You can then use the Properties pane to adjust the orientation of the box (vertical or horizontal) and the number of panes the Gtk.Box contains. Figure 11-5 shows the adjustments necessary for the Gtk.Box properties.

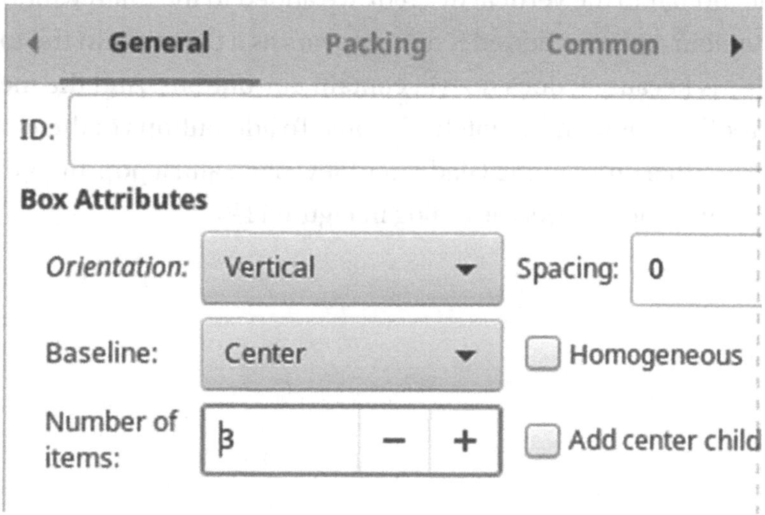

Figure 11-5. *The Default Gtk.Window widget*

By default, three cells are created to hold child widgets, but you can change this to any number of items greater than zero. The default of three is how many child widgets we need.

By default, a Gtk.Box has a vertical orientation but you can change the orientation to horizontal if needed.

Note   Do not worry if you are not sure how many widgets the container will hold. You can add or remove cells in the General tab in the widget Properties pane. You can then change the position of a widget within the box under the Packing tab. You are also still able to edit the user interface with your code after it is built by Gtk. Builder!

After adding the vertical box, you see three separate, empty container meshes; notice the changes in the Properties pane and the widget tree view pane. To these meshes, we will add a toolbar, an address bar, and a tree view.

Adding a Toolbar

The old handle box widget has long been deprecated since most of the widgets it was meant to contain have been enhanced to dynamically hide their content. The Gtk. Toolbar is one of the widgets that has been enhanced in this way. That means we can directly add the toolbar to the vertical Gtk.Box we added to the main window previously.

When the toolbar widget is added it only appears as a thin strip in the top pane of the vertical box. This is because it does not yet contain any buttons. And the method to add buttons to the toolbar is not immediately obvious. To add buttons to the toolbar right-click on the Gtk.Toolbar entry in the Glade tree view pane and a pop-up menu labeled Edit... appears, which then shows the dialog in Figure 11-6.

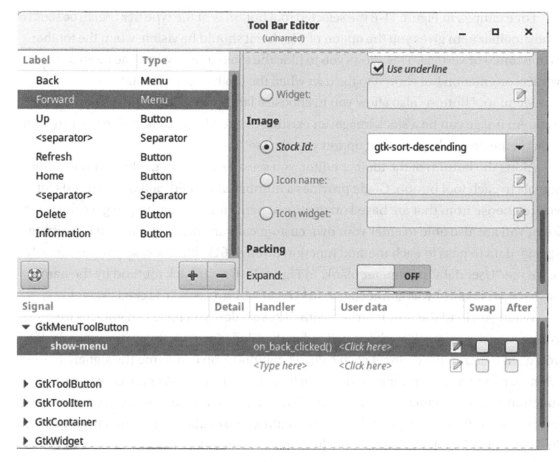

Figure 11-6. *The toolbar editor*

The toolbar editor allows you to add any supported type of item to a toolbar. To add a new item, you need only to click the Add button. This presents you with a pane in the editor dialog with which you can modify the new button's properties. Be careful here as your version of Glade may present you the option of using stock buttons. Stock items have all been deprecated so you must create your own custom buttons instead.

After you add a new tool button, the next step is to choose what type of widget it should be by selecting an option from the Type combo box. The types of toolbar items included in the combo box are a generic tool button containing an image and a label, toggles, radio buttons, menu tool buttons, tool items, and separators. When you select a new type, the dialog immediately changes to allow you to edit properties for the chosen type.

For example, in Figure 11-6 the selected tool button is of the type Gtk.MenuToolButton. Every toolbar item gives you the option of whether it should be visible when the toolbar is horizontal or vertical. This allows you to hide the toolbar item when the toolbar has a vertical orientation but show it to the user when the toolbar is horizontal.

Menu tool buttons also allow you to choose a label and image to display in the tool item. An image can be a stock image, an existing image file, or an identifier of a custom icon theme depending on what option you choose.

Along the bottom of the toolbar editor, you see a tree view that allows you to connect signals to each tool button. Glade provides a number of named callback methods for you to choose from that are based on the signal name and the name you gave the toolbar item. You are also able to enter your own custom callback method name. It is possible to specify data to pass to each method function through Gtk.Builder, so you can usually leave the "User data" parameter blank. In Figure 11-6 a callback method by the name on_back_clicked() was connected to Gtk.MenuToolButton's "clicked" signal.

When you load the user interface with Gtk.Builder, you have two choices for connecting the callback methods defined in the Glade file with those in your code. If you want to manually connect each callback method, you can name the signal handler whatever you choose, as long as the name is unique. However, Gtk.Builder provides a function that automatically connects all of the signals to the appropriate symbols in your executable or Python program. To use this feature, the callback method name you define in Glade must match the name of the function in your code!

The Packing tab includes options to determine padding around the widget, whether the packing is from the start or end of the box, and to determine the widget's position within the container. These properties are exactly equivalent to the settings you used when adding child widgets to Gtk.Box with box.pack_start() and friends.

Tip   You should remember from Chapter 4 that a table was provided that illustrates what the expand and fill properties do to child widgets of a Gtk.Box widget. Glade is a perfect opportunity for you to experiment with packing options to gain a better understanding of how they affect the widget. Therefore, take a moment to experiment with the various packing options!

After completing the toolbar and fixing packing preferences, your application should look like Figure 11-7.

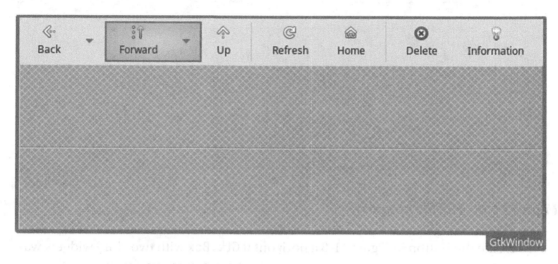

Figure 11-7. *The toolbar in action*

The toolbar shown in Figure 11-7 contains two menu tool buttons used for moving forward and backward through the user's browsing history. There are also tool buttons for moving to the parent directory, refreshing the current view, removing a file, moving to the home directory, and viewing file information. Each of these tool buttons is connected to a callback method that you must implement in your code for the application.

Completing the File Browser

The next step in creating our file browser is to create the address bar that shows the users the current location and allow them to enter a new location. This means that we need a horizontal box with three widgets, as shown in Figure 11-8. The three widgets are a label describing the content held in the Gtk.Entry widget, the Gtk.Entry widget that holds the current location, and a button that moves to the location when pressed.

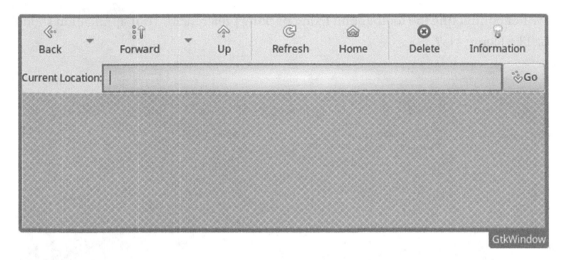

Figure 11-8. *The file browser*

To create the button in Figure 11-8 a horizontal Gtk.Box with two child widgets was added to the button: a Gtk.Image widget set to the GTK_STOCK_JUMP_TO stock image and a Gtk.Label widget named Go.

The last step is to add a Gtk.ScrolledWindow widget to the last cell in the vertical box and a Gtk.TreeView widget to that container. The completed file browser user interface is shown in Figure 11-9. However, we are not yet finished editing the application in Glade.

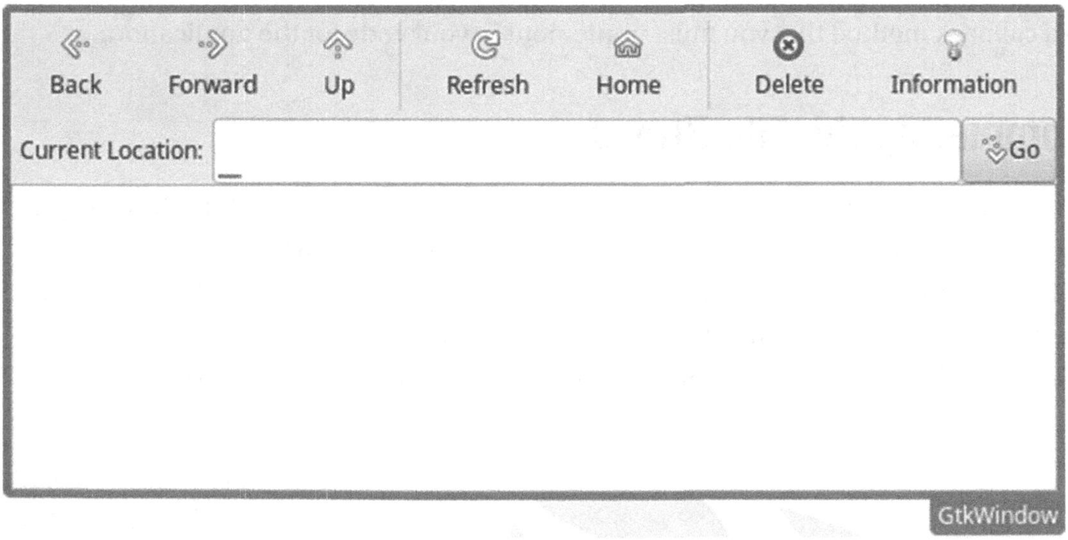

Figure 11-9. *The file browser*

Making Changes

The file browser is completely designed, but now I have decided that it should include a Gtk.StatusBar widget along the bottom of the window! Making changes to the user interface can be tricky, so this section walks you through a few challenging actions.

The first step in adding the status bar is to extend the number of child widgets contained by the main vertical Gtk.Box widget. To do this, choose the vertical box from the widget tree view. In the Properties pane, you can increase the number of children with the "Number of items" property in the General tab. This adds a new empty space at the end of the vertical box into which you can add a status bar widget.

If you need to reorder the children of a vertical or horizontal box, you first need to select the widget you want to move. Then, under the Packing tab in the Properties pane, you can choose a new position by changing the value of its spin button. You are able to see the child widget moving to its new position as you change spin button's value. The positions of surrounding child widgets are automatically adjusted to reflect the changes.

Another problematic task can result if you decide that you need to stuff a container into a location where another widget is already added. For example, let's assume that you have decided to place a horizontal pane in place of the scrolled window in the file browser application. You first need to select the widget from the widget tree view in the main window and remove it by pressing Ctrl+X. After this, an empty box is displayed, in which you can add the horizontal pane. Next, select the pane where the scrolled window should be placed and press Ctrl+V.

Making changes to a user interface used to be a touchy topic with Glade 2, because it did not support undo and redo actions. It used to be very easy to make a mistake and lose hours of work by accidentally deleting your top-level widget, since you could not undo any actions. Now that Glade 3 includes undo and redo support, you do not have to worry as much.

Widget Signals

The last step for this application is to set up signals for all of the widgets. Figure 11-10 shows the Signals tab of the widget properties editor for the Go button. The Gtk.Button widget is connected to the clicked signal, which calls on_button_clicked() when emitted.

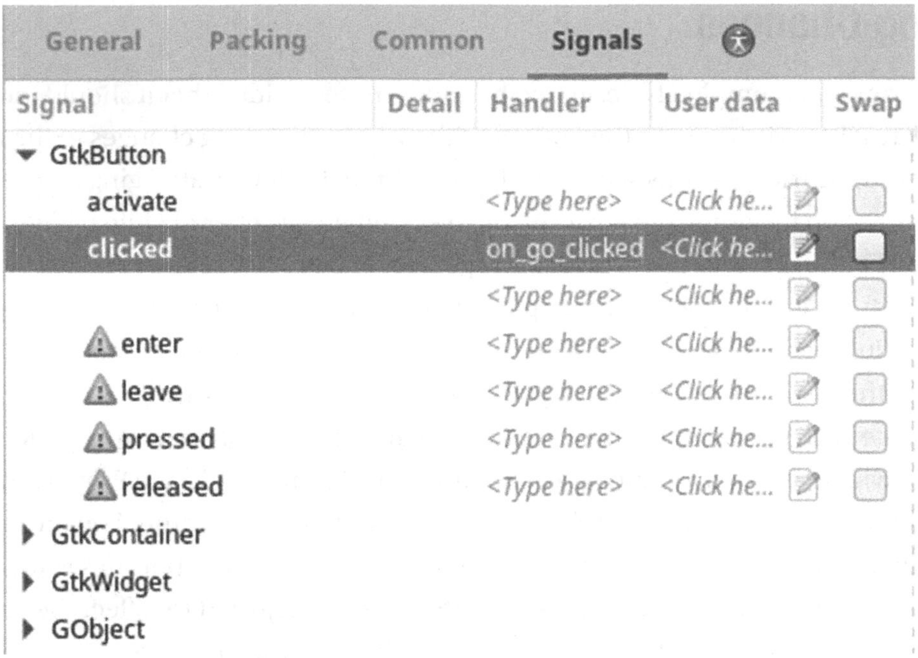

Figure 11-10. *A widget signal editor*

In addition to the "clicked" signal, you need to connect to a few others. Each of the tool items should be connected to Gtk.ToolButton's clicked signal with the exception of the separators. Also, you should connect the Gtk.Entry to activate, which is emitted when the user presses the Enter key when the entry has focus.

Note   This application is only a design for a simple file browser that is meant to show you how to design applications with Glade 3. The code needed for the application to be more than just a design is implemented in Chapter 14.

As for the tree view, you should connect it to row-activated. When a row is activated, the user is shown more information about the file, or it navigates to the chosen directory. A list of the widgets along with their signals and callback methods is provided in Table 11-1 so that you can easily follow along with this example.

Table 11-1. *Widget Signals*

Widget	Description	Signal	Callback Method
Gtk.Button	Go button	"clicked"	on_go_clicked()
Gtk.Entry	Location entry	"activate"	on_location_activate()
Gtk.MenuToolButtonBack		"clicked"	on_back_clicked()
Gtk.MenuToolButtonForward		"clicked"	on_forward_clicked()
Gtk.ToolButton	Up	"clicked"	on_up_clicked()
Gtk.ToolButton	Refresh	"clicked"	on_refresh_clicked()
Gtk.ToolButton	Home	"clicked"	on_home_clicked()
Gtk.ToolButton	Delete	"clicked"	on_delete_clicked()
Gtk.ToolButton	Information	"clicked"	on_info_clicked()
Gtk.TreeView	File browser	"row-activated"	on_row_activated()
Gtk.Window	Main window	"destroy"	on_window_destroy()

Creating a Menu

In addition to toolbars, it is possible to create menus in Glade 3. Figure 11-11 shows the menu bar editor, which is very similar to the toolbar editor. It supports normal menu items and those rendered with images, check buttons, radio buttons, and separators.

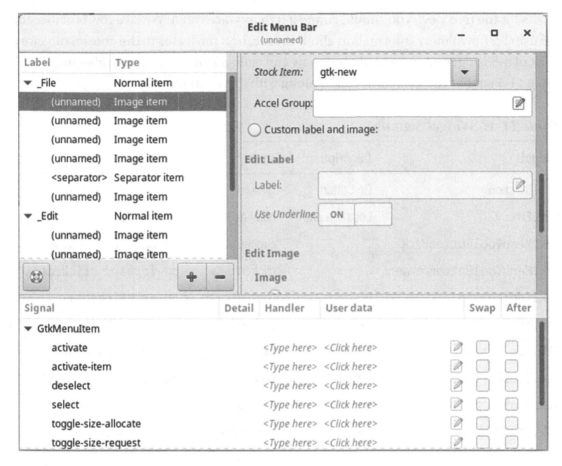

Figure 11-11. *The menu bar editor*

Caution   The Glade 3.22.1 editor currently still uses Stock Items for Menu Items. All Stock Items are deprecated so you really should be using your own custom menu items, only this version of Glade does not support custom menu items. You may need to edit the XML produced by Glade to create your own custom entries.

You now know of three ways to create menus; this raises the question of which one is best. Every method has its advantages and disadvantages, so let's take a look at each method.

You first learned how to create menus manually, molding each object to your needs. This method is good to use with smaller menus, because the code will not take up a lot of space and the implementation is located entirely in one place. However, if your menu grows in size or contains more than just basic items, the code can become tedious to maintain and take up a lot of space.

Next, you learned how to use `Gtk.Builder` with UI definitions to dynamically create menus. This method simplified menu creation, because you could define a large number of actions in a small amount of space. Also, since menus are constructed from UI definitions, allowing the user to edit a menu is extremely simple. This is clearly the preferred method of menu creation if you are not using Glade to design your application.

Glade also presents a very attractive method of menu creation, because after its initial design, maintenance is simple. It also requires no code to create the menu, since `Gtk.Builder` constructs it for you. However, one problem with this method is that it is not as easy to allow the user to alter the layout of menus and toolbars as with the UI file method.

One method that can easily be employed is to pack all of your widgets with respect to the end of the vertical box or whatever container you use as the child of the main window. Then, when your application loads, you can simply pack the menu created by `Gtk.Builder` into the window with `box.pack_start()`. Nevertheless, if you do not need to allow your users to customize the menu, it makes sense to do all menu creation through Glade.

Now that you are finished creating the user interface, you can save it as a `FileBrowser.glade` file, where project can be replaced by a name of your choice. This file can be loaded with respect to the location of the application or from an absolute path.

Using Gtk.Builder

After you design your application in Glade, the next step is to load the user interface with `Gtk.Builder`.

This GTK+ class parses the Glade user interface and creates all of the necessary widgets at runtime.

`Gtk.Builder` provides the methods necessary to create and hold the user interface loaded from an XML file. It can also connect signals added in the Glade file to callback methods within your application.

Another advantage of Gtk.Builder is that overhead is added only during initialization, and this is negligible compared to an interface created directly from code. After initialization, there is virtually no overhead added to the application. For example, Gtk.Builder connects signal handlers internally in the same way as your own code, so this requires no extra processing.

Since Gtk.Builder handles all of the widget initialization and the layout was already designed in Glade 3, the length of your code base can be significantly reduced. Take, for example, Listing 11-1, which would be significantly longer if you had to hand-code everything.

Listing 11-1. Loading the User Interface

```python
#!/usr/bin/python3

import sys
import gi
gi.require_version('Gtk', '3.0')
from gi.repository import Gtk

class SignalHandlers():

    def on_back_clicked(self, button ):
        pass

    def on_forward_clicked(self, button ):
        pass

    def on_up_clicked(self, button ):
        pass

    def on_refresh_clicked(self, button ):
        pass

    def on_home_clicked(self, button ):
        pass

    def on_delete_clicked(self, button ):
        pass
```

```python
    def on_info_clicked(self, button ):
        pass

    def on_go_clicked(self, button ):
        pass

    def on_location_activate(self, button ):
        pass

    def on_row_activated(self, button ):
        pass

    def on_window_destroy(self, button ):
        pass

class Application(Gtk.Application):

    def __init__(self, *args, **kwargs):
        super().__init__(*args, application_id="org.example.myapp",
                         **kwargs)
        self.window = None

    def do_activate(self):
        if not self.window:
            builder = Gtk.Builder()
            builder.add_from_file("./FileBrowser.glade")
            self.window = builder.get_object("main_window")
            self.add_window(self.window)
            builder.connect_signals(SignalHandlers())
            self.add_window(self.window)
        self.window.show_all()

if __name__ == "__main__":
    app = Application()
    app.run(sys.argv)
```

Loading a User Interface

Loading a Glade user interface is done with `builder.add_from_file()`. This is the first `Gtk.Builder` method you should call, although it should be called after getting an instance of `Gtk.Builder`. It parses the user interface provided by the XML file, creates all of the necessary widgets, and provides facilities for translation. The only parameter needed by the `builder.add_from_file()` method is the path to your Glade project file.

```
builder = Gtk.Builder()
builder.add_from_file("./FileBrowser.glade")
```

Next, you need to fetch the `"main_window"`, connect all the signals, and lastly add the window to the `Gtk.Application` class instance.

```
self.window = builder.get_object("main_window")
builder.connect_signals(SignalHandlers())
self.add_window(self.window)
```

The `builder.get_object()` needs one parameter which is the ID you assigned to the `Gtk.Window` main window in your Glade project. From this `Gtk.Builder` can determine all the child widgets that belong to the main window from reading the XML. It can then construct the window from the XML definition.

After constructing the main window, we need to assign all the signal handlers. `Gtk.Builder` can do this automatically if we supply a special Python class that contains nothing but the signal handler methods. The `builder.connect_signals()` method does this by supplying an instance of our signal handler class to it as a parameter.

Finally, we need to add the window constructed by `Gtk.Builder` to our `Gtk.Application`. This window now becomes controlled by our `Gtk.Builder` instance. While it is not a full `Gtk.ApplicationWindow` it acts very much like one as far as controlling the new window. Note that we use the `window.show_all()` to show the window instead of the `window.present()` method because our new window has no `present()` method.

It really is as simple as that. The File Browser window appears immediately and you are off and running. All that is left to do is fill all the signal handler methods, create the store for the `Gtk.TreeView` widget, build the window initialization code, and you have a working application.

Test Your Understanding

These two exercises are especially important for you to become a proficient GTK+ developer. It is not practical to programmatically design every aspect of large applications, because it takes too long.

Instead, you should be using Glade to design the user interface and `Gtk.Builder` to load that design and connect signals. By doing this, you are able to quickly finish the graphical aspects of your applications and get to the backend code that makes your applications work.

Exercise 1: Glade Text Editor

This exercise implements the text editor from the "Test Your Understanding" Exercise 1 section in Glade. The toolbar in the text editor should be implemented completely in Glade.

This exercise should not require extra coding if you still have the exercise solution from the previous chapter. You can also find the solution to "Test Your Understanding" section on the book's web site at `www.gtkbook.com`. This exercise gives you a chance to learn your way around Glade 3 and test out many widget properties.

After you design an application with a toolbar, it is an easy transition to add a menu bar. In larger applications, you should provide both of these options to the user. In the following exercise, you add a menu bar to the text editor application.

Exercise 2: Glade Text Editor with Menus

You have implemented the text editor with a menu bar. In this exercise, redesign the application from that exercise using Glade and Gtk.Builder. First, you should implement the menu with Python and GTK+, which allows you to use both together. Second, you should implement the menu again in Glade.

As with the previous exercise, the solution for Exercise 2 is at `www.gtkbook.com`. Using the downloadable solution allows you skip coding the callback functions because you already did that in the previous chapter.

Summary

In this chapter, we took a short break from coding and looked into issues that you need to consider when designing a graphical user interface. In short, you must always keep your users in mind. You need to know what to expect of your users and cater to their needs in every aspect of the application.

Next, you learned how to design graphical user interfaces using Glade 3. The ability to quickly deploy the graphical aspects of an application is necessary when considering a GUI toolkit, and GTK+ has Glade to fill this need.

Glade allows you to design every aspect of your user interface, including widget properties, layout, and signal handlers. User interfaces are saved as readable XML files that describe the structure of your application.

After designing an application in Glade 3, you can dynamically load the user interface with `Gtk.Builder`. This GTK+ class parses the Glade user interface and creates all the necessary widgets at runtime. It also provides functions for connecting signal handlers declared in Glade to callback methods within your application.

In the next chapter, we are going to get back to coding and delve into the complexities of the `GObject` system. You learn how to create your own `GObject` classes by deriving new widgets and classes, as well as how to create a widget from scratch.

CHAPTER 12

Custom Widgets

By now, you have learned a great deal about GTK+ and its supporting libraries. You have enough knowledge to use the widgets provided by PyGTK to create complex applications of your own.

However, one thing that you have not yet learned is how to create your own widgets. Therefore, this chapter is dedicated to deriving new classes from existing GTK+ classes. You are guided through some examples to show you how easy this is done using PyGTK.

In this chapter, you learn how to derive new classes and widgets from GTK+ widgets. We provide several examples of how to do this and discuss some of the problems you might encounter along the way.

An Image/Label Button

Since GTK+ 3.1, all stock items have been deprecated. While I agree with this decision, I was disappointed that the Gtk.Button was not extended to include an option for a button to display both an image and text. After eliminating the use-stock property, a Gtk.Button can only display text or an image, but not both at the same time.

The workaround for this is easily implemented but is extremely repetitive, and it is not object-oriented at all. You can see an example of how the workaround is implemented in the "Using Push Buttons" section. You can easily see that this solution would be very repetitive if you have a lot of buttons to code, and you are not making good use of code reuse with this implementation.

Another point of contention is that the programmer is forced to look up the real image they want from a string. What if the new implementation did that work for you and all you needed to supply to the new widget was the lookup string? After all, you probably want to use an image from the user's default theme, so just let the new widget do all that work.

© W. David Ashley and Andrew Krause 2019
W. D. Ashley and A. Krause, *Foundations of PyGTK Development*,
https://doi.org/10.1007/978-1-4842-4179-0_12

Figure 12-1 shows an image label button created by the program shown in Listing 12-1. This simple implementation shows how to extend the functionality and style of a standard Gtk.Button.

Figure 12-1. *An ImageLabelButton at work*

Listing 12-1 shows the class implementation for the ImageLabelButton.

Listing 12-1. ImageLabelButton Class Implementation

```
#!/usr/bin/python3

import sys
import gi
gi.require_version('Gtk', '3.0')
from gi.repository import Gtk

class ImageLabelButton(Gtk.Button):

    def __init__(self, orientation=Gtk.Orientation.HORIZONTAL,
                 image="image-missing", label="Missing", *args,
                 **kwargs):
        super().__init__(*args, **kwargs)
        # now set up more properties
        hbox = Gtk.Box(orientation, spacing=0)
        if not isinstance(image, str):
            raise TypeError("Expected str, got %s instead." % str(image))
        icon_theme = Gtk.IconTheme.get_default()
        icon = icon_theme.load_icon(image, -1,
                                Gtk.IconLookupFlags.FORCE_SIZE)
        img = Gtk.Image.new_from_pixbuf(icon)
```

```python
        hbox.pack_start(img, True, True, 0)
        img.set_halign(Gtk.Align.END)
        if not isinstance(label, str):
            raise TypeError("Expected str, got %s instead." % str(label))
        if len(label) > 15:
            raise ValueError("The length of str may not exceed 15
            characters.")
        labelwidget = Gtk.Label(label)
        hbox.pack_start(labelwidget, True, True, 0)
        labelwidget.set_halign(Gtk.Align.START)
        self.add(hbox)

class AppWindow(Gtk.ApplicationWindow):

    def __init__(self, *args, **kwargs):
        super().__init__(*args, **kwargs)
        self.set_border_width(25)
        button = ImageLabelButton(image="window-close", label="Close")
        button.connect("clicked", self.on_button_clicked)
        button.set_relief(Gtk.ReliefStyle.NORMAL)
        self.add(button)
        self.set_size_request(170, 50)

    def on_button_clicked(self, button):
        self.destroy()

class Application(Gtk.Application):

    def __init__(self, *args, **kwargs):
        super().__init__(*args, application_id="org.example.myapp",
                         **kwargs)
        self.window = None

    def do_activate(self):
        if not self.window:
            self.window = AppWindow(application=self,
                                    title="ImageLabelButton")
        self.window.show_all()
        self.window.present()
```

```
if __name__ == "__main__":
    app = Application()
    app.run(sys.argv)
```

The first point to understand is that when a Gtk.Button is created, the style of the button is set when you assign either the image or label property. Once assigned, the style of the button can never be changed. That is also the case for the new ImageLabelButton.

To start our discussion, let's take a closer look at the initialization of the widget. We allow two new properties and override one Gtk.Button existing property. The property label overrides the parent property but is used in the same way as the text for the label widget. The properties orientation and image are new. They are used, respectively, to specify the orientation of the label/image (horizontal or vertical) and the string name to look up the corresponding default theme icon.

The rest of the initialization code is straightforward. Create a Gtk.Box with either the default orientation or the one specified by the keyword argument. Next, if the image keyword is specified, look up the name in the default user theme, fetch the icon, and add the image to Gtk.Box. Next, if the label is specified, create a Gtk.Label and add that to Gtk.Box. Lastly, add the box to the button.

We changed the Gtk.ImageLabelButton class by adjusting the alignment of the image and the label text so that they remain centered together no matter how the button is sized. We used the set_halign() method and turned off the fill and expand properties used in the pack_start() method.

Note that we do not override any other methods or properties of the underlying Gtk.Button. In this case, there is no need to modify the button in any other way. ImageLabelButton behaves as a normal Gtk.Button would. Therefore, we have accomplished our mission of creating a new class of button.

Most importantly, there is some error detection code in the new class to catch invalid data types and values. It cannot be stressed enough that you provide this kind argument checking. The lack of proper error messages and proper error detection can ruin all the work you put into a new class because it does not provide enough debug information to correct even minor mistakes or problems, which will cause your class to fall into disuse.

Custom Message Dialogs

Another reason to subclass GTK+ widgets is to save work by integrating more behavior into the widget. For instance, a standard GTK+ dialog requires a lot of initialization before you ever display the dialog. You can solve a repeated amount of work by integrating a standard look-and-feel to all of your message dialogs.

The way to reduce the amount of work necessary to create a dialog is to create a design that includes all the features you need, with either default settings or parameters that can activate additional options/values. In Listing 12-2, let's look at a customized question dialog to see how this can work.

Listing 12-2. A Customized Question Dialog Implementation

```
class ooQuestionDialog(Gtk.Dialog):

hbox = None
vbox = None

    def __init__(self, title="Error!", parent=None,
                 flags=Gtk.DialogFlags.MODAL, buttons=("NO",
                 Gtk.ResponseType.NO, "_YES",
                       Gtk.ResponseType.YES)):
        super().__init__(title=title, parent=parent, flags=flags,
                     buttons=buttons)
        self.vbox = self.get_content_area()
        self.hbox = Gtk.Box(orientation=Gtk.Orientation.HORIZONTAL,
        spacing=5)

        icon_theme = Gtk.IconTheme.get_default()
        icon = icon_theme.load_icon("dialog-question", 48,
                            Gtk.IconLookupFlags.FORCE_SVG)
        image = Gtk.Image.new_from_pixbuf(icon)
        self.hbox.pack_start(image, False, False, 5)
        self.vbox.add(self.hbox)

    def set_message(self, message, add_msg=None):
        self.hbox.pack_start(Gtk.Label(message), False, False, 5)
        if add_msg != None:
```

```
        expander = Gtk.Expander.new_with_mnemonic( \ "_Click
            me for more information.")
        expander.add(Gtk.Label(add_msg))
        self.vbox.pack_start(expander, False, False, 10)

def run(self):
    self.show_all()
    response = super().run()
    self.destroy()
    return response
```

This dialog has a predefined design that is common to all of our message dialogs. It contains the following elements.

- There are separate classes for each type of message dialog.

- The dialog always contains an icon. The icon displayed is dependent on the type of dialog being displayed (message, information, error, etc.).

- The dialog always displays a primary message.

- The number and type of buttons displayed have a logical default that can be overridden by the user.

- All dialogs default to modal.

- An additional message can also be displayed in the dialog. It is enclosed in an expander that can be used any time the dialog is displayed.

- There are two additional methods supplied with the class. The first method, set_message(), sets both the primary dialog message and an optional additional message. The second method, run(), shows the dialog, runs the dialog, destroys the dialog, and returns the response_id. The run() method is optional if you want a non-modal dialog displayed. Of course, you have to supply additional functionality in the run() dialog to make that happen.

It is very simple to instantiate and run the dialog. The following code performs all the necessary tasks to open the dialog.

```
dialog = ooQuestionDialog(parent=parentwin)
dialog.set_message("This is a test message.\nAnother line.",
                   add_msg="An extra message line.")
response = dialog.run()
```

It is obvious that loading the custom design into the dialog has both advantages and disadvantages. The main disadvantage is combining the design and the functionality together. The big advantage is that should you wish to change the design, there is only one place to modify it.

From this example, it should be an easy exercise for the user to create similar subclasses for error, message, information, and warning dialogs. Just remember that consistency is the key to this task.

Multithreaded Applications

Multithreaded applications are at the core of any high-end GTK+ application, which is any application that utilizes databases, network communication, client-server activities, interprocess communications, and any other process that uses long running transactions. All of these applications require either multiple processes or threads to manage the communications to and from the separate entities to supply and receive information from each other.

GTK+ is a single thread library. It is not thread safe to access its API from multiple threads. All API calls must come from the main thread of the application. This means that long-running transactions can make the user interface seem to freeze, sometimes for very long periods of time.

The key to solving this problem is to move all long-running transactions to other threads. But, this is not easy because it involves setting up threads and supplying some type of thread safe communications for two or more threads or processes to utilize.

Most books on the topic of GUIs usually ignore this problem and concentrate on the GUI itself. This is a great disservice to the reader because just about any GUI application that the reader encounters in their professional life is multithreaded, but the reader has no experience in this type of application.

This book supplies an example to give you a better idea of what a multithreaded application looks like and the basics on how to organize it. The example is not the only way to architect a multithreaded application, but it does supply all the basics for such an application. The details and methods might be different for your project, but you are following the same basic outline supplied by our example.

Listing 12-3 is the example multithreaded application. It is a very simple program that requests information from another thread, and the main thread correctly waits for the supplier thread to provide the data. We describe this example in some detail after the listing.

Listing 12-3. Multithreaded Application

```python
#!/usr/bin/python3

import sys, threading, queue, time
import gi
gi.require_version('Gtk', '3.0')
from gi.repository import Gtk

def dbsim(q1, q2):
    while True:
        data = q1.get()
        # the request is always the same for our purpose
        items = {'lname':"Bunny", 'fname':"Bugs",
                'street':"Termite Terrace", 'city':"Hollywood",
                'state':"California", 'zip':"99999", 'employer':"Warner
                Bros.", 'position':"Cartoon character", 'credits':"Rabbit
                Hood, Haredevil Hare, What's Up Doc?"}
        q2.put(items)
        q1.task_done()

class AppWindow(Gtk.ApplicationWindow):

    def __init__(self, *args, **kwargs):
        super().__init__(*args, **kwargs)
        self.lname    = None
        self.fname    = None
        self.street   = None
```

```python
self.city     = None
self.state    = None
self.zip      = None
self.employer = None
self.position = None
self.credits  = None
self.q1 = queue.Queue()
self.q2 = queue.Queue()
self.thrd = threading.Thread(target=dbsim, daemon=True,
                             args=(self.q1, self.q1, self.q2))
self.thrd.start()

# window setup
self.set_border_width(10)
grid = Gtk.Grid.new()
grid.set_column_spacing(5)
grid.set_row_spacing(5)
# name
label = Gtk.Label.new("Last name:")
label.set_halign(Gtk.Align.END)
grid.attach(label, 0, 0, 1, 1)
self.lname = Gtk.Entry.new()
grid.attach(self.lname, 1, 0, 1, 1)
label = Gtk.Label.new("First name:")
label.set_halign(Gtk.Align.END)
grid.attach(label, 2, 0, 1, 1)
self.fname = Gtk.Entry.new()
grid.attach(self.fname, 3, 0, 1, 1)
# address
label = Gtk.Label.new("Street:")
label.set_halign(Gtk.Align.END)
grid.attach(label, 0, 1, 1, 1)
self.street = Gtk.Entry.new()
grid.attach(self.street, 1, 1, 1, 1)
label = Gtk.Label.new("City:")
label.set_halign(Gtk.Align.END)
```

```
        grid.attach(label, 2, 1, 1, 1)
        self.city = Gtk.Entry.new()
        grid.attach(self.city, 3, 1, 1, 1)
        label = Gtk.Label.new("State:")
        label.set_halign(Gtk.Align.END)
        grid.attach(label, 0, 2, 1, 1)
        self.state = Gtk.Entry.new()
        grid.attach(self.state, 1, 2, 1, 1)
        label = Gtk.Label.new("Zip:")
        label.set_halign(Gtk.Align.END)
        grid.attach(label, 2, 2, 1, 1)
        self.zip = Gtk.Entry.new()
        grid.attach(self.zip, 3, 2, 1, 1)
        # employment status
        label = Gtk.Label.new("Employer:")
        label.set_halign(Gtk.Align.END)
        grid.attach(label, 0, 3, 1, 1)
        self.employer = Gtk.Entry.new()
        grid.attach(self.employer, 1, 3, 1, 1)
        label = Gtk.Label.new("Position:")
        label.set_halign(Gtk.Align.END)
        grid.attach(label, 2, 3, 1, 1)
        self.position = Gtk.Entry.new()
        grid.attach(self.position, 3, 3, 1, 1)
        label = Gtk.Label.new("Credits:")
        label.set_halign(Gtk.Align.END)
        grid.attach(label, 0, 4, 1, 1)
        self.credits = Gtk.Entry.new()
        grid.attach(self.credits, 1, 4, 3, 1)
        # buttons
                    bb = Gtk.ButtonBox(Gtk.Orientation.HORIZONTAL)
        load_button = Gtk.Button.new_with_label("Load")
        bb.pack_end(load_button, False, False, 0)
        load_button.connect("clicked", self.on_load_button_clicked)
        save_button = Gtk.Button.new_with_label("Save")
```

```
    bb.pack_end(save_button, False, False, 0)
    save_button.connect("clicked", self.on_save_button_clicked)
    cancel_button = Gtk.Button.new_with_label("Cancel")
    bb.pack_end(cancel_button, False, False, 0)
    cancel_button.connect("clicked", self.on_cancel_button_clicked)

    # box setup

    vbox = Gtk.Box.new(orientation=Gtk.Orientation.VERTICAL,
    spacing=5) vbox.add(grid)
    vbox.add(bb)
    self.add(vbox)

def on_cancel_button_clicked(self, button):
    self.destroy()

def on_load_button_clicked(self, button):
    self.q1.put('request')
    # wait for the results to be
    queued data = None
    while Gtk.events_pending() or data ==
        None: Gtk.main_iteration()
        try:
            data = self.q2.get(block=False)
        except queue.Empty:
            continue
    self.lname.set_text(data['lname'])
    self.fname.set_text(data['fname'])
    self.street.set_text(data['street'])
    self.city.set_text(data['city'])
    self.state.set_text(data['state'])
    self.zip.set_text(data['zip'])
    self.employer.set_text(data['employer'])
    self.position.set_text(data['position'])
    self.credits.set_text(data['credits'])
    self.q2.task_done()
```

```python
    def on_save_button_clicked(self, button):
        self.lname.set_text("")
        self.fname.set_text("")
        self.street.set_text("")
        self.city.set_text("")
        self.state.set_text("")
        self.zip.set_text("")
        self.employer.set_text("")
        self.position.set_text("")
        self.credits.set_text("")

class Application(Gtk.Application):

    def __init__(self, *args, **kwargs):
        super().__init__(*args, application_id="org.example.myapp",
                         **kwargs)
        self.window = None

    def do_activate(self):
        if not self.window:
            self.window = AppWindow(application=self, title="Multi-Thread")
        self.window.show_all()
        self.window.present()

if __name__ == "__main__":
    app = Application()
    app.run(sys.argv)
```

Before we examine the listing in detail, let's describe the application requirements and see how we satisfied those requirements.

Our application is a simulation of a database client and a server—all in a single multithreaded program. The main window requests data from the threaded server and waits for a response. The server waits for a request and then supplies the data back to the client. The client side of the application is a simple GTK+ application that displays the data fetched from the server. The server is a single Python function running in a thread. It waits for a request, provides the data, and then waits for the next request.

The key to all of this is that the GTK+ client does not freeze, no matter how long the server takes to provide the data back to the client. This allows the application (and all other applications) to continue processing desktop events.

Let's start our examination of the listing right at the top—the `dbsim` server function, which stands for *database simulator*. We kept this function as simple as possible to reveal the basic functionality. The code is an endless loop that waits for a transaction to appear on a queue. `q1.get()` tries to read a transaction off the queue and waits to return when a transaction becomes available. `dbsim` does nothing with the transaction data; instead, it just builds a Python dictionary. It then puts the dictionary on a return queue with the `q2.put(items)`. Finally, processing returns to the top of the forever loop and waits for the next transaction.

The solution shown here works fine for a single client, but breaks down when multiple clients try to access the server because there is no way to synchronize the client requests with the returned data. We would need to enhance the application to provide that level of synchronization.

If you want to experiment with longer transaction times from the server, insert a `time.sleep()` statement between the `q1.get()` and the `q2.put(items)` statements. This provides the proof that the client does not freeze during a long-running transaction.

Now let's see how the client works. The client is a standard GTK+ application, except for the `on_load_button_clicked()` method. This method accesses the database simulator thread to obtain the information to fill out the entry fields displayed on the main window. The first task is to send the request to the database simulator. It does this by placing a request on a queue that is read by the simulator.

Now we come to the hard part. How do we wait for the returned information without putting the main thread to sleep? We do this by placing the method in a loop that processes pending events until the information is available from the server. Let's take a look at that tight loop.

```
while Gtk.events_pending() or data == None:
    Gtk.main_iteration()
    try:
        data = self.q2.get(block=False)
    except queue.Empty:
        continue
```

The `while` statement starts the loop by checking to see if there are pending GTK+ events to process and whether data has been placed in the target variable. If either condition is `True`, the tight loop is entered. Next, we process a single GTK+ event (if one is ready). Next, we try to fetch data from the server. `self.q2.get(block=False)` is a non-blocking request. If the queue is empty, then an exception is raised and then ignored because we need to continue the loop until the data is available.

Once the data is successfully fetched, the `on_load_button_clicked()` method continues by filling out the displayed entry fields with the supplied information.

There is one more piece to this puzzle. Take a look at the statement that created the server thread.

```
self.thrd = threading.Thread(target=dbsim, daemon=True, args=(self.q1,
self.q2))
```

The key part of this statement is the `daemon=True` argument, which allows the thread to watch for the main thread to finish, and when it does, it kills the server thread so that the application ends gracefully.

This application example has all the basic for communication between two threads. We have two queues for requests and returned data. We have a thread that performs all the long-running transactions needed by the client. And finally, we have a client that does not freeze while waiting for information from the server. This is the basic architecture for a multithreaded GUI application.

The Proper Way to Align Widgets

Prior to GTK+ 3.0, the proper way to align widgets was through the `Gtk.Alignment` class. This class was deprecated starting with GTK+ 3.0, thus seeming to eliminate an easy way to align widgets. But in truth, there are two methods in the `Gtk.Widget` class that can align widgets in any container: the `halign()` and the `valign()` methods.

These methods are easy to use and provide the type of alignment that the programmer desires in 90% of cases. Listing 12-4 shows how using the `Gtk.Widget` alignment methods produce all the types of alignment provided by the `halign()` and `valign()` methods.

Listing 12-4. Aligning Widgets

```python
#!/usr/bin/python3

import sys
import gi
gi.require_version('Gtk', '3.0')
from gi.repository import Gtk

class AppWindow(Gtk.ApplicationWindow):

    def __init__(self, *args, **kwargs) :
        super().__init__(*args, **kwargs)
        self.set_border_width(10)
        self.resize(300, 100)
        # create a grid
        grid1 = Gtk.Grid()
        grid1.height = 2
        grid1.width = 2
        grid1.set_column_homogeneous(True)
        grid1.set_row_homogeneous(True)
        self.add(grid1)
        # build the aligned labels
        label1 = Gtk.Label('Top left Aligned')
        label1.can_focus = False
        label1.set_halign(Gtk.Align.START)
        label1.set_valign(Gtk.Align.START)
        grid1.attach(label1, 0, 0, 1, 1)
        label2 = Gtk.Label('Top right Aligned')
        label2.can_focus = False
        label2.set_halign(Gtk.Align.END)
        label2.set_valign(Gtk.Align.START)
        grid1.attach(label2, 1, 0, 1, 1)
        label3 = Gtk.Label('Bottom left Aligned')
        label3.can_focus = False
        label3.set_halign(Gtk.Align.START)
        label3.set_valign(Gtk.Align.END)
```

```
        grid1.attach(label3, 0, 1, 1, 1)
        label4 = Gtk.Label('Bottom right Aligned')
        label4.can_focus = False
        label4.set_halign(Gtk.Align.END)
        label4.set_valign(Gtk.Align.END)
        grid1.attach(label4, 1, 1, 1, 1)

class Application(Gtk.Application):

    def __init__(self, *args, **kwargs):
        super().__init__(*args, application_id="org.example.myapp",
                          **kwargs)
        self.window = None
        gtk_version = float(str(Gtk.MAJOR_VERSION)+'.'+str(Gtk.MINOR_VERSION))
        if gtk_version < 3.16:
            print('There is a bug in versions of GTK older that 3.16.')
            print('Your version is not new enough to prevent this bug from')
            print('causing problems in the display of this solution.')
            exit(0)

    def do_activate(self):
        if not self.window:
            self.window = AppWindow(application=self,
                                    title="Alignment")
            self.window.show_all()
            self.window.present()

if __name__ == "__main__":
    app = Application()
    app.run(sys.argv)
```

When you run this example, you see four different alignments displayed, as shown in Figure 12-2.

Figure 12-2. *Alignment example*

The following code snippet shows how to align a single label widget to the top-left corner of a Gtk.Grid cell.

```
label1.set_halign(Gtk.Align.START)
label1.set_valign(Gtk.Align.START)
```

As you can see, aligning a widget is really simple, and the overhead is reduced because we are not invoking a new class for each aligned widget. This method of aligning widgets should be sufficient for most of your application needs.

Summary

This chapter presented three widget customization examples, which should provide enough information for you to create your own custom widgets. There are many more possibilities to increase the usability and quality of your applications.

CHAPTER 13

More GTK Widgets

You have learned, by now, almost everything this book has to teach you. However, there are a number of widgets that did not quite fit into previous chapters. Therefore, this chapter covers those widgets.

The first two widgets are used for drawing and are named Gtk.DrawingArea and Gtk.Layout. These two widgets are very similar except the Gtk.Layout widget allows you to embed arbitrary widgets into it in addition to using functions for drawing.

In addition, you learn about Gtk.Entry widgets that support automatic completion and calendars. Lastly, you are introduced to widgets that were added in GTK+ 2.10 including status icons, printing support, and recent file managers.

In this chapter, you learn the following.

- How to use the drawing widgets Gtk.DrawingArea and Gtk.Layout

- How to use the Gtk.Calendar widget to track information about months of the year

- How to use widgets introduced in GTK+ 2.10 that provide recent file tracking, printing support, and status icons

- How to implement automatic completion in a Gtk.Entry widget by applying a Gtk.EntryCompletion object

Drawing Widgets

Gtk.DrawingArea only provides one method, Gtk.DrawingArea.new(), which accepts no parameters and returns a new drawing area widget.

```
Gtk.DrawingArea.new()
```

© W. David Ashley and Andrew Krause 2019
W. D. Ashley and A. Krause, *Foundations of PyGTK Development*,
https://doi.org/10.1007/978-1-4842-4179-0_13

To begin using the widget, you only need to use the supplied by the parent widget Gdk.Window to draw on the area. Remember that a Gdk.Window object is also a Gdk. Drawable object.

One advantage of Gtk.DrawingArea is that it derives from Gtk.Widget, which means that it can be connected to GDK events. There are a number of events to which you want to connect your drawing area. You first want to connect to realize so that you can handle any tasks that need to be performed when the widget is instantiated, such as creating GDK resources. The "configure-event" signal notifies you when you have to handle a change in the size of the widget. Also, "expose-event" allows you to redraw the widget when a portion is exposed that was previously hidden. The "expose-event" signal is especially important, because if you want the content of the drawing area to persist over "expose-event" callbacks, you have to redraw its content. Lastly, you can connect to button and mouse click events so that the user can interact with the widget.

Note   To receive certain types of events, you need to add them to the list of widget events that are supported with widget.add_events(). Also, to receive keyboard input from the user, you need to set the widget.set_can_ focus(True) flag, since only focused widgets can detect key presses.

A Drawing Area Example

Listing 13-1 implements a simple drawing program using the Gtk.DrawingArea widget. Since the introduction of GTK+ 3 the Cairo drawing library has replaced the old drawing primitives used in earlier versions of GTK+. This library differs from the old primitives in that it use vector graphics to draw shapes instead of using freehand techniques. Vector graphics are interesting because they don't lose clarity when resized or transformed.

Figure 13-1 is a screenshot of this application.

Figure 13-1. *A drawing area widget with text drawn with the mouse*

While this is a very simple program, it nonetheless shows how to interact with the
Gtk.DrawingArea widget.

Listing 13-1. The Drawing Area Widget

```python
#!/usr/bin/python3

import sys
import cairo
import gi
gi.require_version('Gtk', '3.0')
from gi.repository import Gtk, Gdk
SIZE = 30
class AppWindow(Gtk.ApplicationWindow):

    def __init__(self, *args, **kwargs):
        super().__init__(*args, **kwargs)
        self.set_size_request(450, 550)
        drawingarea = Gtk.DrawingArea()
        self.add(drawingarea)
        drawingarea.connect('draw', self.draw)

    def triangle(self, ctx):
        ctx.move_to(SIZE, 0)
        ctx.rel_line_to(SIZE, 2 * SIZE)
        ctx.rel_line_to(-2 * SIZE, 0)
        ctx.close_path()

    def square(self, ctx):
        ctx.move_to(0, 0)
        ctx.rel_line_to(2 * SIZE, 0)
        ctx.rel_line_to(0, 2 * SIZE)
        ctx.rel_line_to(-2 * SIZE, 0)
        ctx.close_path()

    def bowtie(self, ctx):
        ctx.move_to(0, 0)
        ctx.rel_line_to(2 * SIZE, 2 * SIZE)
        ctx.rel_line_to(-2 * SIZE, 0)
        ctx.rel_line_to(2 * SIZE, -2 * SIZE)
        ctx.close_path()
```

```
def inf(self, ctx):
    ctx.move_to(0, SIZE)
    ctx.rel_curve_to(0, SIZE, SIZE, SIZE, 2 * SIZE, 0)
    ctx.rel_curve_to(SIZE, -SIZE, 2 * SIZE, -SIZE, 2 * SIZE, 0)
    ctx.rel_curve_to(0, SIZE, -SIZE, SIZE, -2 * SIZE, 0)
    ctx.rel_curve_to(-SIZE, -SIZE, -2 * SIZE, -SIZE, -2 * SIZE, 0)
    ctx.close_path()

def draw_shapes(self, ctx, x, y, fill):
    ctx.save()
    ctx.new_path()
    ctx.translate(x + SIZE, y + SIZE)
    self.bowtie(ctx)
    if fill:
        ctx.fill()
    else:
        ctx.stroke()
    ctx.new_path()
    ctx.translate(3 * SIZE, 0)
    self.square(ctx)
    if fill:
        ctx.fill()
    else:
        ctx.stroke()
    ctx.new_path()
    ctx.translate(3 * SIZE, 0)
    self.triangle(ctx)
    if fill:
        ctx.fill()
    else:
        ctx.stroke()
    ctx.new_path()
    ctx.translate(3 * SIZE, 0)
    self.inf(ctx)
    if fill:
        ctx.fill()
```

```
        else:
            ctx.stroke()
        ctx.restore()

    def fill_shapes(self, ctx, x, y):
        self.draw_shapes(ctx, x, y, True)

    def stroke_shapes(self, ctx, x, y):
        self.draw_shapes(ctx, x, y, False)

    def draw(self, da, ctx):
        ctx.set_source_rgb(0, 0, 0)
        ctx.set_line_width(SIZE / 4)
        ctx.set_tolerance(0.1)
        ctx.set_line_join(cairo.LINE_JOIN_ROUND)
        ctx.set_dash([SIZE / 4.0, SIZE / 4.0], 0)
        self.stroke_shapes(ctx, 0, 0)
        ctx.set_dash([], 0)
        self.stroke_shapes(ctx, 0, 3 * SIZE)
        ctx.set_line_join(cairo.LINE_JOIN_BEVEL)
        self.stroke_shapes(ctx, 0, 6 * SIZE)
        ctx.set_line_join(cairo.LINE_JOIN_MITER)
        self.stroke_shapes(ctx, 0, 9 * SIZE)
        self.fill_shapes(ctx, 0, 12 * SIZE)
        ctx.set_line_join(cairo.LINE_JOIN_BEVEL)
        self.fill_shapes(ctx, 0, 15 * SIZE)
        ctx.set_source_rgb(1, 0, 0)
        self.stroke_shapes(ctx, 0, 15 * SIZE)

class Application(Gtk.Application):

    def __init__(self, *args, **kwargs):
        super().__init__(*args, application_id="org.example.myapp",**kwargs)
        self.window = None

    def do_activate(self):
        if not self.window:
            self.window = AppWindow(application=self, title="Drawing Areas")
```

```
    self.window.show_all()
    self.window.present()
if __name__ == "__main__":
    app = Application()
    app.run(sys.argv)
```

The best way to understand how to use Cairo is to imagine that you are an artist using a paintbrush to draw out a shape on canvas.

To begin, you can choose a few characteristics of your brush. You can choose the thickness of your brush and the color you want to paint with. You can also choose the shape of your brush tip. You can choose either a circle or a square.

Once you have chosen your brush, you are ready to start painting. You have to be quite precise when describing what you want to appear.

First, decide where you want to place your brush on the canvas. You do this by supplying an x and a y coordinate. Next, you define how you want your brush stroke to look—an arc, a straight line, and so forth. Finally, you define the point where you want your stroke to end, again by supplying an x and a y coordinate. Triangles and squares are very easy to do!

More complex graphics are generated using variations of the above theme with a few additions, such as Fills (coloring in), transformations (zooming in, moving), and so forth, using the Python interface to Cairo.

Nearly all the work revolves around using the `cairo.Context` (or `cairo_t` in the Cairo C API). This is the object that you send your drawing commands to. There are a few options available to initialize this object in different ways.

It is very important to know that there is a difference between the coordinates that you are *describing* your graphics on and the coordinates that you are *displaying* your graphics on. When giving a presentation, you draw on your transparent acetate beforehand, and then display it on your overhead projector. Cairo calls the transparent acetate that the user space coordinates and the projected image that the device space coordinates.

When initializing the Cairo context object, we tell it how our description should be displayed. To do this, we supply a transformation matrix. Modifying the transformation matrix can lead to some very interesting results.

One of Cairo's most powerful features is that it can output graphics in many different formats (it can use multiple back ends). For printing, we can have Cairo translate our graphics into postscript to send to the printer. For onscreen display, Cairo can translate our graphics into something gtk can understand for hardware-accelerated rendering! It has many more important and useful target back ends. On initializing the `cairo.Context`, we set its target back end, supplying a few details (such as color depth and size), as seen in the next example.

The Layout Widget

In addition to `Gtk.DrawingArea`, GTK+ provides another drawing widget called `Gtk.Layout`. This widget is actually a container and differs from `Gtk.DrawingArea` in that it supports not only drawing primitives but also child widgets. In addition, `Gtk.Layout` provides scrolling support natively, so it does not need a viewport when added to a scrolled window.

Note   One important distinction to note with layouts is that you should draw to `Gtk.Layout`'s bin_window member instead of `Gtk.Widget`'s window . For example, you need to draw to the parent binary window, not the layout window. You can obtain the binary window by calling the `layout.get_bin_window()` method. This allows child widgets to be correctly embedded into the widget.

New `Gtk.Layout` widgets are created with `Gtk.Layout.new()`, which accepts horizontal and vertical adjustments. Adjustments are created for you if you pass None to both function parameters. Since `Gtk.Layout` has native scrolling support, it can be much more useful than `Gtk.DrawingArea` when you need to use it with a scrolled window.

However, `Gtk.Layout` does add some overhead, since it is capable of containing widgets as well. Because of this, `Gtk.DrawingArea` is a better choice if you only need to draw on the widget's `Gdk.Window`.

Child widgets are added to a `Gtk.Layout` container with `layout.put()`, which places the child with respect to the top-left corner of the container. Since `Gtk.Layout` is derived directly from `Gtk.Container`, it is able to support multiple children.

```
layout.put(child_widget, x, y)
```

A call to `layout.move()`can be used later to relocate the child widget to another location in the `Gtk.Layout` container.

Caution   Because you place child widgets at specific horizontal and vertical locations, `Gtk.Layout` presents the same problems as `Gtk.Fixed`. You need to be careful of these when using the layout widget! You can read more about `Gtk.Fixed` widget issues in the "Fixed Containers" section in Chapter 4.

Lastly, if you want to force the layout to be a specific size, you can send new width and height parameters to `layout.set_size()`. You should use this method instead of `layout.set_size_request()`, because it adjusts the adjustment parameters as well.

```
layout.set_size(width, height)
```

Also, unlike size requests, the layout sizing function requires unsigned numbers. This means that you must specify an absolute size for the layout widget. This size should be the total size of the layout, including portions of the widget that are not visible on the screen because they are beyond the bounds of the scrolling area! The size of a `Gtk.Layout` widget defaults to 100×100 pixels.

Calendars

GTK+ provides the `Gtk.Calendar` widget, which is a widget that displays one month of a calendar. It allows the user to move among months and years with scroll arrows, as shown in Figure 13-2. You can also display three-letter abbreviations of the day names and week numbers for the chosen year.

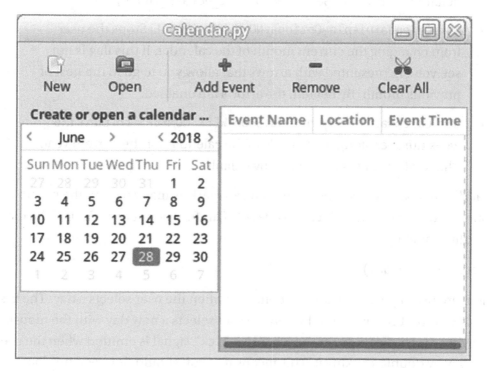

Figure 13-2. *Gtk.Calendar widget*

New `Gtk.Calendar` widgets are created with `Gtk.Calendar.new()`. By default, the current date is selected. Therefore, the current month and year stored by the computer are also displayed. You can retrieve the selected date with `calendar.get_date()` or select a new day with `calendar.select_day()`. To deselect the currently selected day, you should use `calendar.select_day()` with a date value of zero.

To customize how the `Gtk.Calendar` widget is displayed and how it interacts with the user, you should use `calendar.set_display_options()` to set a bitwise list of `Gtk.CalendarDisplayOptions` values. The following are nondeprecated values of this enumeration.

- `Gtk.CalendarDisplayOptions.SHOW_HEADING`: If set, the name of the month and the year are displayed.

- `Gtk.CalendarDisplayOptions.SHOW_DAY_NAMES`: If set, a three-letter abbreviation of each day is shown above the corresponding column of dates. They are rendered between the heading and the main calendar content.

- `Gtk.CalendarDisplayOptions.SHOW_DETAILS`: Shows only a when details are provided. See `calendar.set_detail_func()`.

- `Gtk.CalendarDisplayOptions.NO_MONTH_CHANGE`: Stops the user from changing the current month of the calendar. If this flag is not set, you are presented with arrows that allow you to go to the next or previous month. By default, the arrows are enabled.

- `Gtk.CalendarDisplayOptions.SHOW_WEEK_NUMBERS`: Displays the week number along the left side of the calendar for the current year. The week numbers are hidden by default.

In addition to selecting a single day, you can mark as many days in the month as you want one at a time with `calendar.mark_day()`. This function returns `True` if the day was successfully marked.

```
calendar.mark_day(day)
```

There are two signals available for detecting when the user selects a day. The first signal, `"day-selected"`, is emitted when the user selects a new day with the mouse or the keyboard. The `"day-selected-double-click"` signal is emitted when the user selects a day by double-clicking it. This means that you should not need the `"button-press-event"` signal with the `Gtk.Calendar` widget in most cases.

Printing Support

GTK+ 2.10 introduced a number of new widgets and objects that add printing support to the library. While there are many objects in this API, in most instances, you only need to directly interact with Gtk.PrintOperation, which is a high-level printing API that can be used across multiple platforms. It acts as a front-end interface for handling most print operations.

In this section, we implement an application that prints the content of a text file that the user selects in a Gtk.FileChooserButton widget. Figure 13-3 is a screenshot of the default print dialog on a Linux system. The user selects a file from the disk using a Gtk.FileChooserButton widget, and clicks the Print button in the main window to open this dialog.

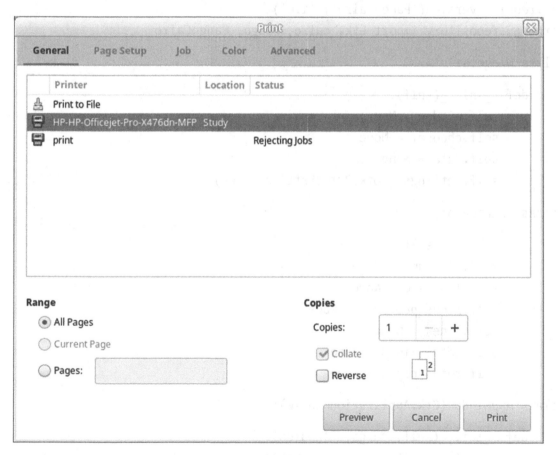

Figure 13-3. *Printing dialog*

Listing 13-2 begins by defining the necessary data structures for the application and setting up the user interface. The `PrintData` class holds information about the current print job, which helps with rendering the final product. `Widgets` is a simple structure that provides access to multiple widgets and the print job information in callback methods.

Listing 13-2. GTK+ Printing Example

```python
#!/usr/bin/python3

import sys
import math
from os.path import expanduser
import gi
gi.require_version('Gtk', '3.0')
gi.require_version('PangoCairo', '1.0')
from gi.repository import Gtk, cairo, Pango, PangoCairo

class Widgets:

    def __init__(self):
        self.window = None
        self.chooser = None
        self.data = None
        self.settings = Gtk.PrintSettings.new()

class PrintData:

    def __init__(self):
        self.filename = None
        self.fontsize = None
        self.lines_per_page = None
        self.lines = None
        self.total_lines = None
        self.total_pages = None

class AppWindow(Gtk.ApplicationWindow):

    def __init__(self, *args, **kwargs):
        super().__init__(*args, **kwargs)
        self.HEADER_HEIGHT = 20.0
```

374

```python
        self.HEADER_GAP = 8.5
        w = Widgets()
        w.window = self
        self.set_border_width(10)
        w.chooser = Gtk.FileChooserButton.new ("Select a File",
                                                 Gtk.FileChooserAction.OPEN)
        w.chooser.set_current_folder(expanduser("~"))
        print = Gtk.Button.new_with_label("Print")
        print.connect("clicked", self.print_file, w)
        hbox = Gtk.Box.new(Gtk.Orientation.HORIZONTAL, 5)
        hbox.pack_start(w.chooser, False, False, 0)
        hbox.pack_start(print, False, False, 0)
        self.add(hbox)

    def print_file(self, button, w):
        filename = w.chooser.get_filename()
        if filename == None:
            return
        operation = Gtk.PrintOperation.new()
        if w.settings != None:
            operation.set_print_settings(w.settings)
        w.data = PrintData()
        w.data.filename = filename
        w.data.font_size = 10.0
        operation.connect("begin_print", self.begin_print, w)
        operation.connect("draw_page", self.draw_page, w)
        operation.connect("end_print", self.end_print, w)
        res = operation.run(Gtk.PrintOperationAction.PRINT_DIALOG,
                              w.window)
        if res == Gtk.PrintOperationResult.APPLY:
            if w.settings != None:
                w.settings = None
            settings = operation.get_print_settings()
        elif res == Gtk.PrintOperationResult.ERROR:
```

```python
            dialog = Gtk.MessageDialog.new(w.window,
                                           Gtk.DialogFlags.DESTROY_WITH_
                                           PARENT,
                                           Gtk.MessageType.ERROR,
                                           Gtk.ButtonsType.S_CLOSE,
                                           "Print operation error.")
            dialog.run()
            dialog.destroy()
    def begin_print(self, operation, context, w):
        w.data.lines = []
        f = open(w.data.filename)
        for line in f:
            w.data.lines.append(line)
        f.close()
        w.data.total_lines = len(w.data.lines)

        height = context.get_height() - self.HEADER_HEIGHT -
        self.HEADER_GAP w.data.lines_per_page = math.floor(height /
        (w.data.font_size + 3)) w.data.total_pages =
        (w.data.total_lines - 1) / w.data.lines_per_page+1
        operation.set_n_pages(w.data.total_pages)

    def draw_page(self, operation, context, page_nr, w):
        cr = context.get_cairo_context()
        width = context.get_width()
        layout = context.create_pango_layout()
        desc = Pango.font_description_from_string("Monospace")
        desc.set_size(w.data.font_size * Pango.SCALE)
        layout.set_font_description(desc)
        layout.set_text(w.data.filename, -1)
        layout.set_width(-1)
        layout.set_alignment(Pango.Alignment.LEFT)
        (width, height) = layout.get_size()
        text_height = height / Pango.SCALE
        cr.move_to(0, (self.HEADER_HEIGHT - text_height) / 2)
        PangoCairo.show_layout(cr, layout)
        page_str = "%d of %d" % (page_nr + 1, w.data.total_pages)
```

```python
            layout.set_text(page_str, -1)
            (width, height) = layout.get_size()
            layout.set_alignment(Pango.Alignment.RIGHT)
            cr.move_to(width - (width / Pango.SCALE),
                        (self.HEADER_HEIGHT - text_height) / 2)
            PangoCairo.show_layout(cr, layout)
            cr.move_to(0, self.HEADER_HEIGHT + self.HEADER_GAP)
            line = page_nr * w.data.lines_per_page
            i = 0
            while i < w.data.lines_per_page and line <
            w.data.total_lines:
                layout.set_text(w.data.lines[line], -1)
                PangoCairo.show_layout(cr, layout)
                cr.rel_move_to(0, w.data.font_size + 3)
                line += 1
                i += 1

    def end_print(self, operation, context, w):
        w.data.lines = None
        w.data = None

class Application(Gtk.Application):

    def __init__(self, *args, **kwargs):
        super().__init__(*args, application_id="org.example.myapp",
                        **kwargs)
        self.window = None

    def do_activate(self):
        if not self.window:
            self.window = AppWindow(application=self,
                                    title="Calendar")
            self.window.show_all()
            self.window.present()

if __name__ == "__main__":
    app = Application()
    app.run(sys.argv)
```

Two values are defined at the top of AppWindow class in Listing 13-2 called HEADER_HEIGHT and HEADER_GAP. HEADER_HEIGHT is the amount of space that is available for the header text to be rendered. This displays information, such as the file name and page number. HEADER_GAP is padding placed between the header and the actual page content.

The PrintData class stores information about the current print job. This includes the location of the file on the disk, the size of the font, the number of lines that can be rendered on a single page, the file's content, the total number of lines, and the total number of pages.

Print Operations

The next step is to implement the print_file callback method that runs when the Print button is clicked. This method is implemented in Listing 13-2. It takes care of creating the PrintData, connecting all the necessary signals, and creating the print operation.

The first step in printing is to create a new print operation, which is done by calling Gtk.PrintOperation.new(). What makes Gtk.PrintOperation unique is that it uses the platform's native print dialog if there is one available. On platforms like UNIX, which do not provide such a dialog, Gtk.PrintUnixDialog or the GNOME dialog is used.

Note   For most applications, you should use the Gtk.PrintOperation methods when possible, instead of directly interacting with the print objects. Gtk.PrintOperation was created as a platform-independent printing solution, which cannot be easily reimplemented without a lot of code.

The next step is to call operation.set_print_settings() to apply print settings to the operation. In this application, the Gtk.PrintSettings object is stored as an attribute in the Widgets class instance. If the print operation is successful, you should store the current print settings so that these same settings can be applied to future print jobs.

You then set up the PrintData class by allocating a new instance. The file name is set to the currently selected file in the Gtk.FileChooserButton, which was already confirmed to exist. The print font size is also set to 10.0 points. In text editing applications, you would usually retrieve this font from Gtk.TextView's current font. In more complex printing applications, the font size may vary throughout a document, but this is a simple example meant only to get you started.

Next, we connect to three Gtk.PrintOperation signals, which are discussed in detail later in this section. In short, begin_print is called before the pages are rendered and can be used for setting the number of pages and doing necessary preparation. The draw_page signal is called for every page in the print job so that it can be rendered. Lastly, the end_print signal is called after the print operation has completed, regardless of whether it succeeded or failed. This callback method cleans up after the print job. A number of other signals can be used throughout the print operation. A full list is in Appendix B.

Once the print operation has been set up, the next step is to begin the printing by calling operation.run(). This method is where you define which task the print operation performs.

operation.run(action, parent)

The Gtk.PrintOperationAction enumeration, shown in the following list, defines which printing task the print operation performs. To print the document, you should use Gtk.PrintOperationAction.PRINT_DIALOG.

- Gtk.PrintOperationAction.ERROR: Some type of error has occurred in the print operation.

- Gtk.PrintOperationAction.PREVIEW: Preview the print job that is performed with the current settings. This uses the same callbacks for rendering as the print operation, so it should take little work to get it up and running.

- Gtk.PrintOperationAction.PRINT: Start printing using the current printing settings without presenting the print dialog. You should only do this if you are 100 percent sure that the user approves of this action. For example, you should have already presented a confirmation dialog to the user.

- Gtk.PrintOperationAction.EXPORTPRINT: Export the print job to a file. To use this setting, you have to set the export-filename property prior to running the operation.

The last two parameters of operation.run() allow you to define a parent window to use for the print dialog to use None to ignore this parameter. This function does not return until all of the pages have been rendered and are sent to the printer.

When the function does give back control, it returns a `Gtk.PrintOperationResult` enumeration value. These values give you instructions on what task you should perform next, and whether the print operation succeeded or failed. The four enumeration values are shown in the following list.

- `Gtk.PrintOperationResult.ERROR`: Some type of error has occurred in the print operation.

- `Gtk.PrintOperationResult.APPLY`: Print settings were changed. Therefore, they should be stored immediately so that changes are not lost.

- `Gtk.PrintOperationResult.CANCEL`: The user cancelled the print operation, and you should not save the changes to the print settings.

- `Gtk.PrintOperationResult.PROGRESS`: The print operation has yet to be completed. You only get this value if you are running the task asynchronously.

It is possible to run the print operation asynchronously, which means that `operation.run()` may return before the pages have been rendered. This is set with `operation.set_allow_async()`. You should note that not all platforms allow this operation, so you should be prepared for this not to work!

If you run the print operation asynchronously, you can use the done signal to retrieve notification when the printing has completed. At this point, you are given the print operation results, and you need to handle it accordingly.

After handling the print operation result, you should also handle the resulting error if it was set and if it exists.

A full list of possible errors under the `Gtk.PrintError` domain can be found in Appendix E.

One unique feature provided by `Gtk.PrintOperation` is the ability to show a progress dialog while the print operation is running. This is turned off by default, but it can be turned on with `operation.set_show_progress()`. This is especially useful if you allow the user to run multiple print operations at the same time.

```
operation.set_show_progress(boolean)
```

It may be necessary at times to cancel a current print job, which can be done by calling `operation.cancel()`. This function is usually used within a `begin_print`, `paginate`, or `draw_page` callback method. It also allows you to provide a Cancel button so that the user can stop in the middle of an active print operation.

`operation_cancel()`

It is also possible to give a unique name to the print job, which identifies it within an external print monitoring application. Print jobs are given names with `operation.set_job_name()`. If this is not set, GTK+ automatically designates a name for the print job and numbers consecutive print jobs accordingly.

If you are running the print job asynchronously, you may want to retrieve the current status of the print job. By calling `operation.get_status()`, a `Gtk.PrintStatus` enumeration value is returned, which gives more information about the status of the print job. The following is a list of possible print job status values.

- `Gtk.PrintStatus.INITIAL`: The print operation has yet to begin. This status is returned while the print dialog is still visible because it is the default initial value.

- `Gtk.PrintStatus.PREPARING`: The print operation is being split into pages, and the begin-print signal was emitted.

- `Gtk.PrintStatus.GENERATING_DATA`: The pages are being rendered. This is set while the draw-page signal is being emitted. No data has been sent to the printer at this point.

- `Gtk.PrintStatus.SENDING_DATA`: Data about the print job is being sent to the printer.

- `Gtk.PrintStatus.PENDING`: All of the data has been sent to the printer, but the job has yet to be processed. It is possible that the printer may be stopped.

- `Gtk.PrintStatus.PENDING_ISSUE`: There was a problem during the printing. For example, the printer could be out of paper, or there could be a paper jam.

- `Gtk.PrintStatus.PRINTING`: The printer is currently processing the print job.

- `Gtk.PrintStatus.FINISHED`: The print job has been successfully completed.

- `Gtk.PrintStatus.FINISHED_ABORTED`: The print job was aborted. No further action is taken unless you run the job again.

The value returned by `operation.get_status()` can be used within applications, since it is a numerical value. However, GTK+ also provides the ability to retrieve a string with `operation.get_status_string()`, which is a human-readable description of the print job status. It is used for debugging output or displaying more information to the user about the print job. For example, it could be displayed on a status bar or in a message dialog.

Beginning the Print Operation

Now that the print operation is set up, it is time to implement the necessary signal callback methods. The "begin-print" signal is emitted when the user initiates printing, which means that all settings have been finalized from the user's point of view.

In Listing 13-2, the `begin_print` callback method first retrieves the contents of the file and splits it into the number of lines. The total number of lines is then calculated, which can retrieve the number of pages.

To calculate the number of pages required by the print operation, you need to figure out how many lines can be rendered on every page. The total height of every page is retrieved with `context.get_height()`, which is stored in a `Gtk.PrintContext` object. `Gtk.PrintContext` stores information about how to draw the page. For example, it stores the page setup, width and height dimensions, and dots per inch in both directions. We go into more detail in the `draw_page` callback method later in this chapter.

Once you have the total height of the page that is available for rendering text, the next step is to divide that height by the font size of the text plus 3 pixels of spacing to be added between each line. The `floor()` function rounds down the number of lines per page so that clipping does not occur along the bottom of every full page.

Once you have the number of lines per page, you can calculate the number of pages. Then, you must send this value to `operation.set_n_pages()` by the end of this callback method. The number of pages are used so that GTK+ knows how many times to call the `draw_page` callback method. This must be set to a positive value so that rendering does not begin until it is changed from its default –1 value.

Rendering Pages

The next step is to implement the `draw_page` callback method, which is called once for every page that needs to be rendered. This callback method requires the introduction of a library called Cairo. It is a vector graphics library that renders print operations, among other things.

Listing 13-2 begins by retrieving the Cairo drawing context for the current `Gtk.PrintContext` with `context.get_cairo_context()`. The returned context object renders print content and then applies it to the `PangoLayout`.

At the beginning of this callback method, we also need to retrieve two other values from the `Gtk.PrintContext`. The first is `context.get_width()`, which returns the width of the document. Notice that we do not need to retrieve the height of the page, since we have already calculated the number of lines that fit on each page. If the text is wider than the page, it is clipped. You have to alter this example to avoid clipping the document.

Caution   The width returned by the `Gtk.PrintContext` is in pixels. You need to be careful because different functions may use alternative scales, such as Pango units or points!

The next step is to create a `PangoLayout` with `context.create_pango_layout()`, which is used for the print context. You should create Pango layouts in this manner for print operations, because the print context already has the correct font metrics applied.

The next operation performed by this function is to add the file name to the top-left corner of the page. To start, `layout.set_text()` sets the current text stored by the layout to the file name. The width of the layout is set to –1 so that the file name does not wrap at forward slash characters. The text is also aligned to the left of the layout with `layout.set_alignment()`.

Now that the text is added to the layout, `cr.move_to()` moves the current point in the Cairo context to the left of the page and the center of the header. Note that the height of the `PangoLayout` must first be reduced by a factor of `Pango.SCALE`!

```
cairo.move_to(x, y)
```

Next, we call `cr.show_layout()` to draw the `PangoLayout` on the Cairo context. The top-left corner of the layout is rendered at the current point in the Cairo context. This is why it was first necessary to move to the desired position with `cr.move_to()`.

```
cairo.show_layout(layout)
```

After rendering the file name, the same method adds the page count to the top-right corner of each page. You should again note that the width returned by the PangoLayout had to be scaled down by Pango.SCALE so that it would be in the same units as other Cairo values.

The next step is to render all of the lines for the current page. We begin by moving to the left of the page, HEADER_GAP units below the header. Then, each line is incrementally rendered to the Cairo context with cr.show_layout(). One interesting thing to note is that the cursor position in the loop is moved with cr.rel_move_to().

```
cairo.rel_move_to(dx, dy)
```

This function moves the current position relative to the previous position. Therefore, after a line is rendered, the current position is moved down one line, which is equal to the font size of the text since the font is monospace.

Tip   By moving the cursor relative to the previous position, it is easy to add an arbitrary amount of spacing between each line of text and the adjacent one as long as this additional height was previously taken into consideration when calculating the number of pages in the begin_print callback method.

When developing with GTK+, you have the whole Cairo library available to you. More basics are covered in the "Cairo Drawing Context" section of this chapter; however, if you are implementing printing in your own applications, you should take the time to learn more about this library from the Cairo API documentation.

Finalizing the Print Operation

After all of the pages have been rendered, the "end-print" signal is emitted. Listing 13-2 shows the end_print callback method, which is used for the signal. It resets modified attributes of the PrintData instance.

Cairo Drawing Context

Cairo is a graphics-rendering library that is used throughout the GTK+ library. In the context of this book, Cairo renders pages during a print operation. This section introduces you to the Pycairo library and some of the classes and drawing methods associated with them.

Pages of a print operation in GTK+ are rendered as Cairo context objects. This object allows you to render text, draw various shapes and lines, and fill clipped areas with color. Let us look at a few methods provided by Cairo for manipulating Cairo drawing contexts.

Drawing Paths

Shapes in Cairo contexts are rendered with paths. A new path is created with `cairo.new_path()`. You can then retrieve a copy of the new path with `cairo.copy_path()` and add new lines and shapes to the path.

`cairo.copy_path()`

There are a number of functions provided for drawing paths, which are listed in Table 13-1. More information about each function can be found in the Cairo API documentation.

Table 13-1. *Cairo Path-Drawing Methods*

Method	Description
cairo.arc()	Draw an arc in the current path. You must provide the radius of the arc, horizontal and vertical positions of its center, and the start and end angle of the curve in radians.
cairo.curve_to()	Create a Bezier curve in the current path. You must provide the end position of the curve and two control points that calculate the curve.
cairo.line_to()	Draw a line from the current position to the specified point. The current position is simply moved if an initial point does not exist.
cairo.move_to()	Move to a new position in the context, which causes a new subpath to be created.
cairo.rectangle()	Draw a rectangle in the current path. You must provide the coordinates of the top-left corner of the rectangle, its width, and its height.
cairo.rel_curve_to()	This function is the same as `cairo.curve_to()`, except it is drawn with respect to the current position.
cairo.rel_line_to()	This function is the same as `cairo.line_to()`, except it is drawn with respect to the current position.
cairo.rel_move_to()	This function is the same as `cairo.move_to()`, except it is drawn with respect to the current position.

When you are finished with a subpath, you can close it with `cairo.path_close()`. This encloses the current path so that it can be filled with a color if necessary.

Rendering Options

The current color used for drawing operations on a source is `cairo.set_source_rgb()`. The color is used until a new color is set. In addition to choosing a color, you can use `cairo.set_source_rgba()`, which accepts a fifth alpha parameter. Each of the color parameters is a floating-point number between 0.0 and 1.0.

After you have moved to a specific point and set the source color, you can fill the current path with `cairo.fill()`, which accepts only the context. Alternatively, you can fill a rectangular area with `cairo.fill_extents()`. This function calculates an area with corners of (x1,y1) and (x2,y2), filling all of the area that is in between those points that is also contained by the current path.

```
cairo.fill_extents(x1, y1, x2, y2)
```

Drawing operations, such as curves, can cause edges to become jagged. To fix this, Cairo provides antialiasing to drawings with `cairo.set_antialias()`.

```
cairo.set_antialias(antialias)
```

Antialiasing settings are provided by the `cairo.Antialias` enumeration. The following is a list of values provided by this enumeration.

- `cairo.Antialias.DEFAULT`: The default antialiasing algorithm is used.

- `cairo.Antialias.NONE`: No antialiasing occurs; instead, an alpha mask is used.

- `cairo.Antialias.GRAY`: Uses only a single color for antialiasing. This color is not necessarily gray but is chosen based on the foreground and background colors.

- `cairo.Antialias.SUBPIXEL`: Uses subpixel shading provided by LCD screens.

This is simply a short introduction to Cairo drawing contexts. For further information about Cairo, you should reference its API documentation at `www.cairographics.org`.

Recent Files

In GTK+ 2.10, a new API was introduced that allows you to keep track of recently opened files across applications. In this section, we are going to implement this functionality in the simple text editing application. This application with a recent file chooser is shown in Figure 13-4. Later, in this chapter's exercise, you are going to add recent file support to your text editor.

Figure 13-4. *Recent file chooser dialog*

The code in Listing 13-3 sets up the text editing application. Two buttons allow you to open an existing file using a Gtk.FileChooserDialog and save your changes.

Then, there is a Gtk.MenuToolButton that provides two functions. When the button is clicked, a Gtk.RecentChooserDialog is displayed that allows you to select a recent file from the list. The menu in the Gtk.MenuToolButton widget is of the type Gtk.RecentChooserMenu, which shows the ten most recent files.

Listing 13-3. Remembering Recently Opened Files

```python
#!/usr/bin/python3

import sys
import urllib
from urllib.request import pathname2url
import os
import gi
gi.require_version('Gtk', '3.0')
from gi.repository import Gtk, Pango

class Widgets():

    def __init__(self):
        self.window = None
        self.textview = None
        self.recent = None

class AppWindow(Gtk.ApplicationWindow):

    def __init__(self, *args, **kwargs):
        super().__init__(*args, **kwargs)
        w = Widgets()
        w.window = self
        self.set_border_width(5)
        self.set_size_request(600, 400)
        w.textview = Gtk.TextView.new()
        fd = Pango.font_description_from_string("Monospace 10")
        self.modify_font(fd)
        swin = Gtk.ScrolledWindow.new(None, None)
        openbutton = Gtk.Button.new_with_label("open")
        save = Gtk.Button.new_with_label("Save")
        icon_theme = Gtk.IconTheme.get_default()
        icon = icon_theme.load_icon("document-open", -1,
                                    Gtk.IconLookupFlags.FORCE_SIZE)
        image = Gtk.Image.new_from_pixbuf(icon)
        w.recent = Gtk.MenuToolButton.new(image, "Recent Files")
```

```
        manager = Gtk.RecentManager.get_default()
        menu = Gtk.RecentChooserMenu.new_for_manager(manager)
        w.recent.set_menu(menu)
        menu.set_show_not_found(False)
        menu.set_local_only(True)
        menu.set_limit(10)
        menu.set_sort_type(Gtk.RecentSortType.MRU)
        menu.connect("selection-done", self.menu_activated, w)
        openbutton.connect("clicked", self.open_file, w)
        save.connect("clicked", self.save_file, w)
        w.recent.connect("clicked", self.open_recent_file, w)
        hbox = Gtk.Box.new(Gtk.Orientation.HORIZONTAL, 5)
        hbox.pack_start(openbutton, False, False, 0)
        hbox.pack_start(save, False, False, 0)
        hbox.pack_start(w.recent, False, False, 0)
        vbox = Gtk.Box.new(Gtk.Orientation.VERTICAL, 5)
        swin.add(w.textview)
        vbox.pack_start(hbox, False, False, 0)
        vbox.pack_start(swin, True, True, 0)
        w.window.add(vbox)

    def save_file(self, save, w):
        filename = w.window.get_title()
        buffer = w.textview.get_buffer()
        (start, end) = buffer.get_bounds()
        content = buffer.get_text(start, end, False)
        f = open(filename, 'w')
        f.write(content)
        f.close()

    def menu_activated(self, menu, w):
        filename = menu.get_current_uri()
        if filename != None:
            fn = os.path.basename(filename)
            f = open(fn, 'r')
            contents = f.read()
```

```
            f.close()
            w.window.set_title(fn)
            buffer = w.textview.get_buffer()
            buffer.set_text(content, -1)
        else:
            print("The file '%s' could not be read!" % filename)

    def open_file(self, openbutton, w):
        dialog = Gtk.FileChooserDialog(title="Open File", parent=w.window,
                                       action=Gtk.FileChooserAction.OPEN,
                                       buttons=("Cancel", Gtk.ResponseType.
                                       CANCEL,"Open", Gtk.ResponseType.OK))
        if dialog.run() == Gtk.ResponseType.OK:
            filename = dialog.get_filename()
            content = ""
            f = open(filename, 'r')
            content = f.read()
            f.close()
            if len(content) > 0:

                # Create a new recently used
                resource. data = Gtk.RecentData()
                data.display_name = None
                data.description = None
                data.mime_type = "text/plain"
                data.app_name =
                os.path.basename(__file__)
                data.app_exec = " " + data.app_name +
                "%u" #data.groups = ["testapp", None]
                data.is_private = False
                url = pathname2url(filename)
                # Add the recently used resource to the default
                recent manager. manager =
                Gtk.RecentManager.get_default()
                result = manager.add_full(url, data)
                # Load the file and set the filename as the title of
```

```
            the window. w.window.set_title(filename)
            buffer =
            w.textview.get_buffer()
            buffer.set_text(content,-1)
    dialog.destroy()

def open_recent_file(self, recent, w):
    manager = Gtk.RecentManager.get_default()
    dialog = Gtk.RecentChooserDialog(title="Open Recent File",
                            parent=w.window,
                            recent_manager=manager,
                            buttons=("Cancel",
                            Gtk.ResponseType.CANCEL,
                            "Open",
                            Gtk.ResponseType.OK))

    # Add a filter that will display all of the files in
    the dialog. filter = Gtk.RecentFilter.new()
    filter.set_name("All Files")
    filter.add_pattern("*") dialog.add_filter(filter)
    # Add another filter that will only display plain
    text files. filter = Gtk.RecentFilter.new()
    filter.set_name("Plain Text")
    filter.add_mime_type("text/plain")
    dialog.add_filter(filter)
    dialog.set_show_not_found(False)
    dialog.set_local_only(True)
    dialog.set_limit(10)
    dialog.set_sort_type(Gtk.RecentSortType.MRU)
    if dialog.run() == Gtk.ResponseType.OK:
        filename = dialog.get_current_uri()
        if filename != None:
            # Remove the "file://" prefix from the beginning of the
            # URI if it exists.
            content = ""
            fn = os.path.basename(filename)
```

```
                    f = open(fn, 'r')
                    contents = f.read()
                    f.close()
                    if len(content) > 0:
                        w.window.set_title(fn)
                        buffer = w.textview.get_buffer()
                        buffer.set_text(content, -1)
                    else:
                        print("The file '%s' could not be read!" % filename)
        dialog.destroy()

class Application(Gtk.Application):

    def __init__(self, *args, **kwargs):
        super().__init__(*args, application_id="org.example.myapp",
                        **kwargs)
        self.window = None

    def do_activate(self):
        if not self.window:
            self.window = AppWindow(application=self, title="Recent Files")
        self.window.show_all()
        self.window.present()

if __name__ == "__main__":
    app = Application()
    app.run(sys.argv)
```

A central class called Gtk.RecentManager handles recent file information. It is possible to create your own from scratch, but if you want to share recent files across applications, you can retrieve the default with Gtk.RecentManager.get_default(). This allows you to share recent files with applications, such as gedit, GNOME's recent documents menu, and others that take advantage of the Gtk.RecentManager API.

We next create a new `Gtk.RecentChooserMenu` widget from the default `Gtk.RecentManager`. This menu displays recent files and (optionally) number the menu items created with `Gtk.RecentChooserMenu.new_for_manager()`. The files are not numbered by default, but this property can be changed by setting "show-numbers" to `True` or by calling `menu.set_show_numbers()`.

`Gtk.RecentChooserMenu` implements the `Gtk.RecentChooser` interface, which provides the functionality you need for interacting with the widget. In Listing 13-3, a number of `Gtk.RecentChooser` properties customize the menu. These also apply to two other widgets that implement the `Gtk.RecentChooser` interface: `Gtk.RecentChooserDialog` and `Gtk.RecentChooserWidget`.

It is possible that recent files in the list have been removed since they were added. In this case, you may not want to display them in the list. You can hide recent files that no longer exist with `rchooser.set_show_not_found()`. This property only works with files that are located on the local machine.

Tip   You may actually want to show files that are not found to the user. If the user selects a file that does not exist, you can then easily remove it from the list after informing the user about the problem.

By default, only local files are shown, which means that they have a `file://` Uniform Resource Identifier (URI) prefix. A URI refers to things, such as file locations or Internet addresses based on their prefixes. Using only the `file://` prefix guarantees that they are located on the local machine. You can set this property to `False` to show recent files that are located at a remote location. You should note that remote files are not filtered out if they no longer exist!

If the list includes a large number of recent files, you probably will not want to list all of them in the menu. A menu with a hundred items is quite large! Therefore, you can use `recentchooser.set_limit()` to set a maximum number of recent items that are displayed in the menu.

```
recentchooser.set_limit(limit)
```

When you set a limit on the number of elements, which files are shown depends on the sort type you defined with `recentchooser.set_sort_type()`. By default, this is set to `Gtk.RecentSortType.NONE`. The following are the available values in the `Gtk.RecentSortType` enumeration.

- `Gtk.RecentSortType.NONE`: The list of recent files is not sorted at all and is returned in the order that they appear. This should not be used when you are limiting the number of elements that are displayed, because you cannot predict which files will be displayed!

- `Gtk.RecentSortType.MRU`: Sorts the most recently added files first in the list. This is most likely the sorting method you want to use, because it places the most recent file at the beginning of the list.

- `Gtk.RecentSortType.LRU`: Sorts the least-recently added files first in the list.

- `Gtk.RecentSortType.CUSTOM`: Uses a custom sorting function to sort the recent files. To use this, you need `recentmanager.set_sort_func()` to define the sorting method.

The last part of this example saves the file under the specified name. When a file is opened in this text editor, the window title is set to the file name. This file name is used to save the file. Therefore, be careful because this simple text editor cannot be used to create new files!

Recent Chooser Menu

You have just learned about the `Gtk.RecentChooserMenu` widget. Listing 13-3 implements the `"selection-done"` callback method that was connected to it. This function retrieves the selected URI and opens the file if it exists.

You can use `recentchooser.get_current_uri()` to retrieve the currently selected recent file, since only one item can be selected. Since we restricted the menu to only displaying local files, we need to remove the `file://` prefix from the URI. If you are allowing remote files to be displayed, you may need to remove different prefixes from the URI, such as `http://`. You can use the Python method `os.path.basename()` to remove URI prefixes.

```
os.path.basename(filename)
os.path.basename(filename)
```

After the prefix is removed, we attempt to open the file. If the file was successfully opened, the window title is set to the file name and the file is opened; otherwise, a warning is presented to the user that the file could not be opened.

Adding Recent Files

When the Open button is pressed, we want to allow the user to select a file to open from a `Gtk.FileChooserDialog`. If the file is opened, it is added to the default `Gtk.RecentManager`.

If the file is successfully opened, `recentmanager.add_full()` adds it as a new recent item to the default `Gtk.RecentManager`. To use this method, you need two items. First, you need the URI, which is created by appending the file name to `file://` to show that it is a local file. This file name can be built with `pathname2url()` from the `url` import.

```
pathname2url(filepath)
```

Secondly, you need an instance of the `Gtk.RecentData` class. The content of this class are a set of attributes that describe the data needed to store the file information to the `Gtk.RecentManager`. `display_name` displays a shortened name instead of the file name, and `description` is a short description of the file. Both of these values can safely be set to `None`.

You then have to specify a MIME type for the file, the name of your application, and the command line used to open the file. The name of your application can be retrieved by calling the Python library method `os.path.basename(__file__)`. There a number of ways to get the program name but you can also safely set this to `None`.

Next, groups is a list of strings that designate what groups the resource belongs to. You are able to use this to filter out files that do not belong to a specific group.

The last member, `is_private`, specifies whether this resource is available to applications that did not register it. By setting this to `True`, you can prevent other applications that use the `Gtk.RecentManager` API from displaying this recent file.

Once you construct the `Gtk.RecentData` instance, it can be added along with the recent file URI as a new resource with `recentmanager.add_full()`. You can also add a new recent item with `recentmanager.add_item()`, which creates a `Gtk.RecentData` object for you.

To remove a recent item, call `recentmanager.remove_item()`. This function returns `True` if a file with the specified URI is successfully removed. If not, an error under theGtk.RecentManagerError domain is set. You can also remove all recent items from the list with `recentmanager.purge_items()`.

```
recentmanagerremove_item(uri)
```

Caution   You should avoid purging all of the items in the default `Gtk.RecentManager`! This removes recent items that are registered by every application, which the user probably does not want since your application should not alter recent resources from other applications.

Recent Chooser Dialog

GTK+ also provides a widget called `Gtk.RecentChooserDialog`, which displays recent files in a convenient dialog. This widget implements the `Gtk.RecentChooser` interface, so it is very similar in functionality to `Gtk.RecentChooserMenu`. In Listing 13-3, open_recent_file shows how to allow the user to open a recent file with this widget.

New `Gtk.RecentChooserDialog` widgets are created in a similar way to dialogs with `Gtk.RecentChooserDialog()`. This function accepts a title for the dialog, a parent window, a `Gtk.RecentManager` widget to display, and pairs of buttons and response identifiers.

Listing 13-3 introduces recent file filters. New `Gtk.RecentFilter` objects are created with `Gtk.RecentFilter.new()`. Filters display only recent files that follow installed patterns.

```
filter.set_name("All Files")
filter.add_pattern("*")
dialog.add_filter(filter)
```

The next step is to set the name of the filter. This name is displayed in the combo box where the user chooses which filter to use. There are many ways to create filters, including with `filter.add_pattern()`, which finds filters with matching patterns. The asterisk character can be used as the wildcard. There are also functions for matching MIME types, image file types, application names, group names, and ages in days. Next, use `recentchooser.add_filter()` to add the `Gtk.RecentFilter` to the recent chooser.

With the `Gtk.RecentChooserDialog` widgets, it is possible to choose multiple files with `recentchooser.set_select_multiple()`. If the user can select multiple files, you want to use `recentchooser.get_uris()` to retrieve all of the selected files.

```
recentchooser.get_uris(length)
```

This function also returns the number of elements in the list of strings.

Automatic Completion

You learned about the Gtk.Entry widget in Chapter 5, but GTK+ also provides the Gtk. EntryCompletion object. Gtk.EntryCompletion is derived from GObject and provides the user with automatic completion in Gtk.Entry. Figure 13-5 shows an example Gtk. Entry that is providing the user with multiple selections. Note that the user also has the option of ignoring the choices and entering an arbitrary string.

Figure 13-5. *Gtk.EntryCompletion automatic completion*

Listing 13-4 implements a Gtk.Entry widget that asks you to enter the name of a GTK+ widget. All of the strings in the Gtk.EntryCompletion widget that have the same prefix as the entered text are displayed as choices. This example shows just how easy it is to get automatic completion up and running.

Listing 13-4. Automatic Completion

```
#!/usr/bin/python3

import sys
import gi
gi.require_version('Gtk', '3.0')
from gi.repository import Gtk, GObject
```

```python
class AppWindow(Gtk.ApplicationWindow):

    def __init__(self, *args, **kwargs):
        super().__init__(*args, **kwargs)
        widgets = ["GtkDialog", "GtkWindow", "GtkContainer",
        "GtkWidget"] self.set_border_width(10)
        label = Gtk.Label.new("Enter a widget in the following GtkEntry:")
        entry = Gtk.Entry.new()
        # Create a GtkListStore that will hold autocompletion
        possibilities. types = (GObject.TYPE_STRING,)
        store = Gtk.ListStore.new(types) for widget in widgets:
        iter = store.append() store.set(iter, 0, widget)
        completion = Gtk.EntryCompletion.new()
        entry.set_completion(completion)
        completion.set_model(store)
        completion.set_text_column(0)
        vbox = Gtk.Box(orientation=Gtk.Orientation.VERTICAL, spacing=0)
        vbox.pack_start(label, False, False, 0)
        vbox.pack_start(entry, False, False, 0)
        self.add(vbox)

class Application(Gtk.Application):

    def __init__(self, *args, **kwargs):
        super().__init__(*args, application_id="org.example.myapp",
                         **kwargs)
        self.window = None

    def do_activate(self):
        if not self.window:
            self.window = AppWindow(application=self, title="Automatic
            Completion")
        self.window.show_all()
        self.window.present()

if __name__ == "__main__":
    app = Application()
    app.run(sys.argv)
```

To implement a Gtk.EntryCompletion, you need to first create a new Gtk.ListStore that displays the choices. The model in this example only has one textual column, but it is acceptable to provide a more complex Gtk.ListStore as long as one column is of the type GObject.TYPE_STRING.

New Gtk.EntryCompletion objects are created with Gtk.EntryCompletion.new(). You can then apply it to an existing Gtk.Entry widget with entry.set_completion(). GTK+ takes care of displaying matches and applying the choices by default.

Next, completion.set_model() applies the tree model to the Gtk.EntryCompletion object. If there was already a model applied to the object, it is replaced. You also have to use completion.set_text_column() to designate which column contains the string, since models do not have to be only a single column. If you do not set the text column, automatic completion will not work because the text column is set to –1 by default.

It is possible to display as much of the prefix as is common to all of the matches with completion.set_inline_completion(). You should note that inline completion is case sensitive, but automatic completion is not! If you are using this, you may want to set completion.set_popup_single_match(), which prevents the pop-up menu from being displayed when there is only a single match.

You can use completion.set_popup_set_width() to force the pop-up menu to be the same width as the Gtk.Entry widget. This corresponds to Gtk.EntryCompletion's popupset_width property.

If there are a lot of matches, you may want to set the minimum match length with completion.set_minimum_key_length(). This is useful when there is such a large number of elements in the list that it would take a long time for the list to be rendered on the screen.

Test Your Understanding

In this chapter's exercise, you finish the text editing application that has been the focus of multiple exercises in past chapters. It requires you to integrate the automatic completion, printing, and recent file capabilities into your application.

Exercise 1: Creating a Full Text Editor

In this exercise, you complete the text editor that you have been creating in the last few chapters. You add three new features to the application.

First, add the automatic completion feature, which should be implemented to remember past searches in the search toolbar. The application has to remember the past searches for only the current instance of the application runtimes. Next, add printing support, which includes printing and print preview abilities. Printing support can be easily implemented with the high-level `Gtk.PrintOperation` class. Lastly, instruct the text editor to remember the last five files loaded using the `Gtk.RecentManager` class.

So that you do not have to rewrite previous aspects of the application, you should use the solution to a Chapter 11 exercise or download that solution from this book's official web site.

Summary

In this chapter, you learned about a number of widgets that did not quite fit into previous chapters. These widgets and objects are summarized in the following list.

- `Gtk.DrawingArea`: An empty widget that is meant to allow you to draw on its `Gdk.Window` object, which is also a `Gdk.Drawable` object.

- `Gtk.Layout`: This widget is like `Gtk.DrawingArea`, except it allows you to embed widgets within its interface as well. It introduces overhead, so you should| not use this widget if you want only drawing capabilities.

- `Gtk.Calendar`: Display a single month for the chosen year. This widget allows the user to select a date, and you can mark multiple dates programmatically.

- `Gtk.PrintOperation`: A high-level printing API that is platform independent. There are many other objects provided for implementing printing support, but most actions should be handled with the `Gtk.PrintOperation` class so that it functions across multiple platforms.

- `Gtk.RecentManager`: A simple class for managing lists of recent files. These lists can be shared across applications. Menu and dialog widgets are provided for displaying recent files.

- `Gtk.EntryCompletion`: Provide automatic completion support to `Gtk.Entry` widgets. The choices are composed of a `Gtk.ListStore` object filled with possible matches.

You have now learned all of the topics that this book intended to introduce. In the next chapter, you are presented with five complete applications that take advantage of topics that were covered in the past 12 chapters.

CHAPTER 14

Integrating Everything

So far, you have had an in-depth view of everything that you can do with GTK+ and associated technologies. In this chapter, we're going to put this knowledge to work by building a few applications.

This chapter introduces five full applications: the file browser that was designed in Chapter 11, a calculator, a ping utility, a hangman game, and a calendar. However, the source code for the examples is not contained in this chapter. The code for each of the applications in this chapter can be downloaded from `www.gtkbook.com`.

I will conclude this final chapter of the book by offering pointers to other learning resources so that you can continue expanding your GTK+ knowledge.

File Browser

In Chapter 11, you implemented the user interface of a file browser application in Glade. The user interface was dynamically loaded, and all the signals were autoconnected with `Gtk.Builder`.

At the end of Chapter 11, you were told that the callback methods would be implemented in this chapter, and we will do so now. Figure 14-1 shows the file browser application when it is first launched. It is displaying the root folder.

© W. David Ashley and Andrew Krause 2019
W. D. Ashley and A. Krause, *Foundations of PyGTK Development*,
https://doi.org/10.1007/978-1-4842-4179-0_14

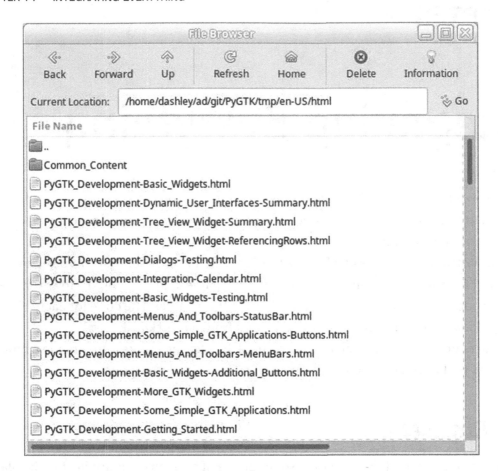

Figure 14-1. *The file browser using Gtk.TreeView*

The file browsing capabilities are of special interest in this application. They are very similar to those in Chapter 9's "Exercise 1: File Browser" section. In that exercise, you created a simple application using a Gtk.TreeView widget that could browse the user's file system. The current location of the file browser is stored in a linked list from which the full path can be built. Each node in the list is one part of the path, and the directory separator is placed between each string to build the full path. A Gtk.Entry widget is also provided to allow the user to edit the path with the keyboard.

Navigation through the file system can be done using a few different methods. The location can be entered in the address bar, although the validity of the location must be verified when the Gtk.Entry widget is activated. In addition to this method, the user can use the Back, Forward, Up, or Home toolbar buttons to navigate through the browsing history, move to the parent directory, or go to the home directory, respectively. Lastly, Gtk.TreeView's row-activated signal allows the user to move into the selected directory or view information about the selected file.

A Gtk.StatusBar widget is placed along the bottom of the window. It keeps track of the total number of items in the current directory and the total size of these items. The sources for this example, along with the four other applications in this chapter, can be downloaded from www.gtkbook.com.

Calculator

A calculator is a simple application that is implemented in most GUI programming books. This example is meant to show you just how easy it is to implement a calculator. Figure 14-2 is a screenshot of the application.

Figure 14-2. *A simple calculator application*

This calculator application was designed in Glade, so the user interface was completed with absolutely no code. Since most of the widgets in this example are Gtk. Button widgets, the clicked and destroy signals were the only two needed.

The calculator allows the user to enter numbers with an optional decimal point, perform four basic operations (add, subtract, multiply, and divide), negate numbers, and calculate square roots and exponents. To cut down on the number of callback methods needed, all the numbers and the decimal place were connected to a single callback method called num_clicked(), and the four basic operations and the power operations were connected to one another. This allows you to take advantage of the fact that these groups of operations need a lot of similar code to work.

When a number or the decimal point button is clicked, the character is appended to the end of the current value, although the length of the number is restricted to ten digits. When an operation button is clicked, the operation is performed, and the new value is stored. It also sets a flag called clear_flag that tells the calculator that a new number should be started when the user presses a number or decimal place.

Ping Utility

In this program, you learn how to use channels in the GLib library to communicate with applications through pipes. A ping utility application is displayed in Figure 14-3; it allows the user to ping an address a specific number of times or continually until the application is stopped.

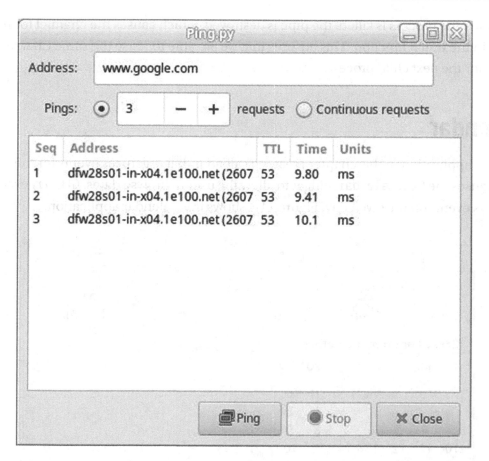

Figure 14-3. *A ping utility application*

In this application, the GLib `spawn_async_with_pipes()` function is used to fork an instance of the ping application with the specified address. The shell command received by this function was parsed with the `shell_parse_argv()` function so that it was in the correct format. The Ping button is disabled, which prevents the user from running multiple instances of the child process.

After spawning the child process, the output pipe is used to create a new Channel object that watches the pipe for read data. When data is ready to be read, it is parsed so that statistics for each ping can be displayed in a `Gtk.TreeView` widget. This continues for the specified number of times or until the user stops the child.

When a child process is running, a Stop button is enabled, which allows the user to kill the child process before it completes. This function simply calls the following instance of the `os.killpg()` function, which forces the child process to close.

When the process is killed, the pipe is destroyed, which causes the channel to shut down in the watch function. This ensures that we are able to reuse the same Channel object for the next child process.

Calendar

The last application in this chapter creates a calendar that organizes events for the user. It uses the Gtk.Calendar widget to allow the user to browse dates. Gtk.TreeView displays events on the given day. Figure 14-4 shows this calendar application.

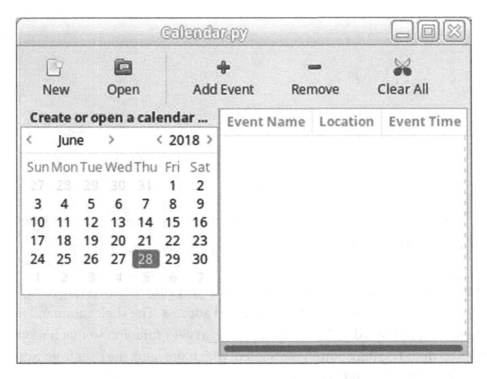

Figure 14-4. *A calendar application with two events*

Most of the code to create the calendar application should look very familiar, because it uses functions introduced in previous chapters. In addition to the familiar functions, the application uses the XML parser provided by XML-SAX to open calendar files, which are stored as XML files. An example calendar file that contains one event is shown in Listing 14-1.

Listing 14-1. Calendar File

```
<calendar>
  <event>
    <name>Release of the Book</name>
    <location>Everywhere</location>
    <day>16</day>
    <month>3</month>
    <year>2007</year>
    <start>All Day</start>
    <end></end>
  </event>
</calendar>
```

A new calendar is created by clicking the New toolbar button, which asks for a calendar file name and location. The calendar is saved every time you add or remove an event, so a Save button is not provided. You can also open an existing calendar by pressing the Open toolbar button.

Markup Parser Functions

To open a calendar, this application uses XML-SAX's parser to retrieve the contents of the file. This parser is very easy to use and supports basic XML files. The first thing you need to do to use the parser is define a new `xmlparser` object. This object has many attributes, including four user-defined functions that you need to code yourself; I cover them one at a time. Any of these functions can be set to `None`.

The first method, `StartElement()`, is called for every open tag, such as `<calendar>` and `<event>`. This function receives the name of the tag element along with arrays of attribute names and values. This allows you to differentiate between starting elements, checking for attributes when appropriate. In the calendar application, this function is used to free all the temporary data stored for the previous event, creating a clean slate for the next event.

```
StartElement(name, attributes)
```

The next method, EndElement(), is called for every close tag, such as </calendar> and </event>. It is also called for tags that have no close tag, such as <tag/>. Similar to the previous method, it accepts the tag name. In the calendar application, it is used to add the event to the global tree if the </event> tag has been reached.

EndElement(name)

The CharacterData() method is called for the data found between StartElement() and EndElement() calls. It accepts the text between the two tags as well as the length of the text. This function is called in the calendar application to read the content of an event.

CharacterData(data)

Note The CharacterData() method is not only called for tags that contain strings but also for tags that call other tags; therefore, this function may have a text parameter filled with spaces and new line characters!

Parsing the XML File

The parsing of the XML text is done with an xmlparser object. You can create a new parser with xml.sax.parse(filename, contenthandler):

xml.sax.parse(filename, contenthandler))

This function creates and returns a new xmlparser object.

XML-SAX can also do XML namespace processing for you. See the documentation for more information.

Further Resources

Congratulations! You have now completed reading this book, and you know enough to develop and manage complex GTK+ applications. However, you may be wondering where you should go from here. There are a number of libraries and resources that will become indispensable as you begin developing applications on your own.

The first resource is the book's web site (www.gtkbook.com). This site includes links to online resources for GTK + developers, as well as tutorials on topics that did not fit in this book. You can use it as a starting point for finding help with GTK+ application development.

Another great resource is the GTK+ web site (`www.gtk.org`). This site includes information about mailing lists, downloads, and bug tracking for GTK+. You can find up-to-date documentation on this site as well.

The GNOME developer's web site (`http://developer.gnome.org`) is also an ideal place to learn more. In addition to GTK+ and its supporting libraries, there are a number of other libraries used to develop applications for GNOME that you will continually run across. The following list briefly summarizes a few of these libraries.

- The PyGObject API Reference (`http://lazka.github.io/pgi-docs`) is a one-stop web site for all things related to Python, GNOME, GTK+, ATK, GDK, and many other libraries.

- The Pycairo API Reference (`http://pycairo.readthedocs.io/en/latest/reference/index.html`) has documentation for all the Python APIs for Cairo.

- The Python web site (`www.python.org`) has documentation for all versions of Python 2.x and 3.x. It includes references, tutorials, how-to's, FAQs, PyPi, and information about the Python Software Foundation.

Summary

You have become familiar with a large portion of GTK+ and its supporting libraries. This knowledge can be used to implement graphical user interfaces for applications on many platforms.

This book is intended to give you a thorough understanding of GTK+, and I hope that it will continue to be a valuable resource as you develop applications. The appendixes are indispensable references for topics that are not always thoroughly documented in the API documentation; they can be used even when you become an expert. The last appendix provides short descriptions of exercise solutions and tips on how to complete them.

Now that you have this knowledge, practice and experience will help you become a great graphical application developer. You have everything you need to continue on your own. I hope you have had as much fun reading this book as I have had writing it!

APPENDIX A

GTK+ Properties

Python provides the property system used by GTK+, which allows you to customize how widgets interact with the user and how they are drawn on the screen. In the following sections, you are provided with a complete reference to the widget and child properties available in GTK+ 3.

GTK+ Properties

Every class derived from `GObject` can create any number of properties. In GTK+, these properties store information about the current state of the widget. For example, `Gtk.Button` has a property called `relief` that defines the type of relief border used by the button in its normal state.

In the following code, `object.relief` was used to retrieve the current value stored by the button's relief property. This method accepts a single property name and returns the value of the property. You can also use `object.relief(value)` to set each object property.

```
relief = button.props.relief
```

There are a great number of properties available to widgets; Tables A-1 through A-132 provide a full properties list for each widget and object in GTK+ 3. Remember that object properties are inherited from parent widgets, so you should investigate a widget's hierarchy for a full list of properties. For more information on each object, you should reference the API documentation.

© W. David Ashley and Andrew Krause 2019
W. D. Ashley and A. Krause, *Foundations of PyGTK Development*,
https://doi.org/10.1007/978-1-4842-4179-0

Caution   In the GTK+ C API, property names may contain one or more dashes. Since these dashes are interpreted by Python as the subtraction operator, all Python property names substitute underscores for dashes in all property names. For instance, the property name logo-icon-name becomes logo_icon_name in a Python program.

Table A-1. *Gtk.AboutDialog Properties*

Property	Type	Description
artists	string	A list of individuals who helped create the artwork used by the application. This often includes information such as an e-mail address or URL for each artist, which is displayed as a link.
authors	string	A list of individuals who helped program the application. This often includes information such as an e-mail address or URL for each programmer, which is displayed as a link.
comments	string	A short string that describes the general functionality of the program. This is displayed in the main dialog window, so it should not be too long.
copyright	string	Copyright information about the application. This is displayed in the main dialog window, so it should not be too long. An example copyright string would be "(C) Copyright 2018 Author".
documenters	string	A list of individuals who helped write documentation for the application. This often includes information such as an e-mail address or URL for each documenter, which is displayed as a link.
license	string	The content of the license for the application. This is displayed with a Gtk.TextView widget in a secondary dialog, so the length of the string does not matter.
license-type	Gtk.License	The license type of the program.

(continued)

Table A-1. (*continued*)

Property	Type	Description
logo	GdkPixbuf	An image that is displayed as the application's logo in the main window. If this is not set, `window.get_default_icon_list()` is used.
logo-icon-name	string	An icon name from the icon theme to use as the logo in the main About dialog. If this is set, it takes precedence over the logo property.
program-name	string	The name of the application to display in the main About dialog. If you do not set this property, `GLib.get_application_name()` is used.
translator-credits	string	A string that holds information about the translator(s) for the current language. It should be set as translatable, so each translator can provide a custom string. This often includes information such as an e-mail address or URL for each translator, which is displayed as a link.
version	string	The version of the application that the user is running.
website	string	A URL to the homepage for the application. This string must be prefixed with `http://`.
website-label	string	A label to display in place of the web site URL. If this is not set, website is set as the URL label.
wrap-license	boolean	If set to `True`, the license content is wrapped.

Table A-2. *GtkAccelGroup Properties*

Property	Type	Description
is-locked	`boolean`	Is the accel group locked.
modifier-mask	`Gdk.ModifierType`	Modifier Mask.

Table A-3. *Gtk.AccelLabel Properties*

Property	Type	Description
accel-closure	GObject.Closure	The closure that should be watched for changes to the keyboard accelerator.
accel-widget	Gtk.Widget	The widget that should be watched for changes to the keyboard accelerator.

Table A-4. *Gtk.Accessible Properties*

Property	Type	Description
widget	Gtk.Widget	The widget referenced by this accessible.

Table A-5. *Gtk.Adjustment Properties*

Property	Type	Description
lower	double	The minimum double value that the adjustment can reach.
page-increment	double	The increment that is shifted when moving one page forward or backward.
page-size	double	The size of a page of the adjustment. You should set this to zero when you use Gtk.Adjustment for Gtk.SpinButton.
step-increment	double	The increment that is moved in an individual step. For example, with Gtk.SpinButton, a single step is taken when an arrow button is pressed.
upper	double	The maximum double value that the adjustment can reach.
value	double	The current value of the adjustment, which is always between lower and upper.

Table A-6. *Gtk.AppChooserButton Properties*

Property	Type	Description
heading	string	The text to show at the top of the dialog.
show-default-item	boolean	Whether the combobox should show the default application on top.
show-dialog-item	boolean	Whether the combobox should include an item that triggers a `Gtk.AppChooserDialog`.

Table A-7. *Gtk.AppChooserDialog Properties*

Property	Type	Description
gfile	`Gio.File`	The `Gio.File` used by the app chooser dialog.
heading	string	The text to show at the top of the dialog.

Table A-8. *Gtk.AppChooserWidget Properties*

Property	Type	Description
default-text	string	The default text appearing when there are no applications.
show-all	boolean	Whether the widget should show all applications.
show-default	boolean	Whether the widget should show the default application.
show-fallback	boolean	Whether the widget should show fallback applications.
show-other	boolean	Whether the widget should show other applications.
show-recommended	boolean	Whether the widget should show recommended applications.

Table A-9. *Gtk.Application Properties*

Property	Type	Description
active-window	`Gtk.Window`	The window that most recently had focus.
app-menu	`Gio.MenuModel`	The `Gio.MenuModel` for the application menu.
menubar	`Gio.MenuModel`	The `Gio.MenuModel` for the menubar.
register-session	boolean	Register with the session manager.

Table A-10. *Gtk.ApplicationWindow Properties*

Property	Type	Description
active-window	Gtk.Window	The window that most recently had focus.
show-menubar	boolean	True if the window should show a menubar at the top of the window.

Table A-11. *Gtk.Arrow Properties*

Property	Type	Description
active-window	Gtk.Window	The window that most recently had focus.
arrow-type	Gtk.ArrowType	The direction the arrow should point.
shadow-type	Gtk.ShadowType	Appearance of the shadow surrounding the arrow.

Table A-12. *Gtk.AspectFrame Properties*

Property	Type	Description
obey-child	boolean	Force aspect ratio to match that of the frame's child.
ratio	float	Aspect ratio if obey_child is False.
shadow-type	float	Appearance of the shadow surrounding the arrow.
xalign	float	X alignment of the child.
yalign	float	Y alignment of the child.

Table A-13. *Gtk.Assistant Properties*

Property	Type	Description
use-header-bar	integer	Use Header Bar for actions.

Table A-14. *Gtk.Box Properties*

Property	Type	Description
baseline-position	`Gtk.BaselinePosition`	The position of the baseline aligned widgets if extra space is available.
homogeneous	boolean	Whether the children should all be the same size.
spacing	integer	The amount of space between children.

Table A-15. *Gtk.Builder Properties*

Property	Type	Description
translation-domain	string	The translation domain used by `gettext()`.

Table A-16. *Gtk.Button Properties*

Property	Type	Description
always-show-image	boolean	Whether the image is always shown.
image	`Gtk.Widget`	Child widget to appear next to the button text.
image-position	`Gtk.PositionType`	The position of the image relative to the text.
label	string	Text of the label widget inside the button, if the button contains a label widget.
relief	`Gtk.ReliefStyle`	The border relief style.
use-underline	boolean	If set, an underline in the text indicates the next character should be used for the mnemonic accelerator key.

Table A-17. *Gtk.ButtonBox Properties*

Property	Type	Description
layout-style	`Gtk.ButtonBoxStyle`	How to lay out the buttons in the box. Possible values are `spread`, `edge`, `start` and `end`.

Table A-18. *Gtk.Calendar Properties*

Property	Type	Description
day	integer	The selected day (as a number between 1 and 31, or 0 to unselect the current day.
detail-height-rows	integer	Details height in rows.
detail-width-chars	integer	Details width in characters.
month	integer	The selected month (as a number between 0 and 11).
no-month-change	boolean	If True, the selected month cannot be changed.
show-day-names	boolean	If True, day names are displayed.
show-details	boolean	If True, details are shown.
show-heading	boolean	If True, a heading is displayed.
show-week-numbers	boolean	If True, week numbers are displayed.
year	integer	The selected year.

Table A-19. *Gtk.CellArea Properties*

Property	Type	Description
edit-widget	Gtk.CellEditable	The widget currently editing the edited cell.
edited-cell	Gtk.CellEditable	The cell that is currently being edited.
focus-cell	Gtk.CellEditable	The cell, which currently has focus.

Table A-20. *Gtk.CellAreaBox Properties*

Property	Type	Description
spacing	integer	Space that is inserted between cells.

Table A-21. *Gtk.CellAreaContext Properties*

Property	Type	Description
area	Gtk.CellArea	The Cell Area this context was created for.
minimum-height	integer	Minimum cached height.
minimum-width	integer	Minimum cached width.
natural-height	integer	Natural cached height.
natural-width	integer	Natural cached width.

Table A-22. *Gtk.CellRenderer Properties*

Property	Type	Description
cell-background	string	Cell background color as a string.
cell-background-set	boolean	Whether the cell background color is set.
minimum-width	integer	Minimum cached width.
editing	boolean	Whether the cell renderer is currently in editing mode.
height	integer	The fixed height.
is-expanded	boolean	Row is an expander row, and is expanded.
is-expander	boolean	Row has children.
mode	Gtk.CellRendererMode	Editable mode of the Gtk.CellRenderer.
sensitive	boolean	xlib.Display the cell sensitive.
visible	boolean	xlib.Display the cell.
width	integer	The fixed width.
xalign	float	The x-align.
xpad	integer	The xpad.
yalign	float	The y-align.
ypad	integer	The ypad.

Table A-23. *Gtk.CellRendererAccel Properties*

Property	Type	Description
accel-key	integer	The keyval of the accelerator.
accel-mode	Gtk.CellRendererAccelMode	The type of accelerators.
accel-mods	Gdk.ModifierType	The modifier mask of the accelerator.
keycode	integer	The hardware keycode of the accelerator.

Table A-24. *Gtk.CellRendererCombo Properties*

Property	Type	Description
has-entry	boolean	If False, don't allow to enter strings other than the chosen ones.
model	Gtk.TreeModel	The model containing the possible values for the combo box.
text-column	integer	A column in the data source model to get the strings from.

Table A-25. *Gtk.CellRendererPixbuf Properties*

Property	Type	Description
gicon	Gio.Icon	The Gio.Icon being displayed.
icon-name	string	The name of the icon from the icon theme.
pixbuf	GdkPixbuf.Pixbuf	The pixbuf to render.
pixbuf-expander-closed	GdkPixbuf.Pixbuf	Pixbuf for closed expander.
pixbuf-expander-open	GdkPixbuf.Pixbuf	Pixbuf for open expander.
stock-detail	string	Render detail to pass to the theme engine.
stock-size	integer	The Gtk.IconSize value that specifies the size of the rendered icon.
surface	cairo.Surface	The surface to render.

Table A-26. *Gtk.CellRendererProgress Properties*

Property	Type	Description
inverted	boolean	Invert the direction in which the progress bar grows.
text	string	Text on the progress bar.
text-xalign	float	The horizontal text alignment, from 0 (left) to 1 (right). Reversed for RTL layouts.
text-yalign	float	The vertical text alignment, from 0 (top) to 1 (bottom).
value	integer	Value of the progress bar.

Table A-27. *Gtk.CellRendererSpin Properties*

Property	Type	Description
adjustment	Gtk.Adjustment	The adjustment that holds the value of the spin button.
climb-rate	float	The acceleration rate when you hold down a button.
digits	integer	The number of decimal places to display.

Table A-28. *Gtk.CellRendererSpinner Properties*

Property	Type	Description
active	boolean	Whether the spinner is active (i.e.. shown) in the cell.
pulse	integer	Pulse of the spinner.
size	Gtk.IconSize	The Gtk.IconSize value that specifies the size of the rendered spinner.

Table A-29. *Gtk.CellRendererText Properties*

Property	Type	Description
align-set	boolean	Whether this tag affects the alignment mode.
alignment	`Pango.Alignment`	How to align the lines.
attributes	`Pango.AttrListe`	A list of style attributes to apply to the text of the renderer.
background	`Gdk.RGBA`	Background color as a `Gdk.RGBA`.
background-set	boolean	Whether this tag affects the background color.
editable	boolean	Whether the text can be modified by the user.
editable-set	boolean	Whether this tag affects text editability.
ellipsize	`Pango.EllipsizeMode`	The preferred place to ellipsize the string, if the cell renderer does not have enough room to display the entire string.
family	string	Name of the font family, e.g. Sans, Helvetica, Times, Monospace.
family-set	boolean	Whether this tag affects the font family.
font	string	Font description as a string, e.g. "Sans Italic 12".
font-desc	`Pango.FontDescription`	Font description as a `Pango.FontDescription` struct.
foreground	string	Foreground color as a string.
foreground-rgba	`Gdk.RGBA`	Foreground color as a `Gdk.RGBA`.
foreground-set	bool	Whether this tag affects the foreground color.
language-set	boolean	Whether this tag affects the language that the text is rendered as.

(*continued*)

Table A-29. (*continued*)

Property	Type	Description
language-set	boolean	Whether this tag affects the language that the text is rendered as.
markup	string	Marked up text to render.
max-width-chars	integer	The maximum width of the cell, in characters.
placeholder-text	string	Text rendered when an editable cell is empty.
rise	integer	Offset of text above the baseline (below the baseline if rise is negative).
rise-set	boolean	Whether this tag affects the rise.
scale	float	Font scaling factor.
scale-set	boolean	Whether this tag scales the font size by a factor.
single-paragraph-mode	boolean	Whether to keep all text in a single paragraph.
size	integer	Font size.
size-points	float	Font size in points.
size-set	boolean	Whether this tag affects the font size.
stretch	`Pango.Stretch`	Font stretch.
stretch-set	boolean	Whether this tag affects the font stretch.
strikethrough	boolean	Whether to strike through the text.
strikethrought-set	boolean	Whether this tag affects strikethrough.
style	`Pango.Style`	Font style.
style-set	boolean	Whether this tag affects the font style.
text	string	Text to render.
underline	`Pango.Underline`	Style of underline for this text.

(*continued*)

Table A-29. (*continued*)

Property	Type	Description
underline-set	boolean	Whether this tag affects underlining.
variant	Pango.Variant	Font variant.
variant-set	boolean	Whether this tag affects the font variant.
weight	integer	Font weight.
weight-set	boolean	Whether this tag affects the font weight.
width-chars	integer	The desired width of the label, in characters.
wrap-mode	Pango.WrapMode	How to break the string into multiple lines, if the cell renderer does not have enough room to display the entire string.
wrap-width	integer	The width at which the text is wrapped.

Table A-30. *Gtk.CellRendererToggle Properties*

Property	Type	Description
activatable	boolean	The toggle button can be activated.
active	boolean	The toggle state of the button
inconsistent	boolean	The inconsistent state of the button.
radio	integer	Draw the toggle button as a radio button.

Table A-31. *Gtk.CellView Properties*

Property	Type	Description
background	string	Background color as a string.
background-rgba	Gdk.RGBA	Background color as a Gdk.RGBA.
background-set	boolean	Whether this tag affects the background color.
cell-area	Gtk.CellArea	The Gtk.CellArea used to layout cells.
cell-area-context	Gtk.CellAreaContext	The Gtk.CellAreaContext used to compute the geometry of the cell view.
draw-sensitive	boolean	Whether to force cells to be drawn in a sensitive state.
fit-model	boolean	Whether to request enough space for every row in the model.
model	Gtk.TreeModel	The model for cell view.

Table A-32. *Gtk.CheckMenuItem Properties*

Property	Type	Description
active	boolean	Whether the menu item is checked.
draw-as-radio	boolean	Whether the menu item looks like a radio menu item.
inconsistent	boolean	Whether to display an "inconsistent" state.

Table A-33. *Gtk.ColorButton Properties*

Property	Type	Description
alpha	integer	The selected opacity value (0 fully transparent, 65535 fully opaque).
show-editor	boolean	Whether to show the color editor right away.
title	string	The title of the color selection dialog.

Table A-34. *Gtk.ColorChooserDialog Properties*

Property	Type	Description
show-editor	boolean	Show editor.

Table A-35. *Gtk.ColorChooserWidget Properties*

Property	Type	Description
show-editor	boolean	Show editor.

Table A-36. *Gtk.ColorSelection Properties*

Property	Type	Description
current-alpha	integer	The current opacity value (0 fully transparent, 65535 fully opaque).
current-rgba	Gdk.RGBA	The current RGBA color.
has-opacity-control	boolean	Whether the color selector should allow setting opacity.
has-palette	boolean	Whether a palette should be used.

Table A-37. *Gtk.ColorSelectionDialog Properties*

Property	Type	Description
cancel-button	Gtk.Widget	The cancel button of the dialog.
color-selection	Gtk.Widget	The color selection embedded in the dialog.
help-button	Gtk.Widget	The help button of the dialog.
ok-button	Gtk.Widget	The OK button of the dialog.

Table A-38. *Gtk.ComboBox Properties*

Property	Type	Description
active	integer	The item that is currently active.
active-id	string	The value of the id column for the active row.
button-sensitivity	Gtk.SensitivityType	Whether the drop-down button is sensitive when the model is empty.
cell-area	Gtk.CellArea	The Gtk.CellArea used to layout cells.
column-span-column	integer	Gtk.TreeModel column containing the column span values.
entry-text-column	integer	The column in the combo box's model to associate with strings from the entry if the combo was created with Gtk.ComboBox.has_entry = True.
has-entry	boolean	Whether combo box has an entry.
has-frame	boolean	Whether the combo box draws a frame around the child.
id-column	integer	The column in the combo box's model that provides string IDs for the values in the model.
model	Gtk.TreeModel	The model for the combo box.
popup-fixed-width	boolean	Whether the pop-up's width should be a fixed width matching the allocated width of the combo box.
popup-shown	boolean	Whether the combo's drop-down is shown.
row-span-column	integer	Gtk.TreeModel column containing the row span values.
wrap-width	integer	Wrap width for laying out the items in a grid.

Table A-39. *Gtk.Container Properties*

Property	Type	Description
border-width	integer	The width of the empty border outside the containers children.

Table A-40. *Gtk.Dialog Properties*

Property	Type	Description
use-header-bar	integer	Use Header Bar for actions.

Table A-41. *Gtk.Entry Properties*

Property	Type	Description
activates-default	boolean	Whether to activate the default widget (such as the default button in a dialog) when **Enter** is pressed.
attributes	`Pango.AttrList`	A list of style attributes to apply to the text of the entry.
buffer	`Gtk.EntryBuffer`	Text buffer object that actually stores entry text.
caps-lock-warning	boolean	Whether password entries show a warning when Caps Lock is on.
completion	`Gtk.EntryCompletion`	The auxiliary completion object.
cursor-position	integer	The current position of the insertion cursor in chars.
editable	boolean	Whether the entry contents can be edited.
has-frame	boolean	`False` removes outside bevel from entry.
im-module	string	Which IM module should be used.
input-hints	`Gtk.InputHints`	Hints for the text field behavior.

(*continued*)

Table A-41. (*continued*)

Property	Type	Description
input-purpose	Gtk.InputPurpose	Purpose of the text field.
max-length	integer	Maximum number of characters for this entry. Zero if no maximum.
overwrite-mode	boolean	Whether new text overwrites existing text.
placeholder-text	string	Show text in the entry when it's empty and unfocused.
populate-all	boolean	Whether to emit "populate-popup" signal for touch pop-ups.
primary-icon-activatable	boolean	Whether the primary icon is activatable.
primary-icon-gicon	Gio.Icon	Gio.Icon for primary icon.
primary-icon-name	string	Icon name for primary icon.
primary-icon-pixbuf	GdkPixbuf.Pixbuf	Primary pixbuf for the entry.
primary-icon-sensitive	boolean	Whether the primary icon is sensitive.
primary-icon-storage-type	Gtk.ImageType	The representation being used for primary icon.
primary-icon-tooltip-markup	string	The contents of the tooltip on the primary icon.
primary-icon-tooltip-text	string	The contents of the tooltip on the primary icon.
progress-fraction	float	The current fraction of the task that's been completed.
progress-pulse-step	float	The fraction of total entry width to move the progress bouncing block for each call to Gtk.Entry.progress_pulse().
scroll-offset	integer	Number of pixels of the entry scrolled off the screen to the left.

(*continued*)

Table A-41. (*continued*)

Property	Type	Description
secondary-icon-activatable	boolean	Whether the secondary icon is activatable.
secondary-icon-gicon	`Gio.Icon`	`Gio.Icon` for secondary icon.
secondary-icon-name	string	Icon name for secondary icon.
secondary-icon-pixbuf	`GdkPixbuf.Pixbuf`	Secondary pixbuf for the entry.
secondary-icon-sensitive	boolean	Whether the secondary icon is sensitive.
secondary-icon-storage-type	`Gtk.ImageType`	The representation being used for secondary icon.
secondary-icon-tooltip-markup	string	The contents of the tooltip on the secondary icon.
secondary-icon-tooltip-text	string	The contents of the tooltip on the secondary icon.
selection-bound	integer	The position of the opposite end of the selection from the cursor in chars.
show-emoji-icon	boolean	Whether to show an icon for Emoji.
tabs	`Pango.TabArray`	A list of tabstop locations to apply to the text of the entry.
text	string	The contents of the entry.
text-length	integer	Length of the text currently in the entry.
truncate-multiline	boolean	Whether to truncate multiline pastes to one line.
visibility	boolean	`False` displays the "invisible str" instead of the actual text (password mode).
width-chars	integer	Number of characters to leave space for in the entry.
xalign	float	The horizontal alignment, from 0 (left) to 1 (right). Reversed for RTL layouts.

Table A-42. *Gtk.EntryBuffer Properties*

Property	Type	Description
length	integer	Length of the text currently in the buffer.
max-length	integer	Maximum number of characters for this entry. Zero if no maximum.
text	string	The contents of the buffer.

Table A-43. *Gtk.EntryCompletion Properties*

Property	Type	Description
cell-area	Gtk.CellArea	The Gtk.CellArea used to layout cells.
inline-completion	boolean	Whether the common prefix should be inserted automatically.
inline-selection	boolean	If set to True, the prefix that is common to all choices is added to the text. For this property to work, text-column must be set.
minimum-key-length	integer	Minimum length of the search key in order to look up matches.
model	Gtk.TreeModel	The model to find matches in.
popup-completion	boolean	Whether the completions should be shown in a pop-up window.
popup-set-width	boolean	If True, the pop-up window has the same size as the entry.
popup-single-match	boolean	If True, the pop-up window appears for a single match.
text-column	integer	The column of the model containing the strings.

Table A-44. *Gtk.EventBox Properties*

Property	Type	Description
above-child	boolean	Whether the event-trapping window of the eventbox is above the window of the child widget as opposed to below it.
visible-window	boolean	Whether the event box is visible, as opposed to invisible and only used to trap events.

Table A-45. *Gtk.EventController Properties*

Property	Type	Description
propagation-phase	Gtk.PropagationPhase	Propagation phase at which this controller is run.
widget	Gtk.Widget	Widget the gesture relates to.

Table A-46. *Gtk.Expander Properties*

Property	Type	Description
expanded	boolean	Whether the expander has been opened to reveal the child widget.
label	string	Text of the expander's label.
label-fill	boolean	Whether the label widget should fill all available horizontal space.
label-widget	Gtk.Widget	A widget to display in place of the usual expander label.
resize-toplevel	boolean	Whether the expander resizes the top-level window upon expanding and collapsing.
use-markup	boolean	The text of the label includes XML markup. See Pango.parse_markup().
use-underline	boolean	If set, an underline in the text indicates the next character should be used for the mnemonic accelerator key.

Table A-47. *Gtk.FileChooserButton Properties*

Property	Type	Description
dialog	Gtk.FileChooser	The file chooser dialog to use.
title	string	The title of the file chooser dialog.
width-chars	integer	The desired width of the button widget, in characters.

Table A-48. *Gtk.FileChooserNative Properties*

Property	Type	Description
accept-label	string	The label on the accept button.
cancel-label	string	The label on the cancel button.

Table A-49. *Gtk.FileChooserWidget Properties*

Property	Type	Description
search-mode	boolean	Search mode.
subtitle	string	Subtitle.

Table A-50. *Gtk.FlowBox Properties*

Property	Type	Description
activate-on-single-click	boolean	Activate row on a single click.
column-spacing	integer	The amount of horizontal space between two children in pixels.
homogeneous	boolean	Whether the children should all be the same size.
max-children-per-line	integer	The maximum amount of children to request space for consecutively in the given orientation.
min-children-per-line	integer	The minimum number of children to allocate consecutively in the given orientation.
row-spacing	integer	The amount of vertical space between two children.
selection-mode	Gtk.SelectionMode	The selection mode.

Table A-51. *Gtk.FontButton Properties*

Property	Type	Description
show-size	boolean	Whether selected font size is shown in the label.
show-style	boolean	Whether the selected font style is shown in the label.
title	string	The title of the font chooser dialog.
Whether the label is drawn in the selected font	boolean	Whether the label is drawn in the selected font.
use-size	boolean	Whether the label is drawn with the selected font size.

Table A-52. *Gtk.FontSelection Properties*

Property	Type	Description
font-name	string	The string that represents this font.
preview-text	string	The text to display in order to demonstrate the selected font.

Table A-53. *Gtk.Frame Properties*

Property	Type	Description
label	string	Text of the frame's label.
label-widget	Gtk.Widget	A widget to display in place of the usual frame label.
label-xalign	float	The horizontal alignment of the label.
shadow-type	Gtk.ShadowType	Appearance of the frame border.

Table A-54. *Gtk.GLArea Properties*

Property	Type	Description
auto-render	boolean	Whether the Gtk.GLArea renders on each redraw.
context	Gdk.GLContext	The GL context.
has-alpha	boolean	Whether the color buffer has an alpha component.
has-depth-buffer	boolean	Whether a depth buffer is allocated.
has-stencil-buffer	boolean	Whether a stencil buffer is allocated.
use-es	boolean	Whether the context uses OpenGL or OpenGL ES.

Table A-55. *Gtk.Gesture Properties*

Property	Type	Description
n-points	integer	Number of points needed to trigger the gesture.
window	Gdk.Window	Gdk.Window to receive events about.

Table A-56. *Gtk.GestureLongPress Properties*

Property	Type	Description
delay-factor	float	Factor by which to modify the default timeout.

Table A-57. *Gtk.GesturePan Properties*

Property	Type	Description
orientation	Gtk.Orientation	Allowed orientations.

Table A-58. *Gtk.GestureSingle Properties*

Property	Type	Description
button	integer	Button number to listen to.
exclusive	boolean	Whether the gesture is exclusive.
touch-only	boolean	Whether the gesture handles only touch events.

Table A-59. *Gtk.Grid Properties*

Property	Type	Description
baseline-row	integer	The row to align to the baseline when valign is `Gtk.Align.BASELINE`.
column-homogeneous	boolean	If `True`, the columns are all the same width.
column-spacing	integer	The amount of space between two consecutive columns.
row-homogeneous	boolean	If `True`, the rows are all the same height.
row-spacing	integer	The amount of space between two consecutive rows.

Table A-60. *Gtk.HeaderBar Properties*

Property	Type	Description
custom-title	`Gtk.Widget`	Custom title widget to display.
decoration-layout	string	The layout for window decorations.
decoration-layout-set	boolean	Whether the decoration-layout property has been set.
has-subtitle	boolean	Whether to reserve space for a subtitle.
show-close-button	boolean	Whether to show window decorations.
spacing	integer	The amount of space between children.
subtitle	string	The subtitle to display.
title	string	The title to display.

Table A-61. *Gtk.IMContext Properties*

Property	Type	Description
input-hints	`Gtk.InputHints`	Hints for the text field behavior.
input-purpose	`Gtk.InputPurpose`	Purpose of the text field.

Table A-62. *Gtk.IconView Properties*

Property	Type	Description
activate-on-single-click	boolean	Activate row on a single click.
cell-area	Gtk.CellArea	The Gtk.CellArea used to layout cells.
column-spacing	integer	Space that is inserted between grid columns.
columns	integer	Number of columns to display.
item-orientation	Gtk.Orientation	How the text and icon of each item are positioned relative to each other.
item-padding	integer	Padding around icon view items.
item-width	integer	The width used for each item.
markup-column	integer	Model column used to retrieve the text if using Pango markup.
model	Gtk.TreeModel	The model for the icon view.
pixbuf-column	integer	Model column used to retrieve the icon pixbuf from.
reorderable	boolean	View is reorderable.
row-spacing	integer	Space that is inserted between grid rows.
selection-mode	Gtk.SelectionMode	The selection mode.
spacing	integer	Space that is inserted between cells of an item.
text-column	integer	Model column used to retrieve the text from.
tooltip-column	integer	The column in the model containing the tooltip texts for the items.

Table A-63. *Gtk.ListBox Properties*

Property	Type	Description
activate-on-single-click	boolean	Activate row on a single click.
selection-mode	Gtk.SelectionMode	The selection mode.

Table A-64. *Gtk.ListBoxRow Properties*

Property	Type	Description
activatable	boolean	Whether this row can be activated.
selectable	boolean	Whether this row can be selected.

Table A-65. *Gtk.LockButton Properties*

Property	Type	Description
permission	Gio.Permission	The Gio.Permission object controlling this button.
text-lock	string	The text to display when prompting the user to lock.
text-unlock	string	The text to display when prompting the user to unlock.
tooltip-lock	string	The tooltip to display when prompting the user to lock.
tooltip-not-authorized	string	The tooltip to display when prompting the user cannot obtain authorization.
tooltip-unlock	string	The tooltip to display when prompting the user to unlock.

Table A-66. *Gtk.Menu Properties*

Property	Type	Description
accel-group	Gtk.AccelGroup	The accel group holding accelerators for the menu.
accel-path	string	An accel path used to conveniently construct accel paths of child items.
active	integer	The currently selected menu item.
anchor-hints	Gdk.AnchorHints	Positioning hints for when the menu might fall off-screen.
attach-widget	Gtk.Widget	The widget the menu is attached to.
menu-type-hint	Gdk.WindowTypeHint	Menu window type hint.

(continued)

Table A-66. (*continued*)

Property	Type	Description
monitor	integer	The monitor that the menu pops up on.
rect-anchor-dx	integer	Rect anchor horizontal offset.
rect-anchor-dy	integer	Rect anchor vertical offset.
reserve-toggle-size	boolean	A boolean that indicates whether the menu reserves space for toggles and icons.

Table A-67. *Gtk.MenuBar Properties*

Property	Type	Description
child-pack-direction	Gtk.PackDirection	The child pack direction of the menubar.
pack-direction	Gtk.PackDirection	The pack direction of the menubar.

Table A-68. *Gtk.MenuButton Properties*

Property	Type	Description
align-widget	Gtk.Container	The parent widget that the menu should align with.
direction	Gtk.ArrowType	The direction the arrow should point.
menu-model	Gio.MenuModel	The model from which the pop-up is made.
popover	Gtk.Popover	The pop-over.
popup	Gtk.Menu	The drop-down menu.
use-popover	boolean	Use a pop-over instead of a menu.

Table A-69. *Gtk.MenuItem Properties*

Property	Type	Description
accel-path	string	Sets the accelerator path of the menu item.
label	string	The text for the child label.
submenu	Gtk.Menu	The submenu attached to the menu item, or None if it has none.
use-underline	boolean	If set, an underline in the text indicates the next character should be used for the mnemonic accelerator key.

Table A-70. *Gtk.MenuShell Properties*

Property	Type	Description
take-focus	boolean	A boolean that determines whether the menu grabs the keyboard focus.

Table A-71. *Gtk.MenuToolButton Properties*

Property	Type	Description
menu	Gtk.Menu	The drop-down menu.

Table A-72. *Gtk.MessageDialog Properties*

Property	Type	Description
buttons	Gtk.ButtonsType	The buttons shown in the message dialog.
message-area	Gtk.Widget	Gtk.Box that holds the dialog's primary and secondary labels.
message-type	Gtk.MessageType	Whether the color buffer has an alpha component.
secondary-text	String	The secondary text of the message dialog
secondary-use-markup	boolean	The secondary text includes Pango markup.
text	string	The primary text of the message dialog.
use-markup	boolean	The primary text of the title includes Pango markup.

Table A-73. *Gtk.ModelButton Properties*

Property	Type	Description
active	boolean	Active.
centered	boolean	Whether to center the contents.
icon	Gio.Icon	The icon.
iconic	boolean	Whether to prefer the icon over text.
inverted	boolean	Whether the menu is a parent.
menu-name	string	The name of the menu to open.
role	Gtk.ButtonRole	The role of this button.
text	string	The text.

Table A-74. *Gtk.MountOperation Properties*

Property	Type	Description
is-showing	boolean	Are we showing a dialog?
parent	Gtk.Window	The parent window.
screen	Gdk.Screen	The screen where this window is displayed.

Table A-75. *Gtk.NativeDialog Properties*

Property	Type	Description
modal	boolean	If True, the dialog is modal (other windows are not usable while this one is up)
title	string	The title of the dialog.
transient-for	Gtk.Window	The transient parent of the dialog.
visible	boolean	Whether the dialog is currently visible.

Table A-76. *Gtk.Notebook Properties*

Property	Type	Description
enable-popup	boolean	If True, pressing the right mouse button on the notebook pops up a menu that you can use to go to a page.
group-name	string	Group name for tab drag and drop.
page	integer	The index of the current page.
scrollable	boolean	If True, scroll arrows are added if there are too many tabs to fit.
show-border	boolean	Whether the border should be shown.
show-tabs	boolean	Whether tabs should be shown.
tab-pos	Gtk.PositionType	Which side of the notebook holds the tabs.

Table A-77. *Gtk.NumerableIcon Properties*

Property	Type	Description
background-icon	Gio.Icon	The icon for the number emblem background.
background-icon-name	string	The icon name for the number emblem background.
count	integer	The count of the emblem currently displayed.
label	string	The label to be displayed over the icon.
style-context	Gtk.StyleContext	The style context to theme the icon appearance.

Table A-78. *Gtk.PadController Properties*

Property	Type	Description
action-group	Gio.ActionGroup	Action group to launch actions from.
pad	Gdk.Device	Pad device to control.

Table A-79. *Gtk.Paned Properties*

Property	Type	Description
max-position	integer	Largest possible value for the "position" property.
min-position	integer	Smallest possible value for the "position" property.
position-set	boolean	True if the Position property should be used.
wide-handle	boolean	Whether the paned should have a prominent handle.

Table A-80. *Gtk.PlacesSidebar Properties*

Property	Type	Description
local-only	boolean	Whether the sidebar only includes local files.
location	Gio.File	The location to highlight in the sidebar.
open-flags	Gtk.PlacesOpenFlags	Modes in which the calling application can open locations selected in the sidebar.
populate-all	boolean	Whether to emit "populate-popup" for pop-ups that are not menus.
show-desktop	boolean	Whether the sidebar includes a built-in shortcut to the Desktop folder.
show-enter-location	boolean	Whether the sidebar includes a built-in shortcut to manually enter a location.
show-other-locations	boolean	Whether the sidebar includes an item to show external locations.
show-recent	boolean	Whether the sidebar includes a built-in shortcut for recent files.
show-starred-location	boolean	Whether the sidebar includes an item to show starred files.
show-trash	boolean	Whether the sidebar includes a built-in shortcut to the Trash location.

Table A-81. *Gtk.Plug Properties*

Property	Type	Description
embedded	boolean	Whether the plug is embedded.
socket-window	Gdk.Window	The window of the socket the plug is embedded in.

Table A-82. *Gtk.Popover Properties*

Property	Type	Description
constrain-to	Gtk.PopoverConstraint	Constraint for the popover position.
modal	boolean	Whether the popover is modal.
pointing-to	Gdk.Rectangle	Rectangle the bubble window points to.
position	Gtk.PositionType	Position to place the bubble window.
position	Gtk.Widget	Widget the bubble window points to.

Table A-83. *Gtk.PopoverMenu Properties*

Property	Type	Description
visible-submenu	string	The name of the visible submenu.

Table A-84. *Gtk.PrintOperation Properties*

Property	Type	Description
allow-async	boolean	True if print process may run asynchronous.
current-page	integer	The current page in the document.
custom-tab-label	string	Label for the tab containing custom widgets.
default-page-setup	Gtk.PageSetup	The Gtk.PageSetup used by default.
embed-page-setup	boolean	True if page setup combos are embedded in Gtk.PrintUnixDialog.

(continued)

Table A-84. (*continued*)

Property	Type	Description
export-filename	string	Export filename.
has-selection	boolean	True if a selection exists.
job-name	string	A string used for identifying the print job.
n-pages	integer	The number of pages in the document.
n-pages-to-print	integer	The number of pages that print.
print-settings	Gtk.PrintSettings	The Gtk.PrintSettings used for initializing the dialog.
show-progress	boolean	True if a progress dialog is shown while printing.
status	Gtk.PrintStatus	The status of the print operation.
status-string	string	A human-readable description of the status.
support-selection	boolean	True if the print operation supports print of selection.
track-print-status	boolean	True if the print operation continues to report on the print job status after the print data has been sent to the printer or print server.
unit	Gtk.Unit	The unit in which distances can be measured in the context.
use-full-page	boolean	True if the origin of the context should be at the corner of the page and not the corner of the imageable area.

Table A-85. *Gtk.ProgressBar Properties*

Property	Type	Description
ellipsize	Pango.EllipsizeMode	The preferred place to ellipsize the string, if the progress bar does not have enough room to display the entire string, if at all.
fraction	float	The fraction of total work that has been completed.
inverted	boolean	Invert the direction in which the progress bar grows.
pulse-step	float	The fraction of total progress to move the bouncing block when pulsed.
show-text	boolean	Whether the progress is shown as text.
text	string	Text to be displayed in the progress bar.

Table A-86. *Gtk.RadioButton Properties*

Property	Type	Description
group	Gtk.RadioButton	The radio button whose group this widget belongs to.

Table A-87. *Gtk.RadioMenuItem Properties*

Property	Type	Description
group	Gtk.RadioMenuItem	The radio menu item whose group this widget belongs to.

Table A-88. *Gtk.RadioToolButton Properties*

Property	Type	Description
group	Gtk.RadioToolButton	The radio tool button whose group this button belongs to.

Table A-89. *Gtk.Range Properties*

Property	Type	Description
adjustment	Gtk.Adjustment	The Gtk.Adjustment that contains the current value of this range object.
fill-level	float	The fill level.
inverted	boolean	Invert direction slider moves to increase range value.
lower-stepper-sensitivity	Gtk.SensitivityType	The sensitivity policy for the stepper that points to the adjustment's lower side.
restrict-to-fill-level	boolean	Whether to restrict the upper boundary to the fill level.
round-digits	integer	The number of digits to round the value to.
show-fill-level	boolean	Whether to display a fill level indicator graphics on trough.
upper-stepper-sensitivity	Gtk.SensitivityType	The sensitivity policy for the stepper that points to the adjustment's upper side.

Table A-90. *Gtk.RecentChooserMenu Properties*

Property	Type	Description
show-numbers	boolean	Whether the items should be displayed with a number.

Table A-91. *Gtk.RecentManager Properties*

Property	Type	Description
filename	string	The full path to the file to be used to store and read the list.
size	integer	The size of the recently used resources list.

Table A-92. *Gtk.RendererCellAccessible Properties*

Property	Type	Description
renderer	`Gtk.CellRenderer`	The cell renderer represented by this accessible.

Table A-93. *Gtk.Revealer Properties*

Property	Type	Description
child-revealed	boolean	Whether the child is revealed and the animation target reached.
reveal-child	boolean	Whether the container should reveal the child.
transition-duration	integer	The animation duration, in milliseconds.
transition-type	`Gtk.RevealerTransitionType`	The type of animation used to transition.

Table A-94. *Gtk.Scale Properties*

Property	Type	Description
digits	integer	The number of decimal places that are displayed in the value.
draw-value	boolean	Whether the current value is displayed as a string next to the slider.
has-origin	boolean	Whether the scale has an origin.
value-pos	`Gtk.PositionType`	The position in which the current value is displayed.

Table A-95. *Gtk.ScaleButton Properties*

Property	Type	Description
adjustment	`Gtk.Adjustment`	The `Gtk.Adjustment` that contains the current value of this scale button object.
icons	string	List of icon names.
size	`Gtk.IconSize`	The icon size.
value	float	The value of the scale.

Table A-96. *Gtk.ScrolledWindow Properties*

Property	Type	Description
hadjustment	Gtk.Adjustment	The Gtk.Adjustment for the horizontal position.
hscrollbar-policy	Gtk.PolicyType	When the horizontal scrollbar is displayed.
max-content-height	integer	The maximum height that the scrolled window allocates to its content.
max-content-width	integer	The maximum width that the scrolled window allocates to its content.
min-content-height	integer	The minimum height that the scrolled window allocates to its content.
min-content-width	integer	The minimum width that the scrolled window allocates to its content.
overlay-scrolling	boolean	Overlay scrolling mode.
propagate-natural-height	boolean	Propagate Natural Height.
propagate-natural-width	boolean	Propagate Natural Width.
shadow-type	Gtk.ShadowType	Style of bevel around the contents.
vadjustment	Gtk.Adjustment	The Gtk.Adjustment for the vertical position.
vscrollbar-policy	Gtk.PolicyType	When the vertical scrollbar is displayed.
window-placement	Gtk.CornerType	Where the contents are located with respect to the scrollbars.

Table A-97. *Gtk.SearchBar Properties*

Property	Type	Description
search-mode-enabled	boolean	Whether the search mode is on and the search bar shown.
has-origin	boolean	Whether to show the close button in the toolbar.

Table A-98. *Gtk.SeparatorToolItem Properties*

Property	Type	Description
draw	boolean	Whether the separator is drawn, or just blank.

451

Table A-99. *Gtk.Settings Properties*

Property	Type	Description
gtk-alternative-button-order	boolean	Whether buttons in dialogs should use the alternative button order.
gtk-alternative-sort-arrows	boolean	Whether the direction of the sort indicators in list and tree views is inverted compared to the default (where down means ascending).
gtk-application-prefer-dark-theme	boolean	Whether the application prefers to have a dark theme.
gtk-cursor-blink	boolean	Whether the cursor should blink.
gtk-cursor-blink-time	integer	Length of the cursor blink cycle, in milliseconds.
gtk-cursor-blink-timeout	integer	Time after which the cursor stops blinking, in seconds.
gtk-cursor-theme-name	string	Name of the cursor theme to use, or None to use the default theme.
gtk-cursor-theme-size	integer	Size to use for cursors, or 0 to use the default size.
gtk-decoration-layout	string	The layout for window decorations.
gtk-dialogs-use-header	boolean	Whether built-in GTK+ dialogs should use a header bar instead of an action area.
gtk-dnd-drag-threshold	integer	Number of pixels the cursor can move before dragging.
gtk-double-click-distance	integer	Maximum distance allowed between two clicks for them to be considered a double click (in pixels).
gtk-double-click-time	integer	Maximum time allowed between two clicks for them to be considered a double click (in milliseconds).
gtk-enable-accels	boolean	Whether menu items should have accelerators.
gtk-enable-animations	boolean	Whether to enable toolkit-wide animations.
gtk-enable-event-sounds	boolean	Whether to play any event sounds at all.

(continued)

Table A-99. (*continued*)

Property	Type	Description
gtk-enable-input-feedback-sounds	boolean	Whether to play event sounds as feedback to user input.
gtk-enable-input-feedback-sounds	boolean	Whether a middle click on a mouse should paste the 'PRIMARY' clipboard content at the cursor location.
gtk-entry-password-hint-timeout	integer	How long to show the last input character in hidden entries.
gtk-enable-primary-paste	boolean	Whether a middle click on a mouse should paste the 'PRIMARY' clipboard content at the cursor location.
gtk-entry-select-on-focus	boolean	Whether to select the contents of an entry when it is focused.
gtk-error-bell	boolean	When True, keyboard navigation and other errors cause a beep.
gtk-font-name	string	The default font family and size to use.
gtk-fontconfig-timestamp	integer	Timestamp of current fontconfig configuration.
gtk-icon-theme-name	string	Name of icon theme to use.
gtk-im-module	string	Which IM module should be used by default.
gtk-key-theme-name	string	Name of key theme to load.
gtk-keynav-use-caret	boolean	Whether to show cursor in text.
gtk-label-select-on-focus	boolean	Whether to select the contents of a selectable label when it is focused.
gtk-long-press-time	integer	Time for a button/touch press to be considered a long press (in milliseconds).
gtk-modules	string	List of currently active GTK modules.
gtk-primary-button-warps-slider	boolean	Whether a primary click on the trough should warp the slider into position.

(*continued*)

Table A-99. (*continued*)

Property	Type	Description
gtk-print-backends	string	List of the GtkPrintBackend backends to use by default.
gtk-print-preview-command	string	Command to run when displaying a print preview.
gtk-recent-files-enabled	boolean	Whether GTK+ remembers recent files.
gtk-recent-files-max-age	integer	Maximum age of recently used files, in days.
gtk-shell-shows-app-menu	boolean	Set to True if the desktop environment is displaying the app menu, False if the app should display it itself.
gtk-shell-shows-desktop	boolean	Set to True gtk-shell-shows-desktop, False if not.
gtk-shell-shows-menubar	boolean	Set to True if the desktop environment is displaying the menubar, False if the app should display it itself.
gtk-sound-theme-name	string	XDG sound theme name.
gtk-split-cursor	boolean	Whether two cursors should be displayed for mixed left-to-right and right-to-left text.
gtk-theme-name	string	Name of theme to load.
gtk-titlebar-double-click	string	The action to take on titlebar double-click.
gtk-titlebar-middle-click	string	The action to take on titlebar middle-click.
gtk-titlebar-right-click	string	The action to take on titlebar right-click.
gtk-xft-antialias	integer	Whether to antialias Xft fonts; 0=no, 1=yes, −1=default.
gtk-xft-dpi	integer	Resolution for Xft, in 1024 * dots/inch. −1 to use default value.
gtk-xft-hinting	integer	Whether to hint Xft fonts; 0=no, 1=yes, −1=default.
gtk-xft-hintstyle	string	What degree of hinting to use; hintnone, hintslight, hintmedium, or hintfull.
gtk-xft-rgba	string	Type of subpixel antialiasing; none, rgb, bgr, vrgb, vbgr.

Table A-100. *Gtk.ShortcutLabel Properties*

Property	Type	Description
accelerator	string	Accelerator.
disabled-text	string	Disabled text.

Table A-101. *Gtk.ShortcutsGroup Properties*

Property	Type	Description
accel-size-group	Gtk.SizeGroup	Accelerator Size Group.
height	integer	Height.
title	string	Title.
title-size-group	Gtk.SizeGroup	Title Size Group.
view	string	View.

Table A-102. *Gtk.ShortcutsSection Properties*

Property	Type	Description
max-height	integer	Maximum Height.
section-name	string	Section Name.
title	string	Title.
view-name	string	View Name.

Table A-103. *Gtk.ShortcutsShortcut Properties*

Property	Type	Description
accel-size-group	Gtk.SizeGroup	Accelerator Size Group.
accelerator	string	The accelerator keys for shortcuts of type 'Accelerator'.
action-name	string	The name of the action.
direction	Gtk.TextDirection	Text direction for which this shortcut is active.
icon	Gio.Icon	The icon to show for shortcuts of type 'Other Gesture'.
icon-set	boolean	Whether an icon has been set.
shortcut-type	Gtk.ShortcutType	The type of shortcut that is represented.
subtitle	string	A short description for the gesture.
subtitle-set	boolean	Whether a subtitle has been set.
title	string	A short description for the shortcut.
title-size-group	Gtk.SizeGroup	Title Size Group.

Table A-104. *Gtk.ShortcutsWindow Properties*

Property	Type	Description
section-name	string	Section Name.
view-name	string	View Name.

Table A-105. *Gtk.SizeGroup Properties*

Property	Type	Description
mode	Gtk.SizeGroupMode	The directions in which the size group affects the requested sizes of its component widgets.

Table A-106. *Gtk.SpinButton Properties*

Property	Type	Description
adjustment	Gtk.Adjustment	The adjustment that holds the value of the spin button.
climb-rate	float	The acceleration rate when you hold down a button.
digits	integer	The number of decimal places to display.
numeric	boolean	Whether non-numeric characters should be ignored.
snap-to-ticks	boolean	Whether erroneous values are automatically changed to a spin button's nearest step increment.
update-policy	Gtk.SpinButtonUpdatePolicyt	Whether the spin button should update always, or only when the value is legal.
value	float	Reads the current value, or sets a new value.
wrap	boolean	Whether a spin button should wrap upon reaching its limits.

Table A-107. *Gtk.Spinner Properties*

Property	Type	Description
active	boolean	Whether the spinner is active.

Table A-108. *Gtk.Stack Properties*

Property	Type	Description
hhomogeneous	boolean	Horizontally homogeneous sizing.
homogeneous	boolean	Homogeneous sizing.
interpolate-size	boolean	Whether or not the size should smoothly change when changing between differently sized children.
transition-duration	integer	The animation duration, in milliseconds.
transition-running	boolean	Whether or not the transition is currently running.
transition-type	Gtk.StackTransitionType	The type of animation used to transition.
vhomogeneous	boolean	Vertically homogeneous sizing.
visible-child	Gtk.Widget	The widget currently visible in the stack.
visible-child-name	string	The name of the widget currently visible in the stack.

Table A-109. *Gtk.StackSidebar Properties*

Property	Type	Description
stack	Gtk.Stack	Associated stack for this Gtk.StackSidebar.

Table A-110. *Gtk.StackSwitcher Properties*

Property	Type	Description
icon-size	integer	Symbolic size to use for named icon.
stack	Gtk.Stack	Associated stack for this Gtk.StackSidebar.

Table A-111. *Gtk.StyleContext Properties*

Property	Type	Description
paint-clock	Gdk.FrameClock	The associated Gdk.FrameClock.
parent	Gtk.StyleContext	The parent style context.
screen	Gdk.Screen	The associated Gdk.Screen.

Table A-112. *Gtk.Switch Properties*

Property	Type	Description
active	boolean	Whether the switch is on or off.
state	boolean	The backend state.

Table A-113. *Gtk.TextBuffer Properties*

Property	Type	Description
copy-target-list	Gtk.TargetList	The list of targets this buffer supports for clipboard copying and DND source.
cursor-position	integer	The position of the insert mark (as offset from the beginning of the buffer).
has-selection	boolean	Whether the buffer has some text currently selected.
paste-target-list	Gtk.TargetList	The list of targets this buffer supports for clipboard pasting and DND destination.
tag-table	Gtk.TextTagTable	Text Tag Table.
text	string	Current text of the buffer.

Table A-114. *Gtk.TextMark Properties*

Property	Type	Description
left-gravity	bool	Whether the mark has left gravity.
name	string	Mark name.

Table A-115. *Gtk.TextTag Properties*

Property	Type	Description
accumulative-margin	bool	Whether left and right margins accumulate.
background	string	Background color as a string.
background-full-height	bool	Whether the background color fills the entire line height or only the height of the tagged characters.
background-full-height-set	bool	Whether this tag affects background height.
background-rgba	Gdk.RGBA	Background color as a Gdk.RGBA.
background-set	boolean	Whether this tag affects the background color.
direction	Gtk.TextDirection	Text direction, e.g. right-to-left or left-to-right.
editable	boolean	Whether the text can be modified by the user.
editable-set	boolean	Whether this tag affects text editability.
fallback	boolean	Whether font fallback is enabled.
fallback-set	boolean	Whether this tag affects font fallback.
family	string	Name of the font family, e.g. Sans, Helvetica, Times, Monospace.
family-set	boolean	Whether this tag affects the font family.
font	string	Font description as a string, e.g. "Sans Italic 12".
font-desc	Pango.FontDescription	Font description as a Pango.FontDescription class.

(*continued*)

Table A-115. (*continued*)

Property	Type	Description
font-features-set	boolean	Whether this tag affects font features.
foreground	string	Foreground color as a string.
foreground-rgba	Gdk.RGBA	Foreground color as a Gdk.RGBA.
foreground-set	boolean	Whether this tag affects the foreground color.
indent	integer	Amount to indent the paragraph, in pixels.
indent-set	boolean	Whether this tag affects indentation.
invisible	boolean	Whether this text is hidden.
invisible-set	boolean	Whether this tag affects text visibility.
justification	Gtk.Justification	Left, right, or center justification.
justification-set	boolean	Whether this tag affects paragraph justification.
language	string	The language this text is in, as an ISO code. Pango can use this as a hint when rendering the text. If not set, an appropriate default is used.
language-set	boolean	Whether this tag affects the language that the text is rendered as.
left-margin	integer	Width of the left margin in pixels.
left-margin-set	boolean	Whether this tag affects the left margin.
letter-spacing	integer	Extra spacing between graphemes.
letter-spacing-set	boolean	Whether this tag affects letter spacing.

(*continued*)

Table A-115. (*continued*)

Property	Type	Description
name	string	Name used to refer to the text tag. None for anonymous tags.
paragraph-background	string	Paragraph background color as a string.
paragraph-background-rgba	Gdk.RGBA	Paragraph background RGBA as a Gdk.RGBA.
paragraph-background-set	boolean	Whether this tag affects the paragraph background color.
pixels-above-lines	integer	Pixels of blank space above paragraphs.
pixels-above-lines-set	boolean	Whether this tag affects the number of pixels above lines.
pixels-below-lines	integer	Pixels of blank space below paragraphs.
pixels-below-lines-set	boolean	Whether this tag affects the number of pixels below lines.
pixels-inside-wrap	integer	Pixels of blank space between wrapped lines in a paragraph.
pixels-inside-wrap-set	boolean	Whether this tag affects the number of pixels between wrapped lines.
right-margin	integer	Width of the right margin in pixels.
right-margin-set	boolean	Whether this tag affects the right margin.
rise	integer	Offset of text above the baseline (below the baseline if rise is negative) in Pango units.
rise-set	boolean	Whether this tag affects the rise.

(*continued*)

Table A-115. (*continued*)

Property	Type	Description
scale	float	Font size as a scale factor relative to the default font size. This properly adapts to theme changes etc. so is recommended. Pango predefines scales, such as PANGO_SCALE_X_ LARGE, which is defined in C as the value (1.2 * 1.2).
scale-set	boolean	Whether this tag scales the font size by a factor.
size	integer	Font size in Pango units.
size-points	float	Font size in points.
size-set	boolean	Whether this tag affects the font size.
stretch	Pango.Stretch	Font stretch as a Pango.Stretch, e.g. Pango.Stretch.CONDENSED
stretch-set	boolean	Whether this tag affects the font stretch.
strikethrough	boolean	Whether to strike through the text.
strikethrough-rgba	Gdk.RGBA	Color of strikethrough for this text.
strikethrough-rgba-set	boolean	Whether this tag affects strikethrough color.
strikethrough-set	boolean	Whether this tag affects strikethrough.
style	Pango.Style	Font style as a Pango.Style, e.g. Pango.Style.ITALIC.
style-set	boolean	Whether this tag affects the font style.
tabs	Pango.TabArray	Custom tabs for this text.

(*continued*)

Table A-115. (*continued*)

Property	Type	Description
tabs-set	boolean	Whether this tag affects tabs.
underline	`Pango.TabArray`	Style of underline for this text.
underline-rgba	`Gdk.RGBAy`	Color of underline for this text.
underline-rgba-set	boolean	Whether this tag affects underlining color.
underline-set	boolean	Whether this tag affects underlining.
variant	`Pango.Variant`	Font variant as a Pango.Variant, e.g. `Pango.Variant.SMALL_CAPS`
variant-set	boolean	Whether this tag affects the font variant.
weight	integer	Font weight as an integer, see predefined values in `Pango.Weight`; for example, `Pango.Weight.BOLD`.
weight-set	boolean	Whether this tag affects the font weight.
wrap-mode	`Gtk.WrapMode`	Whether to wrap lines never, at word boundaries, or at character boundaries.
wrap-mode-set	boolean	Whether this tag affects line wrap mode.

Table A-116. *Gtk.TextView Properties*

Property	Type	Description
accepts-tab	bool	Whether Tab results in a tab character being entered.
bottom-margin	integer	Height of the bottom margin in pixels.
buffer	Gtk.TextBuffer	The buffer that is displayed.
cursor-visible	boolean	If the insertion cursor is shown.
editable	boolean	Whether the text can be modified by the user.
im-module	string	Which IM module should be used.
indent	integer	Amount to indent the paragraph, in pixels.
input-hints	Gtk.InputHints	Hints for the text field behavior.
input-purpose	Gtk.InputPurpose	Purpose of the text field.
justification	Gtk.Justification	Left, right, or center justification.
left-margin	integer	Width of the left margin in pixels.
monospace	boolean	Whether to use a monospace font.
overwrite	boolean	Whether entered text overwrites existing contents.
pixels-above-lines	Integer	Pixels of blank space above paragraphs.
pixels-below-lines	integer	Pixels of blank space below paragraphs.
pixels-inside-wrap	integer	Pixels of blank space between wrapped lines in a paragraph.
populate-all	boolean	Whether to emit the "populate-popup" signal for touch pop-ups.
right-margin	integer	Width of the right margin in pixels.
tabs	Pango.TabArray	Custom tabs for this text.
top-margin	integer	Height of the top margin in pixels.
wrap-mode	Gtk.WrapMode	Whether to wrap lines never, at word boundaries, or at character boundaries.

Table A-117. *Gtk.ThemingEngine Properties*

Property	Type	Description
name	string	Theming engine name.

Table A-118. *Gtk.ToggleButton Properties*

Property	Type	Description
active	boolean	If the toggle button should be pressed in.
draw-indicator	boolean	If the toggle part of the button is displayed.
inconsistent	boolean	If the toggle button is in an "in between" state.

Table A-119. *Gtk.ToggleToolButton Properties*

Property	Type	Description
active	boolean	If the toggle button should be pressed in.

Table A-120. *Gtk.ToolButton Properties*

Property	Type	Description
icon-name	string	The name of the themed icon displayed on the item.
icon-widget	Gtk.Widget	Icon widget to display in the item.
label	string	Text to show in the item..
label-widget	Gtk.Widget	Widget to use as the item label.
use-underline	boolean	If set, an underline in the label property indicates that the next character should be used for the mnemonic accelerator key in the overflow menu.

Table A-121. *Gtk.ToolItem Properties*

Property	Type	Description
is-important	boolean	Whether the toolbar item is considered important. When `True`, toolbar buttons show text in `Gtk.ToolbarStyle.BOTH_HORIZ` mode.
visible-horizontal	boolean	Whether the toolbar item is visible when the toolbar is in a horizontal orientation.
visible-vertical	boolean	Whether the toolbar item is visible when the toolbar is in a vertical orientation.

Table A-122. *Gtk.ToolItemGroup Properties*

Property	Type	Description
collapsed	boolean	Whether the group has been collapsed and items are hidden.
ellipsize	`Pango.EllipsizeMode`	Ellipsize for item group headers.
header-relief	`Gtk.ReliefStyle`	Relief of the group header button.
label	string	The human-readable title of this item group.
label-widget	`Gtk.Widget`	A widget to display in place of the usual label.

Table A-123. *Gtk.ToolPalette Properties*

Property	Type	Description
icon-size	`Gtk.IconSize`	Size of icons in this tool palette.
icon-size-set	boolean	Whether the icon-size property has been set.
toolbar-style	`Gtk.ToolbarStyle`	Style of items in the tool palette.

Table A-124. *Gtk.Toolbar Properties*

Property	Type	Description
icon-size	Gtk.IconSize	Size of icons in this toolbar.
icon-size-set	boolean	Whether the icon-size property has been set.
show-arrow	boolean	If an arrow should be shown if the toolbar doesn't fit.
toolbar-style	Gtk.ToolbarStyle	How to draw the toolbar.

Table A-125. *Gtk.TreeModelFilter Properties*

Property	Type	Description
child-model	Gtk.TreeModel	The model for the filtermodel to filter.
virtual-root	Gtk.TreePath	The virtual root (relative to the child model) for this filtermodel.

Table A-126. *Gtk.TreeModelSort Properties*

Property	Type	Description
model	Gtk.TreeModel	The model for the TreeModelSort to sort.

Table A-127. *Gtk.TreeSelection Properties*

Property	Type	Description
mode	Gtk.SelectionMode	Selection mode.

Table A-128. *Gtk.TreeView Properties*

Property	Type	Description
activate-on-single-click	boolean	Activate row on a single click.
enable-grid-lines	Gtk.TreeViewGridLines	Whether grid lines should be drawn in the tree view.
enable-search	boolean	View allows user to search through columns interactively.
enable-tree-lines	boolean	Whether tree lines should be drawn in the tree view.
expander-column	Gtk.TreeViewColumn	Set the column for the expander column.
fixed-height-mode	boolean	Speeds up Gtk.TreeView by assuming that all rows have the same height.
headers-clickable	boolean	Column headers respond to click events.
headers-visible	boolean	Show the column header buttons.
hover-expand	boolean	Whether rows should be expanded/collapsed when the pointer moves over them.
hover-selection	boolean	Whether the selection should follow the pointer.
level-indentation	integer	Extra indentation for each level.
model	Gtk.TreeModel	The model for the tree view.
reorderable	boolean	View is reorderable.
rubber-banding	boolean	Whether to enable selection of multiple items by dragging the mouse pointer.
search-column	integer	Model column to search through during interactive search.
show-expanders	boolean	View has expanders.
tooltip-column	integer	The column in the model containing the tooltip texts for the rows.

Table A-129. *Gtk.TreeViewColumn Properties*

Property	Type	Description
alignment	float	X Alignment of the column header text or widget.
cell-area	Gtk.CellArea	The Gtk.CellArea used to layout cells.
clickable	boolean	Whether the header can be clicked.
expand	boolean	Column gets share of extra width allocated to the widget.
fixed-width	integer	Current fixed width of the column.
max-width	integer	Maximum allowed width of the column.
min-width	integer	Minimum allowed width of the column.
reorderable	boolean	Whether the column can be reordered around the headers.
resizable	boolean	Column is user-resizable.
sizing	Gtk.TreeViewColumnSizing	Resize mode of the column.
sort-column-id	integer	Logical sort column ID this column sorts on when selected for sorting.
sort-indicator	boolean	Whether to show a sort indicator.
sort-order	Gtk.SortType	Sort direction the sort indicator should indicate.
spacing	integer	Space that is inserted between cells.
title	string	Title to appear in column header.
visible	boolean	Whether to display the column.
widget	Gtk.Widget	Widget to put in column header button instead of column title.
width	integer	Current width of the column.
x-offset	integer	Current X position of the column.

Table A-130. *Gtk.VolumeButton Properties*

Property	Type	Description
use-symbolic	boolean	Whether to use symbolic icons.

Table A-131. *Gtk.Widget Properties*

Property	Type	Description
app-paintable	boolean	Whether the application paints directly on the widget.
can-default	boolean	Whether the widget can be the default widget.
can-focus	boolean	Whether the widget can accept the input focus
composite-child	boolean	Whether the widget is part of a composite widget.
events	Gdk.EventMask	The event mask that decides what kind of Gdk. EventMask this widget gets.
expand	boolean	Whether widget wants to expand in both directions.
focus-on-click	boolean	Whether the widget should grab focus when it is clicked with the mouse.
halign	Gtk.Align	How to position in extra horizontal space.
has-default	boolean	Whether the widget is the default widget.
has-focus	boolean	Whether the widget has the input focus.
has-tooltip	boolean	Whether this widget has a tooltip.
height-request	integer	Override for height request of the widget, or −1 if natural request should be used.
hexpand	boolean	Whether widget wants more horizontal space.
hexpand-set	boolean	Whether to use the hexpand property.
is-focus	boolean	Whether the widget is the focus widget within the toplevel.
margin	integer	Pixels of extra space on all four sides.
margin-bottom	integer	Pixels of extra space on the bottom side.
margin-end	integer	Pixels of extra space on the end.

(continued)

Table A-131. *(continued)*

Property	Type	Description
margin-start	integer	Pixels of extra space on the start.
margin-top	integer	Pixels of extra space on the top side.
name	string	The name of the widget.
no-show-all	boolean	Whether `Gtk.Widget.show_all()` should not affect this widget.
opacity	float	The opacity of the widget, from 0 to 1.
parent	`Gtk.Container`	The parent widget of this widget. Must be a Container widget.
receives-default	boolean	If `True`, the widget receive the default action when it is focused.
scale-factor	integer	The scaling factor of the window.
sensitive	boolean	Whether the widget responds to input.
tooltip-markup	string	The contents of the tooltip for this widget.
tooltip-text	string	The contents of the tooltip for this widget.
valign	`Gtk.Align`	How to position in extra vertical space.
vexpand	boolean	Whether widget wants more vertical space.
vexpand-set	boolean	Whether to use the vexpand property.
visible	boolean	Whether the widget is visible.
width-request	integer	Override for width request of the widget, or -1 if natural request should be used.
window	`Gdk.Window`	The widget's window if it is realized.

Table A-132. *Gtk.Window Properties*

Property	Type	Description
accept-focus	boolean	True if the window should receive the input focus.
application	Gtk.Application	The Gtk.Application for the window.
attached-to	Gtk.Widget	The widget where the window is attached.
decorated	boolean	Whether the window should be decorated by the window manager.
default-height	integer	The default height of the window, used when initially showing the window.
default-width	integer	The default width of the window, used when initially showing the window.
deletable	boolean	Whether the window frame should have a close button.
destroy-with-parent	boolean	If this window should be destroyed when the parent is destroyed.
focus-on-map	boolean	True if the window should receive the input focus when mapped.
focus-visible	boolean	Whether focus rectangles are currently visible in this window.
gravity	Gdk.Gravity	The window gravity of the window.
has-toplevel-focus	boolean	If this window's titlebar should be hidden when the window is maximized.
icon	GdkPixbuf.Pixbuf	Icon for this window.
icon-name	string	Name of the themed icon for this window.
is-active	boolean	Whether the toplevel is the current active window.
is-maximized	boolean	Whether the window is maximized.

(continued)

Table A-132. *(continued)*

Property	Type	Description
mnemonics-visible	boolean	Whether mnemonics are currently visible in this window.
modal	boolean	If `True`, the window is modal (other windows are not usable while this one is up).
resizable	boolean	If `True`, users can resize the window.
role	string	Unique identifier for the window to be used when restoring a session.
screen	`Gdk.Screen`	The screen where this window is displayed.
skip-pager-hint	boolean	`True` if the window should not be in the pager.
skip-taskbar-hint	boolean	`True` if the window should not be in the task bar.
startup-id	string	Unique startup identifier for the window used by startup-notification.
title	string	The title of the window.
transient-for	`Gtk.Window`	The transient parent of the dialog.
type	`Gdk.WindowTypeHint`	Hint to help the desktop environment understand what kind of window this is and how to treat it.
urgency-hint	bool	`True` if the window should be brought to the user's attention.
window-position	`Gtk.WindowPosition`	The initial position of the window.

Child Widget Properties

A few containers in GTK+ have properties that are assigned to every child of the container. Table A-133 through Table A-149 describes these properties.

Caution In the GTK+ C API property, names may contain one or more dashes. Since these dashes are interpreted by Python as the subtraction operator, all Python property names substitute underscores for dashes in all property names. For instance, the property name logo-icon-name becomes logo_icon_name in a Python program.

Table A-133. *Gtk.ActionBar Child Properties*

Property	Type	Description
pack-type	Gtk.PackType	A Gtk.PackType indicating whether the child is packed with reference to the start or end of the parent.
position	Integer	The index of the child in the parent.

Table A-134. *Gtk.Assistant Child Properties*

Property	Type	Description
complete	boolean	Whether all required fields on the page have been filled out.
has-padding	boolean	Whether the assistant adds padding around the page.
header-image	GdkPixbuf.Pixbuf	Header image for the assistant page.
page-type	Gtk.AssistantPageType	The type of the assistant page.
sidebar-image	GdkPixbuf.Pixbuf	Sidebar image for the assistant page.
title	string	The title of the assistant page.

Table A-135. *Gtk.Box Child Properties*

Property	Type	Description
expand	boolean	Whether the child should receive extra space when the parent grows.
fill	boolean	Whether extra space given to the child should be allocated to the child or used as padding.
pack-type	Gtk.PackType	A Gtk.PackType indicating whether the child is packed with reference to the start or end of the parent.
padding	integer	Extra space to put between the child and its neighbors, in pixels.
position	integer	The index of the child in the parent.

Table A-136. *Gtk.ButtonBox Child Properties*

Property	Type	Description
non-homogeneous	boolean	If True, the child is not subject to homogeneous sizing.
secondary	boolean	If True, the child appears in a secondary group of children, suitable for, e.g., help buttons.

Table A-137. *Gtk.Fixed Child Properties*

Property	Type	Description
x	integer	X position of child widget.
y	integer	Y position of child widget.

Table A-138. *Gtk.Grid Child Properties*

Property	Type	Description
height	integer	The number of rows that a child spans.
left-attach	integer	The column number to attach the left side of the child to.
top-attach	integer	The row number to attach the top side of a child widget to.
width	integer	The number of columns that a child spans.

Table A-139. *Gtk.HeaderBar Child Properties*

Property	Type	Description
pack-type	Gtk.PackType	A Gtk.PackType indicating whether the child is packed with reference to the start or end of the parent.
position	integer	The index of the child in the parent.

Table A-140. *Gtk.Layout Child Properties*

Property	Type	Description
x	integer	X position of child widget.
y	integer	Y position of child widget.

Table A-141. *Gtk.Menu Child Properties*

Property	Type	Description
bottom-attach	integer	The row number to attach the bottom of the child to.
left-attach	integer	The column number to attach the left side of the child to.
right-attach	integer	The column number to attach the right side of the child to.
top-attach	integer	The row number to attach the top side of a child widget to.

Table A-142. *Gtk.Notebook Child Properties*

Property	Type	Description
detachable	boolean	Whether the tab is detachable.
menu-label	string	The string displayed in the child's menu entry.
position	integer	The index of the child in the parent.
reorderable	boolean	Whether the tab is reorderable by user action.
tab-expand	boolean	Whether to expand the child's tab.
tab-fill	boolean	Whether the child's tab should fill the allocated area.
tab-label	string	The string displayed on the child's tab label.

Table A-143. *Gtk.Overlay Child Properties*

Property	Type	Description
index	integer	The index of the overlay in the parent, −1 for the main child.
pass-through	boolean	Pass through input, does not affect main child.

Table A-144. *Gtk.Paned Child Properties*

Property	Type	Description
resize	boolean	If True, the child expands and shrinks along with the paned widget.
shrink	boolean	If True, the child can be made smaller than its requisition.

Table A-145. *Gtk.PopoverMenu Child Properties*

Property	Type	Description
position	integer	The index of the child in the parent.
submenu	string	The name of the submenu.

Table A-146. *Gtk.Stack Child Properties*

Property	Type	Description
icon-name	string	The icon name of the child page.
name	string	The name of the child page.
needs-attention	boolean	Whether this page needs attention.
position	integer	The index of the child in the parent.
title	string	The title of the child page.

Table A-147. *Gtk.ToolItemGroup Child Properties*

Property	Type	Description
expand	boolean	Whether the item should receive extra space when the group grows.
fill	boolean	Whether the item should fill the available space.
homogeneous	boolean	Whether the item should be the same size as other homogeneous items.
new-row	boolean	Whether the item should start a new row.
position	integer	Position of the item within this group.

Table A-148. *Gtk.ToolPalette Child Properties*

Property	Type	Description
exclusive	boolean	Whether the item group should be the only expanded at a given times.
expand	boolean	Whether the item group should receive extra space when the palette grows.

Table A-149. *Gtk.Toolbar Child Properties*

Property	Type	Description
expand	boolean	Whether the item should receive extra space when the toolbar grows.
homogeneous	boolean	Whether the item should be the same size as other homogeneous items.

APPENDIX B

GTK+ Signals

GTK+ is a system that relies on signals and callback methods/functions. A signal is a notification to your application that the user has performed some action. When a signal is emitted, you can tell GTK+ to run a method/function called a callback method/function.

To connect a signal, you can use the `object.connect()` function, which accepts three parameters. The `signal_name` is a string representing the signal. A list of signal names can be found in the tables throughout this appendix.

```
object.signal(signal_name, handler, data)
```

The second parameter is the name of the callback method/function that is called when the signal is emitted. The form for each callback function is found in the GTK+ API documentation; however, many of the function prototypes have incomplete documentation, so you can find more information about nonstandard parameters in the signal reference tables throughout this appendix.

The last parameter of `object.connect()` allows you to send data of an arbitrary type to the callback method/function.

This appendix provides a complete list of events and signals available to GTK+ objects and widgets. The first section provides information about the GDK event types available to `Gtk.Widget` and derivative classes (see Table B-1). The sections that follow provide a complete list of signal names and a description for every object with signals in GTK+.

© W. David Ashley and Andrew Krause 2019
W. D. Ashley and A. Krause, *Foundations of PyGTK Development*,
https://doi.org/10.1007/978-1-4842-4179-0

Events

Events are a special type of signal that are emitted by the X Window System. Once emitted, they are sent from the window manager to your application to be interpreted by the signal system provided by GLib.

In doing this, you can use the same signal connection and callback function methods as with normal signals. One difference is that event callback functions return a boolean value. If you return True, no further action will happen. If you return the default value of False, GTK+ will continue to handle the event. Table B-1 lists the Gtk.Widget event types.

Table B-1.   *Gtk.Widget Event Types*

Signal Name	Gdk.EventType Value	Description
delete-event	Gdk.EventType.DELETE	The window manager requested that the top-level window be destroyed. This can be used to confirm the deletion of the window.
destroy-event	Gdk.EventType.DESTROY	The widget's Gdk.Window was destroyed. You should not use this signal, because the widget is usually disconnected before it can be emitted.
expose-event	Gdk.EventType.EXPOSE	A new part of the widget was shown and needs to be drawn. This is emitted when the window was previously obscured by another object.
motion-notify-event	Gdk.EventType.MOTION_NO	The IFY mouse cursor has moved while within the proximity of the widget.
button-press-event	Gdk.EventType.BUTTON_PRESS	A mouse button was clicked once. This is emitted along with Gdk.EventType.2BUTTON_PRESS and Gdk.EventType.3BUTTON_PRESS events.
button-press-event	Gdk.EventType.2BUTTON_PRESS	A mouse button was clicked twice. This also emits Gdk.EventType.BUTTON_PRESS, so you need to check the event type in the method/callback function.

(continued)

Table B-1. (*continued*)

Signal Name	Gdk.EventType Value	Description
button-press-event	Gdk.EventType. 3BUTTON_PRESS	A mouse button was clicked twice. This also emits Gdk.EventType.BUTTON_PRESS, so you need to check the event type in the method/callback function.
button-release-event	Gdk.EventType. BUTTON_RELEASE	A previously clicked mouse button was released.
key-press-event	Gdk.EventType. KEY_PRESS	A keyboard key was pressed. You can return True to prevent any text from being entered or actions being taken because of the key press.
key-release-event	Gdk.EventType. KEY_RELEASE	A previously pressed keyboard key was released. This is usually not as useful as "key-press-event".
enter-notify-event	Gdk.EventType. ENTER_NOTIFY	The mouse cursor entered the proximity of the widget.
leave-notify-event	Gdk.EventType. LEAVE_NOTIFY	The mouse cursor exited the proximity of the widget.
focus-in-event	Gdk.EventType. FOCUS_CHANGE	Keyboard focus entered the widget from another widget within the window.
focus-out-event	Gdk.EventType. FOCUS_CHANGE	Keyboard focus left the widget for another widget within the window.
configure-event	Gdk.EventType. CONFIGURE	The size, position, or stacking order of the widget changed. This is normally emitted when a new size is allocated for the widget.
map-event	Gdk.EventType. MAP	The widget was mapped to the display.
unmap-event	Gdk.EventType. UNMAP	The widget was unmapped from the display.
property-notify-event	Gdk.EventType. PROPERTY_NOTIFY	A property of the widget has been changed or deleted. You can use this to track changes to a specific widget property stored by GObject.

(*continued*)

Table B-1. (*continued*)

Signal Name	Gdk.EventType Value	Description
selection-clear-event	Gdk.EventType. SELECTION_CLEAR	The application no longer has ownership of a selection, so it needs to be cleared.
selection-request-event	Gdk.EventType. SELECTION_REQUEST	The selection of the widget was requested by another application.
selection-notify-event	Gdk.EventType. SELECTION_NOTIFY	The owner of a selection responded to a selection conversion request.
proximity-in-event	Gdk.EventType. PROXIMITY_IN	An input device has come in contact with a sensing surface, such as a pen on a touch screen.
proximity-out-event	Gdk.EventType. PROXIMITY_OUT	An input device, such as a pen on a touch screen, has broken off contact with a sensing surface.
event	Gdk.EventType. DRAG_ENTER	The mouse pointer entered the widget while a drag action was in progress.
event	Gdk.EventType. DRAG_LEAVE	The mouse pointer left the widget while a drag action was in progress.
event	Gdk.EventType. DRAG_MOTION	The mouse pointer moved within the widget while a drag action was in progress.
event	Gdk.EventType. DRAG_STATUS	The current status of a drag action was changed.
event	Gdk.EventType. DROP_START	A drop action on the widget began.
event	Gdk.EventType. DROP_FINISHED	A drop action on the widget completed.
client-event	Gdk.EventType. CLIENT_EVENT	An event for the widget was received from another application.
visibility-notify-event	Gdk.EventType. VISIBILITY NOTIFY	The visibility of the widget changed. For example, some portion of it has been covered or uncovered.

(*continued*)

Table B-1. (*continued*)

Signal Name	Gdk.EventType Value	Description
no-expose-event	`Gdk.EventType.` `NO_EXPOSE`	The source region was completely available when parts of a drawable area were copied.
scroll-event	`Gdk.EventType.` `SCROLL`	The widget has been scrolled in one direction or another. This allows you to update the widget's visible area.
window-state-event	`Gdk.EventType.` `WINDOW_STATE`	The state of the widget has changed. If the widget is a top-level window, this can happen when it is minimized, maximized, made sticky, made into an icon, and so forth.
event	`Gdk.EventType.` `SETTING`	A setting was added, removed, or modified for the widget.
event	`Gdk.EventType.` `OWNER_CHANGE`	The owner of the widget has changed. This event was introduced in GTK+ 2.6.
grab-broken-event	`Gdk.EventType.` `GRAB_BROKEN`	The widget was grabbed by the pointer or the keyboard, but it was broken. This can happen when the window becomes invisible or when a user attempts to repeat a grab. This event was introduced in GTK+ 2.8.

Widget Signals

Tables B-2 through B-69 provide a complete list of signals for each class in GTK+ that has signals. In addition to signal names, a description is provided for each item. If the signal does not follow the standard signal prototype, the additional parameters are listed; these additional parameters do not include the user data pointer.

Table B-2. *Gtk.AccelGroup Signals*

Signal Name	Additional Parameters	Description
accel-activate	`GObject.Object` `acceleratable`, integer keyval, `Gdk.ModifierType` modifier	The accel-activate signal is an implementation detail of `Gtk.AccelGroup` and not meant to be used by applications.
accel-changed	`GObject.Object` `acceleratable`,integer keyval, `Gdk.ModifierType` modifier	The accel-changed signal is emitted when an entry is added to or removed from the accel group.

Table B-3. *Gtk.AccelMap Signals*

Signal Name	Additional Parameters	Description
changed	string accel_path, integer accel_key, `Gdk.ModifierType` accel_mods	Notifies about a change in the global accelerator map.

Table B-4. *Gtk.Adjustment Signals*

Signal Name	Additional Parameters	Description
changed	None	Emitted when one or more of the `Gtk.Adjustment` properties have been changed, other than the `Gtk.Adjustment` value property.
value-changed	None	Emitted when the `Gtk.Adjustment` value property has been changed.

Table B-5. *Gtk.AppChooserButton Signals*

Signal Name	Additional Parameters	Description
custom-item-activated	string item_name	Emitted when a custom item, previously added with `Gtk.AppChooserButton.append_custom_` is activated from the drop-down menu.

Table B-6. *Gtk.AppChooserWidget Signals*

Signal Name	Additional Parameters	Description
application-activated	`Gio.AppInfo application`	Emitted when an application item is activated from the widget's list.
application-selected	`Gio.AppInfo application`	Emitted when an application item is selected from the widget's list.
populate-popup	`Gtk.Menu menu, Gio. AppInfo application`	Emitted when a context menu is about to pop up over an application item.

Table B-7. *Gtk.Application Signals*

Signal Name	Additional Parameters	Description
window-added		Emitted when a `Gtk.Window` is added to application through `Gtk.Application.add_window()`.
window-removed	`window`	Emitted when a `Gtk.Window` is removed from application,
		either as a side-effect of being destroyed or explicitly through `Gtk.Application.remove_ window()`.

Table B-8. *Gtk.Assistant Signals*

Signal Name	Additional Parameters	Description
apply	None	The Apply button or the Forward button was clicked any `Gtk.Assistant` page.
cancel	None	The Cancel button was clicked any `Gtk. Assistant` page.
close	None	The Close button or the Apply button was clicked the last page in the `Gtk.Assistant`.
escape	None	
prepare	`Gtk.Widget page`	A new page is about to become visible. This signal was emitted so that you can perform any preparation tasks before it is visible to the user.

Table B-9. *Gtk.Button Signals*

Signal Name	Additional Parameters	Description
activate		The "activate" signal on Gtk.Button is an action signal and emitting it causes the button to animate press then release.
clicked		Emitted when the button has been activated (pressed and released).

Table B-10. *Gtk.Calendar Signals*

Signal Name	Additional Parameters	Description
day-selected	None	Emitted when the user selects a day.
day-selected-double-click	None	Emitted when the user double-clicks a day.
month-changed	None	Emitted when the user clicks a button to change the selected month on a calendar.
next-month	None	Emitted when the user switched to the next month.
next-year	None	Emitted when user switched to the next year.
prev-month	None	Emitted when the user switched to the previous month.
prev-year	None	Emitted when user switched to the previous year.

Table B-11. *Gtk.CellArea Signals*

Signal Name	Additional Parameters	Description
add-editable	`Gtk.CellRenderer renderer,` `Gtk.CellEditable editable,` `Gdk.Rectangle cell_area,` `Gtk.TreePath path`	Indicates that editing has started on renderer and that editable should be added to the owning cell-layouting widget at cell_area.
apply-attributes	`Gtk.TreeModel model, Gtk.` `TreeIter iter,` boolean is_ expander, boolean is_expanded	This signal is emitted whenever applying attributes to area from model.
focus-changed	`Gtk.CellRenderer renderer,` `Gtk.TreePath path`	Indicates that focus changed on this area.
remove-editable	`Gtk.CellRenderer renderer,` `Gtk.CellEditable editable`	Indicates that editing finished on renderer and that editable should be removed from the owning cell-layouting widget.

Table B-12. *Gtk.CellRenderer Signals*

Signal Name	Additional Parameters	Description
editing-canceled	None	This signal is emitted when the user cancels the process of editing a cell.
editing-started	`GtkCellEditable` `editable,` string path	This signal is emitted when a cell starts to be edited.

Table B-13. *Gtk.CellRendererAccel Signals*

Signal Name	Additional Parameters	Description
accel-cleared	string path_string	Emitted when the user has removed the accelerator.
accel-edited	string path_string, integer accel_ key, `Gdk.ModifierType accel_` `mods`, integer hardware_keycode	Emitted when the user has selected a new accelerator.

Table B-14. *Gtk.CellRendererCombo Signals*

Signal Name	Additional Parameters	Description
changed	string path_string, Gtk. TreeIter new_iter	This signal is emitted each time after the user selected an item in the combo box, either by using the mouse or the arrow keys.

Table B-15. *Gtk.CellRendererText Signals*

Signal Name	Additional Parameters	Description
edited	string path_string, string new_text	This signal is emitted after renderer has been edited.

Table B-16. *Gtk.CellRendererToggle Signals*

Signal Name	Additional Parameters	Description
toggled	string path_string	The "toggled" signal is emitted when the cell is toggled.

Table B-17. *Gtk.CheckMenuItem Signals*

Signal Name	Additional Parameters	Description
toggled	None	This signal is emitted when the state of the check box is changed.

Table B-18. *Gtk.Clipboard Signals*

Signal Name	Additional Parameters	Description
owner-change	Gdk.EventOwnerChange event	The "owner-change" signal is emitted when GTK+ receives an event that indicates that the ownership of the selection associated with clipboard has changed.

Table B-19. *Gtk.ColorButton Signals*

Signal Name	Additional Parameters	Description
color-set	None	The "color-set" signal is emitted when the user selects a color.

Table B-20. *Gtk.ColorSelection Signals*

Signal Name	Additional Parameters	Description
color-changed	None	This signal is emitted when the color changes in the Gtk.ColorSelection according to its update policy.

Table B-21. *Gtk.ComboBox Signals*

Signal Name	Additional Parameters	Description
changed	None	The changed signal is emitted when the active item is changed.
format-entry-text	string path	For combo boxes that are created with an entry (See Gtk.ComboBox.has-entry).
move-active	Gtk.ScrollType scroll_type	The "move-active" signal is a keybinding signal that is emitted to move the active selection.
popdown	None	The "popdown" signal is a keybinding signal that is emitted to popdown the combo box list.
popup	None	The "popup" signal is a keybinding signal that is emitted to pop up the combo box list.

Table B-22. *Gtk.Container Signals*

Signal Name	Additional Parameters	Description
add	`Gtk.Widget child`	A child widget was added or packed into the container. This signal is emitted even if you do not explicitly call `object.container_add()` but use the widget's built-in packing functions instead.
check-resize	None	The container checks whether it needs to be resized before adding a child widget.
remove	`Gtk.Widget child`	A child widget was removed from the container.
set-focus-child	`Gtk.Widget child`	A container's child widget gained focus from the window manager.

Table B-23. *Gtk.CssProvider Signals*

Signal Name	Additional Parameters	Description
parsing-error	`Gtk.CssSection section`	Signals that a parsing error occurred.

Table B-24. *Gtk.Dialog Signals*

Signal Name	Additional Parameters	Description
close	None	The "close" signal is a keybinding signal that is emitted when the user uses a keybinding to close the dialog.
response	integer	Emitted when an action widget is clicked, the dialog receives a delete event, or the application programmer calls `Gtk.Dialog.response()`.

Table B-25. *Gtk.Entry Signals*

Signal Name	Additional Parameters	Description
activate	None	The "activate" signal is emitted when the user hits the **Enter** key.
backspace	None	The "backspace" signal is a keybinding signal that is emitted when the user asks for it.
copy-clipboard	None	The "copy-clipboard" signal is a keybinding signal that is emitted to copy the selection to the clipboard.
cut-clipboard	None	The "cut-clipboard" signal is a keybinding signal that is emitted to cut the selection to the clipboard.
delete-from-cursor	Gtk.DeleteType type, integer num_deletions	d C The "icon-press" signal is emitted when an activatable icon is clicked.
icon-press	Gtk.EntryIconPosition pos, Gtk. EntryIconPosition event	The "icon-press" signal is emitted when an activatable icon is clicked.
icon-release	Gtk.EntryIconPosition pos, Gtk. EntryIconPosition event	The "icon-release" signal is emitted on the button release from a mouse click over an activatable icon.
insert-at-cursor	string new_text	The "insert-at-cursor" signal is a keybinding signal that is emitted when the user initiates the insertion of a fixed string at the cursor.

(continued)

Table B-25. (*continued*)

Signal Name	Additional Parameters	Description
insert-emoji	None	The "insert-emoji" signal is a keybinding signal that is emitted to present the Emoji chooser for the entry.
move-cursor	`Gtk.MovementStep step`, integer num_steps, boolean extended	The "move-cursor" signal is a keybinding signal that is emitted when the user initiates a cursor movement.
paste-clipboard	None	The "paste-clipboard" signal is a keybinding signal that is emitted to paste the contents of the clipboard into the text view.
populate-popup	`Gtk.Widget popup`	The "populate-popup" signal is emitted before showing the context menu of the entry.
preedit-changed	string preedit	If an input method is used, the typed text is not immediately be committed to the buffer.
toggle-overwrite	None	The "toggle-overwrite" signal is a keybinding signal that is emitted to toggle the overwrite mode of the entry.

Table B-26. *Gtk.EntryBuffer Signals*

Signal Name	Additional Parameters	Description
deleted_text	integer position, integer n_chars	This signal is emitted after text is deleted from the buffer.
inserted_text	integer position, string chars, integer n_chars	This signal is emitted after text is inserted into the buffer.

Table B-27. *Gtk.EntryCompletion Signals*

Signal Name	Additional Parameters	Description
action_activated	integer index	Emitted when an action is activated.

Table B-28. *Gtk.Expander Signals*

Signal Name	Additional Parameters	Description
activate	None	Emitted when an action is activated.

Table B-29. *Gtk.FileChooserButton Signals*

Signal Name	Additional Parameters	Description
file_set	None	The "file-set" signal is emitted when the user selects a file. Note that this signal is only emitted when the user changes the file.

Table B-30. *Gtk.FileChooserWidget Signals*

Signal Name	Additional Parameters	Description
desktop_folder	None	The "desktop-folder" signal is a keybinding signal that is emitted when the user asks for it. This is used to make the file chooser show the user's Desktop folder in the file list.
down_folder	None	The "down-folder" signal is a keybinding signal that is emitted when the user asks for it.
home_folder	None	The "home-folder" signal is a keybinding signal that is emitted when the user asks for it.
location_popup	string path	The "location-popup" signal is a keybinding signal that is emitted when the user asks for it.
location_popup_on_paste	None	The "location-popup-on-paste" signal is a keybinding signal that is emitted when the user asks for it.
location_toggle_popup	None	The "location-toggle-popup" signal is a keybinding signal that is emitted when the user asks for it.
places_shortcut	None	The "places-shortcut" signal is a keybinding signal that is emitted when the user asks for it.

(continued)

Table B-30. (*continued*)

Signal Name	Additional Parameters	Description
quick_bookmark	integer bookmark_ index	The "quick-bookmark" signal is a keybinding signal that is emitted when the user asks for it.
recent_shortcut	None	The "recent-shortcut" signal is a keybinding signal that is emitted when the user asks for it.
search_shortcut	None	The "search-shortcut" signal is a keybinding signal that is emitted when the user asks for it.
show_hidden	None	The "show-hidden" signal is a keybinding signal that is emitted when the user asks for it.
up_folder	None	The "up-folder" signal is a keybinding signal that is emitted when the user asks for it.

Table B-31. *Gtk.FlowBox Signals*

Signal Name	Additional Parameters	Description
activate_cursor_child	None	The "activate-cursor-child" signal is a keybinding signal that is emitted when the user activates the box.
child_activated	`Gtk.FlowBoxChild child`	The "child-activated" signal is emitted when a child has been activated by the user.
move_cursor	`Gtk.MovementStep step`, integer count	The "move-cursor" signal is a keybinding signal that is emitted when the user initiates a cursor movement.
select_all	None	The "select-all" signal is a keybinding signal that is emitted to select all children of the box, if the selection mode permits it.

(*continued*)

Table B-31. (*continued*)

Signal Name	Additional Parameters	Description
selected_children_changed	None	The "selected-children-changed" signal is emitted when the set of selected children changes.
toggle_cursor_child	None	The "toggle-cursor-child" signal is a keybinding signal that toggles the selection of the child that has the focus.
unselect_all	None	The "unselect-all" signal is a keybinding signal that is emitted to unselect all children of the box, if the selection mode permits it.

Table B-32. *Gtk.FlowBoxChild Signals*

Signal Name	Additional Parameters	Description
activate	None	The "activate" signal is emitted when the user activates a child widget in a Gtk.FlowBox, either by clicking or double-clicking, or by using the Space or Enter key.

Table B-33. *Gtk.FontButton Signals*

Signal Name	Additional Parameters	Description
font_set	None	The "font-set" signal is emitted when the user selects a font. When handling this signal, use Gtk.FontButton.get_font_name() to find out that font was just selected.

Table B-34. *Gtk.GLArea Signals*

Signal Name	Additional Parameters	Description
create_context	Gdk.GLContext context	The "create-context" signal is emitted when the widget is being realized, and allows you to override how the GL context is created. This is useful when you want to reuse an existing GL context, or if you want to try creating different kinds of GL options.
render	None	The "render" signal is emitted every time the contents of the Gtk.GLArea should be redrawn.
resize	integer width, integer height	The "resize" signal is emitted once when the widget is realized, and then each time the widget is changed while realized. This is useful in order to keep GL state up to date with the widget size, like for instance camera properties that may depend on the width/height ratio.

Table B-35. *Gtk.Gesture Signals*

Signal Name	Additional Parameters	Description
begin	Gdk.EventSequence sequence	This signal is emitted when the gesture is recognized. This means the number of touch sequences matches Gtk.Gesture.n-points(), and the Gtk.Gesture.check handler() returned True.
render	Gdk.EventSequence sequence	This signal is emitted whenever a sequence is cancelled. This usually happens on active touches when Gtk.EventController.reset() is called on gesture (manually, due to grabs...), or the individual sequence was claimed by parent widgets' controllers.

(continued)

Table B-35. (*continued*)

Signal Name	Additional Parameters	Description
end	Gdk.EventSequence sequence	This signal is emitted when the gesture is recognized. This means the number of touch sequences matches Gtk.Gesture.n-points(), and the Gtk.Gesture.check handler() returned True.
sequence_state_ changed	Gdk.EventSequence sequence, Gtk. EventSequenceState state	This signal is emitted whenever a sequence state changes.

Table B-36. *Gtk.GestureDrag Signals*

Signal Name	Additional Parameters	Description
drag_begin	Gtk.GestureDrag gesture_ drag, float startx, float starty	This signal is emitted whenever dragging starts.
drag_end	Gtk.GestureDrag gesture_ drag, float startx, float starty	This signal is emitted whenever the dragging is finished.
drag_update	Gtk.GestureDrag gesture_ drag, float startx, float starty	This signal is emitted whenever the dragging point moves.

Table B-37. *Gtk.GestureLongPress Signals*

Signal Name	Additional Parameters	Description
cancelled	None	Gtk.GestureLongPress "pressed" happened.
pressed	float x, float y	This signal is emitted whenever a press goes unmoved/unreleased longer than what the GTK+ defaults tell.

Table B-38. *Gtk.GestureMultiPress Signals*

Signal Name	Additional Parameters	Description
pressed	integer n_press, float x, float y	This signal is emitted whenever a button or touch press happens.

Table B-39. *Gtk.GesturePan Signals*

Signal Name	Additional Parameters	Description
pan	`Gtk.PanDirection direction`, float offset	This signal is emitted once a panning gesture along the expected axis is detected.

Table B-40. *Gtk.GestureRotate Signals*

Signal Name	Additional Parameters	Description
pan	float angle, float angle_delta	This signal is emitted when the angle between both tracked points changes.

Table B-41. *Gtk.GestureSwipe Signals*

Signal Name	Additional Parameters	Description
swipe	float velocity_x, float velocity_y	This signal is emitted when the recognized gesture is finished, velocity and direction are a product of previously recorded events.

Table B-42. *Gtk.GestureZoom Signals*

Signal Name	Additional Parameters	Description
scale_changed	float scale	This signal is emitted whenever the distance between both tracked sequences changes.

Table B-43. *Gtk.IMContext Signals*

Signal Name	Additional Parameters	Description
commit	string str	The "commit" signal is emitted when a complete input sequence has been entered by the user. This can be a single character immediately after a key press or the final result of pre-editing.
delete_surrounding	integer offset, integer n_chars	The "delete-surrounding" signal is emitted when the input method needs to delete all or part of the context surrounding the cursor.
preedit_changed	None	The "preedit-changed" signal is emitted whenever the preedit sequence currently being entered has changed. It is also emitted at the end of a preedit sequence, in that case Gtk.IMContext.get_preedit_string() returns the empty string.
preedit_end	None	The "preedit-end" signal is emitted when a pre-editing sequence has been completed or canceled.
retrieve_surrounding	None	The "retrieve-surrounding" signal is emitted when the input method requires the context surrounding the cursor. The callback should set the input method surrounding context by calling the Gtk.IMContext.set_surrounding() method.

Table B-44. *Gtk.IconTheme Signals*

Signal Name	Additional Parameters	Description
changed	None	Emitted when the current icon theme is switched or GTK + detects that a change has occurred in the contents of the current icon theme.

Table B-45. *Gtk.IconView Signals*

Signal Name	Additional Parameters	Description
activate_cursor_item	None	A keybinding signal that is emitted when the user activates the currently focused item.
item_activated	Gtk.TreePath path	The "item-activated" signal is emitted when the method Gtk.IconView.item_activated() is called, when the user double clicks an item with the "activate-on-single-click" property set to False, or when the user single clicks an item when the "activate-on-single-click" property set to True. It is also emitted when a non-editable item is selected and one of the keys: Space, Return or Enter is pressed.
move_cursor	Gtk.MovementStep step, integer count	The "move-cursor" signal is a keybinding signal that is emitted when the user initiates a cursor movement.
select_all	None	A keybinding signal that is emitted when the user selects all items.
select_cursor_item	None	A keybinding signal that is emitted when the user selects the item that is currently focused.
selection_changed	None	The "selection-changed" signal is emitted when the selection (i.e. the set of selected items) changes.
toggle_cursor_item	None	A keybinding signal that is emitted when the user toggles whether the currently focused item is selected or not. The exact effect of this depend on the selection mode.
unselect_all	None	A keybinding signal that is emitted when the user unselects all items.

Table B-46. *Gtk.InfoBar Signals*

Signal Name	Additional Parameters	Description
close	None	The "close" signal is a keybinding signal that is emitted when the user uses a keybinding to dismiss the info bar.
response	integer response_id	Emitted when an action widget is clicked or the application programmer calls `Gtk.Dialog.response()`. The `response_id` depends on that action widget was clicked.

Table B-47. *Gtk.Label Signals*

Signal Name	Additional Parameters	Description
activate_current_link	None	A keybinding signal that is emitted when the user activates a link in the label.
activate_link	string uri	The signal that is emitted to activate a URI. Applications may connect to it to override the default behavior, which is to call `Gtk.show_uri_on_window()`
copy_clipboard	None	The "copy-clipboard" signal is a keybinding signal that is emitted to copy the selection to the clipboard.
move_cursor	`Gtk.MovementStep step,` integer count, boolean extend_selection	The "move-cursor" signal is a keybinding signal that is emitted when the user initiates a cursor movement. If the cursor is not visible in entry, this signal causes the viewport to be moved instead.
populate_popup	`Gtk.Menu menu`	The "populate-popup" signal is emitted before showing the context menu of the label. Note that only selectable labels have context menus.

Table B-48. *Gtk.LevelBar Signals*

Signal Name	Additional Parameters	Description
offset_changed	string name	Emitted when an offset specified on the bar changes value as an effect to `Gtk.LevelBar.add_offset_value()` being called.

Table B-49. *Gtk.LinkButton Signals*

Signal Name	Additional Parameters	Description
activate_link	None	The "activate-link" signal is emitted each time the `Gtk.LinkButton` has been clicked.

Table B-50. *Gtk.ListBox Signals*

Signal Name	Additional Parameters	Description
activate_cursor_row	None	
move_cursor	`Gtk.MovementStep object`, integer p0	
row_activated	`Gtk.ListBoxRow row`	The "row-activated" signal is emitted when a row has been activated by the user.
row_selected	`Gtk.ListBoxRow row`	The "row-selected" signal is emitted when a new row is selected, or (with a None row) when the selection is cleared.
select_all	None	The "select-all" signal is a keybinding signal that is emitted to select all children of the box, if the selection mode permits it.
selected_rows_changed	None	The "selected-rows-changed" signal is emitted when the set of selected rows changes.
toggle_cursor_row	None	
unselect_all	None	The "unselect-all" signal is a keybinding signal that is emitted to unselect all children of the box, if the selection mode permits it.

Table B-51. *Gtk.ListBoxRow Signals*

Signal Name	Additional Parameters	Description
activate	None	If you want to be notified when the user activates a row (by key or not), use the `Gtk.ListBox` "row-activated" signal on the row's parent `Gtk.ListBox`.

Table B-52. *Gtk.Menu Signals*

Signal Name	Additional Parameters	Description
move_scroll	`Gtk.ScrollType scroll_type`	
popped_up	object flipped_rect, object final_rect, boolean flipped_x, boolean flipped_y	Emitted when the position of menu is finalized after being popped up using `Gtk.Menu.popup_at_rect()`, `Gtk.Menu.popup_at_widget()`, or `Gtk.Menu.popup_at_pointer()`.

Table B-53. *Gtk.MenuItem Signals*

Signal Name	Additional Parameters	Description
move_scroll	`Gtk.ScrollType scroll_type`	The user scrolled the menu with one of the `Gtk.ScrollType` values.
activate	None	Emitted when the item is activated.
activate_item	None	Emitted when the item is activated, but also if the menu item has a submenu. For normal applications, the relevant signal is `Gtk.MenuItem` "activate".
deselect	None	
select	None	
toggle_size_allocate	integer object	The menu item was allocated with a new size.
toggle_size_request	integer object	The menu item requested a new size.

Table B-54. *Gtk.MenuShell Signals*

Signal Name	Additional Parameters	Description
activate_current	boolean force_hide	An action signal that activates the current menu item within the menu shell.
cancel	None	An action signal that cancels the selection within the menu shell. Causes the Gtk.MenuShell "selection- done" signal to be emitted.
cycle_focus	Gtk.DirectionType direction	A keybinding signal that moves the focus in the given direction.
deactivate	None	This signal is emitted when a menu shell is deactivated.
insert	Gtk.Widget child, integer position	The "insert" signal is emitted when a new Gtk. MenuItem is added to a Gtk.MenuShell. A separate signal is used instead of Gtk. Container "add" because of the need for an additional position parameter.
move_current	Gtk. MenuDirectionType direction	A keybinding signal that moves the current menu item in the direction specified by direction.
move_selected	integer distance	The "move-selected" signal is emitted to move the selection to another item.
selection_done	None	This signal is emitted when a selection has been completed within a menu shell.

Table B-55. *Gtk.MenuToolButton Signals*

Signal Name	Additional Parameters	Description
show_menu	None	The "show-menu" signal is emitted before the menu is shown.

Table B-56. *Gtk.NativeDialog Signals*

Signal Name	Additional Parameters	Description
response	integer	Emitted when the user responds to the dialog.

Table B-57. *Gtk.Notebook Signals*

Signal Name	Additional Parameters	Description
change_current_page	integer	The page currently shown by Gtk.Notebook was changed.
create_window	Gtk.Widget page, integer x, integer y	The "create-window" signal is emitted when a detachable tab is dropped on the root window.
focus_tab	Gtk.NotebookTab	The focus was moved by
move_focus_out	Gtk.DirectionType object	The focus was moved out of the Gtk.NotebookTab widget in the given direction.
page_added	Gtk.Widget child, integer page_num	the "page-added" signal is emitted in the notebook right after a page is added to the notebook.
page_removed	Gtk.Widget child, integer page_num	The "page-removed" signal is emitted in the notebook right after a page is removed from the notebook.
page_reordered	Gtk.Widget child, integer page_num	The "page-reordered" signal is emitted in the notebook right after a page has been reordered.
reorder_tab	Gtk.DirectionType direction, boolean p0	
select_page	boolean	A new page was selected for
switch_page	Gtk.Widget child, integer page_num	Emitted when the user or a function changes the current page.

Table B-58. *Gtk.Overlay Signals*

Signal Name	Additional Parameters	Description
get_child_position	Gtk.Widget widget	The "get-child-position" signal is emitted to determine the position and size of any overlay child widgets. A handler for this signal should fill allocation with the desired position and size for widget, relative to the 'main' child of overlay.

Table B-59. *Gtk.Paned Signals*

Signal Name	Additional Parameters	Description
accept_position	None	The "accept-position" signal is a keybinding signal that is emitted to accept the current position of the handle when moving it using key bindings.
cancel_position	None	The "cancel-position" signal is a keybinding signal that is emitted to cancel moving the position of the handle using key bindings. The position of the handle is reset to the value prior to moving it.
cycle_child_focus	boolean reversed	The "cycle-child-focus" signal is a keybinding signal that is emitted to cycle the focus between the children of the paned.
cycle_handle_focus	boolean reversed	The "cycle-handle-focus" signal is a keybinding signal that is emitted to cycle whether the paned should grab focus to allow the user to change position of the handle by using key bindings.
move_handle	Gtk.ScrollType scroll_type	The "move-handle" signal is a keybinding signal that is emitted to move the handle when the user is using key bindings to move it.
toggle_handle_focus	None	The "toggle-handle-focus" is a keybinding signal that is emitted to accept the current position of the handle and then move focus to the next widget in the focus chain.

Table B-60. *Gtk.PlacesSidebar Signals*

Signal Name	Additional Parameters	Description
drag_action_ask	integer action	The places sidebar emits this signal when it needs to ask the application to pop up a menu to ask the user for that drag action to perform.
drag_action_ requested	`Gdk.DragContext, Gio.File dest_file, Gio.File src_file_list`	When the user starts a drag-and-drop operation and the sidebar needs to ask the application for that drag action to perform, then the sidebar emits this signal.
drag_perform_drop	`Gio.File dest_file, Gio.File src_file_ list`, integer action	The places sidebar emits this signal when the user completes a drag-and-drop operation and one of the sidebar's items is the destination. This item is in the `dest_ file`, and the `source_file_list` has the list of files that are dropped into it and that should be copied/moved/etc. based on the specified action.
mount	`Gio.MountOperation mount_operation`	The places sidebar emits this signal when it starts a new operation because the user clicked some location that needs mounting. In this way the application using the `Gtk. PlacesSidebar` can track the progress of the operation and, for example, show a notification.
open_location	`Gio.File location, Gtk.PlacesOpenFlags open_flags`	The places sidebar emits this signal when the user selects a location in it. The calling application should display the contents of that location; for example, a file manager should show a list of files in the specified location.

(continued)

Table B-60. (*continued*)

Signal Name	Additional Parameters	Description
populate_popup	`Gtk.Widget container, Gio.File selected_ item, Gio.Volume selected volume`	The places sidebar emits this signal when the user invokes a contextual pop-up on one of its items. In the signal handler, the application may add extra items to the menu as appropriate. For example, a file manager may want to add a "Properties" command to the menu.
show_connect_to_ server	None	The places sidebar emits this signal when it needs the calling application to present a way to connect directly to a network server. For example, the application may bring up a dialog box asking for a URL like "sftp:// ftp.example.com". It is up to the application to create the corresponding mount by using, for example, `Gio.File.mount_enclosing _volume()`.
show_enter_location	None	The places sidebar emits this signal when it needs the calling application to present a way to directly enter a location. For example, the application may bring up a dialog box asking for a URL like "`http://http. example.com`".
show_error_message	string primary, string secondary	The places sidebar emits this signal when it needs the calling application to present an error message. Most of these messages refer to mounting or unmounting media, for example, when a drive cannot be started for some reason.

(*continued*)

Table B-60. (*continued*)

Signal Name	Additional Parameters	Description
show_other_ locations_with_flags	Gtk.PlacesOpenFlags open_flags	The places sidebar emits this signal when it needs the calling application to present a way to show other locations e.g. drives and network access points. For example, the application may bring up a page showing persistent volumes and discovered network addresses.
show_starred_ location	Gtk.PlacesOpenFlags object_flags	The places sidebar emits this signal when it needs the calling application to present a way to show the starred files. In GNOME, starred files are implemented by setting the nao:predefined-tag-favorite tag in the tracker database.
unmount	Gio.MountOperation mount_operation	The places sidebar emits this signal when it starts a new operation because the user for example ejected some drive or unmounted a mount. In this way the application using the Gtk.PlacesSidebar a track the progress of the operation and, for example, show a notification.

Table B-61. *Gtk.Plug Signals*

Signal Name	Additional Parameters	Description
plug	None	Emitted when the plug becomes embedded in a socket.

Table B-62. *Gtk.Popover Signals*

Signal Name	Additional Parameters	Description
closed	None	

Table B-63. *Gtk.PrintOperation Signals*

Signal Name	Additional Parameters	Description
begin_print	`Gtk.PrintContext context`	Emitted after the user has finished changing print settings in the dialog, before the actual rendering starts.
create_custom_widget	None	Emitted when displaying the print dialog. If you return a widget in a handler for this signal it is added to a custom tab in the print dialog. You typically return a container widget with multiple widgets in it.
custom_widget_apply	`Gtk.Widget widget`	Emitted right before Gtk. PrintOperation "begin-print" if you added a custom widget in the Gtk. PrintOperation "create-custom-widget" handler. When you get this signal you should read the information from the custom widgets, as the widgets are not guaranteed to be around at a later time.
done	`Gtk. PrintOperationResult result`	Emitted when the print operation run has finished doing everything required for printing.

(*continued*)

Table B-63. (*continued*)

Signal Name	Additional Parameters	Description
draw_page	`Gtk.PrintContext` `context`, integer page_nr	Emitted for every page that is printed. The signal handler must render the page_nr's page onto the Cairo context obtained from context using `Gtk.PrintContext.get_` `cairo_context(`
end_print	`Gtk.PrintContext` `context`	Emitted after all pages have been rendered. A handler for this signal can clean up any resources that have been allocated in the `Gtk.PrintOperation` "begin-print" handler.
paginate	`Gtk.PrintContext` `context`	Emitted after the `Gtk.PrintOperation` "begin-print" signal, but before the actual rendering starts. It keeps getting emitted until a connected signal handler returns `True`.
preview	`preview, Gtk.` `PrintContext` `context, Gtk.Window` `parent`	`Gtk.PrintOperationPreview` is emitted when a preview is requested from the native dialog.
request_page_setup	`Gtk.PrintContext` `context`, integer pagre_ nr, `Gtk.PageSetup` `setup`	Emltted once for every page that is printed, to give the application a chance to modify the page setup. Any changes done to setup are enforced only for printing this page.
status_changed	None	Emitted at between the various phases of the print operation. See `Gtk.PrintStatus` for the phases that are being discriminated. Use `Gtk.PrintOperation.get_` `status()` to find out the current status.
update_custom_widget	`Gtk.Widget widget,` `Gtk.PageSetup setup,` `Gtk.PrintSettings` `settings`	Emitted after change of selected printer. The actual page setup and print settings are passed to the custom widget, which can actualize itself according to this change.

Table B-64. *Gtk.RadioButton Signals*

Signal Name	Additional Parameters	Description
group_changed	None	Emitted when the group of radio buttons that a radio button belongs to changes. This is emitted when a radio button switches from being alone to being part of a group of 2 or more buttons, or vice-versa, and when a button is moved from one group of 2 or more buttons to a different one, but not when the composition of the group that a button belongs to changes.

Table B-65. *Gtk.RadioMenuItem Signals*

Signal Name	Additional Parameters	Description
group_changed	None	The radio button switched to a new group, or it was removed from a radio group altogether.

Table B-66. *Gtk.Range Signals*

Signal Name	Additional Parameters	Description
adjust_bounds	float value	Emitted before clamping a value, to give the application a chance to adjust the bounds.
change_values	`Gtk.ScrollType scroll_type`, float value	The `Gtk.Range` "change-value" signal is emitted when a scroll action is performed on a range. It allows an application to determine the type of scroll event that occurred and the resultant new value. The application can handle the event itself and return `True` to prevent further processing. Or, by returning `False`, it can pass the event to other handlers until the default GTK+ handler is reached.
move_slider	`Gtk.ScrollType step`	Virtual function that moves the slider. Used for keybindings.
value_changed	None	Emitted when the range value changes.

Table B-67. *Gtk.RecentManager Signals*

Signal Name	Additional Parameters	Description
changed	None	Emitted when the current recently used resources manager changes its contents, either by calling Gtk.RecentManager. add_item() or by another application.

Table B-68. *Gtk.Scale Signals*

Signal Name	Additional Parameters	Description
format_value	float value	Signal that allows you to change how the scale value is displayed. Connect a signal handler that returns an allocated string representing value. That string is then used to display the scale's value.

Table B-69. *Gtk.ScaleButton Signals*

Signal Name	Additional Parameters	Description
popdown	None	The "popdown" signal is a keybinding signal that is emitted to popdown the scale widget.
popup	None	The "popup" signal is a keybinding signal that is emitted to pop up the scale widget.
value_changed	float value	The "value-changed" signal is emitted when the value field has changed.

Table B-70. *Gtk.ScrolledWindow Signals*

Signal Name	Additional Parameters	Description
edge_overshot	Gtk.PositionType pos	The "edge-overshot" signal is emitted whenever user initiated scrolling makes the scrolled window firmly surpass (i.e., with some edge resistance) the lower or upper limits defined by the adjustment in that orientation.
edge_reached	Gtk.PositionType pos	The "edge-reached" signal is emitted whenever user-initiated scrolling makes the scrolled window exactly reaches the lower or upper limits defined by the adjustment in that orientation.
move_focus_out	Gtk.ScrollType scroll, boolean horizontal	The "move-focus-out" signal is a keybinding signal that is emitted when focus is moved away from the scrolled window by a keybinding. The Gtk.Widget "move-focus" signal is emitted with direction_type on this scrolled windows toplevel parent in the container hierarchy. The default bindings for this signal are and .
scroll_child	Gtk.DirectionType direction_type	The "scroll-child" signal is a keybinding signal that is emitted when a keybinding that scrolls is pressed. The horizontal or vertical adjustment is updated that triggers a signal that the scrolled windows child may listen to and scroll itself.

Table B-71. *Gtk.SearchEntry Signals*

Signal Name	Additional Parameters	Description
next_match	None	The "next-match" signal is a keybinding signal that is emitted when the user initiates a move to the next match for the current search string.
previous_match	None	The "previous-match" signal is a keybinding signal that is emitted when the user initiates a move to the previous match for the current search string.
search_changed	None	The Gtk.SearchEntry "search-changed" signal is emitted with a short delay of 150 milliseconds after the last change to the entry text.
stop_search	None	The "stop-search" signal is a keybinding signal that is emitted when the user stops a search via keyboard input.

Table B-72. *Gtk.ShortcutsWindow Signals*

Signal Name	Additional Parameters	Description
close	integer object	The "close" signal is a keybinding signal that is emitted when the user uses a keybinding to close the window.

Table B-73. *Gtk.Socket Signals*

Signal Name	Additional Parameters	Description
plug_added	None	This signal is emitted when a client is successfully added to the socket.
plug_removed	None	This signal is emitted when a client is removed from the socket. The default action is to destroy the Gtk.Socket widget, so if you want to reuse it you must add a signal handler that returns True.

Table B-74. *Gtk.SpinButton Signals*

Signal Name	Additional Parameters	Description
change_value	`Gtk.ScrollType scroll`	The "change-value" signal is a keybinding signal that is emitted when the user initiates a value change.
input	None	The "input" signal can be used to influence the conversion of the users input into a double value. The signal handler is expected to use `Gtk.Entry.get_text()` to retrieve the text of the entry and set new_value to the new value.
output	None	The "output" signal can be used to change to formatting of the value that is displayed in the spin buttons entry.
value_changed	None	The "value-changed" signal is emitted when the value represented by spinbutton changes. Also see the `Gtk.SpinButton` "output" signal.
wrapped	None	The "wrapped" signal is emitted right after the spinbutton wraps from its maximum to minimum value or vice-versa.

Table B-75. *Gtk.Statusbar Signals*

Signal Name	Additional Parameters	Description
text_popped	integer context_id, string text	Emitted whenever a new message is popped off a status bar's stack.
text_pushed	integer context_id, string text	Emitted whenever a new message is pushed onto a status bar's stack.

Table B-76. Gtk.StyleContext Signals

Signal Name	Additional Parameters	Description
changed	None	The "changed" signal is emitted when there is a change in the Gtk.StyleContext.

Table B-77. Gtk.Switch Signals

Signal Name	Additional Parameters	Description
activate	None	The "activate" signal on Gtk.Switch is an action signal and emitting it causes the switch to animate. Applications should never connect to this signal, but use the "notify_active" signal.
state_set	boolean state	The "state-set" signal on Gtk.Switch is emitted to change the underlying state. It is emitted when the user changes the switch position. The default handler keeps the state in sync with the Gtk.Switch active property.

Table B-78. Gtk.TextBuffer Signals

Signal Name	Additional Parameters	Description
apply_tag	Gtk.TextTag tag, Gtk.TextIter start, Gtk.TextIter end	The "apply-tag" signal is emitted to apply a tag to a range of text in a Gtk.TextBuffer. Applying actually occurs in the default handler.
begin_user_action	None	The "begin-user-action" signal is emitted at the beginning of a single user-visible operation on a Gtk.TextBuffer.
changed	None	The "changed" signal is emitted when the content of a Gtk.TextBuffer has changed.
end_user_action	None	The "end-user-action" signal is emitted at the end of a single user-visible operation on the Gtk.TextBuffer.

(*continued*)

Table B-78. (*continued*)

Signal Name	Additional Parameters	Description
insert_child_anchor	`Gtk.TextIter location,` `Gtk.TextChildAnchor` `anchor`	The "insert-child-anchor" signal is emitted to insert a `Gtk.TextChildAnchor` in a `Gtk.TextBuffer`. Insertion actually occurs in the default handler.
insert_pixbuf	`Gtk.TextIter location,` `GdkPixbuf.Pixbuf` `pixbuf`	The "insert-pixbuf" signal is emitted to insert a `GdkPixbuf.Pixbuf` in a `Gtk.TextBuffer`. Insertion actually occurs in the default handler.
insert_text	`Gtk.TextIter location,` string test, integer len	The "insert-text" signal is emitted to insert text in a `Gtk.TextBuffer`. Insertion actually occurs in the default handler.
mark_deleted	`Gtk.TextMark mark`	The "mark-deleted" signal is emitted as notification after a `Gtk.TextMark` is deleted.
mark_set	`Gtk.TextIter location,` `Gtk.TextMark mark`	The "mark-set" signal is emitted as notification after a `Gtk.TextMark` is set.
modified_changed	None	The "modified-changed" signal is emitted when the modified bit of a `Gtk.TextBuffer` flips.
paste_done	`Gtk.Clipboard` `clipboard`	The "paste-done" signal is emitted after paste operation has been completed. This is useful to properly scroll the view to the end of the pasted text. See `Gtk.TextBuffer.paste_clipboard()` for more details.
remove_tag	`Gtk.TextTag tag, Gtk.` `TextIter start, Gtk.` `TextIter end`	The "remove-tag" signal is emitted to remove all occurrences of tag from a range of text in a `Gtk.TextBuffer`. Removal actually occurs in the default handler.

Table B-79. *Gtk.TextTag Signals*

Signal Name	Additional Parameters	Description
event	`GObject.Object object, Gdk.Event event, Gtk. TextIter iter`	The "event" signal is emitted when an event occurs on a region of the buffer marked with this tag.

Table B-80. *Gtk.TextTagTable Signals*

Signal Name	Additional Parameters	Description
tag_added	`Gtk.TextTag tag`	A `GtkTextTag` object was added to the tag table.
tag_changed	`Gtk.TextTag tag`, boolean size_changed	A property of a tag contained by the tag table was changed. The size of the displayed text can be changed by other properties besides the size, such as weight and font family.
tag_removed	`Gtk.TextTag tag`	A `Gtk.TextTag` object was removed from the tag table.

Table B-81. *Gtk.TextView Signals*

Signal Name	Additional Parameters	Description
backspace	None	The "backspace" signal is a keybinding signal that is emitted when the user asks for it.
copy_clipboard	None	The "copy-clipboard" signal is a keybinding signal that is emitted to copy the selection to the clipboard.
cut_clipboard	None	The "cut-clipboard" signal is a keybinding signal that is emitted to cut the selection to the clipboard.
delete_from_cursor	`Gtk.DeleteType type`, integer count	Text was deleted from around cursor.

(continued)

Table B-81. (*continued*)

Signal Name	Additional Parameters	Description
extend_selection	`granularity, Gtk.TextIter location, Gtk.TextIter start, Gtk.TextIter end`	`Gtk.TextExtendSelection` The "extend-selection" signal is emitted when the selection needs to be extended at location.
insert_at_cursor	`string string`	The "insert-at-cursor" signal is a keybinding signal that is emitted when the user initiates the insertion of a fixed string at the cursor.
insert_emoji	None	The "insert-emoji" signal is a keybinding signal that is emitted to present the Emoji chooser for the text view.
move_cursor	`Gtk.MovementStep step`, integer count, boolean extended_ selection	The "move-cursor" signal is a keybinding signal that is emitted when the user initiates a cursor movement. If the cursor Is not visible in text view, this signal causes the viewport to be moved instead.
move_viewport	`Gtk.ScrollStep step`, integer count	The "move-viewport" signal is a keybinding signal that can be bound to key combinations to allow the user to move the viewport, i.e. change what part of the text view is visible in a containing scrolled window.
paste_clipboard	None	The "paste-clipboard" signal is a keybinding signal that is emitted to paste the contents of the clipboard into the text view.
populate_popup	`Gtk.Widget popup`	The "populate-popup" signal is emitted before showing the context menu of the text view.
preedit_changed	`string preedit`	If an input method is used, the typed text is not immediately committed to the buffer. So if you are interested in the text, connect to this signal.

(*continued*)

Table B-81. (*continued*)

Signal Name	Additional Parameters	Description
select_all	boolean select	The "select-all" signal is a keybinding signal that is emitted to select or unselect the complete contents of the text view.
set_anchor	None	The "set-anchor" signal is a keybinding signal that is emitted when the user initiates setting the "anchor" mark. The "anchor" mark is placed at the same position as the "insert" mark.
toggle_cursor_ visible	None	The "toggle-cursor-visible" signal is a keybinding signal that is emitted to toggle the Gtk. TextView cursor-visible property.
toggle_overwrite	None	The "toggle-overwrite" signal is a keybinding signal that is emitted to toggle the overwrite mode of the text view.

Table B-82. *Gtk.ToggleButton Signals*

Signal Name	Additional Parameters	Description
toggled	None	Should be connected if you wish to perform an action whenever the Gtk. ToggleButton's state is changed.

Table B-83. *Gtk.ToggleToolButton Signals*

Signal Name	Additional Parameters	Description
toggled	None	Emitted whenever the toggle tool button changes state.

Table B-84. *Gtk.ToolButton Signals*

Signal Name	Additional Parameters	Description
clicked	None	This signal is emitted when the tool button is clicked with the mouse or activated with the keyboard.

Table B-85. *Gtk.ToolItem Signals*

Signal Name	Additional Parameters	Description
create_menu_proxy	None	This signal is emitted when the toolbar needs information from tool item about whether the item should appear in the toolbar overflow menu.
toolbar_reconfigured	None	This signal is emitted when some property of the toolbar that the item is a child of changes.

Table B-86. *Gtk.Toolbar Signals*

Signal Name	Additional Parameters	Description
focus_home_or_end	boolean focus_home	A keybinding signal used internally by GTK+. This signal can't be used in application code.
orientation_changed	`Gtk.Orientation orientation_changed`	Emitted when the orientation of the toolbar changes.
popup_context_menu	`Gtk.Orientation orientation`	Emitted when the user right-clicks the toolbar or uses the keybinding to display a pop-up menu.
style_changed	`Gtk.ToolbarStyle style`	Emitted when the style of the toolbar changes.

Table B-87. *Gtk.TreeSelection Signals*

Signal Name	Additional Parameters	Description
changed	None	Emitted whenever the selection has (possibly) changed. Please note that this signal is mostly a hint.

Table B-88. *Gtk.TreeView Signals*

Signal Name	Additional Parameters	Description
columns_changed	None	The number of columns of the treeview has changed.
cursor_changed	None	The position of the cursor (focused cell) has changed.
expand_collapse_ cursor_row	boolean object, boolean p0, boolean p1	A row located at the cursor position needs to expanded or collapsed.
move_cursor	Gtk.MovementStep step, integer direction	The Gtk.TreeView "move-cursor" signal is a keybinding signal that is emitted when the user presses one of the cursor keys.
row_activated	Gtk.TreePath path, Gtk.TreeViewColumn column	The "row-activated" signal is emitted when the method Gtk.TreeView.row_activated() is called, when the user double clicks a treeview row with the "activate-on-single-click" property set to False, or when the user single clicks a row when the "activate-on-single-click" property set to True.
row_collapsed	Gtk.TreeIter iter, Gtk.TreePath path	The given row has been collapsed (child nodes are hidden).
row_expanded	Gtk.TreeIter iter, Gtk.TreePath path	The given row has been expanded (child nodes are shown).

(continued)

Table B-88. (*continued*)

Signal Name	Additional Parameters	Description
select_all	None	All of the rows within the tree view were selected. This can be done by pressing Ctrl+A or Ctrl +.
select_cursor_ parent	None	The user pressed the **Backspace** key while the row had cursor focus.
select_cursor_ row	boolean object	A noneditable row was selected by pressing one of the following key bindings: space bar, Shift +space bar, Return, or Enter.
start_interactive_ search	None	The user pressed **Crtl+F** while the tree view had focus.
test_collapse_ row	Gtk.TreeIter iter, Gtk.TreePath path	The given row is about to be collapsed (hide its children nodes). Use this signal if you need to control the collapsibility of individual rows.
test_expand_ row	Gtk.TreeIter iter, Gtk.TreePath path	The given row is about to be expanded (show its children nodes). Use this signal if you need to control the expandability of individual rows.
toggle_cursor_ row	None	The user pressed Ctrl+spacebar while a row had focus.
unselect_all	None	All of the rows in a tree view were deselected by pressing Shift +Ctrl+A or Shift+Ctrl+/.

Table B-89. *Gtk.TreeViewColumn Signals*

Signal Name	Additional Parameters	Description
clicked	None	The user pressed the tree view column's header button. This usually causes the tree view's rows to be sorted according to that column in views that support sorting.

Table B-90. *Gtk.Widget Signals*

Signal Name	Additional Parameters	Description
accel_closures_changed	None	
button_press_event	`Gdk.EventButton event`	The "button-press-event" signal is emitted when a button (typically from a mouse) is pressed.
button_release_event	`Gdk.EventButton event`	The "button-release-event" signal is emitted when a button (typically from a mouse) is released.
can_activate_accel	integer signal_id	Determines whether an accelerator that activates the signal identified by signal_id can currently be activated.
child_notify	`GObject.ParamSpec child_property`	The "child-notify" signal is emitted for each 'child property [child-properties]' that has changed on an object. The signal's detail holds the property name.
configure_event	`Gdk.EventConfigure event`	The "configure-event" signal is emitted when the size, position or stacking of the widget's window has changed.
damage_event	`Gdk.EventExpose event`	Emitted when a redirected window belonging to widget is drawn into. The region/area members of the event shows what area of the redirected drawable was drawn into.
delete_event	`Gdk.Event event`	The "delete-event" signal is emitted if a user requests that a toplevel window is closed.

(continued)

Table B-90. (*continued*)

Signal Name	Additional Parameters	Description
destroy	None	Signals that all holders of a reference to the widget should release the reference that they hold. May result in finalization of the widget if all references are released.
destroy_event	`Gdk.Event event`	The "destroy-event" signal is emitted when a `Gdk.Window` is destroyed. You rarely get this signal, because most widgets disconnect themselves from their window before they destroy it, so no widget owns the window at destroy time.
direction_changed	`Gtk.TextDirection previous_direction`	The "direction-changed" signal is emitted when the text direction of a widget changes.
drag_begin	`Gdk.DragContext context`	The "drag-begin" signal is emitted on the drag source when a drag is started. A typical reason to connect to this signal is to set up a custom drag icon with e.g. `Gtk.Widget.drag_source_set_icon_pix`
drag_data_delete	`Gdk.DragContext context`	The "drag-data-delete" signal is emitted on the drag source when a drag with the action `Gdk.DragAction.MOVE` is successfully completed.

(continued)

Table B-90. (*continued*)

Signal Name	Additional Parameters	Description
drag_data_get	`Gdk.DragContext context,` `Gtk.SelectionData data,` integer info, integer time	The "drag-data-get" signal is emitted on the drag source when the drop site requests the data that is dragged.
drag_data_received	`Gdk.DragContext context,` integer x, integer y, `Gtk.` `SelectionData data,` integer info, integer time	The "drag-data-received" signal is emitted on the drop site when the dragged data has been received.
drag_drop	`Gdk.DragContext context,` integer x, integer y, integer time	The "drag-drop" signal is emitted on the drop site when the user drops the data onto the widget.
drag_end	`Gdk.DragContext context`	The "drag-end" signal is emitted on the drag source when a drag is finished.
drag_failed	`Gdk.DragContext context,` `Gtk.DragResult result`	The "drag-failed" signal is emitted on the drag source when a drag has failed.
drag_leave	`Gdk.DragContext context,` integer time	The "drag-leave" signal is emitted on the drop site when the cursor leaves the widget.
drag_motion	`Gdk.DragContext context,` integer x, integer y, integer time	The "drag-motion" signal is emitted on the drop site when the user moves the cursor over the widget during a drag.
draw	`cairo.Context cr`	This signal is emitted when a widget is supposed to render itself.
enter_notify_event	`Gdk.EventCrossing event`	The "enter-notify-event" is emitted when the pointer enters the widget's window.

(*continued*)

Table B-90. (*continued*)

Signal Name	Additional Parameters	Description
event	Gdk.Event event	The GTK+ main loop emits three signals for each GDK event delivered to a widget: one generic "event" signal, another, more specific, signal that matches the type of event delivered (e.g. Gtk. Widget "key-press-event") and finally a generic Gtk.Widget "event-after" signal.
event_after	Gdk.Event event	After the emission of the Gtk. Widget "event" signal and (optionally) the second more specific signal, "event-after" is emitted regardless of the previous two signals handlers return values.
focus	Gtk.DirectionType direction	The widget received focus.
focus_in_event	Gdk.EventFocus event	The "focus-in-event" signal is emitted when the keyboard focus enters the widget's window.
focus_out_event	Gdk.EventFocus event	The "focus-out-event" signal is emitted when the keyboard focus leaves the widget's window.
grab_broken_event	Gdk.EventGrabBroken event	Emitted when a pointer or keyboard grab on a window belonging to widget is broken.

(*continued*)

Table B-90. (*continued*)

Signal Name	Additional Parameters	Description
grab_focus	None	The widget forced focus on itself by calling `widget.grab_focus()`. This signal can also be initiated with mnemonic accelerators.
grab_notify	boolean was_grabbed	The "grab-notify" signal is emitted when a widget becomes shadowed by a GTK+ grab (not a pointer or keyboard grab) on another widget, or when it becomes unshadowed due to a grab being removed.
hide	None	The "hide" signal is emitted when widget is hidden, for example with `Gtk.Widget.hide()`.
hierarchy_changed	`Gtk.Widget previous_toplevel`	The "hierarchy-changed" signal is emitted when the anchored state of a widget changes.
key_press_event	`Gdk.EventKey event`	The "key-press-event" signal is emitted when a key is pressed. The signal emission reoccurs at the key-repeat rate when the key is kept pressed.
key_release_event	`Gdk.EventKey event`	The "key-release-event" signal is emitted when a key is released.
keynav_failed	`Gtk.DirectionType direction`	Emitted if keyboard navigation fails. See `Gtk.Widget.keynav_failed()` for details.

(*continued*)

Table B-90. (*continued*)

Signal Name	Additional Parameters	Description
leave_notify_event	`Gdk.EventCrossing event`	The "leave-notify-event" is emitted when the pointer leaves the widget's window.
map	None	The "map" signal is emitted when widget is going to be mapped.
map_event	`Gdk.EventAny event`	The "map-event" signal is emitted when the widget's window is mapped. A window is mapped when it becomes visible on the screen.
mnemonic_activate	boolean group_cycling	The default handler for this signal activates widget if `group_cycling` is `False`, or just makes widget grab focus if `group_cycling` is `True`.
motion_notify_event	`Gdk.EventMotion event`	The "motion-notify-event" signal is emitted when the pointer moves over the widget's `Gdk.Window`.
move_focus	`Gtk.Widget old_parent`	The "parent-set" signal is emitted when a new parent has been set on a widget.
popup_menu	None	This signal is emitted whenever a widget should pop up a context menu.
property_notify_event	`Gdk.EventProperty event`	The "property-notify-event" signal is emitted when a property on the widget's window has been changed or deleted.

(*continued*)

Table B-90. (*continued*)

Signal Name	Additional Parameters	Description
proximity_in_event	Gdk.EventProximity event	To receive this signal the Gdk. Window associated to the widget needs to enable the Gdk. EventMask.PROXIMITY _IN_ MASK mask.
proximity_out_event	Gdk.EventProximity event	To receive this signal the Gdk. Window associated to the widget needs to enable the Gdk. EventMask.PROXIMITY _OUT_ MASK mask.
query_tooltip	integer x, integer y, boolean keyboard_mode, Gtk. Tooltip tooltip	Emitted when Gtk.Widget has-tooltip is True and the hover timeout has expired with the cursor hovering "above" widget; or emitted when widget got focus in keyboard mode.
realize	None	The "realize" signal is emitted when widget is associated with a Gdk.Window, which means that Gtk.Widget.realize() has been called or the widget has been mapped (that is, it is going to be drawn).
screen_changed	Gdk.Screen previous_screen	The "screen-changed" signal is emitted when the screen of a widget has changed.

(*continued*)

Table B-90. (*continued*)

Signal Name	Additional Parameters	Description
scroll_event	`Gdk.EventScroll event`	The "scroll-event" signal is emitted when a button in the 4 to 7 range is pressed. Wheel mice are usually configured to generate button press events for buttons 4 and 5 when the wheel is turned.
selection_clear_event	`Gdk.EventSelection event`	The "selection-clear-event" signal is emitted when the widget's window has lost ownership of a selection.
selection_get	`Gtk.SelectionData data`, integer info, integer time	Selection data was requested from the widget.
selection_notify_event	`Gtk.SelectionData data`	
selection_received	`Gtk.SelectionData data`, integer time	
selection_request_event	`Gdk.EventSelection event`	The "selection-request-event" signal is emitted when another client requests ownership of the selection owned by the widget's window.
show_help	`Gtk.WidgetHelpType help_type`	The user requested help with the widget by pressing Ctrl +F1. Help types are defined by Gtk.WidgetHelpType, which is composed of Gtk.WidgetHelpType. HELP _TOOLTIP and Gtk. WidgetHelpType.WHATS _THIS.
size_allocate	`Gdk.Rectangle allocation`	The widget was given a new size allocation.

(*continued*)

Table B-90. (*continued*)

Signal Name	Additional Parameters	Description
state_flags_changed	Gtk.StateFlags flags	
style_updated	None	The "style-updated" signal is a convenience signal that is emitted when the Gtk.StyleContext "changed" signal is emitted on the widget's associated Gtk.StyleContext.
touch_event	None	
unmap	None	The "unmap" signal is emitted when widget is going to be unmapped, which means that either it or any of its parents up to the toplevel widget have been set as hidden.
unmap_event	Gdk.EventAny event	The "unmap-event" signal is emitted when the widget's window is unmapped. A window is unmapped when it becomes invisible on the screen.
unrealize	None	The "unrealize" signal is emitted when the Gdk.Window associated with widget is destroyed.
visibility_notify_event	Gdk.EventVisibility event	The "visibility-notify-event" is emitted when the widget's window is obscured or unobscured.
window_state_event	Gdk.EventWindowState event	The "window-state-event" is emitted when the state of the toplevel window associated to the widget changes.

Table B-91. *Gtk.Window Signals*

Signal Name	Additional Parameters	Description
activate-default	None	The "activate-default" signal is a keybinding signal that is emitted when the user activates the default widget of window.
activate-focus	None	The "activate-focus" signal is a keybinding signal that is emitted when the user activates the currently focused widget of window.
enable-debugging	None	The "enable-debugging" signal is a keybinding signal that is emitted when the user enables or disables interactive debugging.
keys-changed	None	The "keys-changed" signal is emitted when the set of accelerators or mnemonics that are associated with window changes.
set-focus	Gtk.Widget	The focus was changed to a different child in the window.

GTK+ Styles

GTK+ provides many ways to customize the styles of widgets. Most widget style customization is done through style properties.

This appendix provides a reference to the default Pango Text Attribute Markup Language and `Gtk.TextTag` styles.

Default RC File Styles

Until GTK+ 3.x, styles were governed by the `Gtk.Style` class, RC files that defined user styles, the Pango markup language, and the `Gtk.TextTag` class. Since the introduction of GTK+ 3.x, RC files and the `Gtk.Style` class have been deprecated. A new class, `Gtk.StyleContext`, was introduced to replace the `Gtk.Style` class, but RC files remain deprecated and have no replacement.

Pango

The Pango Text Attribute Markup Language allows you to change text styles with XML tags in certain widgets, such as `Gtk.Label`, using the `set_markup` method.

The `<span>` tag can be used with many attributes to define the styles of text. For example, `<span font_desc='Sans Bold 12'>Text</span>` sets the text between the tags with the specified font. Table C-1 lists the `<span>` tag's supported attributes.

© W. David Ashley and Andrew Krause 2019
W. D. Ashley and A. Krause, *Foundations of PyGTK Development*,
https://doi.org/10.1007/978-1-4842-4179-0

Table C-1. *Span Tag Attributes*

Attribute	Description
background	A value that describes the background color. Possible values include the hexadecimal RGB value in the form #RRGGBB or a supported color name like blue.
face	A font family name, such as Sans or Monospace. This tag is the same thing as font_family.
fallback	When enabled, which is the default, the system tries to find the font that most closely matches the specified font. You should not turn this off, but if it is necessary, you should use a value of False.
font_desc	A font description string that would be supported by Pango. FontDescription, such as "Sans Bold 12".
font_family	A font family name, such as Sans or Monospace. This tag is the same thing as face.
foreground	A value that describes the foreground color. Possible values include the hexadecimal RGB value in the form #RRGGBB or a supported color name like blue.
lang	A language code that states what language the text string is in.
rise	This value allows you to create superscripts and subscripts by specifying a vertical displacement, in 10,000ths of an em unit. Negative values create a subscript, and positive values create a superscript.
size	The size of the font, in 1,024ths of a point. You can also use xx-small, x-small, small, medium, large, x-large, xx-large, larger, or smaller. Absolute sizes are usually easier to specify by using font_desc.
stretch	How much the text is stretched. Possible values include ultracondensed, extracondensed, condensed, semicondensed, normal, semiexpanded, expanded, extraexpanded, and ultraexpanded.
strikethrough	You should specify true to place a single line through the text or false to turn it off.

(continued)

Table C-1. (*continued*)

Attribute	Description
strikethrough_color	A value that describes the strikethrough line color. Possible values include the hexadecimal RGB value in the form #RRGGBB or a supported color name like blue.
variant	A value of normal or smallcaps, which allows text to be rendered as all capital letters.
weight	The weight of the text. Possible values include ultralight, light, normal, bold , ultrabold , heavy , and a numeric weight value.

Pango also provides a number of convenience tags. These tags can be used in place of various attributes. As with the tag, you must always provide a closing tag (e.g.,).

- <b>: Make the font bold, which is equivalent to .

- <big>: Make the font larger than the current font, which is equivalent to .

- <i>: Equivalent to , which makes the font italic.

- <s>: Strike through the text, which is equivalent to , which makes the font italic.

- <sub>: Make the text string subscript. This uses the default value for subscript text.

- <sup>: Make the text string superscript. This uses the default value for superscript text.

- <small>: Make the font larger than the current font, which is equivalent to .

- <small>: Make the font larger than the current font, which is equivalent to .

- `<tt>`: Make the font a monospace font. This can be used for code segments or other strings that require monospaced characters.

- `<u>`: Underline the text, which is equivalent to `<span underline="single">`.

Gtk.TextTag Styles

Text tags allow you to define styles for specific sections of Gtk.TextBuffer. Table C-2 is a complete list of styles supported by Gtk.TextBuffer along with a description of what type of values each style supports using the `create_tag` and `apply_tag` methods.

Table C-2. *Gtk.TextTag Style Properties*

Property	Type	Description
accumulative-margln	boolean	Whether left and right margins accumulate.
background	string	The background color as a hexadecimal string. Strings should be specified in the following format: #RRGGBB.
background-full-height	boolean	Indicates whether the background color fills the entire line height or only the height of each individual character.
background-full-height-set	boolean	Whether this tag affects background height.
background-full-height-set	boolean	Whether this tag affects background height.
background-set	boolean	Whether this tag affects the background color.
direction	Gtk.TextDirection	Text direction (e.g., right-to-left or left-to-right).

(continued)

Table C-2. (*continued*)

Property	Type	Description
editable	boolean	Indicates whether the text can be modified.
editable-set	boolean	Whether this tag affects text editability.
fallback	boolean	Whether font fallback is enabled.
fallback-set	boolean	Whether this tag affects font fallback.
family	string	Name of the font family (e.g., Sans, Helvetica, Times, Monospace).
family-set	boolean	Whether this tag affects the font family.
font	string	Font description as a string (e.g., Sans Italic 12).
font-desc	`Pango.FontDescription`	Font description as a `Pango.FontDescription` class.
font-features	string	OpenType Font Features to use.
font-features-set	boolean	Whether this tag affects font features.
foreground	string	Foreground color as a string.
foreground-rgba	`Gdk.RGBA`	Foreground color as a `Gdk.RGBA`.
foreground-set	boolean	Whether this tag affects the foreground color.
indent	integer	Amount to indent the paragraph, in pixels.
indent-set	boolean	Whether this tag affects indentation.
invisible	boolean	Whether this text is hidden.
invisible-set	boolean	Whether this tag affects text visibility.
justification	`Gtk.Justification`	Left, right, or center justification.
justification-set	boolean	Whether this tag affects paragraph justification.

(*continued*)

Table C-2. (*continued*)

Property	Type	Description
language	string	The language this text is in, as an ISO code. Pango can use this as a hint when rendering the text. If not set, an appropriate default is used.
language-set	boolean	Whether this tag affects the language the text is rendered in.
left-margin	integer	Width of the left margin in pixels.
left-margin-set	boolean	Whether this tag affects the left margin.
letter-spacing	integer	Extra spacing between graphemes.
letter-spacing-set	boolean	Whether this tag affects letter spacing.
name	string	Name used to refer to the text tag. None for anonymous tags.
paragraph-background	string	Paragraph background color as a string.
paragraph-background-rgba	Gdk.RGBA	Paragraph background RGBA as a Gdk.RGBA.
paragraph-background-set	boolean	Whether this tag affects the paragraph background color.
pixels-above-lines	integer	Pixels of blank space above paragraphs.
pixels-above-lines-set	boolean	Whether this tag affects the number of pixels above lines.
pixels-below-lines	integer	Pixels of blank space below paragraphs.
pixels-below-lines-set	boolean	Whether this tag affects the number of pixels above lines.

(*continued*)

Table C-2. (*continued*)

Property	Type	Description
pixels-inside-wrap	integer	Pixels of blank space between wrapped lines in a paragraph.
pixels-inside-wrap-set	boolean	Whether this tag affects the number of pixels between wrapped lines.
right-margin	integer	Width of the right margin in pixels.
right-margin-set	boolean	Whether this tag affects the right margin.
rise	integer	Offset of text above the baseline (below the baseline if rise is negative) in Pango units.
rise-set	boolean	Whether this tag affects the rise.
scale	float	Font size as a scale factor relative to the default font size. This properly adapts to theme changes, and so forth, so it is recommended.
scale-set	boolean	Whether this tag scales the font size by a factor.
size	integer	Font size in Pango units.
size-points	float	Font size in points.
size-set	boolean	Whether this tag affects the font size.
stretch	`Pango.Stretch`	Font stretch as a `Pango.Stretch` (e.g., `Pango.Stretch.CONDENSED`).
stretch-set	boolean	Whether this tag affects the font stretch.
strikethrough	boolean	Whether to strike through the text.
strikethrough-rgba	`Gdk.RGBA`	Color of strikethrough for this text.
strikethrough-rgba-set	boolean	Whether this tag affects strikethrough color.

(*continued*)

Table C-2. (*continued*)

Property	Type	Description
style	Pango.Style	Font style as a Pango.Style, (e.g., Pango.Style.ITALIC).
style-set	boolean	Whether this tag affects the font style.
tabs	Pango.TabArray	Custom tabs for this text.
tabs-set	boolean	Whether this tag affects tabs.
underline	Pango.Underline	Style of underline for this text.
underline-rgba	Gdk.RGBA	Color of underline for this text.
underline-rgba-set	boolean	Whether this tag affects underlining color.
underline-set	boolean	Whether this tag affects underlining.
variant	Pango.Variant	Font variant as a Pango.Variant (e.g., Pango.Variant.SMALL_CAPS).
variant-set	boolean	Whether this tag affects the font variant.
weight	integer	Font weight as an integer, see predefined values in Pango.Weight; for example, Pango.Weight.BOLD.
weight-set	boolean	Whether this tag affects the font weight.
wrap-mode	Gtk.WrapMode	Whether to wrap lines never, at word boundaries, or at character boundaries.
wrap-mode-set	boolean	Whether this tag affects line wrap mode.

Exercises Solutions and Hints

This appendix walks you through the solutions for each of the exercises found in this book, although the full code for the solutions can be downloaded from www.gtkbook.com. If you get stuck, this appendix gives you the tools to solve the exercises before you look at the code. You can then reference the downloadable solutions to see how I implemented each of the exercise applications.

Note As the exercises become more complex, the solutions may differ greatly from your implementations. Even if your application works successfully, you should check out the downloadable solutions for comparison.

Chapter 3, Exercise 1: Using Events and Properties

The solution for this exercise should appear very similar to the exercises found throughout Chapter 3. To begin, your application should include the following four basic steps that are required by every Python GTK+ application.

1. Create the Gtk.Application instance.

2. Create the Gtk.ApplicationWindow instances.

3. Show the Gtk.ApplicationWindow instance using the show_all() method.

4. Activate the Gtk.ApplicationWindow instance using the present() method.

In addition to these basic steps, you must also add a `Gtk.Label` widget to the top-level window. This label widget can be set as selectable with `set_selectable()`. Next, you should connect the `Gtk.ApplicationWindow` widget to the "key-press-event" signal, which is called every time the user presses a key when the window has focus.

Note   The "key-press-event" does not work if it is connected to the `Gtk.Label` widget! In Chapter 4, you learn that the label widget cannot receive GDK events because it does not have its own `Gdk.Window`.

In the "key-press-event" callback method, you can use the following Python code to determine whether the label is currently displaying the first or last name.

```
if string1.lower() == string2.lower():
```

The window and label text should be switched accordingly. You should then return `False` so that the application continues to handle the "key-press-event".

Another solution is to just swap the window title and label text unconditionally. This is the approach used in the supplied exercise solution.

Chapter 4, Exercise 1: Using Multiple Containers

This exercise helps you gain experience using a variety of container widgets that were covered in Chapter 4, including `Gtk.Notebook` and `Gtk.Box`. Let's analyze the content of each of these containers.

The `Gtk.Notebook` container should contain four tabs. Each tab in a notebook is associated with a label widget and a child widget. The `append_page()` method can be used to add new pages to a notebook. Each of these tabs should contain a `Gtk.Button` widget that is connected to the clicked signal. When a button is clicked, the notebook should move to the next page, wrapping around when the last page is reached. Connecting each clicked signal to the same callback function can do this.

Within the callback method, which is called `next_tab()` in the downloadable solution, you first need to check the page number. If the page number is less than three, you can simply call `next_page()` to move to the next page; otherwise, you can use `set_current_page()` to set the page number to zero. This same method can be used for moving to the previous page in the notebook.

The next container is a horizontal Gtk.Box that holds two buttons. The first button should move to the previous page in the Gtk.Notebook container when pressed. You can use the same method for moving to the next page for moving to the previous page, although it has to be reversed. The other button should close the window and exit the application when clicked. These buttons can be packed with pack_end() so that they appear against the right side of the horizontal box instead of the left side.

The last container in the application is a vertical Gtk.Box widget that should hold the Gtk.Notebook and horizontal Gtk.Box widgets. This vertical box can be packed into the top-level Gtk.Window widget to complete the application's user interface.

Chapter 4, Exercise 2: Even More Containers

This exercise solution is very similar to the previous exercise. The first difference is that the Gtk.Notebook tabs should be hidden with set_show_tabs(). Then, a Gtk.Expander container should be placed between each Gtk.Button widget and the Notebook tab. This allows you to show and hide the button found in each tab. The expander's label can also be used to tell you which tab is currently displayed.

The last difference is that, instead of using a vertical Gtk.Box widget to pack the notebook and horizontal box, you should use a vertical Gtk.Paned widget. This container allows you to redistribute the allocated space for each of its two children by dragging the horizontal separator located between the two widgets.

Chapter 5, Exercise 1: Renaming Files

In this exercise, you need to use several widgets that you learned about in Chapter 5, including the stock buttons Gtk.Entry and Gtk.FileChooserButton. The purpose of this exercise is to allow the user to rename the selected file with a function built into Python.

The first step is to set up your user interface, which includes three interactive widgets. The first is a file chooser button, created with Gtk.FileChooserButton.new(). The chooser's action should be set to Gtk.FileChooserAction.OPEN. This allows you to select only a single file. The set_current_folder() function can be used to set the current folder of the file chooser button to the user's home directory, found using the Python method os.path.expanduser('~').

This Gtk.FileChooserButton widget should be connected to the "selection-changed" signal. Within its callback function, you need to verify whether the file can be renamed. This can be done with a Python method called os.access(). The following call can use used within your application.

```
ret = os.access("/tmp/foo.txt", os.F_OK | os.W_OK)
```

If the file cannot be accessed or changed by the current user, the Gtk.Entry and Gtk.Button widgets should be disabled. This can be done by sending the opposite Boolean value as mode to the widget via the method set_sensitive().

The next widget in the exercise is a Gtk.Entry , which allows the user to enter a new name for the widget. This is a new name for the file excluding the location, since this file name is appended to the Gtk.FileChooserButton's location when the file is renamed. The last widget, the Gtk.Button, should call the renaming function when clicked.

Within the button's callback method, you first need to retrieve the current file and location from the file chooser button. The location, along with the content of the Gtk.Entry widget, can be used to build a new absolute path for the file. Lastly, you should use the Python os.rename(src, dest) function to rename the file. You should note that you must import the Python os module for any of the functions to work!

```
import os
```

Chapter 5, Exercise 2: Spin Buttons and Scales

This exercise is very different from the previous exercise; it lets you practice with the Gtk.CheckButton, Gtk.SpinButton, and Gtk.Scale widgets. When the check button is activated, the values of the spin button and horizontal scale should be synchronized; otherwise, they can move independently of each other.

To do this, the first step is to create two identical adjustments, one for each range widget. The toggle button in the solution is active on application launch so that the values are immediately synced.

The next step is to connect each of the range widgets to the same callback method/function for the "value-changed" signal. Within this function, the first step is to retrieve the current values of the spin button and scale. If the toggle button is active, these values are compared. Action is only taken if the values are not the same so that the value-changed signal is not repeatedly emitted.

Lastly, the callback function can use the Python built-in `isinstance()` function to figure out which type of widget holds the new value. Based on the result of the test, the other widget should be given the new value.

Chapter 6, Exercise 1: Implementing File Chooser Dialogs

In this chapter's only exercise, you are supposed to re-create the four types of file chooser dialogs by embedding a `Gtk.FileChooserWidget` widget into a `Gtk.Dialog` widget. The results of each action can simply be printed to standard output.

The main application window includes four buttons, one for each of the `Gtk.FileChooserWidget` action types, where the `Gtk.FileChooserAction.OPEN` action allows you to select multiple files. These buttons can be packed into a vertical box and then into the top-level window.

Each of the callback functions follows the same pattern. It first creates a `Gtk.Dialog` widget and packs a `Gtk.FileChooserWidget` above the dialog's action area by packing the dialog's vbox member with `pack_start()`.

The next step is to run the dialog with `run()`. If the returned result is the response associated with acceptance of the action, you should output what would occur with `print()`. For example, you should tell the user that the file is saved; the folder has been created; the files is opened; or the folder was selected. In a `Gtk.FileChooserAction.OPEN` action, you should output all the selected files.

Chapter 8, Exercise 1: Text Editor

This exercise is the first instance of the text editor application that you encounter. It asks you to implement all of the functionality of the text editor.

Note   The downloadable exercise solution includes only very basic functionality of a text editor. It is meant to get you started if you are having trouble. However, you are encouraged to continue to expand your text editor implementation beyond the provided solution!

There are a number of callback functions implemented for the text editor. These are the ability to create a new file; open an existing file; save the file; cut, copy, and paste selected text; and search for text in the document.

To create a new document, you should first ask the user whether or not the application should continue with a Gtk.MessageDialog widget. If the user chooses to continue, the downloadable exercise solution simply clears the Gtk.TextBuffer object and destroys the dialog; otherwise, the dialog is just destroyed.

Opening a document in the provided solution does not ask the user for confirmation, since it is easy to cancel the operation from the Gtk.FileChooserDialog widget. The file chooser dialog has an action type of Gtk.FileChooserAction.OPEN. When a file is selected, its contents are read with the Python method read() and written into the text buffer. Saving in the exercise solution asks for a new file name every time the button is pressed. It calls write() to save the text to the selected file.

The clipboard functions are similar to those provided in Chapter 8's clipboard example. It uses the built-in text buffer functions for cut, copy, and paste actions. These actions are performed on the default clipboard, Gdk.SELECTION_CLIPBOARD.

Chapter 9, Exercise 1: File Browser

In this chapter's exercise, you implement a very simple file browser. It allows the user to browse throughout the system's file structure and differentiate between files and folders. This exercise is meant to give you practice using the Gtk.TreeView widget. In Chapter 14, it greatly expands into a more functional file browser.

The first step is to configure the tree view, which includes a single column. This column includes two cell renderers, one for a GdkPixbuf and one for the file or folder name, so you have to use the expanded method of tree view column creation that was discussed in Chapter 9. The first cell renderer should use Gtk.CellRendererPixbuf and the second, Gtk.CellRendererText.

The tree model, a Gtk.ListStore is created with two columns with types of GdkPixbuf.Pixbuf and GObject.TYPE_STRING.

After the tree model is created in the downloadable exercise solution, the populate_tree_model() method is called, which displays the root folder of the file system on startup. The current path displayed by the file browser is stored in a global linked list called current_path. If the list is empty, the root folder is displayed; otherwise, a path is built out of the list's content, and the ".." directory entry is added to the tree model.

Then, GDir is used to walk through the contents of the directory, adding each file or folder to the tree model. You can use os.path.isdir(location) to check whether each is a file or folder, displaying the correct icon depending on the result.

The last step is to handle directory moves, which is done with Gtk.TreeView's "row-activated" signal. If the selection is the ".." entry, then the last element in the path is removed, and the tree model repopulated; otherwise, the new path is built out of the current location and the selection. If the selection is a folder, then the tree model is repopulated in the new directory. If it is a file, then the action is ignored and nothing else is done.

Chapter 10, Exercise 1: Toolbars

This exercise alters Listing 10-1 (a simple pop-up menu) by replacing the buttons along the side with a Gtk.Toolbar created with Gtk.Builder. The following XML file can be used for creating the toolbar.

```
<?xml version='1.0' encoding='utf-8' ?>
<interface>
  <requires lib='gtk+' version='3.4'/>
  <object class='GtkToolbar' id='toolbar'>
    <property name='visible'>True</property>
    <property name='can_focus'>False</property>
    <child>
      <object class='GtkToolButton' id='toolbutton_new'> <property name=
      'visible'>True</property> <property name='can_focus'>False</property>
        <property name='tooltip_text' translatable='yes'>New Standard
        </property>
        <property name='action_name'>app.on_newstandard</property>
        <property name='icon_name'>document-new</property>
      </object>
      <packing>
        <property name='expand'>False</property>
        <property name='homogeneous'>True</property>
      </packing>
    </child>
```

```
<child>
  <object class='GtkToolButton' id='toolbutton_open'> <property
  name='visible'>True</property> <property name='can_focus'>False
  </property>
    <property name='tooltip_text' translatable='yes'>Open Standard
    </property> <property name='action_name'>app.on_openstandard</property>
    <property name='icon_name'>document-open</property> </object>
  <packing>
    <property name='expand'>False</property>
    <property name='homogeneous'>True</property>
  </packing>
</child>
<child>
  <object class='GtkToolButton' id='toolbutton_save'> <property
  name='visible'>True</property> <property name='can_focus'>False
  </property>
    <property name='tooltip_text' translatable='yes'>Save Standard
    </property> <property name='action_name'>app.on_savestandard</property>
    <property name='icon_name'>document-save</property> </object>
  <packing>
    <property name='expand'>False</property>
    <property name='homogeneous'>True</property>
  </packing>
</child>
<child>
  <object class='GtkSeparatorToolItem' id='toolbutton_separator'>
  <property name='visible'>True</property>
    <property name='can_focus'>False</property> </object>
</child>
<child>
  <object class='GtkToolButton' id='toolbutton_cut'> <property
  name='visible'>True</property> <property name='can_focus'>False
  </property>
    <property name='tooltip_text' translatable='yes'>Cut Standard
    </property> <property name='action_name'>win.on_cutstandard</property>
    <property name='icon_name'>edit-cut</property> </object>
```

```
      <packing>
        <property name='expand'>False</property>
        <property name='homogeneous'>True</property>
      </packing>
    </child>
    <child>
      <object class='GtkToolButton' id='toolbutton_copy'> <property
      name='visible'>True</property> <property name='can_focus'>False
      </property>
        <property name='tooltip_text' translatable='yes'>Copy Standard
        </property> <property name='action_name'>win.on_copystandard</property>
        <property name='icon_name'>edit-copy</property> </object>
      <packing>
        <property name='expand'>False</property>
        <property name='homogeneous'>True</property>
      </packing>
    </child>
    <child>
      <object class='GtkToolButton' id='toolbutton_paste'> <property
      name='visible'>True</property> <property name='can_focus'>False
      </property>
        <property name='tooltip_text' translatable='yes'>Paste Standard
        </property> <property name='action_name'>win.on_pastestandard
        </property>
        <property name='icon_name'>edit-paste</property> </object>
      <packing>
        <property name='expand'>False</property>
        <property name='homogeneous'>True</property>
      </packing>
    </child>
  </object>
</interface>
```

Within your application, you next need to create signal callback methods to process the signals generated by the callbacks. The rest of the text editor's implementation is the same as in Listing 10-1.

Chapter 10, Exercise 2: Menu Bars

This exercise is an alteration of Listing 10-1, where the buttons along the side are moved to a Gtk.MenuBar widget created with Gtk.Builder. The following UI file can be used for creating the toolbar.

```
<?xml version="1.0" encoding="UTF-8"?>
<!-- Generated with glade 3.22.1 -->
<interface>
  <requires lib="gtk+" version="3.20"/>
  <object class="GtkMenuBar" id='menubar'>
    <property name="visible">True</property>
    <property name="can_focus">False</property>
    <child>
      <object class="GtkMenuItem">
        <property name="visible">True</property>
        <property name="can_focus">False</property>
        <property name="label" translatable="yes">_File</property>
        <property name="use_underline">True</property> <child
        type="submenu">
      <object class="GtkMenu">
        <property name="visible">True</property>
        <property name="can_focus">False</property>
          <child>
            <object class="GtkImageMenuItem"> <property name="label">
            gtk-new</property> <property name="visible">True</property>
            <property name="can_focus">False</property> <property
            name="use_stock">True</property>
              <signal name="activate" handler="app.on_menu_new"
              swapped="no"/> </object>
          </child>
          <child>
            <object class="GtkImageMenuItem">
              <property name="label">gtk-open</property>
              <property name="visible">True</property>
              <property name="can_focus">False</property>
```

```
          <property name="use_stock">True</property>
          <signal name="activate" handler="app.on_menu_open"
          swapped="no"/> </object>
      </child>
      <child>
        <object class="GtkImageMenuItem">
          <property name="label">gtk-save</property>
          <property name="visible">True</property>
          <property name="can_focus">False</property>
          <property name="use_stock">True</property>
          <signal name="activate" handler="app.on_menu_save"
          swapped="no"/> </object>
      </child>
    </object>
  </child>
</object>
</child>
<child>
  <object class="GtkMenuItem">
    <property name="visible">True</property>
    <property name="can_focus">False</property>
    <property name="label" translatable="yes">_Edit</property>
    <property name="use_underline">True</property> <child type="submenu">
      <object class="GtkMenu">
        <property name="visible">True</property>
        <property name="can_focus">False</property>
        <child>
          <object class="GtkImageMenuItem"> <property name="label">
          gtk-cut</property> <property name="visible">True</property>
          <property name="can_focus">False</property> <property
          name="use_stock">True</property>
            <signal name="activate" handler="win.on_menu_cut"
            swapped="no"/>
          </object>
        </child>
```

```
        <child>
          <object class="GtkImageMenuItem">
            <property name="label">gtk-copy</property>
            <property name="visible">True</property>
            <property name="can_focus">False</property>
            <property name="use_stock">True</property>
            <signal name="activate" handler="win.on_menu_copy"
            swapped="no"/> </object>
        </child>
        <child>
          <object class="GtkImageMenuItem">
            <property name="label">gtk-paste</property>
            <property name="visible">True</property>
            <property name="can_focus">False</property>
            <property name="use_stock">True</property>
            <signal name="activate" handler="win.on_menu_paste"
            swapped="no"/> </object>
        </child>
      </object>
    </child>
  </object>
</child>
</object>
</interface>
```

Within your application, you next need to create an the callback methods/functions that is associated with each of the toolbar items in the UI file. The rest of the exercise is the same as in Listing 10-1.

Chapter 11, Exercise 1: Glade Text Editor

This exercise expands on the Glade main window (see Listing 11-1), yet again by asking you to redesign the whole user interface in Glade. Instead of using buttons, you should implement a toolbar for text editing functions. You can then use Gtk.Builder to load the graphical user interface and connect the necessary signals. Figure D-1 is a screenshot of the application for this exercise using a toolbar.

Figure D-1. *The text editor application with a toolbar designed in Glade*

Within your application, you next need to create signal callback methods to process the signals generated by the callbacks. The rest of the text editor's implementation is the same as in Listing 10-1.

Chapter 11, Exercise 2: Glade Text Editor with Menus

This exercise also expands on Listing 11-1. You to redesign the whole user interface in Glade. This time, though, instead of using buttons, you should implement a menu bar for text editing functions. You can then use `Gtk.Builder` to load the graphical user interface and connect the necessary signals. Figure D-2 is a screenshot of the application for this exercise using a menu bar.

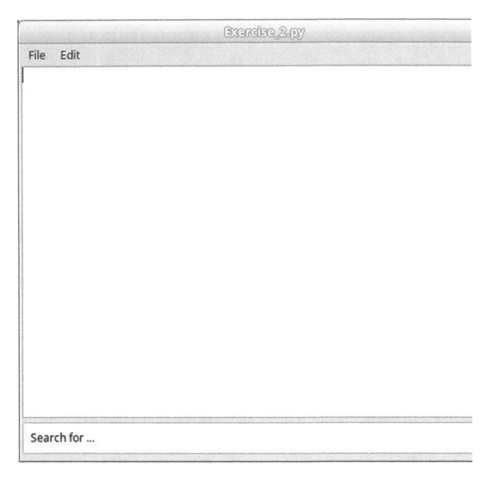

Figure D-2. The text editor application with a menu bar in Glade

Chapter 13, Exercise 1: Full Text Editor

This last text editor exercise is an extension of Listing 13-1, "The Drawing Area Widget."
In it, you should add two additional features. The first is printing support, which allows
the user to print the current text in the Gtk.TextBuffer widget. The printing support in
the downloadable solution for this exercise is very similar to the printing example built
in Chapter 13, so you should check out that example's description for more information
about how this solution works.

The other additional feature is a recent file chooser menu for the Open toolbar item. To create this, you must convert the Open toolbar item to a `Gtk.MenuToolItem` widget. The default recent manager, obtained with `recentmanager.get_default()`, can be used to provide the recent files. Then, you can create the recent file chooser menu with `Gtk.RecentChoooserMenu.new_for_manager()`. This menu should be added to the Open menu tool button's `Gtk.Menu`. You can use the `selection-done` signal to figure out which menu item is selected and what file should be opened.

Index

A

Adjustment, *see* Gtk.Adjustment

B

Button, check, *see* Gtk.CheckButton
Button, color, *see* Gtk.ColorButton
Button, file chooser, *see* Gtk.
FileChooserButton
Button, font, *see* Gtk.FontButton
Button, push, *see* Gtk.Button
Button, radio, *see* Gtk.RadioButton
Button, spin, *see* Gtk.SpinButton
Button, toggle, *see* Gtk.ToggleButton

C, D

Check button, *see* Gtk.CheckButton
Chooser button, file, *see* Gtk.
FileChooserButton
Chooser, file, *see* Gtk.FileChooser
Color button, *see* Gtk.ColorButton

E

Entry, text, *see* Gtk.Entry

F

File chooser, *see* Gtk.FileChooser
File chooser button, *see* Gtk.
FileChooserButton

File filter, *see* Gtk.FileFilter
Filter, file, *see* Gtk.FileFilter
Font button, *see* Gtk.FontButton

G, H, I, J, K, L, M, N, O

Gdk.Color, 93–94, 223
   methods
     new(), 94
GLib, 1, 26, 33, 81, 153, 223, 406–407, 482
Gtk.Adjustment, 85–86, 91, 176, 264, 416,
     423, 449–451, 457, 486
   methods
     new(), 85
Gtk.Button, 33–34, 37, 39–40, 49, 69–71,
     74, 76, 78, 92, 104, 196, 212, 314,
     335, 337, 345–346, 348, 406, 413,
     419, 488, 546–548
   methods
     set_relief(), 74
   Stock items, 71
Gtk.CheckButton, 74, 76–79,
     104, 146, 548
   methods
     new(), 77
     new_with_mnemonic(), 77
Gtk.Color, 92
   methods
     new_with_color(), 94
Gtk.ColorButton, 92–94, 105, 139, 427, 491
   methods

P, Q

R

S

T, U, V, W, X, Y, Z

Printed in the United States
By Bookmasters